Dominique Lapierre

A Thousand Suns

Translated from the French
by Kathryn Spink

WARNER BOOKS

A Time Warner Company

Originally published in French as *Mille Soleils* by Editions Robert Laffont

Copyright © 1997 by Dominique Lapierre
English translation copyright © 1999 by Pressinter, S.A.
All rights reserved.

Warner Books, Inc., 1271 Avenue of the Americas, New York, NY 10020
Visit our Web site at www.twbookmark.com

 A Time Warner Company

Printed in the United States of America

First Trade Printing: February 2000

10 9 8 7 6 5 4 3 2 1

The Library of Congress has cataloged the hardcover edition as follows:

Lapierre, Dominique
[Mille soleils. Engish]
A thousand suns / Dominique Lapierre
p. cm.
ISBN 0-446-52535-9
1. Lapierre, Dominique.   2. French—Foreign countries—
Biography.
I. Title.
CT1018.L3165A313   1999
909.82'5—dc21   98-39026
CIP
ISBN 0-446-67595-4 (pbk.)

Book design by Giorgetta Bell McRee

INTERNATIONAL ACCLAIM FOR
A THOUSAND SUNS

"Riveting and grippingly written . . . an intriguing look at some of this century's most interesting people. . . . Lapierre is a terrific tour guide."
—Kirkus Reviews

"A fascinating blend of history and journalistic reporting methods."
—Midwest Book Review

"Vivid accounts . . . an inspiring eyewitness to a half-century of history."
—King Features

"A novelist's eye for detail and a fluid, compelling style. . . . Lapierre offers some of the most exciting history in years, much of which remains eerily topical . . . cracking good adventures coupled with deep insight."
—Vancouver Sun

"Three stars! A remarkable book. . . . The subtitle is no exaggeration; Lapierre seems to have been everywhere and met everybody."
—Rapport

"A big feast of words, adventures, and emotions. In this book, Lapierre does more than write. He spreads hope."
—Le Figaro, Paris

"This spectacular book holds the reader breathless from beginning to end . . . [from] an author who knows how to blend his talent with the generosity of his heart."
—France Soir, Paris

"Magnificent! . . . The gripping characters of A THOUSAND SUNS have all gone to the end of their dreams, to the extremes of their faith and struggle."
—El Pais, Madrid

"What is really striking in A THOUSAND SUNS is the energy, the dynamism, the originality, the panache of the various stories. This book is a feast."
—La Stampa, Turin

To Larry,
companion of so many
unforgettable adventures,
and to Alexandra,
his goddaughter and my daughter,
who has in her turn picked up the pen,
to carry on telling those epic stories
that inspire people to dream.

Acknowledgments

First and foremost I would like to express my immense gratitude to my wife, Dominique, who shared in most of the adventures related in this book and who was of invaluable help to me in the preparation of *A Thousand Suns*.

I would also like to thank Colette Modiano, Paul and Manuela Andreota, Antoine Caro and Jessica Papin, who spent long hours correcting my manuscript and encouraging me.

I could never have written this book without the enthusiastic support of my literary agent, Morton Janklow, and that of my long-standing and faithful American publisher, Larry Kirshbaum, and his colleagues around the world. I would also like to express my special gratitude to my translator, Kathryn Spink, herself the author of remarkable books on Mother Teresa, Brother Roger of Taizé and Jean Vanier.

My profound appreciation also goes to all those supporting my humanitarian work in India. These extraordinary individuals are too numerous to mention here, but I would like them to know that their generosity is my inspiration.

Contents

Author's Note to the Reader

My extensive historical research and my assignments as a journalist have meant that I have often been lucky enough to witness spectacular events and, above all, come into contact with extraordinary people. Nearly all these encounters have shown me humanity's strength and grandeur.

You will no doubt find yourself wondering what the connection is between an Andalusian bullfighter dancing with death and the actual, dreadful death of a friend shot down by Russian bullets in Budapest; between a black mechanic in New Orleans who resurrected a car belonging to an adolescent obsessed with old vehicles and a leper child in Calcutta who emerged triumphant from his wretchedness; between an American convict fighting against execution on death row and the Great Soul who liberated the largest colonial empire of modern times; between an idealist who lay down his life to save the African elephants and a Nazi general who refused to carry out Hitler's orders to lay waste the capital of France.

There is no a priori connection, except perhaps the will, buried in human hearts, to fight for what we believe in.

Most of the people I talk about in this book have illumined and shaped my life. With their taste for noble causes and their rage to overcome adversity, they have awakened my curiosity, nurtured my dreams, aroused my spirit of resistance and enriched my existence. It is this richness that I would like to share with you in these pages.

One day, while waiting for a bus under the monsoon torrents of South India, I read a proverb on the wall which said: "There are always a thousand suns beyond the clouds."

May the reading of *A Thousand Suns* convince you of the universal relevance of this message.

D.L.

A
THOUSAND
SUNS

There are always a thousand suns beyond the clouds.

—INDIAN PROVERB

1

The Grandiose and Mad Dream of a Twentieth-Century Don Quixote

In that spring of 1960, fifteen years after the collapse of Nazi Germany and Fascist Italy, two political tyrannies still held sway in Western Europe. Democratic nations seemed resigned to the dictatorships of General Francisco Franco in Spain and his colleague Professor Antonio de Oliveira Salazar in Portugal. But one February day of that year, their regimes were shaken by an unprecedented event. One of the immediate consequences of this event was to project the shy fledgling reporter that I was into the eye of a media cyclone. It was my first major assignment with the French news magazine *Paris Match*.

Five hundred journalists from all over the world had descended like a swarm of locusts upon the hotels of the Brazilian port of Recife. Even Red China had sent reporters and photographers. We were covering the hijacking on the high seas of the Portuguese cruise ship the *Santa Maria*, with its 630 passengers and crew of 390.

The man responsible for this feat, sixty-seven-year-old Captain Henrique Galvào, was a former officer and administrator in the Portuguese African colonies. Through this act of modern-day piracy, the captain and his small band of black-bereted Portuguese and Spanish revolutionaries wanted to attract world attention to the fascist regimes of Antonio Salazar and Francisco Franco. They had hoped to steer the ship to Angola and there foment an uprising to overthrow the dictatorships in Lisbon and Madrid.

Their attempt had failed

Surrounded by a pack of American warships, the *Santa Maria* cruised off the Brazilian coast, hoping to unload its hostages. No one knew where and when the release would take place, nor how the captain and his companions' adventure would end. Every police officer in Brazil was on alert, and word was that a commando of the PIDE, the Portuguese secret police, had arrived from Lisbon to assassinate Galvào as soon as he set foot on land.

The assignment my editor in chief had given me was quite straightforward—and identical to that given to reporters from all the other papers. Get on board the ship, secure a photo scoop and an exclusive on the pirate captain's account of his extravagant adventure. A big, fair-haired fellow, armed with camera bags, was waiting for me at the airport. A veteran of the Indo-Chinese War and half a dozen other conflicts, a specialist in difficult missions, twenty-eight-year-old Charles Bonnay was one of our profession's top photographers. His presence alone was enough to suggest that I had not come to Brazil for a picnic.

"Do you know where this bloody captain and his boat are?" I asked rather ingenuously.

Charles guffawed. His teeth gleamed white against his tanned face. "Somewhere on the high seas, a hundred to a hundred and fifty miles from here. The American navy is refusing to give out any information. We'll have to find him ourselves!"

His rash suggestion took us to the port of Recife, where we hired a fishing boat. Aristotle Onassis's yacht would have cost us less than the old lobster trawler on board which we spent the day spewing up our guts in a twelve-foot swell, without seeing a trace of the pirated liner. The next morning Charles's patience had run out. He gripped my arm.

"Get me a parachute. We'll look for the ship by plane and I'll jump onto it."

"A parachute?" I repeated incredulously.

I knew that Bonnay had taken part in airborne operations in

Tonkin and in Egypt during the Anglo-French Suez expedition of 1956, but the idea of dropping him out of the sky onto the deck of a passenger ship seemed completely crazy.

"What about the sharks?" I worried. "This area's infested with them."

Bonnay dismissed my objection disdainfully.

"They can't be any worse than the Vietcong."

Locating the *Santa Maria* by plane and boarding her on the open sea was obviously our best chance of beating our competitors. We made for the local air base. The base commander, a slightly built colonel with lots of braid, received us effusively. Our request seemed to amuse him enormously.

"I'll lend you my own parachute," he told Charles. "How much do you weigh?"

"A hundred and ninety-eight pounds," responded Charles, forgetting the few extra pounds he had put on in the Brazilian bistros since his arrival.

"A hundred and ninety-eight? That's a shame. I only weigh one forty-three, and the flying surface of my parachute is geared to that weight. You might come down a bit fast."

"Never mind," Charles replied, "the water will break my fall."

We took the little colonel's parachute away with us and set off in search of the Recife flying club to rent a plane. On the way I got Charles to stop outside a hardware store, where I bought a large kitchen knife.

"At least you'll be able to cut the parachute webbing if you fall in the water," I said, handing him the instrument.

"You think of everything," my colleague marveled.

"Wait," I continued, "I've got something else for you."

I handed him a large plastic bag containing a very fine pink powder.

"What's that?" asked Charles. "Cocaine?"

"No, it's shark repellent powder. You sprinkle it in the water around you and the little bastards clear off as fast as they can. The guy promised me it was effective for five or six minutes—just enough time for you to get out of the water, because afterward they come back, fiercer than ever."

The photographer responded with a slight, sardonic smile.

Reporters for *Life*, the *New York Times*, the London *Times*, the Tokyo *Asahi* and a few other major newspapers had already snapped up the flying club's best planes. We were left with an old battered Piper Cub. Its pilot, a muscular black man who looked like Muhammad Ali, assured us that it was capable of crossing the Atlantic with a single flap of its wings. He wanted five hundred dollars payable in advance, for two hours' offshore searching.

Charles put his parachute on his back, fastened the straps, then attached the watertight case containing his photographic equipment to his right leg. I looked anxiously at his luggage: the added weight would accelerate my friend's fall even more.

The sea was so blue it was almost black, iridescent in places with trails of white foam. Apart from a light-tonnage tanker and some cargo boats, there was not a ship to be seen on the horizon. Soon we were completely alone above the vastness, without any points of reference. The land had disappeared. I listened nervously to the throb of the engine. An hour went by. The pilot announced he was going to turn back. Immediately the plane began to veer around to the right. That was when Charles gave a shout.

"Look!"

There was the *Santa Maria*, as majestic and colossal as a cathedral, with its large yellow funnels with their green and red stripes. A few hundred yards to starboard a U.S. Navy destroyer was escorting her. Charles signaled to the pilot to lose altitude and bank around the liner. I could see passengers waving vigorously to us. From the air, I saw that the ship had been rechristened. Her new name was printed in enormous red letters on the upper quarterdeck. She was called the *Santa Libertade*.

Charles carefully examined the sea conditions. The water was as flat as a mill pond, indicating the almost total absence of any wind. If he were to jump from directly above the ship, he would have a good chance of landing on the upper deck. He made a sign to the pilot to pull slightly on the joystick to ensure that the plane was high enough to give the parachute time to open. My colleague's coolness amazed me. The idea of dropping into a shark-infested sea seemed not to perturb him at all.

The liner's decks and gangways were packed with people. Some were waving flags and banners. One of them said: "Free Spain and Portugal from the fascists." There seemed to be a certain agitation on the American destroyer also.

"Okay, old man, see you in Recife. Put the champagne in the fridge!" With these words Charles jumped into the void. I heaved a sigh of relief as I saw the white corolla open almost immediately, just over the ship. Yet his descent seemed terribly fast. What if he fell into the funnel? I saw Charles pulling on his webbing and thought his fall slowed down a little. But it might only have been an illusion. My nails dug into the palms of my hands. The last few feet seemed to flash past at lightning speed. Below, people were waving their arms ever more frenziedly. A few seconds to go and my colleague would crash on the deck. I was terrified. Suddenly the corolla disappeared from view. I scoured the outline of the boat, then the surrounding sea. Finally I found him again, floating in the waves between the *Santa Maria* and the American warship.

From high up in my battered little airplane, I saw then a sight that would be forever engraved upon my memory. The speed of his fall and the weight of his case had dragged Charles several feet below the water. He was an excellent swimmer and reappeared on the surface a few seconds later. But the weight of the damp parachute was in danger of sinking him. The passengers were yelling their encouragement. Captain Galvào had already lowered a lifeboat into the sea. The commander of the American destroyer had done the same, and the two embarkations sped toward the castaway. One of the American sailors was standing in the bow of his launch with a gun pointing at the sea, ready to fire at the first shark closing in. With a pounding heart I followed the progress of the two boats to Charles. They looked as if they were racing. The contest was unfair. The Portuguese seaman's biceps could not possibly compete with the U.S. Navy launch's powerful engine. I could imagine my colleague's anger and frustration at the sight of his rescuers coming to rob him of his international scoop. I even saw him shove their launch away with his foot. It was unheard-of. I learned afterward that he had actually shouted at the Americans to "Beat it!"

The destroyer had lowered a second launch into the water, this one equipped with grappling irons and boat hooks. Despite all his courage, Charles was going to be caught like a common swordfish. Dodging his punches and even his kitchen knife, four sailors managed to grab hold of him and hoist him aboard their boat. He was transferred to the warship, where he was given dry clothes. Then, after confiscating his cameras, the commander had my photographer locked up in the ship's prison.

THE U.S. NAVY RELEASED my unfortunate colleague three days later when the pirated liner arrived in the port of Recife. Determined to avenge him, I carried two thousand dollars in small banknotes which I intended to offer Captain Galvào in exchange for the exclusive story of his capture of the *Santa Maria*. Along the quay, however, the liner was even more difficult to reach than out at sea. As soon as the passengers and crew had disembarked, dozens of helmeted Brazilian police formed an impenetrable cordon around it. The pirate leader had remained on board with his men. There was a rumor saying that he intended to take the boat out to sea, sink it and go down with it. Hundreds of impatient journalists were pressed up against the security barriers, ready to do anything to get on board and interview and photograph the heroes of the extraordinary episode.

"We'll have to rustle up a disguise," Charles declared, always one step ahead with his ideas. No sooner had he uttered these words than a fire engine stopped alongside us. Two leather jackets and gleaming helmets were hanging at a window. We exchanged a look of complicity. It took us less than ten seconds to don the providentially provided clothing. Thereafter, getting through police controls and scaling the gangplank posed no problems. Who would stop two firemen doing their rounds? Even if their brigade boots were Gucci moccasins?

We found the "pirate captain" in the first-class bar, calmly sipping a whiskey with his chief of staff. The "corsairs" with him looked more like unshaven bunker hands than the heroes of a revolutionary crusade. By contrast Galvào impressed us with his presence. Tall and thin, his chiseled face lit up by steely blue eyes beneath bushy eyebrows, he had the bearing of a Renaissance *condottiere*. His hair was elegantly plastered back, scarcely gray; it made him look younger than his years. Most striking of all was the mixture of authority and distinction apparent in his unfurrowed brow, strong chin and thin lips. Velázquez or Philippe de Champaigne would have been happy to paint this altogether virile and romantic character. His life had been a succession of adventures inspired by his passions.

Born on the banks of the Tagus River that had given birth to so many explorers, at twenty Henrique Galvào had embraced a career in the army. Military life had soon seemed too restrictive to his impetuous character full of libertarian ideas. Ten years later, believing he was fighting for a just and good cause, he had taken part in a military putsch that swept away a decadent, corrupt republic and brought to power an obscure but honest economics professor at the University of Coimbra, a man by the name of Antonio de Oliveira Salazar. Galvào's reward had been a post as governor of a province in Angola, then the pearl of the Portuguese colonial empire in Africa. He spent six years with little to do, six years that had turned the young officer into a formidable hunter (it was said he had killed a hundred elephants and at least fifty lions) and one of the most prolific Portuguese writers. Taking advantage of the long evenings, he had devoured hundreds of literary works, learned French, Spanish, English and half a dozen other languages and committed thousands of verses from Virgil, Byron, Goethe and Hugo to memory. Wielding his pen with as much dexterity as his hunting rifle, he had tried his hand at every conceivable genre, producing novels, short stories, plays and even verse drama.

Above all else, however, his African experience had introduced a young officer enamored of justice and freedom to the corruption of an oppressive colonial system. Officially Portugal did not have an empire, only "provinces overseas." Twenty times the size of the parent country, these provinces were the most extensive territories owned by the white man in black Africa. The huge coffee and cotton plantations of Angola and Mozambique were in the clutches of a handful of colonists, as were their diamond, copper and manganese mines; and their ivory, animal skin and precious wood resources, which provided a privileged few in Portugal with riches no other colonial nation was extracting from its empire. In response to any criticism, the Portuguese retorted that in none of their overseas provinces was there segregation between black and white communities. Mixed-race marriages were not forbidden, and Africans were not turned away from hotel rooms because of the color of their skin. Provided an African spoke Portuguese, dressed in European clothes and paid taxes, he could even claim *assimilado* status and enjoy the same privileges as the white people from the home country. This, at least, was the theory. The reality, as Galvào was to find out, was very different. Less than one in a hundred blacks in Angola and Mozambique were officially regarded as *assimilado*. The ninety-nine others put up with living and work conditions that were close to slavery. Illiteracy afflicted nearly all of the indigenous population. There was not one secondary school in the whole of Portuguese Africa. Promoted to inspector of the colonial administration, Galvào never stopped denouncing its defects. But his accusatory reports were ignored by authorities not inclined to appreciate critics.

One day, in disgust, he had spoken directly to members of the Lisbon parliament. His revelations about the collusion between the colonial administration and drug traffickers caused an uproar. The authorities exacted harsh revenge. Forced out of office into retirement, Galvào had been obliged to leave Africa. Punishment made him all the more determined to do everything he could to combat the dictatorship of the man he had helped bring to power. His career as a revolutionary had begun. The PIDE, Salazar's secret police, kept a close watch on any opponents of the regime. During a raid on the former governor's home, its agents found in the bottom of a Chinese porcelain vase a paper giving a detailed outline of plans for a putsch to overthrow the head of state. The text was in Galvào's own handwriting. In vain he claimed it was a play he had written, set in an imaginary country. The document provided a good excuse to put its author out of action once and for all. Henrique Galvào was locked up in a dungeon in the prison-fortress of Caixas. Feigning madness, he managed to get himself transferred to a psychiatric hospital. Foiling the vigilance of his guards, there he received numerous friends and political sympathizers, not to mention elegant ladies from Lisbon's society, attracted to the distinguished revolutionary's charm.

Eighteen months later he escaped the mental hospital by borrowing a doctor's white smock. Then, disguised as a delivery boy, he had knocked on the door of the Argentinean embassy to ask for political asylum. Salazar, the dictator, allowed his irksome adversary to leave. "Let him go as far away as possible and be forgotten!" he declared.

Salazar underestimated his opponent. No sooner had Galvào arrived on the other side of the Atlantic than he wrote an open letter to Portugal's dictator, which was printed in numerous international newspapers.

"I have slipped from your clutches, my dear Salazar, from your fearsome hatred, from your all-powerful Gestapo, from your special judges and tribunals, from your petty newly rich tyrants, your idolatrous mercenaries, your army of occupation, your prisons and concentration camps, from your self-interested yes-men, your speeches that allow no answers and your pompous lies."

Galvào next called Salazar to account for a regime that, he claimed, had "reduced a simple and good-hearted people to the spiritual and material poverty of totalitarian countries." He condemned the policies of a regime that fostered the lowest standard of living in Europe, a corrupt administration, an army devoid of both moral courage and military spirit, a government made up of mediocrity and colonial politics that were feudal.

"We are under the illusion that we are living in peace," he concluded, "but this peace, like that of Soviet Russia and its satellite states, is the peace of sheep and cemeteries."

The author of this indictment harbored no illusions. It would take more than an open letter to break the silence surrounding the dictatorship and rally the Portuguese and the rest of the world to action. Tyranny could only be toppled by some spectacular event: the capture of the *Santa Maria* and its six hundred passengers was the means to this end.

The Kidnapped Pirate

The sudden entrance of two journalists disguised as firemen into the ship's bar seemed to amuse the pirate captain and his companions. After accepting a whiskey, I explained in French the purpose of our presence to Henrique Galvào and took a bundle of notes out of my pocket.

"Captain, may I offer you this in exchange for the exclusive story of your capture of the *Santa Maria*?" I asked. The sum in question was two thousand dollars.

Galvào considered the wad of green bills with some surprise. After a moment's thought, he looked up at me.

"*C'est d'accord,*" he agreed. "I'll give you the exclusive rights to my story but I'd want us to talk somewhere other than on this ship. Here we could well be disturbed."

The idea of spiriting away the man pursued by the world's press and all the police in Brazil and Portugal for my own benefit was irresistibly appealing.

"I can offer you the hospitality of my modest hotel room," I said at once.

The Portuguese acquiesced, and I led the captain out on deck so that Charles could make up for his attempt to board the ship at sea with a spectacular series of photos. After that, with the help of his men, we got away in the bottom of a covered dinghy. One hour later a taxi dropped us outside my hotel. All the rooms in the big hotels in Recife already taken, I had had to put up some fifteen miles from the center, in a lower-rated establishment. It bore, nonetheless, the appealing name Boa Viagem (Pleasant Journey). Entering my room, I found it difficult to believe that I had managed to "kidnap" one of history's most celebrated pirates.

The game was far from won, however. First because I was almost blind. An insect had stung me in my right eye, causing a very painful infection. Galvào took charge of my bottle of eye lotion and treated me himself. Ten times in the course of that night he was to renew the treatment without which I would have had difficulty recording his story. This passing infirmity concerned me less, however, than the mysterious coming and going of footsteps in the corridor. Every two or three minutes the steps stopped outside the door to my room. The tips of black shoes would appear then in the ray of light filtering in from outside. I was sure an ear was pressing against the panel to listen to us. Was it a Salazar secret agent? My room would be ideal for one of those discreet executions the secret services seemed to favor. All they had to do was break down the door and use a gun with a silencer. Since murderers were seldom fond of witnesses, I was practically certain to be eliminated in the process.

I communicated my concern to my guest but received only a casual shrug of his shoulders. "If Salazar were to have me assassinated, he would seriously embarrass Brazil," he said. "I think he's too intelligent to make that sort of blunder."

The Portuguese's warm, velvety voice was so compelling that I eventually forgot about the danger. He spoke a polished French that he took pleasure in embellishing with subjunctives and rare and refined expressions. His delight at being able to express himself in the language of his idols, Voltaire and Hugo, manifested itself in every sentence.

"I was a man alone, penniless, without political support, without relatives or friends," he began. "When Argentina granted me political asylum, I was forbidden to engage in any activity against the Lisbon government. I couldn't go to Brazil, where Salazar had had me declared persona non grata. On the advice of two compatriots in exile, I finally went to live in Caracas, in Venezuela. There I met some favorably disposed Portuguese prepared to join me in my crusade and a small group of Spanish republicans who had fled their country after the civil war. I suggested to them that we create an Iberian Revolutionary Directory of Liberation in response to the pact Salazar had struck with Franco. But to do what? Europe was a long way away, and the world was completely uninterested in our cause. I dreamed of action. But what kind of action? Soon I had run out of money to pay even my rent. Friends took me in. I found a small administrative job with a building company. I was earning a thousand bolivars a month, half the price of a secondhand submachine gun.

"One morning when I was feeling particularly racked with doubt and melancholy, I chanced upon a few lines tucked away in the middle of the Caracas *Diario*, Venezuela's principal daily newspaper. They announced that the Portuguese liner the *Santa Maria* had arrived in the Venezuelan port of La Guaira, where she stopped each month on a cruise that included Lisbon, Curaçao and Miami. This enflamed my imagination. If we could get control of that ship and take her to Africa to raise a liberation army, we could oust Salazar and Franco. The whole world would be made aware. The Portuguese and Spanish opposition would be forced to get involved. In short, it would be a tremendous shock that might just jolt my countrymen into believing in imminent liberation. So I decided to seize the *Santa Maria*.

"I confided in my closest companions. Together we planned the operation in the utmost secrecy because we were being spied on day and night by Franco's and Salazar's secret agents. My first concern was to give the operation a name. Like Don Quixote, I was convinced we needed a lady's patronage before embarking on any great adventure. 'Knights without love are bodies without souls,' don't you think? So I gave our project the name of Cervantes's heroine. The operation would be called Dulcinea."

The captain lit another cigarette from the one he had just finished, and went on.

"I sent my men to glean whatever information they could. They disguised themselves as dockers and climbed aboard the *Santa Maria* at her next port of call. They investigated everything that might be of interest to us. What fuel resources did the ship have? Where did it take on supplies, fresh water and fuel oil? What was the average number of passengers on each voyage? What were the crew's political opinions? Were there secret police on board? Was there any contingency plan in the event of an outside attack? Were there any armor-plated doors to prevent access to the bridge? In the meantime, passing myself off as a respectable grandfather wanting to treat my grandchildren to a cruise at sea, I went to get all the available brochures and maps from the cruise line's local representative. The company had even been careless enough to have a huge model of the *Santa Maria* made and put on display in the lobby of the Hulton travel agency, right in the center of Caracas. With my eyes concealed behind thick dark glasses and my head hidden in an assortment of hats, every day I studied that mock-up of the *Santa Maria*, until I knew the layout of the boat down to every last detail. Those hours of minute observation of the replica of the vessel will remain one of my most poignant memories."

Four Old Guns for the Act of Piracy of the Century

"At last, one day, I actually went on board," Galvào continued. "With espadrilles and a floral shirt, I looked the perfect tourist. For two hours I was able to roam from one end of the boat to the other, unnoticed. I climbed up to the bridge. It was deserted. For a few seconds I even took hold of the wheel. Then I went down a level and caught sight of the ship's captain talking to someone in his cabin.

"The boat had eight decks. We would only have to take possession of the top two levels—the deck with the wheelhouse and radio room and the level where the officers' cabins were—to gain total control of the ship. Only two flights of steps gave access to those two sensitive levels. Two armed men placed at the foot to each would prevent any counterattack. I left the *Santa Maria* convinced that capturing her would be child's play.

"In order to train, equip and arm a proper commando for Operation Dulcinea—roughly a hundred men—I figured I would need at least thirty thousand dollars. The pitiful savings I'd been accumulating for months didn't even amount to a third of that sum. I had to resign myself to reducing our total strength to a mere twenty-five men. Our armaments were laughable. They were made up of a Thompson submachine gun that had cost us three hundred dollars; an automatic pistol, so worn out it must have been fired in every single one of the South American revolutions; four old rifles; half a dozen revolvers; and just about as many grenades.

"The most crucial problem was buying tickets for the voyage. A third-class ticket from Venezuela to Lisbon cost eight hundred bolivars, or two hundred dollars. Three days before D Day we still needed six hundred dollars to buy the last three tickets. I had put off Operation Dulcinea until the following month.

"At last, the great day arrived. Only one of us was to go on board without a ticket. Me. My name was too well known. Its appearance on the passenger list might upset the whole operation. To make sure no one recognized me, I decided to make myself up with a false mustache and not go on board until the Curaçao stop, a few minutes before the *Santa Maria* raised anchor for Miami. So I took a plane to the small Dutch island, to wait there for the boat to arrive.

"As for my companions, they were to embark as planned at La Guaira, in Venezuela. They had divided their weapons up into separate pieces in several suitcases. Each of those suitcases was marked with a small white cross. We had bribed a customs officer to help us. The sign was to ensure they weren't searched.

"In Curaçao I checked into a small boardinghouse near the

quay. I had only fifteen florins, just enough to pay for one night. From my window I could see the channel the *Santa Maria* would pull into at eight o'clock the next morning. I didn't sleep that night. Had my men been able to board? Were their suitcases with the weapons on board? Had some of Salazar's agents gone onto the ship at the last minute? Were we suddenly going to find ourselves confronted with increased security?

"Next morning, a little before eight, from my window I saw the swing bridge that gave the ships access to the quay opening. The *Santa Maria* was there, magical, marvelous, just like Don Quixote's Dulcinea. She berthed a long way away and I had to wait over an hour before my second-in-command, Commander Jorge Soto Mayor, our specialist in navigational matters, was able to come ashore and reassure me that the embarkation had gone perfectly smoothly. Soto Mayor was a former officer in the Spanish Republican Navy, covered with decorations. During the civil war, at the helm of his destroyer, he had sunk Franco's battle cruiser *Baléares*. He was the one to whom I had entrusted the responsibility of steering the *Santa Maria* to the coast of Africa.

"That evening at six o'clock, four hours before departure for Miami, wearing the same broad-brimmed straw hat I'd worn the day I slipped out of the psychiatric hospital in Lisbon, I went on board the liner with Soto Mayor. On me I had a visitor's pass, issued by the company's local agent. Once I saw that no one had recognized me, there was no doubt left in my mind: the *Santa Maria* was mine."

Completely oblivious to the worrisome footsteps in the corridor outside my room, Captain Galvào relived his adventure like the principal actor in a stage play.

"A companion took me to one of the third-class cabins we had booked," he continued. "It was stiflingly hot in there because the ventilation system had broken down. It had no portholes and was in the middle of the lower deck, just above the engines. It wasn't possible to see our departure from that windowless room. But suddenly I felt a tremendous vibration shake the vessel. The maneuvering of machinery had begun.

All at once I felt absolutely serene. The most difficult part was over.

"I changed my tourist attire for a shirt and pair of khaki linen trousers, more suitable for my role as a *libertador*. Then I hurried along the gangway to the third-class deck where my men were waiting for me.

"It was nine o'clock at night. I had fixed the time to take over the boat at one-thirty in the morning, when the passengers and officers, tired after two stops in close succession, would for the most part have gone to bed. We were all to meet a few minutes before the deadline on the quarterdeck of the main deck. I had split my forces into two assault groups. The first, under the command of Soto Mayor, would take possession of the bridge, the wheelhouse and the radio room. The second would seize the lower level and neutralize the officers in their cabins. It was there that we expected the fiercest resistance. I had therefore decided to take command of the group assigned to this phase of the operation. Once those two objectives had been achieved, the rest of the men would take up position at the accesses to the various staircases to prevent any attempt at a counterattack on the part of the crew.

"Just before midnight, I proceeded to distribute the weapons. Rojo and Fernandez, two veterans of the Spanish civil war, were given the two submachine guns. The others parceled out the guns, revolvers and hand grenades among themselves. The youngest and least experienced had to make do with machetes, knives and bludgeons.

"At twenty-eight minutes past one in the morning, I arrived on the main deck, our meeting place. My twenty-five companions were there with their weapons. It was a magnificent night, worthy of what we were about to do. I whispered good luck to each one. The youngest in the group, José Ramos, who was only eighteen, was the son of a communist teacher in Porto. He asked me to give him a blessing. He was armed with one of those machetes the Brazilian *seringueiros* use to harvest rubber from the heveas trees. We all slipped on our red and green arm badges, the Portuguese colors. The officers attached their epaulettes. We put on our black berets. I consulted my watch and said: 'Let's go!' "

Forty-five Minutes to Take Over a Floating Palace

Forty-six-year-old Mario Simoes Maya, the ship's captain, was fast asleep in his cabin paneled with rare African wood. Because Curaçao was where fuel, fresh water and supplies were taken on, and a large number of passengers embarked, it was invariably the most tiring stop of the trip. The chief engineer, the purser and most of the officers on his staff were also asleep in their air-conditioned cabins.

Just above them, on the bridge level, the officer on duty, Lieutenant José Nascimento Costa, the twenty-seven-year-old son of an Algarve peasant, studied the darkness. Costa was the happiest of men. That morning, the ship's radio had relayed him a telegram. His wife, Lourdes, had just delivered an eight-pound boy, Antonio. Sailor José Antonio de Souza, aged twenty-four, was at the helm behind him.

Suddenly a group of armed men surged from the starboard steps and threw themselves at them. A brutal conflict ensued, punctuated with gunfire. Struck in the head and chest, Lieutenant Costa fell to the ground. He would never meet his son. Next to him, helmsman de Souza sprawled in a pool of blood. The attack was over in a flash. It had killed one man and seriously injured another, but the *Santa Maria*'s bridge was in the hands of the revolutionaries. Taking control of the navigation station, Soto Mayor seized the helm and put the ship through a ninety-degree turn to starboard, to point its 35,000 tons in the direction of the African coast. The radio room was also in the hands of the pirates: no cry for help would alert the world.

The shots had woken Captain Maya. Concluding that drunken revelers were amusing themselves with firecrackers, he promptly turned over on his pillow and went back to sleep. But a banging on his door got him out of bed.

"It had taken us less than forty-five minutes to assume control of the *Santa Maria*, its staff, its 390-man crew and its 630 passengers asleep in their cabins or in their deck chairs," Captain Galvào said. "That floating palace had become the first piece of my homeland to be liberated. As I scanned the darkness, I thought of Byron leaving for Greece to free the land of Homer from the yoke of the Turks."

Apart from the officers on the top deck, not one of the 630 passengers and none of the crew had heard the gunshots. Emerging from their cabin for breakfast, Bob and Gladys Boulton, two Americans from New Orleans, noticed an inscription painted on the floor of the afterdeck. The name of their ship had changed overnight. The *Santa Maria* had become the *Santa Libertade*. When everyone was seated in the various dining rooms, the sound of a striking gong was heard over the speakers of the public address system. A voice announced:

"This is Commander Henrique Galvào, leader of the Iberian Revolutionary Directory for Liberation, speaking to you.

"Passengers and crew members, I have to inform you that you are now in a piece of Portugal freed from Salazar's fascist dictatorship," he declared. "We shall not give ourselves up to anyone, but we will vouch for your safety and even your comfort. We shall do everything we can to enable you to leave the boat as soon as possible. In the meantime we are not asking you to help us, but to help yourselves by remaining perfectly calm."

The passengers looked at each other, dumbstruck. It was impossible, incredible, inconceivable: in the middle of the twentieth century, they were actually in the hands of pirates!

The master of the *Santa Libertade* then gave orders for the cruise to continue as normal. He made arrangements for a gala evening, at which he and his staff would be the guests of honor. He made sure that the program of daily entertainment carried on as usual: aperitifs to musical accompaniment, clay pigeon shooting competitions on A-deck, miniature horse racing, bridge tournaments, dance parties by the swimming pool. For many of the female passengers, the sudden appearance of these handsome, fit, young revolutionaries with irreproachable manners was not an unexciting surprise, especially as most of them were excellent dancers. As for the ship's kitchen, it continued to offer the same wide range of dishes. In fact, the only change presented to the passengers was the information that they were no longer aboard the *Santa Maria* en route to Miami, but "on board the *Santa Libertade* en route to freedom."

A Forfeit for the Sake of an Innocent Man

"Once the various problems of security, administration and the organization of the passengers' lives had been sorted out, only one thing preoccupied me: getting as far as possible before the world discovered what we'd done," Galvào continued. "For that, we needed four days' secrecy. Since sailing time between Curaçao and Miami was usually three days, I decided to gain a fourth by telegraphing the company's agent in Miami to say that slight engine damage had obliged us to reduce our speed. Then I ordered total radio silence from the ship.

"We had just passed the islands of Martinique and Saint Lucia when the ship's doctor came to tell me that the sailor wounded during the taking of the vessel would die if he didn't have an urgent operation. He had a bullet in his liver and another in his small intestine. I immediately assembled my officers on the top deck. Should we or should we not land the wounded man and risk being discovered? I knew that from a military point of view I was under no obligation. By saving one life I would be endangering a thousand others. My officers pressed me to continue on our way. But in my heart of hearts I didn't feel I had the right to let an innocent man die. In resisting our attack, he had been the only one, apart from the duty officer, to show a measure of courage. So I gave the order to turn around and stop two miles off the coast of Saint Lucia and lower a dinghy into the sea with three sailors and a medic to take the wounded man ashore. I also had the body of the officer killed the previous night placed in the boat. With the departure of that boat, I knew the secret of Operation Dulcinea was blown."

THE COUNT OF OXFORD and Acquit, the fifty-seven-year-old administrator of the small British island of Saint Lucia, began each day by allowing his binoculars to roam over the glorious bay that opened out to sea before him. That morning something unusual caught his attention.

"A Portuguese ship!" he muttered.

The count saw the large white liner approach slowly from the north, turn about and come to a halt out to sea. He saw a rowboat lowered into the water and several people get into it. He saw the ship promptly move away while the boat made for land.

Something odd was going on on this small piece of Britain. Without further ado, he made swiftly for the quay. The rowboat had just come ashore.

Unable to understand a single word of Portuguese, the Englishman sent for a local interpreter. That was how he heard the news that would focus the eyes of the world on the map of the Atlantic.

"Piracy!" he exclaimed, before speeding off in his car to his friend Commodore Shand, who was in charge of the sector's navy.

Her Majesty's frigate the *Rothesay*, anchored in the port, received orders to weigh anchor immediately and pursue the liner. Under a storm-red sky, a pirate hunt like those of olden times began in Caribbean waters. In response to a radio alert, the American navy diverted the destroyers *Damato* and *Wilson* and had two search planes take off from Puerto Rico. But the abductors of the *Santa Maria* had a substantial lead, and the size of their escape zone made it difficult to locate them. Their ship was just a tiny dot in the middle of an expanse of ocean six times the size of France.

The incredible news spread like wildfire. The Lisbon newspapers ran riot. *"Os Pirataes!"* (The Pirates) ran the headlines in poster-sized letters. In the Portuguese capital the legend of

Galvào, the enfant terrible of the thirties and forties, sprang to everyone's lips to the accompaniment of inscrutable smiles. Beside himself with anger, Salazar placed his armed forces in a state of alert and deployed every craft the Portuguese navy could induce to float to the Atlantic. General Franco joined in the pursuit with several destroyers. Henrique Galvào could flatter himself: forces worthy of the Invincible Armada were being mobilized against his *Potemkin*.

"Call her *Libertade!*"

"I'd arranged with my second-in-command, Soto Mayor, to have the *Santa Libertade* sail in zigzags to throw off any possible pursuers," the captain continued his story. "As of the third day I rationed the fresh water and reduced the meals served in first and second class. I authorized all the children traveling in third class to come and take their meals with the children in the higher classes. Apart from that, life on board continued as normal. It was not until the third day that our radio picked up a first message. It came from the American television network NBC. I agreed to talk to one of their correspondents by radiotelephone. That first contact opened a floodgate of requests. All the world's media wanted to interview me. I was offered pots of gold in exchange for our position. Television companies wanted to send in reporters by parachute. It was madness. But curiously enough, we had still not been spotted. We actually managed to remain incognito until the fifth day, when a Danish cargo ship crossed our path. We were halfway to the African coast. The vessel signaled our position. And that was the end of our stolen freedom.

"Two hours later an American plane flew low over us. Its pilot informed me by radio that the American authorities were ordering me to take the *Santa Libertade* to San Juan in Puerto Rico. I replied sharply that I did not take orders from any authorities. All the same, I offered to receive an emissary on board to discuss the fate of the forty-two American nationals on the ship.

"The strength of my reaction seemed to surprise the officer in the plane. He told me the commander in chief of the United States Atlantic fleet would maintain constant contact with me.

"We carried on toward Africa nonetheless. Despite the rationing of fresh water, the atmosphere on board continued to be excellent. A passenger in third class brought a baby into the world in the ship's sick bay. I rushed to wet the baby's head. 'What are you going to call her?' I asked the mother. It was a girl. The young woman hesitated. 'Call her *Libertade*!' I suggested.

"That exhilarating day ended on an unpleasant note. Salazar and Franco had joined forces to ask Britain and the U.S. to block our passage by every possible means. Two American torpedo boats patrolling off the Ivory Coast had changed course to come and meet us. There was no longer any hope of our reaching Africa. I assembled my men to confront them with this harsh reality. The American commander in chief of the Atlantic fleet suggested we evacuate the passengers. I responded that there was nothing I would like better, provided it was done in a neutral port, where I could be sure of the safety of the passengers, our ship and ourselves. I suggested the Brazilian port of Recife.

"That evening, I arranged for a farewell dinner in the various dining rooms on board. I had given orders for the tables to be decorated with small Portuguese and Spanish Republican flags. While the orchestra played 'Auld Lang Syne' the *Santa Libertade* dropped anchor three miles from the access channel to the port of Recife.

"When dinner ended, I found myself suddenly engulfed by a tide of people. At one point I thought they wanted to throw me overboard. I was wrong. The passengers of the *Santa Libertade* wanted me to autograph their menus as a souvenir of the cruise of a lifetime."

NEXT DAY, ALONG WITH HUNDREDS of fellow journalists and photographers and thousands of local residents who had come from all over the city—just as they had done two and a half centuries previously—to watch the arrival of the corsair, I saw the spectacular berthing of the great white liner that had been monopolizing world news for twelve days. Slowly it approached the quay amid a swarm of tugs, sirens blaring. Behind her, a spectacular mauve-black storm cloud rose out of the sea like an immense aureole. From the decks, gangways and portholes came the sound of shouting, laughter, singing and crying, in the tropical heat and the tension of an impending storm. On the quay two hundred naval fusiliers were having the greatest difficulty containing the crowd. When the ship finally stopped, there was a mad rush. Children were passed from arm to arm. Bags, bundles and suitcases rained down from all sides. People jostled with each other to get at the ladders, threw themselves onto the gangways, stumbled over each other in an indescribable confusion and cacophony.

From the top deck, wearing his legendary black beret, Captain Henrique Galvào watched impassively as his dream came to an end.

"The Brazilian admiral had promised to place a tug at my disposal to enable me to return to international waters once the passengers and crew had disembarked," the captain continued. "My mind was made up. If the epic story of the *Santa Libertade* had to end there because we had thought it better to save a human life, there would still be a wreck to act as an eternal reminder of this great ship and the handful of men devoted to liberty who had taken it this far. I had decided to evacuate all my men, then scuttle the *Santa Libertade*.

"When people had finished disembarking, the Brazilian admiral came to tell me his country's authorities could not provide me with a tug to enable us to leave. I had been betrayed. The admiral did, however, offer me and my men Brazil's hospitality and an honorable way out.

"Then began a long last night on board the great empty ship.

In front of witnesses we counted out the forty thousand dollars in the ship's safe, and I had the seals affixed. For our last meal, we combined our culinary talents, and my men went quietly to bed for the first time for many days. Afterward I climbed up to the bridge. The night was as magnificent as the one on which we had seized the ship. Before me, Recife shone with a thousand lights, and I thought back over all that had happened in the last few days. I was satisfied with what we had achieved and only sad that our adventure had had to stop there. I was more determined than ever to draw the attention of the world to our cause. I was convinced that one day I or others would succeed in finishing what we had begun and free Portugal and Spain from their tyrannies.

"To me and a few others, the *Santa Maria* would forever after be called the *Santa Libertade*.

"So there you have the story of our adventure."

IT WAS NEARLY FIVE O'CLOCK in the morning. The ocean outside my window was still swathed in darkness. I had scribbled at least forty pages of closely spaced notes. The captain must have smoked three packs of cigarettes. He had also emptied the whole bottle of eye lotion into my infected eye. His features betrayed no tiredness, just a vague lassitude that I attributed to melancholy. I was hungry.

"Let's go for a bite to eat!" I proposed after thanking him for his gripping account. "Along the beach there are taverns that stay open all night."

He welcomed the suggestion. I examined the ray of light under the door. The black shoes were no longer there. I turned the key cautiously in the lock and went out onto the landing. The corridor was empty. On tiptoes, like conspirators, we made it to the elevator. Downstairs the lobby was deserted.

The captain laughed. "Salazar's police keep banking hours! They've gone to bed."

There was not a living soul on the boulevard running along

the seafront. We had been walking for a while when I heard the throb of an engine behind us. I turned around. A big black American limousine with its lights off was slowly following us. It was driving down the middle of the road. I looked in vain for a side street or passageway where we could escape. But on one side there was the beach and the sea and on the other villas with closed shutters.

"Captain, we're being followed," I said anxiously.

I had seen too many American films not to imagine what would happen next. Already I had the vision of submachine guns popping out of the windows. My companion's calmness served only to intensify my fear. "He doesn't get it," I thought. "With his black beret and his epaulettes covered with braid and pips, he thinks he's still on the bridge of his ship. We're going to be shot like rabbits." Fortunately, about ten yards away I spotted the bluish glow of a tavern sign. I gripped the captain by the arm and stepped up my pace. The car was still following us. A few seconds to go and we might find safety. The café-restaurant had a split stable door like a Wild West saloon. The lighting was so dim you could hardly make out people's faces. A jukebox was blasting out samba music. The place smelled of beer and palm wine, but it was reputed to serve the best grilled crab and lobster in Brazil. Girls in miniskirts, with cheeks daubed with makeup, were enticing clients to drink. I caught sight of an unoccupied table at the back of the room with two chairs backed against the wall. If our pursuers burst in, at least we would see them coming. Wasn't it a golden rule of gangsters when they sat at a restaurant table always to keep one eye on the door?

Henrique Galvào seemed smugly pleased, like a young officer mixing with low company in one of his garrison's brothels. While the cook grilled our lobsters, I went to the bar to telephone his second-in-command, Soto Mayor, to come quickly and look to his leader's safety. After several attempts, I managed to speak to the Spaniard and tell him about the mysterious car. Relieved, I went back to our table. My chair was occupied by a pretty prostitute with green almond-shaped eyes. Obviously she had not recognized the famous captain. She was examining the lines on his right hand.

"She tells me I have the willpower to change the course of the Amazon," Galvào translated with a laugh, "and she can see me . . ."

I did not hear what followed. Captain Jorge Soto Mayor and two of his men had just burst into the restaurant. Heaving such a sigh of relief that the girl started, I called the café's proprietor.

"Quickly, champagne all around, and three more lobsters!"

SURE ENOUGH, just as the indomitable Portuguese captain had promised, the end of the *Santa Libertade* venture was not the end of his crusade to free his country from its dictator. He took refuge in Morocco. Still hoping to attract public attention through spectacular deeds, a few months later he had a Casablanca–Madrid plane diverted in midflight to drop thousands of pamphlets on the Portuguese capital. He was immediately arrested and deported by the Moroccan authorities. In February 1962 a special Portuguese tribunal sentenced him in absentia to twenty-two years' imprisonment for seizing the *Santa Maria*.

Banned from several countries, subject to various extradition proceedings instigated by the Portuguese government, Henrique Galvào returned to Brazil. On his arrival in Rio, however, the police were waiting for him. By order of the country's new president, he was assigned to live in the city of Belo Horizonte, where he was prohibited from engaging in any political activity. After several months of purgatory, he was eventually given permission to settle in São Paulo, where his wife, Maria, and their adopted daughter, Lourdes, came to join him. It was there that he passed away on June 25, 1970, at the age of seventy-five. He had supported the fight for Portugal's liberation with letters and messages to the very end.

His death preceded that of his old enemy, Antonio de Oliveira Salazar, by a month and two days, and that of General Francisco Franco by five years and five months. With the passing of the two dictators, the captain's dream of freedom and democracy for the Iberian Peninsula was finally fulfilled.

2

A Small Piece of Paradise
under a Parasol Pine

This spectacular maritime hijacking and the ferocious press coverage it prompted made me realize what an incredibly competitive field I had chosen for a career. I needed a break. Instead of packing me straight off to Algeria to cover the war between France and the Algerian rebels, my editor in chief granted me a few days on the world-famous sands of Saint-Tropez.

This once-quiet fishing village, long a paradise for painters, had become an extravagant playground for jet-setting society led by movie star Brigitte Bardot. My editor in chief's generosity was especially timely: I had an appointment with the notary for the small harbor town to make a dream come true. I hoped to finalize the purchase of a piece of vineyard and a tiny farmer's cabin on the peninsula.

The saga of this purchase had been going on for three years. It had begun with a challenge, an absurd suggestion made by an elderly lady so in love with her peninsula that she was constantly scheming to have her friends take up residence there.

"You like coming to spend your time off in this paradise so much, you're going to be very pleased," she informed me one day in a confidential tone. "When I was out walking my dogs, I bumped into a farmer who owns some vineyards and scrubland just behind the beach of Pampelonne. I don't think he would be entirely opposed to the idea of . . ."

"Of selling?"

"You guessed it."

I was speechless. Finally I managed to ask: "Do you have any idea how much a young reporter earns?"

The august dowager dismissed my objection with a wave of her hand.

"There's a farmer's cabin where you could make a bedroom and a small office for yourself and four acres of land." She mentioned a price far greater than two years of my salary. "If you play your cards right, however, you could probably have the lot for"—she hesitated—"a third or a fourth of his asking price. And possibly even pay in installments."

Only someone out of his mind could have taken so fanciful an idea seriously and involved himself in such an undertaking. But the object—a piece of that magical peninsula—was, in my view, worth all the hardships and sacrifices involved. Three years of hard bargaining would follow.

Eugène Giovanni, the seller, was a man of about sixty, dry and gnarled like the stems of the vines he had spent his life pruning. Like many of the inhabitants of the region, he was of Italian origin. His parents had fled the poverty of their native Piedmont at the turn of the century to take refuge in this corner of Provence. Like many of their compatriots, they had worked hard on the vine-growing estates and put down roots. The most fortunate of them had been able to buy a patch of land on which to plant vegetables and a few vines. For many, the arrival of Mussolini's troops in 1940 had been the occasion of joyous reunions with their nearest and dearest. For a good part of the war, occupiers and occupied had drunk and danced and sung beneath the vine trellises of the peninsula.

Unfortunately my would-be seller, that Italian rascal, had a distinct liking for pastis, the licorice-flavored alcohol so much in favor in the south of France. In order to discuss conditions for the purchase of his property and wrest a few concessions from him, I had to go and see him at dawn. After seven o'clock in the morning the effects of the pastis would have clouded his brain for the day. Sometimes I had to hammer on his door for ten minutes to get him to open up. Eventually the barking of his mongrel terrier and the terrified bleating of the five nanny goats he kept under his roof would drag him from his bed. He would appear then on the threshold in an old darned shirt. *"Non è una ora di cristiano"* ("It is not a Christian hour for being called out of bed"), he would grumble, looking up at a still-dark sky.

His cabin was comprised only of one room with a bed, two chairs, a table and a fireplace that served as a stove. It took me several visits to get used to the smell of pastis and goat droppings that caught me by the throat as I entered. And several more to steel myself to the burning, black pastis-flavored liquid that he called his morning coffee. He had poured several bottles of his favorite aperitif into his well to make quite sure that the water he washed in and used for his morning coffee would taste and smell of aniseed!

At any rate, my persistence was rewarded. I managed to obtain very nearly the price and payment terms the elderly lady's fanciful promises had led me to hope for. I needed only to sign the deed of sale. I weighed the full implications of a formality that would allow me to enter the very closed circle of local society. The long-standing residents of Saint-Tropez would be able to bestow upon me the prestigious label of *local stranger,* a subtle distinction that would differentiate me forever from the *strangers from outside*, those invaders attracted more by the whiff of scandal associated with the small harbor than its deeper qualities.

THE NOTARY'S HOUSE at the end of the rue Gambetta was a stately two-story building, with pierced Venetian shutters and windows with small panes. Above the green serpentine door frame a plaque revealed that one of the town's glorious sons, General Jean-François Allard, an officer under Napoleon and commander of the Indian armies of the sultan of Lahore, had had the house built in 1835. I hesitated before pressing the doorbell. A kind of stage fright seized me. The sharp tapping of a battery of old typewriters seemed to come straight out of a sound track from a 1930s film. In a vast room hung with curtains to subdue the light and the sounds from outside, a dozen employees worked away like ants. The smell of fresh wax polish pervaded this temple of industry. As soon as I entered, a stoutish man with oversleeves, the absolute antithesis of the pampered and glamorous creatures that frequented the local boutiques and cafés, lay down his piles of files to greet me. Ferdinand Mignone occupied the position of head clerk in the practice. The fine round writing of his old-fashioned pen had been drawing up the deeds for real estate transactions on the peninsula for a generation.

"Well now, there you are at last!" he exclaimed in the singsong accent of Provence. "Your seller is tearing his hair out. He was already afraid you had fallen out of love with our peninsula. Let's quickly go and reassure him!"

The farmer was waiting for me in the notary's office.

"Greetings, my Parisian friend," he said, keeping his cigarette in the corner of his mouth.

In honor of the occasion Eugène Giovanni had dressed himself up in a suit that was slightly too large for him and plastered his hair with a grease that smelled of caramel.

"Now that we have buyer and seller together, we can commence," the notary began with the simultaneously solemn and smooth-tongued authority of his profession. "As the law requires, I shall read you the deed."

Giovanni acquiesced by clearing his throat. The brightness of his eyes and the trembling of his hands left me in no doubt: he had plied himself with a good half dozen pastis in the cafés in the Place des Lices before coming to our meeting.

"A plot of vineyard, heath and scrub with a total area of four acres, 101 square yards demarcated in the north by a parasol pine, and in the south by . . ." The notary read at a gallop, as if these specifications should be self-evident to each of the parties before him.

The notary was wrong. I had never managed to induce Giovanni to show me the exact boundaries of his property. I don't think he knew them himself. To no avail, I had searched through all the deeds sanctioning the various transactions relating to that corner of the peninsula for the last century and longer. Sometimes a text would mention a cross on a rock, a stone marker, an old oak tree, but seldom a precise distance between these reference points. The land in this remote corner of the Mediterranean coast had never been of any great value. A few pine trees, a few briars more or less, scarcely made any difference. During World War II, unscrupulous landowners had taken advantage of the lack of clarity over the boundaries to extend their land by nibbling away sometimes several dozen yards from a neighbor imprisoned in Germany. It was said that many acres of property had changed hands in this way.

The notary was coming to the end of his reading. I was waiting for Giovanni's reaction to the statement regarding the intervals between installment payments which I had had so much difficulty negotiating. I was afraid that three years would suddenly seem like an eternity to him. But the notary was shrewd enough to speed up his discourse. All went smoothly.

I was then able to write Giovanni a first check.

"That'll buy a few bottles of pastis," I said.

"You're not wrong, my friend!" agreed Giovanni.

The notary invited us to sign the bottom of the deed. As he guided Giovanni's hand, intense emotion flooded me at the sight of that clumsy paraph being inscribed next to my name. The notary's voice rang out.

"This sale is only valid if Mr. Giovanni's mother, usufructuary of the property, agrees to countersign the transaction," he announced.

"Why is this person not here?" I asked, surprised.

"She's an invalid," the notary explained. "She lives in an old people's home next to the hospital. We shall have to go to her bedside."

Our arrival in the communal room of the home provoked a lively curiosity. Soon a whole group of elderly people had gathered around us. Mme Giovanni was a little old lady dressed all in black, with a fine face lit up by two large blue eyes that shone with an intense brilliance. She was so hard of hearing that the notary had to raise his voice. But the old woman waved her walking stick to interrupt him.

"So you're the one who's going to live on our hill," she said in a strong Italian accent. "You're a very lucky man. There's no piece of countryside more beautiful." She motioned me to draw closer. "On our hill, just in front of our cabin, there's a parasol pine," she said, almost in a whisper. "That pine is the most beautiful and the tallest of all the pines on the peninsula. It's at least two hundred years old, perhaps more. One day I caught my Eugène making for the tree with a saw in his hand. He wanted to cut it down because it was casting a shadow over the vegetable patch. I rushed at him. I told my boy that that tree was the good Lord ascending from earth to heaven. I forbade him to touch it. I told him that it would bring us misfortune. I snatched the saw from his hands . . ."

Tears flowed down her wrinkled cheeks as we gazed at her in silence. My heart went out to her.

"Monsieur, I beg you now to respect that tree," she continued very slowly. "It will be your roots. It will be your benediction."

As soon as I had pocketed my deed of ownership, I went to pay my respects to the parasol pine. The old lady was right. It was a noble tree. Its majestic trunk with pinkish brown bark, striped with dark bands like a tiger's hide, supported such a full crown of greenery that it could be seen from every hill on the peninsula. Twisted with age, its powerful branches intertwined with one another under a vault so dense that it stopped the light. At its base the contorted roots extended flush with the ground like the tentacles of an octopus, before plunging deep into the earth in search of nourishment. So greedy was this tree that not a blade of grass grew for yards around. A pachyderm of the plant world, one of nature's giants, it commanded admiration and respect.

Sitting against its trunk, I breathed in the scent of its needles. I spoke to it long and lovingly. I urged it to continue to flourish, to brace itself against the furious onslaughts of the mistral wind, to shower down upon our heads the manna of its delicious pine kernels beloved of children and confectioners, to protect us with its soothing shade from the harshness of the Provençal sun. Above all, I asked it to remain our sentinel, our witness. In short, I asked that it be a benediction for us, just as the woman who had been its companion for sixty years had promised. To encourage it, I decided to rechristen my small piece of countryside the Great Pine.

Other, more modest parasol pines formed superb mushrooms of greenery at either end of the vineyard. Large holm oaks with graceful dentated leaves and branches harbored families of squirrels. There were cork oaks with trunks stripped of their thick elastic bark, and maritime pines with needles yellowed by the mysterious Japanese bug that had decimated this variety of tree all over the region. Alongside the rows of vines Eugène had lovingly cultivated, islets of wild vegetation and scrub had grown: cytisus bushes, rock roses, sweet-smelling boxtree boughs and wild laurels with their long triangular leaves. Somewhere a thyme shoot released a waft of perfume: its scent blended with that of lavender and rosemary, the kind the Greek and Roman colonizers of the peninsula burned in their censers. Farther on, the red and black berries of a clump of mastic trees, Don Quixote's fetish shrub, pervaded the air with the fruity scent so characteristic of Provence.

A place of a thousand treasures, that herbarium was strewn with bits of pottery, fragments of hewn stone and glass, pieces of flint, some of which I felt certain dated back to the dawn of time. Generations of Phoenicians, Phocaeans, Greeks, Romans and Saracens had succeeded each other on this ancient peasant land. My small piece of vineyard was only the most recent avatar of what had once been land on which grains, olive groves and almond trees grew, and which had little by little decked itself out in the magnificent vineyards that now produced the famous Côtes de Provence wines in bottles curved like a woman's hips.

The scrubland surrounding the vineyard was alive with butterflies, beetles, snails, caterpillars, praying mantises and grasshoppers. Spiderwebs hung like wisps of cotton wool from the low branches of the briars. Rabbit, toad, field-mouse, fox and snake droppings bore witness to the presence of a host of small predators on the wasteland, but in vain I watched at holes and burrows. Apart from a fat ocellus lizard feasting on a family of wood lice driven out from under a stone, none of them deigned to show themselves in broad daylight. By contrast, numerous birds frolicked in the sky over the Great Pine. Pigeons, jays and warblers fluttered between the parasols and the cork oaks.

How long would it take me to discover all the secrets of my small paradise? Probably a lifetime. Nothing could have inveigled me into such an adventure more pleasurably than the deafening cacophony that set the countryside abuzz that day. The raucous song of the cicadas proclaimed my joy at having purchased the Great Pine.

GIOVANNI'S REPLACEMENT by a young Parisian journalist did not seem to provoke much of a reaction from my neighbors. Although my arrival passed unnoticed, I felt it only polite to introduce myself to those about me. I immediately fell for the truculent vine grower whose property bordered my own to the west. Antoine Navaro was a rotund character full of Mediterranean exuberance. His cheeks were the same shade of purple as his wine, and his voice sang rather than spoke.

"If there is a God, it's here that he has created his heaven," he declared, waving his arms in the direction of his vines. "Welcome!"

He filled two large glasses to the brim with rosé, and we clinked them happily. Antoine was a noble man. From the books that filled the rooms of his old wisteria-covered farmhouse it was clear that his vineyards were not the only thing he cultivated. He received so many books from several book clubs that no new literary work escaped the curiosity of his small, vivacious eyes. He was visibly delighted that someone slightly out of the ordinary was moving into his neighborhood. He plied me with questions about my latest assignments. Had I met members of the Algerian rebellion against France? What solution could the Americans find to their war in Vietnam? Was Fidel Castro going to set the world ablaze? Our meeting promised to be a protracted one, but Antoine had all the time in the world. In order to better savor my answers, he led me into his wine storehouse, where a delightful coolness prevailed amid a striking aroma of wine. He drew two glasses of rosé from one of the barrels, offered me an armchair and stretched out in a large Oriental hammock suspended between two wine presses, in which he took his daily siesta. With his eyes half closed and his pudgy fingers folded over the front of twill overalls distended by his paunch, he looked like a Buddha. Just two and a half miles from the eccentricities of Saint-Tropez, I found myself on another planet.

A similar sense of otherworldliness prevailed when I went to visit the scatterbrain who lived a little farther away in a farmhouse turned into an animal reserve. At one time, Gonzague de Chastelas must have been a very handsome man, but his glum expression, rasping voice, alcohol-bloated face, hairy torso and the animal smell he gave off were no longer engaging. In the fifties this strange character had been a renowned Parisian art gallery owner. One day he had abandoned his fashionable house decorated with antique furniture and rare objects in the Marais district to resurface as manager of a real estate agency in Saint-Tropez. While out walking his dogs, he spotted a tiled roof tucked away beneath the parasol pines. The house and its vineyard were for sale. Gonzague liquidated his agency, packed his bags and jumped into his white convertible sports car, drove two and a half miles and embarked on the venture of a lifetime: creating his own personal zoo.

He had been completely successful. He had stocked his domain with hundreds of birds of all kinds. There were majestic emus with the airs of ostriches, ibises, crested cranes, pink flamingos, peacocks, parrots and an infinite variety of ducks, geese, pigeons and other winged creatures. Sheep, goats, a tame boar, two black mares, three ponies, a miniature horse, a donkey that occupied his living room, a tribe of cats and dogs—whom, on summer evenings, he walked in his underpants—completed his menagerie.

Splendid Gonzague! He received me at the gateway to the property he had aptly named The Zoo like a maharaja at the border to his state. In honor of the occasion, the elderly shepherd who served as his factotum, valet, gin rummy partner and whipping boy had removed the donkey from the living room and placed a bottle of pastis and two glasses on a Louis XVI walnut chest of drawers which served as a feed trough. Gonzague was in a dreadful mood that day. "Dogs! All dogs," he stormed. I wasn't certain whether he referred to animals or people. In the end I learned that his horticulturist, whom he refused to pay because the plants he provided had died, had forced him to put his house up for sale. Yellow notices about a forthcoming estate auction were already appearing in Saint-Tropez and neighboring districts. The asking price was so attractive that half the peninsula was likely to come running. In a movement of compassion, I took his hand. Shrieking at the top of his voice, he extricated himself. The shepherd came running.

"Marcelin, call the police! This man wants to take advantage of me in my misfortune."

The shepherd looked somewhat surprised but obeyed. Fortunately the police station number was busy.

"Pay up!" I said then. "Pay whatever is being asked of you. The sale will automatically be canceled."

My words struck him like a bolt out of the blue. His face relaxed into a serene expression that almost erased his ugliness.

"Thank you," he said. "I hadn't thought of that."

TO THE EAST OF MY PROPERTY lived another colorful character. In honor of the eternal beret with the green pom-pom he was always wearing, people in the neighborhood called him "the

Scotsman." In fact he was Belgian. Nathanael van Boven must have been over eighty. Thirty years before the arrival of Brigitte Bardot, he had been king of the peninsula's nightlife. At that time, the Admiral, his famous café with musical entertainment, his jazz joints and discotheques were the recognized Meccas for those who enjoyed Saint-Tropez nightlife. When World War II ended, he had managed to increase his nocturnal empire by systematically colonizing the sublime Pampelonne beach with camping sites. His crowning glory, the Kon Tiki, was an immense tent and caravan site where ten to fifteen thousand tourists from all over Europe flocked together every summer in wild promiscuity. Convinced the Saint-Tropez myth must inevitably fade, one day van Boven sold everything and decided to retire. He had the means to buy the most sumptuous estate on the peninsula, but he chose instead to make his home in a small country house of summary comfort. Since then his hobby had been cultivating cacti. He grew every variety imaginable in tins salvaged from the municipal dump. He devoted his days to them, talking to them tenderly, changing their position according to the movement of the sun, watering them with an eyedropper, turning them around a quarter circle or semicircle like precious bottles of vintage champagne.

He greeted me with a white metal can in each hand containing what looked like a small green candle bristling with spikes.

"Please accept these modest welcoming gifts," he declared in a colorful Belgian accent. "They're candelabra cacti. Plant them on either side of your door. They'll protect you like sentries. Do you realize," he asked, changing the subject, "you got a damn good deal? I made the mistake of retiring too soon. Tomorrow a patch of ground in Saint-Tropez will be worth more than a whole block in Manhattan . . ."

My tour of the neighborhood concluded at the home of the local patriarch whose vast vineyards, woods and scrublands bordered a large part of my little plot. With its grandiose drive lined with hundred-year-old palm trees, its double hedge of scarlet and white laurels, its bougainvillea bushes that covered the buildings with a superb violet drape, the approach to Alphonse Cuissard's house lacked neither presence nor dignity. A Moroccan workman led me to a shed, where the master of the house was busy repairing a plowshare. With his solid peasant build, fresh pink cheeks and knowing expression, old man Cuissard did not look his seventy-five years. He ignored me, as indifferent to my arrival as he was to a hornet beating against the window of his workshop. He continued with his work, taking short puffs at the corn-colored Gitane protruding from the right corner of his mouth. I was about to turn on my heels when he condescended to notice my presence.

"So you're the Parisian that bastard Giovanni sold his plot to?" he growled, bringing his hammer down on his anvil again.

From Iraqi revolutionaries to Argentinean Tuparamos, I was to soft-soap quite a number of hard nuts. But in the presence of this Provençal potentate, I felt at a loss and even slightly guilty. By treating me as a "Parisian," he had instantly rejected, excluded and condemned me.

I had thought I was acquiring a piece of paradise. Instead I was to be sent hurriedly to purgatory! The day after our meeting, Georges, the local music-loving postman, brought me a registered letter. In it Cuissard informed me that the boundaries of my land were not those the seller had indicated to me. He claimed ownership of one of the plots I had bought. He was threatening legal proceedings. My dream was in danger of ending before it had properly begun.

3

A Green Room on the Shores of the Pacific

The road formed a dark ribbon between the sapphire expanse of the Pacific Ocean and a majestic row of giant palm trees. The California coast was a setting fit for daydreams and pleasant idleness. Tropical scents suffused the mild air, and the world seemed both sweet and harmonious. That was when I caught sight of the imposing fortress on its wave-washed promontory. How anyone had the gall to build so grim a structure in so heavenly a location! Beyond the defensive walls and barred windows of San Quentin penitentiary more than five thousand criminals were serving sentences, many condemned to spend their lives there. For about thirty men, the fifth story of a top-security building represented the last stop before the gas chamber.

In the spring of 1960 one of those men was a criminal by the name of Caryl Chessman. Although he was not a murderer, he had spent twelve years on death row. Eight times he had succeeded in deferring his meeting with the executioner, on the last two occasions within hours of the fateful moment. His desperate struggle to prove his innocence had made him the world's most famous prisoner. From New York to Rio de Janeiro, from Los Angeles to Paris, his predicament roused people's passions. According to California penal code, the simultaneously committed triple crime of sexual assault, kidnapping and robbery of which he was accused could warrant the death penalty. America might remain divided, but the rest of the planet was unanimous in its desire to spare his life. Could there be any punishment more inhuman than living for twelve years at the door to the gas chamber? For a man who had not committed murder? Two-thirds of the letters and telegrams that arrived each day on the governor of California's desk from every corner of the globe begged for clemency. Brazil alone sent more than 2.5 million signatures. The Belgian royal family, the Vatican, artists, intellectuals, scientists, industrialists, clerics and thousands of ordinary citizens telephoned to ask for Chessman's pardon. In a page-one headline the influential Buenos Aires newspaper *Critica* declared the Chessman case to be "the worst to confront the world for a long time." An editorial in the *London News Chronicle* warned: "Caryl Chessman's ordeal is a source of humiliation to the great American nation." Another English newspaper, the *Daily Herald*, wrote: "On the day Chessman is executed, it will be rather unpleasant to be American." In the Netherlands the best-selling musical album was a lament titled "Epitaph for Caryl."

The fever was no less high in the United States. The cover of *Time* had carried a portrait of Chessman, and the magazine devoted continuing coverage to what the country called "the Chessman affair." From one end of the land to another, thousands of jukeboxes played "The Ballad of Caryl Chessman." Three times its refrain repeated an appeal to "Let him live!" In Sacramento, the capital of California, hundreds of demonstrators lined the steps of the capitol building. Their banners castigated "ritual murder in the gas chambers." Under the governor's windows militants had started a hunger strike. A cavalcade of cars brought him a petition signed by 384 university professors, calling for the immediate closure of all gas chambers. A rodeo champion rode from town to town, collecting signatures. The streets of San Francisco were invaded by protesters calling for respect for civil rights.

Who was this man under sentence of death who had so captured the attention of the world? In the winter of 1948 a man in a car had been attacking couples parking at night on the deserted roads above Los Angeles. He would approach their car, directing a portable red revolving light at them. Believing it was a police patrol, his victims put up no resistance. That was when a threatening .45 revolver would appear.

"Pocketbook, wallet, jewelry, quickly!" a voice would order.

Theft was not the worst of his crimes. He had forced two young women, Regina Johnson, aged twenty-two, and Mary-Alice Meza, a seventeen-year-old high school student, to get into his car and perform oral sex on him, a crime that the law described as "an unnatural sex act." For entire nights undercover officers had hidden themselves away in places the criminal seemed to haunt. An officer had even dressed up as a woman to try to trap him. Radio stations broadcast his description. They were looking for a man who drove a late-model Ford and used a police light. The suspect was of Mediterranean type, with a tanned complexion. Between twenty-five and thirty years of age, he stood approximately five feet ten inches tall and weighed 145 to 175 pounds. He had brown crew-cut hair, dark eyes, a narrow, aquiline nose, crooked teeth and a pointed chin. Distinguishing feature: a scar above his brow ridge. Extreme caution was recommended. The criminal was armed and dangerous. The police were convinced they were not dealing with a first-time offender. Victims studied pictures of known criminals operating in the area to no avail.

The day after the attack on young Mary-Alice Meza, two men entered a clothing store in Redondo Beach, a southern suburb of Los Angeles, brandishing a revolver. After knocking the owner unconscious, emptying the cash register and snatching up some clothes, they made off in a late-model Ford. Some hours later two police officers, patrolling Vermont Avenue in the direction of Hollywood Boulevard, spotted a vehicle fitting the description of that of the robbers'. They set off in pursuit, sirens blaring. The chase ended in a scene worthy of a Hollywood gangster film. After a fierce shoot-out, two of the three occupants of the Ford were captured. The importance of the arrests did not escape the police. The driver of the car was one of California's most wanted gangsters, Caryl Chessman. One of his specialties was to hold up and rob the clients of Los Angeles's fashionable brothels. In the glove compartment of the car he was driving, police found a .45 revolver and a red revolving light. They came to the conclusion that they had at last put their hands on "the Red Light Bandit."

Chessman was accused of armed robbery, kidnapping and sexual assault, and his prosecutor demanded the death penalty. After a trial marked with numerous legal irregularities, he was sentenced to the gas chamber. Since then, all his appeals had been rejected. On the April morning that I pulled up to San Quentin, Caryl Chessman had a fortnight left to live. He was thirty-nine years old.

THIS UNUSUAL PRISONER had described his fight against execution and the ordeal of his wait on the threshold of the gas chamber in a book titled *Cell 2455—Death Row*. Like most of his readers, I had been deeply disturbed by his account. I had followed the developments of the affair with a mixture of horror and fascination. It had inspired several of my articles. As the condemned man's execution drew nearer, my reports provoked an ever-growing reaction among my readers in France. In response to the mail that poured in, my newspaper launched a petition to commute Caryl Chessman's sentence. We received more than 100,000 replies.

"Take all those petitions to the governor of California," my editor in chief directed me one morning. "And get Chessman to meet you on death row."

My editor in chief was never troubled by undue doubt. And while I was not certain I could accomplish the meeting so easily, his idea thrilled me. I knew that in America, prisoners under sentence of death had the right to meet journalists and even to appear on television. I knew also that for the past few weeks, Chessman had turned down all requests for interviews from U.S. journalists because of the hateful articles they had written about him. My non-American status might stand me in good stead. I got hold of the number of San Quentin penitentiary and called the chief warden in person. He asked me to give him some time to consult his prisoner.

"Mr. Chessman will be glad to receive you next Wednesday at 3:30 P.M.," he informed me when I called back. "Your meeting will take place in the visiting room of death row."

AT THE MAIN ENTRANCE to the penitentiary two guards in olive-green uniforms had been notified that I was coming. They had rosy cheeks and looked so benign, they might have been taken for two Club Med hosts. Even their rifles seemed inoffensive.

"Good journey?" inquired the one with the most braid, as he picked up a telephone. "Chess is expecting you."

He showed me the way to a metal detector and led me into a courtyard attractively adorned with a hedge of yellow and red rosebushes. Leaving on our left the high whitewashed walls of the old Spanish fort around which the penitentiary had been built, we proceeded through a double iron gate into a vast rectangular yard, a real concrete valley bounded by several multistory buildings, bristling with watchtowers.

The yard was empty at that time, but I could make out the sound of voices and felt the disquieting sensation of hundreds of pairs of eyes observing me from the cell windows. The guard had me pass in front of a series of cement plates. In each one was lodged an electronic eye capable of detecting a fragment of metal as small as a pin. I had to deposit my keys, change and cigarette lighter in a box. At last we arrived in front of an armored double door with a peephole. After some minutes, it opened to reveal a deep, dark cavern protected by barred gates and more armored doors.

I advanced toward the first iron gate. Guards came to unbolt it and lead me to the gaping mouth of a steel cage, the elevator to the rotunda of the north building. The ascent to the fifth floor was so slow that I had time to get used to the freezing horror of the place. The elevator deposited us at the entrance of a corridor, the other end of which was closed off by a double iron gate. The gate gave access to the narrow cell-lined passage known as death row. At the entrance to the landing, an armed guard kept watch from a cage protected by two sets of bars. Nothing that went on in the "row" could escape him. Next door was a small room, brilliantly lit by fluorescent lights, with a table and four chairs. An iron grille served as a door. The walls and ceiling were painted green. This, at last, was the visiting room for prisoners under sentence of death.

4,341 Days in a Slaughterhouse

"Abandon hope all ye who enter herein," inscribed Dante on the opening page of his *Inferno*. Death row in San Quentin was a hell far more dreadful than that conceived by the Italian writer. Chessman had described it as a somber and hostile necropolis cut off from real life, a dismal hole in which people clung desperately to existence before being killed, a scrap heap for the haunted, wounded and lost. The destructive psychological effect of a death sentence was compounded by the funereal, pitiless nature of surroundings in which people lived as if suspended between two worlds. The man I was about to meet had spent 4,341 days in this slaughterhouse where the specter of death was a constant companion.

Yet everything there seemed peaceful and orderly. The guards were courteous. The barred doors opened and closed again without undue noise, the visiting room smelled of fresh paint. Of course this impression was deceptive; at any moment some unexpected crisis could arise. Without provocation the occupants of this microcosm could explode with sudden, murderous violence. Here the prospect of a planned death drove the weakest to madness. Chessman had seen many of his fellow prisoners go to pieces under the torture of waiting. He had heard their prayers, their screams, their curses. He had seen them roll naked on the floor in their own excrement, hurl themselves at other men's throats, smash their washbasins, their toilet bowls, and destroy everything in their cells. He had heard their heart-rending pleas for mercy and watched as the corpses of prisoners who had slashed their veins and bled like pigs were carried away. Stranger still were instances in which vestiges of life outside the prison existed side by side with those images of horror. The previous Christmas, when Chessman had been approaching his seventh appointment with the executioner, the prison warden had had a magnificent Christmas tree, sparkling with garlands, baubles, candles and luminous stars, erected at the entrance to the row. Returning from their walk, the condemned men had come timidly to touch its branches and sniff the wild, unreal scent of the forest.

That spring, twenty-four prisoners waited with Caryl Chessman to be brought to the ground floor—to the "green room" used for executions. In the course of his twelve-year detention, Chessman had seen more than two hundred of his fellow inmates embark on this final journey. Some had been friends. For three years Bald Henry, a former factory worker condemned to death for the rape and murder of a little girl, had stagnated five cells away from him. Chessman had placed all his legal knowledge at the disposal of this "poor man with the soul of a bird and the body of a colossus." Eventually Chessman's argument for "diminished responsibility" convinced the governor of California to commute Henry's sentence. When the governor telephoned to issue Bald Henry's reprieve and subsequent transfer to a psychiatric asylum, the young rapist had just been strapped into the chair in the gas chamber. The executioner barely had time to release him before it was too late.

Chessman had had another friend, whom he had known only by his nickname. The Phantom Killer was a puny creature with a thin voice who used to roam the streets of Los Angeles with a .38 Smith & Wesson in his pocket. He would fire at random at passersby, without any real intention of killing anyone, but just to frighten himself. One day a woman was hit in the heart. It took the police two years to catch her murderer, dispatch him to death row and have him executed.

Chessman had also grown attached to the giant of a man who occupied a cell near his for years. Originally from Arkansas, Big

Red had come to work in the rich orchards of California's San Joaquin Valley. He was an unpretentious, easygoing man. One night, after a drinking bout, he had been taken to a police station and locked up with two drunks. In a fit of violence he knocked one of them out. The man died. Big Red found himself on San Quentin's death row. A fanatical supporter of President Eisenhower, he campaigned for his reelection among his fellow prisoners and the guards. To feel his idol close to him as he died, he had requested to take a portrait of the former general with him into the gas chamber. The favor had been denied, but Big Red died reassured about the future of America. His candidate had just been reelected.

There were two chairs in San Quentin's gas chamber, and it was not unheard-of for two condemned men to be executed at the same time. Four years earlier, at the time of his sixth appointment with the executioner, Chessman was to have died next to Frank, a slightly built convict who had cut the throat of a fellow inmate in another prison. Shortly before Chessman's transfer to the gas chamber, the chief warden had informed him he had been granted another stay of execution. So Frank had gone to the green room alone, shouting as he left the row: "Good luck, Chess!" He seemed resigned. After three years on the row, knowing he had, as he put it, no more chance of getting out of there alive than "a snowball in hell," he was glad to put an end to it all. Chessman had seen such a reaction many times. The sinister atmosphere of the row, the confusing complexities of legal proceedings, the feeling of being caught in a trap like a rat, eventually drove many a condemned man to say: "To hell with it all!" No one had ever taken any interest in Frank's predicament. No one had written to the governor to request clemency for him. Like the vast majority of the condemned, he let himself be gassed with no more fuss than a dog put to sleep at a pound.

Others were not so equivocal about their end. Léandress Rilly, a young black man, had killed a shopkeeper in the course of a burglary that went wrong. Twenty years old and terrified of dying, he struggled to the last. He even managed to tear himself free and get out of the chair before the gas was introduced.

Guards had been obliged to interrupt the execution to strap him down again. By the time the deadly vapors reached his lungs, he had freed one arm. Chessman could not forget his screams.

It was one of the fundamental truths of the row: every condemned person reacted differently to the final moment. Some left the row swaggering, head erect, greeting their fellow prisoners with two fingers held high in a V for victory; others left hurling insults and curses; yet others recited prayers. Harry, a placid farm laborer, who in a moment of madness had shot and killed the girl with whom he was platonically in love, left the row with a Bible in his shackled hands, singing psalms at the top of his voice. Jack, a fresh-faced, beardless youth, kept on asking why no one came to his rescue. Stanley, who had murdered an elderly woman, was still indignant about the "bad joke" of which he thought he was the victim. "You're making a mistake!" insisted Doil, a twenty-seven-year-old black man who had been the lookout while his pals killed the owner of a store during a robbery: "I wasn't the one who pulled the trigger." Tom, a truck driver who had strangled his wife's lover, went to his death without showing he was upset in any way, smoking one of the cheap fat cigars that had fouled the row for years. Eddy, a prisoner riddled with cancer, had seemed to welcome the release the gas chamber promised.

Some were first-time offenders; others were true professionals. Yet others were pathetic creatures driven to murder by sexual perversions or psychological disorders. They had killed with firearms, bludgeons, knives, axes and their bare hands. Three-quarters of death row inmates had only state-appointed lawyers to defend them. Most had been put to death on the first date fixed for their execution. A few had procured one or two reprieves, but death had caught up with them all.

CARYL CHESSMAN WAS THE CHAMPION of stayed executions. Having turned himself into an expert on California criminal law, he had managed to secure eight reprieves in twelve years. His success had earned him the animosity of a large proportion of his countrymen, who were scandalized that a man sentenced to death could be allowed to avoid punishment. Newspapers declaimed "perversion of the course of justice" and called for the urgent introduction of new legislation "to make Chessman finally pay his debt to society." Four times he faced the ritual preparation for capital punishment: he had made his last wishes known, received envoys from an eye bank who came to ask him to donate his corneas, made arrangements for his cremation and the disposal of his ashes with the undertaker's representative. He knew the procedures by heart. To the chief warden of the penitentiary, who one day asked him whether he thought he could really avoid the gas chamber, he replied: "My journey in the company of hatred is over. I have had my life saved from justice too often to react emotionally. Death has lost all significance for me. I am as ready to die as to go on living, that's all." Then, quoting from Swinburne's "The Garden of Proserpine," he had concluded: "I am tired of tears and laughter, and of men who laugh and weep." Another evening, while waiting for word on a possible stay of execution, he listened as a radio commentator described the death he would face. "At times like that," he noted in his diary, "you have a choice between terror and madness."

His fight to prove he was not the infamous Red Light Bandit had made some people happy. Before each one of his appointments with the executioner, the Los Angeles bookmakers took bets. They generally gave six to one for a week before the fateful date, but the odds lengthened as the day of reckoning drew nearer. The previous time, the odds had risen to twenty-four to one. On February 18, 1960, not a gambler in Los Angeles was prepared to risk a single dollar on the survival of the famous prisoner. When his guards came to lead him to the ground-floor cage for his last night, seven paces away from the gas chamber where he was due to be executed the next morning, it seemed the bettors would be vindicated.

It was then that a radio bulletin announced what no one had dared to imagine. It was a little after midnight. Caryl Chessman had begun his last night on earth. Two hundred and fifty miles away, in the heart of Sacramento, the state capital, Governor Edmund Brown had withdrawn to his study to try and resolve Caryl Chessman's endless confrontation with the law.

"It was a long and difficult debate with my conscience," he would confide, "but all the facts of the problem pointed to a single certainty: the death penalty was a bad thing."

Brown had therefore called for a special session of the state legislature to suggest that California consider the possibility of a law abolishing the death penalty. Then he postponed Chessman's execution for sixty days so that in the event of a favorable vote, Chessman would be spared. The next morning he asked the people of California themselves to express their views on capital punishment through the voices of their representatives.

The reactions came instantaneously and with a vehemence that was unusual even for a state accustomed to political excess. California's blood was up. The press again took to the warpath. Delegates in every camp demanded the governor's resignation, or even his indictment. A number of Brown's collaborators and political supporters, although for the most part against capital punishment, judged the timing to be bad. As it happened, four-fifths of the seats in the California Assembly were shortly to come up for reelection. The governor's initiative could cause dissension within the Democratic Party and tarnish the political profile of one of their emblematic figures. After all, wasn't Brown his party's best chance in the next race for the White House?

The governor defended his project courageously on the Assembly's rostrum. He knew the leaders of his party were divided on the question of capital punishment. He knew, above all, that their primary aim was to stifle any controversy and protect him against the negative repercussions to which he had exposed himself. When he realized the delegates would never vote for the abolition of the death penalty, he suggested an alternative: suspend the implementation of the death penalty for three and a half years; then decide.

His proposal was submitted to a commission of representatives. In a heated sixteen-hour marathon the commission heard arguments both for and against capital punishment. Its most ardent supporters included judges, police and even clerics. One prosecuting attorney tried to demonstrate the advantages of quite simply eliminating criminals serving life sentences. "One of these blades still bears traces of the blood of a guard stabbed straight in the heart," he declared, exhibiting a collection of weapons found in prisoners' cells.

A police superintendent alerted the commission to the dangers of "believing that the unique objective of the penal code is to ensure the rehabilitation of offenders." A pastor swept away their last scruples by declaring that "if governments exist, it is in order to enable God to dispense just punishment." In the face of such an onslaught, the arguments of those opposed to the death penalty, supported by statistics demonstrating its ineffectiveness as a deterrent, stood no chance of mustering even the smallest majority. The governor's proposed moratorium was rejected by eight votes to seven. This surprised no one. Everyone agreed that if the case of the celebrated San Quentin prisoner had not been interwoven with the matter in question, the result would probably have been different.

The governor was not slow to recognize that a significant proportion of Americans shared this viewpoint. A torrent of telegrams and letters rained down on his desk. As an execution approached, his mail was usually teeming with appeals for clemency. This time the reverse was true.

The fact that Chessman had been charged with a sex crime exacerbated the animosity of many of the correspondents. The fact, too, that for the first time in the annals of the law, so many years had elapsed without sentence being enacted was for some "proof that it had not been possible to carry out proper and expeditious justice." No one put forward the hypothesis that these stays of execution might have been justified by some error on the part of the law, universally considered to be infallible. Instead, everyone reiterated what the newspapers never stopped claiming, namely that Caryl Chessman was "an evil genius" who compounded his crimes by refusing to submit to just punishment. Rare were those who recognized in the long delay proof of the respect America had for the rights of the individual. Many felt that Chessman had manipulated the legal system, that he had taken advantage of its weakness. In other words, Americans judged Caryl Chessman a bad loser. The *Los Angeles Times* summed up this point of view, stating that "this particularly perverse and adept criminal has called to question the functioning of our legal system and stained our laws with discredit." It was no longer a matter of killing Chessman in order to expiate his crimes, but rather in order to rehabilitate the system his stratagems and tricks had made the object of derision. In order to restore public confidence in its courts and laws, Caryl Chessman had to die.

The most contemptible arguments were brought to bear. "Chessman is a Jew and Jews always manage to get away with it," claimed one letter, while another castigated "civil rights defenders and other communists who contaminate America's true values by coming to Chessman's defense." Another spoke for a widespread section of public opinion when it declared that "Chessman must die because he's a dirty bastard." Even religion came into it. "I am a Catholic and I shall never go to church again if his sentence is commuted," one woman promised. Reminding people that the apostle Paul had been put to death despite his innocence, one Baptist pastor inquired: "Are we to abolish our laws just because an innocent man might be decapitated?" A petition signed by twelve graduates of the University of California demanded quite simply that Chessman be killed "so that he stops being a burden to the taxpayers."

A number of the letters invoked the usual myths supporting the death penalty. A mother asked: "Is it surprising to find that crime is constantly on the increase when any adolescent can point a finger at Chessman and say: 'That man has escaped just punishment'?" Perhaps the most disturbing thing the letters revealed was the fact that people questioned a man's most fundamental right—the right to fight for his own life.

GOVERNOR BROWN DECLARED himself "extremely disappointed" at the failure of his attempt to have the death penalty abolished in the state of California. As a consequence he announced he had "no more power to intervene in the Chessman affair." He ordered the resumption of executions. In San Quentin the first appointment in the green room fell to a twenty-nine-year-old truck driver, Charlie Brubaker, perpetrator of a double murder. A week later it was Lawrence Wade, a thirty-two-year-old black saxophonist who had killed an Oakland liquor shop owner in the course of a burglary. The second of May was selected for Chessman.

A few days before Brubaker's execution, an unusual incident caused a commotion on the row. Returning from his daily walk, Chessman had found a goldfish bowl full of water in his cell. From behind the glass, two globular eyes surveyed him fixedly. It was a little silver herring like the ones people fished for in San Francisco Bay.

"Guys! There's a fish in my place!"

A chorus of sarcastic remarks and whistles greeted the news. Had Chessman cracked up?

"Liar!" a voice rang out.

Chessman decanted the herring from the bowl into a peanut butter jar and brandished the receptacle at arm's length through the bars.

"Look, you bunch of assholes! Just take a look!"

Chessman placed the container on the cement floor of the row. He pushed it delicately toward his neighbor and asked him to have it passed on from cell to cell. Then he called out: "Charlie, it's for you!" He hoped the fish's presence would relieve the misery of the truck driver's last days. In five years Brubaker had received only one visit, from his mother, a poor woman who had been driven half-mad by her son's crime and punishment.

Forwarded with infinite care, the jar and its occupant

reached their destination. Then Brubaker's gruff voice boomed out like a clap of thunder:

"Chess, what's your bloody herring called?"

At a loss, Chessman hesitated. Memories of his reading tumbled through his mind. "Prometheus! It's called Prometheus!" he responded triumphantly, delighted to have come up with the name of the mythological hero who had managed to break free of his chains.

"What's the point? I won't be here anymore."

I heard the clank of a lock. Caryl Chessman stood in front of me, in his blue-jean uniform, taller, more solidly built than I had envisaged, his face pale and rather repellent with its broken nose, deep wrinkles and slightly drooping lower lip. His heavy hand took mine and he invited me to sit down. Then with a gentle voice which contrasted oddly with his appearance, he welcomed me.

With a gaze that was dark, percussive and deep, he looked around the visiting room.

"How beautiful Paris must be at this time of the year."

The remark took me by surprise. What relevance could the passing of the seasons possibly have in this hellhole? I agreed, a little embarrassed.

In the presence of this prisoner, in the prime of his life and perfectly in control of himself, I felt like a small boy at a loss. What questions could I possibly ask this man who, in a few days, was due to undergo a ritual and programmed death?

The conversation began awkwardly. The harsh light from the ceiling prompted me to ask a question that immediately sounded silly to my own ears.

"Can you see daylight from your cell?"

"Yes, a tiny patch of sky. Sometimes I even catch a glimpse of a seagull, calling as it passes."

"Where there's life, there's hope, no?"

A disappointed smile crumpled the corner of his mouth. "Not really." He offered me a cigarette, then added, with the detachment of a doctor pronouncing a diagnosis: "You know, after spending twelve years shut up in a cell half the size of this room, you eventually give up building castles in the air."

"But after so many years haven't you finished by adapting yourself to your situation?"

Again, I immediately regretted this stupid question. What was more, I knew what the answer would be. In his first book Chessman had described how he had learned to live with all the groaning and yelling, the prayers uttered aloud, the blaspheming and cursing on death row. If he had managed not to go under, it was because his existence in this morbid place had been in many respects different from the normal life of a man about to be executed. By devoting himself to writing he had managed to channel his energy and subdue his anxieties. His subsequent books had given his life meaning and direction. He had never given up following world events, and those years of coexistence with death had enabled him to calm his hatred, appease his spirit of revolt.

He kept silent for a long time and then smiled. "Every morning when I wake up, it's like coming to my cell for the first time," he said.

His face was peaceful. When I asked him to describe the atmosphere on the row at the moment, he took several drags on his cigarette.

"Quite good. I should say that several of the guards have been there for years. I know all about their lives and their problems. We've formed bonds of friendship. Sure, they lock up the cells. But they do it noiselessly, without any aggressiveness. They do it because it's their job."

"And your fellow prisoners?"

Chessman's expression became serious.

"Last week there were still six of us waiting for imminent execution. Lawrence Wade, the saxophonist next door, was put to death on Friday. It'll be my turn on May 2." He specified the date as if it were the most natural thing in the world. "Then, on

13, 20, 28 . . . There are five of us due to go over the next few days . . . Yes, that's right, five."

A silence imposed itself. I ventured a diversion.

"I've heard that since the death of your saxophonist neighbor, you've inherited a cellmate. Is it true?"

"You want to talk about Prometheus? Prometheus, the herring?"

I nodded in confirmation. Chessman laughed heartily.

"He's a demanding bugger. I can't go out for my walk without him letting me know he doesn't like to be left alone. Every time I come back, I find all the water splashed out of his bowl, with Prometheus about to expire. Despite the proximity of the sea, getting hold of seawater in this prison is not easy. For two days now, I've been putting the television on for him before I leave my cell. That keeps him a bit quieter. They brought me a set the day before yesterday. It's a privilege reserved for the inhabitants of death row once the execution procedure has started. Now and then I look at the news but when you're this close to dying, daily realities lose much of their meaning. When they predict traffic jams on the weekend, you know it doesn't concern you. You hear the next exciting programs announced and you say to yourself: 'What's the point? I won't be here anymore.'"

"I suppose all the other prisoners on the row have been sentenced for murder . . ."

"That's right. All except me."

"How many of them have any chance of being pardoned?"

"You can never tell . . . not until the very last minute."

"Are they friendly to you, the old-timer?"

"Not all of them. Some are envious of my fame. You must realize that most of them are in a terrifying state of psychological distress. No one from their families ever comes to see them. One young black guy who has been here for thirteen months hasn't even had a visit from a lawyer yet."

"If you were given the choice today between death and life imprisonment, I mean imprisonment without any hope of release, imprisonment to the end of your days, what would you choose?"

The response took the form of a explosion:

"Life! I have enough work to keep me busy for several years! Years at the end of which I might be able to become a real writer. I've got at least four novels in my head and a play." Seeing my astonishment, he went into more detail: "A theater play about the life of one of your countrymen . . . Guess who. I'll give you a clue: this man was born on the day Joan of Arc was burned at the stake."

This American criminal's cultural knowledge amazed me. I tried to concentrate but the setting and the circumstances of this unusual test were too stressful to help me find an answer. Chessman was amused by my ignorance.

"François Villon!" he exclaimed triumphantly. "Like me, your poet was condemned to death. Without wanting to sound pretentious, I feel a profound communion with him."

"Have you already started writing, or is this just an idea for the future?"

"I haven't got a single word down on paper yet, but there are three good acts in my head."

He took a pencil out of his pocket and showed it to me, as if to say, "All I have to do is get down to it." Pointing to the barred door through which we could see a rifle resting on the guard's knees, he added in a low voice: "The worst part about it is that I'm officially forbidden to write. Since the publication of my first book, they've tightened up the rules. I'm under constant surveillance. If they find any writing on me or in my cell that isn't related to my defense, I'm instantly sent to solitary." He sighed. "Not being able to write freely is worse for me than waiting for death itself."

I delved for some distraction that was neither trite nor ridiculous. "At least you can have visitors, whereas in France a person condemned to death is not allowed to see anyone apart from a lawyer or close relatives. You even have the right to meet journalists."

He stood up, walked around his chair and sat down again. I had touched a sore point. His face had darkened. "I do have a few good, faithful friends in the press," he admitted. "Several of them have even put their careers at risk to defend me. But the vast majority of their colleagues have such an obvious antipathy toward me that communication is impossible. Some of them have been pursuing me like a pack of hounds for years. And, you see, the psychological conditions of life here mean that I can't cope easily with hatred. That's why for some time now, I've almost systematically refused to answer journalists' questions."

He watched my pen moving over my notebook and gave me a friendly smile. "With you it's different. You aren't caught up in all the intrigue and compromising of local politics. You're like a breath of fresh air in my reclusive life. And your presence is proof that people on the other side of the world care about the plight of a stranger shut away in the depths of this prison."

"AND NOW, CARYL, WITH A WEEK to go to your execution, what do you feel?"

It was my second visit. There were to be six in all.

"What do I feel?" he repeated, shrugging his shoulders with a smile. "Neither frantic hope nor absolute despair. I feel capable of walking into the gas chamber with my head held high and facing death calmly. I'm trying not to live in a permanent state of anguish, haunted by my imminent death. It's not easy . . ."

His face wore a slight sneer, as if his expression could erase any grandiloquence in what he had just said.

"Caryl, what do you want most from now on?"

"Peace of mind for the few days I have left to live." After a silence, he added: "What else could I wish for?"

"Is there a woman in your life?" I asked.

I knew that some years earlier Chessman had been passionately in love. Her name was Judy. "With her little girl looks, her sparkling laughter, her warm, alluring beauty, Judy had everything a man could hope for in a woman," he had written. Judy was a waitress in a drugstore. The rebellious young car thief, who had just spent two years in an extremely harsh rehabilitation center, had found with her what he had thought existed only in novels and films: happiness. He had made great plans: to change his life, find a job, marry Judy and have a child with her. To his much-loved mother, Hallie, he would restore the faith she had lost in her renegade son. The couple planned to make their home in Los Angeles with the poor woman, who lived in a state of appalling suffering, paralyzed as a result of a car accident.

A newspaper article had undone all these noble intentions. Reading that new developments in neurological surgery were enabling some handicapped people to recover the use of their legs, Caryl had brought the surgeon who wrote the scientific report to his mother's bedside. The doctor admitted that improvement was possible but that it would involve numerous delicate and costly operations. He estimated the cost at several thousand dollars.

Forgetting all his good resolutions, Caryl Chessman undertook to obtain the money for his mother's operation. He stole a car and, armed with a revolver, started to hold up the clients of the gambling dens and brothels in the affluent parts of Los Angeles. He very swiftly accumulated enough money to pay the surgeon's fee and the hospital charges for his beloved mother. But three operations could not restore life to her limbs. His mother would remain a cripple for life.

Caryl drowned his despair in ever more reckless acts of violence. He committed up to eight robberies in a single night. Arrested and tried immediately, he was sentenced to sixteen years' incarceration. He had not yet celebrated his twentieth birthday. His mother died of grief. As for Judy, whom he saw several times through the glass of his prison visiting room, he managed to convince her that she should give him up.

After seven years in confinement, he was paroled, only to fall soon again into the hands of the law. Since Judy, had he found love again? He smiled, and then his face assumed an expression of sadness.

"A woman's love is a luxury you can't allow yourself when you're on the list of those condemned to death. Think of the distress, the tension, the horror of waiting, for a woman who loves you . . ."

Impressed by so much lucidity, I inquired whether he had found relief from his ordeal from another source. He had written once how a Bible he found on the bunk in his cell had helped him tolerate his first experience of imprisonment. He had learned numerous verses of Ecclesiastes by heart, repeating them unflaggingly as he paced up and down in his cell like a wild animal: *To every thing there is a season, and a time to every purpose under the heaven: A time to be born, and a time to die . . . A time to kill, and a time to heal . . . A time to love, and a time to hate* . . . Where did he stand now?

"Caryl, how do you see the afterlife?"

"As a total void," he replied without the least hesitation. "I'm not a believer. I'm not against religion. I can't swear to anything. I simply don't have the answer." He paused. "I think we all have a time on earth, and that we leave . . . That's all."

SOMETIMES, WHEN CHESSMAN seemed tense or anxious, I would try to come up with an absurd question.

"If you suddenly had the chance to escape, what would you do?" I asked him one day.

The response came back at me like a bullet: "I'd make for Brazil where I have friends waiting for me . . . I'd like to be able to visit Europe . . . Do you think I would be regarded as undesirable in France?"

I reassured him. His long torment and his keenness to survive had earned him enough sympathy in France to ensure a friendly reception. The thought brought a light of whimsical joy to his face, which encouraged me to lure him further away from this sinister penitentiary. To a man who would be put to death in a few days, I dared to talk about life and the future. It was almost surreal. I described to him the beauty of the Parisian girls savoring the spring sunshine on the café terraces. I portrayed for him the pink mist that rises from the waters of the Seine as twilight approaches, I evoked the fragrance of the chestnut trees blooming in the gardens on the Champs-Elysées, I spoke to him of the magic of Paris, a city that was falling asleep even as we talked. I also helped him to imagine the beauty of Saint-Tropez harbor which I had just left, the sublime light of Provence on the vineyards and the parasol pines.

The clanking of a key in the lock put an end to our imaginary escapade. Before being taken away, Chessman took my hands in his. "Dominique, come back tomorrow, without fail!" he said warmly.

IT WAS OUR FOURTH MEETING. From the very beginning of our talks I had been obsessed with one particular question: why had this man who possessed both sparkling intelligence and abundant charm needed to pass himself off as a police officer and brandish a revolver to obtain a woman's favors?

Chessman was anxious to have me know how the Los Angeles police had made people believe he was the Red Light Bandit.

"I was dragged at nightfall outside the home of young Mary-Alice Meza, one of that man's victims. She lived on the fourth floor. She was called to the window. It was barely possible to see. I'd been arrested and put in solitary confinement for two days and hadn't been able to wash or shave. I'd been beaten black-and-blue and my nose had been broken. From the street a police officer pointed to me in between his two uniformed colleagues and called out to the girl: 'Your assailant is one of these three men. Do you recognize him?' That's how I became the Red Light Bandit. And yet I wasn't anything like the description the girl had given the police."

I was astonished. "So why did you sign a confession?"

He pointed to his nose.

"To put a stop to gun-butt blows in the head and kicks in the stomach, one would ultimately admit to anything . . ."

An "Unknown" Person Called Terranova

Twenty-seven days before the fatal second of May, a New York monthly magazine by the name of *Argosy*, specializing in criminal matters, sent one of its crack journalists to San Quentin to report on Caryl Chessman's last days. William Woodfield emerged from the penitentiary convinced an innocent man was about to be killed. He called his editor in chief and persuaded him to let him reopen the inquiry: he wanted to find fresh evidence to prove that Chessman was not the Red Light Bandit. Woodfield was given a free hand and the support of his colleague, Milt Malchin, a veteran of investigative journalism. The two men jumped into the story with passion. They quickly discovered the photograph the police had taken of Chessman three days after his arrest. The picture revealed a sizable bruise on the right side of his forehead. It flagrantly contradicted the medical report produced at the trial claiming that the accused showed no trace of injury after questioning. The jury never saw the photo. The prosecution used the medical report to prove that Chessman's initial confession had not been obtained through police brutality.

Woodfield and Malchin also managed to lay hands on the initial statements the victims of the Red Light Bandit made to the police. These statements were not consistent with what their signatories subsequently told the court in the course of the trial. A certain Thomas Bartle had indicated that the individual had "several front teeth that were crooked." It was a detail that could scarcely have eluded him: he was a dentist. This distinguishing feature in itself should have disqualified Chessman—who was blessed with even teeth—on the spot. But this piece of information had never appeared in the file submitted to the court.

The *Argosy* journalists brought other disturbing facts to light. On studying the victims' statements kept secret by the police, they noticed that the description of the Red Light Bandit's vehicle did not tally with the Ford Chessman had been driving at the time of his arrest. One had been described as a light-colored two-door coupé, while the other was a dark four-door sedan.

The testimony that had carried the most weight in the jury's vote in favor of the death sentence had been that of Mary-Alice Meza, who had allegedly gone insane as a consequence of the sexual assaults to which the Red Light Bandit had subjected her. Of all his victims, she was the one he had kept longest in his car. She had been able to observe the arrangement of the interior and had explained that on the dashboard, which remained lit up, she had noticed a "round speedometer." When a police officer had shown her a picture of a similar dashboard, she had confirmed, "Yes, that's what it was like." At the trial her testimony had been taken as crucial. Woodfield and Malchin discredited it. The car Chessman was driving could not have been that of Meza's assailant, because on the previous day the speedometer had been taken out for repair. The two journalists had managed to get proof of this from a local mechanic's invoice book.

From a "Confidential" file found with the Los Angeles county sheriff, Woodfield and Malchin further established that some victims of the Red Light Bandit had stated that they were attacked by *two* men. Who was the other individual whose existence the police had concealed since Chessman's arrest?

These revelations raised serious questions about the Los Angeles Police Department, regarded at the time as the most corrupt in the United States. As for the acts of brutality committed by its members, they were so frequent that the department was beset by scandals. Numerous police officers had ended up in prison.

Working day and night thanks to an abundant supply of coffee, the two journalists followed up every line of inquiry that might prove that Chessman was not the Red Light Bandit. At his trial the prosecution had not been able to catch him in a lie or categorically prove his guilt. The victims' fingerprints had not been found in Chessman's car. No trace of blood had been discovered on the seats, even though the two victims of sexual assault had stated that they were having their periods at the time of the attack. Six days after Chessman's arrest, however, two detectives had mysteriously found two hairs in the car that an expert for the prosecution attributed to one of the victims.

All the same, would proving the condemned man's innocence be enough to prevent his execution? The two journalists doubted it. Above all, they needed to find the person who was really guilty. Fortune smiled on them. Although the document had disappeared from police records, they managed to dig out the transcript of the very first interview with Chessman, conducted a few hours after his capture.

"The guy you're looking for is Terranova," Chessman had said. "The red light and the sexual assaults, that's all him." He had then provided a detailed description of the individual concerned. At the time, the police had claimed to have no record of a criminal fitting this profile. In their eyes, as in those of the judges and the members of the jury who had condemned Chessman to death, "Terranova" was a myth, a phantom, a pure invention of the accused.

Woodfield and Malchin were to discover that Charles Severine Terranova was well and truly real. His crooked teeth and the scar over his left eye fitted the description provided by the victims of the Red Light Bandit. This criminal, so curiously unknown to police, had in fact a record of thirteen convictions for crimes committed in the Los Angeles area. Terranova had been released in 1955 after seven years' incarceration. Since then he had disappeared. But Woodfield and Malchin had found his photograph, a portrait in which the scar over the left eye, referred to by several victims of the Red Light Bandit, was clearly distinguishable.

The two journalists were overwhelmed by the enormous implications of their discoveries. If they were to keep them exclusive to their monthly, they would deprive Caryl Chessman of a chance of escaping the gas chamber: the next issue of *Argosy* was not due out until June. Woodfield and Malchin rushed to meet Chessman's lawyers. They all agreed: these revelations were to be relayed immediately to Governor Brown. There was not an hour to lose. The two journalists took the first plane for Sacramento.

Their journey got off to a bad start. When they presented

themselves at their flight check-in, Malchin saw a very corpulent man approach the stewardess and ask to see the passenger
list. The hostess replied that she did not have the authority to
let him have it. The man did not insist and vanished into the
crowd. Malchin gave no more thought to the incident until a
message over the loudspeaker invited all passengers on his
flight to come to the airline desk. They were then informed
that, due to a bomb threat, their departure would be delayed.
FBI agents searched the aircraft for three hours. No suspect device was discovered, but the two journalists learned their lesson. They decided to take the precaution of traveling
separately. Malchin would take the plane; Woodfield would
make the journey by car.

NEVER BEFORE HAD THE CORRIDORS of the Sacramento capitol
building known such a stir. One week before the fateful date,
it seemed that all the American and international press had
arranged to meet outside Governor Brown's office. An astute,
distinguished-looking African American man was trying to appease the journalists' impatience. A Harvard-educated attorney, Cecil Poole, aged thirty-one, standing six feet two inches
with a thin Clark Gable mustache, was in charge of criminal
pardons on the governor's staff. It was he who first examined all
pleas for reprieve or for commutation of the death sentence.
His authority was absolute and the governor always followed
his recommendations.

Immediately after my first meeting with Chessman, I, too,
had gone to Sacramento, to submit to the governor the 100,000
petitions I had brought with me from Paris. I had been received by Cecil Poole. The governor's adviser could not sup-
press a look of displeasure at the sight of the bundles of
petitions I deposited in front of him.

"A lot of fuss about nothing," he growled.

"A man's life is not nothing," I ventured. "Especially when
the man is not a murderer."

"Mr. Lapierre, you are French, and you are not familiar with American legislation," Poole replied politely. "Mr. Chessman has been tried and sentenced in accordance with our laws. You must agree that our justice system has shown exceptional leniency. Mr. Chessman has been the beneficiary of twelve years' respite in which to make good his claims. I do not think that the law in your country is given to showing such patience with criminals it has found liable to the guillotine."

I drew his attention to the fact that, in France, the crimes with which Caryl Chessman was charged were not punishable with death. I reminded him that the Red Light Bandit's "kidnappings" in fact consisted of making his victims get out of one car and into another.

Poole let out a small sneer. I thought I saw a hostile glint in his expression. I wondered whether this educated black man was not, in a sense, trying to settle his score with whites. So many black people filled the death rows of American prisons without ever being lucky enough to have anyone take an interest in their plight. Chessman himself had recounted the stories of so many poor bastards who let themselves be quietly led away to the gas chambers, strapped to an electric chair or hanged, to the complete indifference of press and public. Why should a criminal be spared now just because the color of his skin had earned him the compassion of the world?

"I shall pass on these signatures to the governor and ask him to see you," said Cecil Poole.

He stood up: the meeting was over.

THE TWO *ARGOSY* JOURNALISTS entered the office of the man responsible for pardons, carrying two attaché cases full of documents amassed in the course of their inquiry. Their drawn features and crumpled suits betrayed their exhausted state. But they felt confident. In a few hours the governor would be aware of their spectacular discoveries. He would be able to revise his position and ask the State Supreme Court for Chessman's pardon and a review of his trial.

Woodfield and Malchin were mistaken. Cecil Poole categorically refused to believe that, after so many years, two journalists could bring to light so much new evidence. He leafed reluctantly through the documents, pausing from time to time to consult an item in one of the record files behind him. When he came to the photograph of Chessman with a bruise on his forehead that the medical report had disavowed, he acknowledged sportingly: "That is indeed new." The discovery of Terranova's existence and the revelations about his criminal past also seemed to interest him.

"You've brought us two previously unrevealed pieces of evidence," he concluded. "I'll look at all your information over the weekend, and tell you on Monday what I think of it."

The two journalists hurried away to share their optimism with Chessman.

THAT SAME EVENING, I MET the condemned man again. He was usually very pale, so I was surprised at how well he looked. He could not hide his excitement and relief.

"The *Argosy* investigators' disclosures are going to be a bombshell, Dominique," he said. "What they've discovered proves I was the victim of a conspiracy on the part of the Los Angeles police who were fed up with my holdups on the brothels they were protecting. My lawyers are at last going to present irrefutable proof to clear me of the Red Light Bandit's crimes. This time it won't be a question of a reprieve but a fresh trial! A trial that will make me a free man!"

Casting a glance at the guard who was twiddling his whistle around his index finger beyond the barred gate, I leaned over to whisper to Chessman. "Have you confirmed to the *Argosy* reporters that this Terranova you mentioned during your first interview is really the Red Light Bandit?"

My question made him start. "Certainly not!"

"Why do you persist in leaving a shadow of doubt over the precise identity of this bandit? It's known that you gave it to your lawyer Rosalie Asher some weeks ago, with the request that she make it public fifty years after your execution. Why don't you speak out now? It wouldn't make any difference to him. His crimes are covered by the statute of limitations. Whereas for you it's a matter of life or death."

I felt embarrassed. How could I dare give advice to a man who, in twelve years, had postponed his appointment with death eight times; a man who had shown himself more adept and more determined than the pack of judges, prosecutors and journalists set on seeing him into the green room?

Chessman smiled and offered me a cigarette. My visiting time was up. The guard had already unbolted the barred door to take him back to his cell.

"See you tomorrow!" he called out to me with a smile.

"I'd rather go to the gas chamber."

"I don't want to owe either my life or my freedom to being an informant," Chessman declared next day without any preamble.

Our conversation the previous day had obviously shaken him.

"For as long as the Supreme Court doesn't recognize my innocence of the crimes I was sentenced to death for twelve years ago, I shall officially be the Red Light Bandit. Once I've been pronounced innocent, it'll be the police's job to find the real culprit and not mine."

"You're talking as if you had years in front of you, Caryl. May 2 is just six days away."

"You're right, but you've got to understand me. I'm out of the jungle now and I don't want to go back in. I died a thousand deaths when I was accused of the disgraceful crimes committed by the Red Light Bandit. At the time, I had no reason to live. I was a sick man held captive by my violent instinct. I know now what a psychopath and a fool I was. I hope I don't sound pompous, but I think I can say that I finally 'found' myself. Now I have my writings. Now, I hope, I've earned the right to call you and quite a number of other people my friends."

He paused. His expression was melancholy.

"Whether the Red Light Bandit's name is Terranova or some other name doesn't change a thing. He may be alive, he may be dead. Suppose he's dead, that someone was obliged to kill him in self-defense. Just giving him that label wouldn't prove anything. Suppose, on the other hand, he's alive, that you manage to corner him and say: 'Chessman says you're the Red Light Bandit.' He's going to laugh in your face and say: 'Chessman's getting himself off the hook.'

"Don't forget," Chessman continued, "his victims only saw him once, at night, often when he was wearing a mask, in terrifying conditions, and that, twelve years ago. I was the one they fingered, not him. It's my face that people associate with his crimes. The victims would be quite capable of testifying in all good faith today that their assailant was not this Terranova. That it was me. My denunciation would only look like a last-minute attempt by a desperate man to cloud the issue."

"Apart from his name, don't you have any evidence to prove his guilt?"

"Of course," replied Chessman nodding his head sadly. "But to use it effectively, in a way that would really count, I would have to implicate too many people. To establish that I'd colluded with him in all kinds of criminal activities, I'd be forced to cite names, dates, places. Well, there are people involved who were my friends. One of them even saved my life. Another did a stretch rather than send me to the slammer. Should I rat on them now, mess up their lives by bringing them before a court? I'd also have to call to the stand guys who'd want me dead, and who have connections. It would mean dragging everyone into the shit. I'd have to reveal their dealings—past and present. If I were to save my hide under those conditions, I'd be disgusted with myself for the rest of my days. I'd be an informant, a stool pigeon, a traitor. It would undo all the good I've done by my writing. I'd rather go to the gas chamber."

He fell silent, took a deep breath and concluded almost in a whisper: "That's my answer to your question."

THE MAN IN CHARGE OF PARDONS, Cecil Poole, kept his word. He gave up his Sunday to study the paperwork provided by the two *Argosy* journalists. But by Monday morning his conviction remained intact. He informed Woodfield and Malchin that nothing in their file could make him change his mind and suddenly believe in Chessman's innocence. He did, however, promise to pass the file on to the governor and ask him to give them an audience. It was a promise that left Chessman, his lawyers and the *Argosy* reporters under no illusions: Brown would never go against the opinion of his closest adviser. It was then that Chessman had an idea. While his lawyers prepared a new request for habeas corpus based on Woodfield and Malchin's discoveries, the journalists would pack a powerful punch by publicizing their findings at a press conference. Their revelations might just swing public opinion in favor of the condemned man. Above all, they might produce further evidence leading to other lines of inquiry.

Their success exceeded all their expectations. That very evening, all the California newspapers devoted their front pages to the two journalists' shock announcements. Special news flashes interrupted radio programs. Reports emphasized the importance of the information provided. In divulging the existence of Charles Severine Terranova, Woodfield and Malchin provided his criminal record number, both in California and in the FBI index, together with a detailed list of all his previous convictions.

This media coup brought the two journalists valuable additional information. They eagerly prepared a new file for the governor. But a telephone call from Woodfield's wife abruptly dampened their optimism. The young woman had received an anonymous call. "Is Bill there?" a man's voice asked. She replied that her husband had gone to Sacramento to meet the governor.

"Tell him it would be better if he didn't pass on what he's just learned. Otherwise he might just not want to look at you again. A face spattered with sulfuric acid is not a very pretty sight." The warning was clear. Woodfield told his wife to leave at once and hide with friends.

BECAUSE OF THE MEDIA FERVOR of the previous day, that morning the governor's waiting room looked more like a station concourse at rush hour. Along with several dozen colleagues I waited for a statement from the man who had the power to save Chessman. A secretary appeared at last to say that the governor would receive us. Brown stood behind a long light-colored wooden table, smiling calmly, his jacket unbuttoned and his red-spotted tie loosened. His slightness and easygoing manner contrasted oddly with the imposing stature of his adviser, Cecil Poole, who was glued to his side. Carefully lined up against the wall was an impressive row of boxes bulging with letters and telegrams. On each box a label in red marker pen indicated "For" or "Against." There were ten times as many boxes "For" the death of Caryl Chessman.

Never again would a governor give so short a press conference. Obviously influenced by his adviser, Edmund Brown confined himself to announcing that he would not be taking any new initiative in favor of the condemned man. He would let justice follow its course. Examination of the documents provided by the *Argosy* reporters had not changed his opinion one iota.

Despite the tears of rage fogging their glasses, Woodfield and Malchin would not give up. They still had five days before Chessman was executed. They scrambled to San Quentin in the hope of extracting some decisive piece of information from him.

"You're on the right track," the condemned man confirmed, "but I'm not going to be the one to point a finger at anybody."

"You mean to say you'd rather die in the gas chamber than survive with the reputation of being a stool pigeon?" marveled Woodfield.

"It might seem crazy to you," Chessman replied. "All the same, that's it."

On Friday April 29, three days prior to the deadline, we had our sixth meeting. I knew it might be our last.

"Do you know, Dominique, I sat up most of the night reading *Capital Punishment* by your fellow countryman Albert Camus! What a book! What a writer!" Camus expressed the opinion that the death penalty cannot be justified in terms of its exemplary value because virtually everywhere in the world executions are carried out almost secretly.

"Do you think there would be less crime if they were public?" I asked.

"Certainly not! Arthur Koestler gave the best answer to that question when he pointed out that at the time when pickpockets were hanged in the public squares of England, other pickpockets were doing the rounds of the spectators. Later, executions were carried out in secret almost everywhere. It had been recognized that they stimulated sadistic instincts in the onlookers. It was also a tacit admission of their pointlessness."

"When you were going around holding people up, when you were waving your revolver about, right, left and center, did it never occur to you that you might end up in the gas chamber one day? Did that possibility frighten you at all?"

He looked up at the ceiling and answered as if he were talking to himself. "When I was a youngster, people drummed into me so often that if I carried on with my stupidity I'd end up being gassed that the idea of the gas chamber made no impression on me. A young man who is drawn to violence is never put off by fear of the consequences, no matter how dreadful they might be. At least two hundred men have gone past my cell on their way to their last journey, and I can tell you: I've never met a single one who'd admit he'd thought about the punishment his action might earn him before doing what he did.

"The people who are afraid of the gas chamber are 'normal' people, people . . . I was going to say, people like you and me." The incongruous comparison made him smile. "Only honest people are afraid of capital punishment. Not the others." He gave me a sudden intense look. "What about you? Have you never felt the urge to kill someone?"

I nodded that I had.

"Right," he continued animatedly. "So what was it that prevented you from doing it? Why would someone else not hesitate? Society's mistake lies in not looking at what makes some youngsters commit crime, what it is that makes them rebel against the established order, in contempt of their very lives."

While conceding that laws were necessary, Chessman believed that society was unconsciously promoting crime by asking that laws be ever more rigorously applied and calling for larger and harsher prisons.

"It is infinitely easier and more humane to try and save a young delinquent than to destroy his soul or harden him so that, sooner or later, he'll become a professional criminal and a killer," he concluded vehemently.

Chessman knew what he was talking about. He had spent a third of his life behind bars. I had no argument to put to him. I wanted to take advantage of the few minutes we had left to return to whether or not the death penalty was effective as a deterrent. It seemed to me that the unusual amount of publicity surrounding the Chessman affair, with its endless suffering, its last-minute stays of execution and its whole cortege of horrors, must have struck fear in the hearts of at least a few would-be criminals. I asked the question.

"What will my execution prove?" he replied sharply. "Nothing, except that the occupant of cell 2455 is dead. And what will that death prove? Nothing either. There will still be crime and there will still be criminals. I'm ready to die. But before I hear those cyanide balls plopping into the pan of acid, I'd like to have contributed in some small way to solving the problem of crime. If my personal destiny is only of concern to me, that of the thousands of young people in prison tempted to follow in my footsteps concerns society as a whole. The cases of all those potential Chessmans should be looked at to see how they can be helped. Then people might realize that what is at stake is far more than the execution of one man, that they're dealing rather with a whole culture of revolvers spewing out fire, of tires squealing on the asphalt, of hands stuck up in the air, of penal institutions, cells and bars, and death chambers painted in soft green. I am undoubtedly going to be put to death, but I believe my execution will only evade the problem I posed."

"We were talking a little while ago about Camus," I said. "While he denounced the death penalty as a crime, he also suggested that those societies that applied it should use an anesthetic to execute those condemned to death. Have you ever thought about the way you would prefer to die?"

"The more you try to give the death penalty the veneer of civility, the less likely its abolition becomes. Execution by barbiturates or something of that kind wouldn't shock people anymore. For the death penalty to go, the human conscience must be horrified by the atrocity of organized killing."

"Is that why you've invited four journalist friends to your execution?"

"Absolutely! I know my 'invitations' have been criticized. People have chosen to see them as morbid exhibitionism, even sadism. In fact, I wasn't thinking of me when I asked those two women to be present at the horrible spectacle." His voice hardened. "I'd like them to be scarred forever by the horror of what they'll see. I want them to communicate that horror to everyone who reads their articles. I think it could be useful . . ."

Chessman must have discerned the doubt on my face.

"Here in America, death doesn't have quite the same value as in Europe. In Europe death has always been a reality people have to live with. Because of the wars, millions have been confronted by it at some point in their lives. Here, death remains an abstraction. It never occurs to most Americans that they might suddenly find themselves face-to-face with it. They don't ask themselves what their reaction might be. Instead of taking those who volunteer—out of a spirit of vindictiveness, morbid curiosity or out-and-out sadism—to witness executions, they should invite men and women who think death is something important . . . those who think that capital punishment is a form of murder. The judges, jurors and lawyers who call for the death penalty should be made to come. I believe that all their fine theories about its social usefulness would soon go out the window if they were actually to see a human being executed. Their presence alone would make them feel they'd taken part in the killing."

The guard was already unbolting the door to the visiting room, but Chessman continued with fervor:

"Dominique, get it into your head that society's duty is not so much to punish the offender but to prevent the offense itself. For that you have to look at the mechanisms that make a man stray into crime. If my appeal to the Supreme Court is rejected, I shall write a long letter on this subject to my friend Mary Crawford of the *San Francisco News Call Bulletin*. It will be my last message. I ask you, as a favor, to print it in your paper."

He got up and we shook hands.

"I will," I said, then crossed my fingers for good luck.

"See you on Monday, Caryl!"

The Greenish Vapors Are More Easily Distinguishable Against a White Background

The funereal vigil had begun. The appearance of two Bell Telephone Company vans provoked an onrush of journalists. What were they doing here on Sunday? I soon guessed when I saw two banks of telephones set up on either side of the door to the building of the gas chamber. Above each phone a notice indicated: *United Press, New York Times, Washington Post, Los Angeles Times* . . . Thanks to these special lines, my American colleagues would be able to spread news of Caryl Chessman's death as soon as his heart stopped beating.

The telephone workers left and a feeling of menace and uncertainty hovered over the penitentiary yard. The arrival of Rosalie Asher's old Chevrolet heightened our unease. I had become quite friendly with the sweet young woman whose boyish haircut and fashionable glasses gave her the look of a *Vogue* model. Rosalie was one of Chessman's two lawyers. She was also his confidante, the person who had been closest to him for many years. Burning with an almost mystical certainty that he was not the Red Light Bandit, she had never tired of devising with him fresh reasons for a stay of execution and a retrial. Rosalie fought like a *passionaria*. Her devotion and unrelenting commitment had earned her the animosity of a large section of the press and a prolific mail in which, each day, she found more insults and slanders than encouragement.

The news she was bringing her client that morning was not good. On the previous day she and George Davis, the condemned man's other defense lawyer, had seen the governor again. The meeting had gone badly. Brown had refuted the two lawyers' arguments one by one. He had sarcastically rejected the photo of Terranova which Rosalie had had enlarged for his benefit so that the scar above the left eye and the crooked teeth would be clearly visible. "Trick photography!" he exclaimed, irritated. Rosalie assured me, however, that in her heart of hearts there was still a glimmer of hope. Davis and she had an appointment first thing next day with a California Supreme Court judge. She would fight to the very last second.

The young woman waved a friendly greeting at the other journalists and, escorted by two guards, made for death row. Our wait began again in this strange setting: a death chamber bordered by rosebushes in full bloom, against a background of ocean studded with white sails.

This particularly poignant assignment had given me the chance to link up with several American colleagues. The "guests" for Chessman's execution, the blond Mary Crawford of the *San Francisco News Call Bulletin* and her friend Pony Black, a petite redhead with green eyes who worked for the *Los*

Angeles Examiner, had been fierce adversaries of Chessman before being convinced he was not the Red Light Bandit. They had then passionately proclaimed his innocence, courageously explaining their about-face to a hostile public. *San Francisco Chronicle* correspondent Ed Montgomery, a gangly strapping fellow with a hearing aid, was another ardent supporter of the condemned man. He, too, was to be present at the execution.

I GLANCED AT MY WATCH. It was just three o'clock in the afternoon. Chessman had been at work since dawn. He had typed his last letters on his indefatigable little Underwood, for six years the companion of his literary escapes. One letter was addressed to Will Stevens, the editorial writer of the *San Francisco Examiner,* the fourth journalist he had invited to his execution. They had agreed on a coded signal that would let Stevens know whether death by asphyxiation with cyanide gas was an appalling ordeal or an agreeable way of drifting into the hereafter.

"By the time you read this letter," Chessman wrote to his friend, "I shall have exchanged a twelve year nightmare for oblivion. And you will have witnessed the last, definitive, fatal, ritual act. I hope and believe that you will be able to say that I died with dignity, without animal fear and without bravado. Even as I die I want to express my hope that those who have made themselves heard on my behalf will continue to fight against the gas chambers. . . . In my own way, I have done everything within my power to make the world aware of the existence of these places of torture. I have to die in the knowledge that I am leaving behind me others who are living out their last days on Death Row. Well, I protest that by ritually and premeditatedly killing, man casts shame on civilization, without resolving anything . . ."

He finished his letter with the "solemn and unreserved" affirmation that he was not the "infamous Red Light Bandit."

"California has condemned an innocent man. She has persisted in refusing to admit the possibility of a mistake and, what is more, to correct it. When the time is right, the world will have proof of her cruel error. . . ."

Chessman had just started a second letter when the tall, thin figure of Mike van Brunt, assistant warden of the penitentiary, appeared at the bars.

"Caryl, it's time."

Chessman took the sheet of paper out of the typewriter and stood up. "I wasn't expecting you so early," he said. "But I'm ready." He pointed to a pile of books at the back of his cell. "Could you pass those volumes on to the next occupant of cell 2455? They're lawbooks. He'll need them . . ."

His gaze halted at the peanut butter jar that was serving as an aquarium for Prometheus, the herring he had inherited on the death of his saxophonist neighbor. "Would you also be so kind as to take this fish to prisoner James Hooton so he can have his company until his execution?"

Before leaving, Chessman took a long look around the concrete and steel cage in which he had spent a third of his life. "I'm ready," he repeated, tucking the envelope containing his correspondence and a pad of writing paper under his arm.

He stepped resolutely out into the row. As he passed, hands gripped the bars of the cells, others reached out to him.

"Good-bye, old brother!" called one prisoner.

"Chin up, *viejito*!" cried another.

"Go to hell!" yelled a third. One day in a brawl, Chessman had left the man half-dead in the prison recreation yard.

He went by without stopping, brushing his companions' hands. At the end of the corridor he turned right. Two guards took him into a small green-painted room, where he was summarily searched. Then, still accompanied by the assistant warden, he entered the long corridor and stopped in front of the elevator operated by a prisoner.

He reached the ground floor within seconds. Next day there would be just seven steps left to take to the macabre chair. The ceiling of the small cage in which he was shut up for his last night was so low that he had to duck his head to stand. Its only furnishings consisted of a mattress and a lavatory built into one of its corners.

A guard brought him some trousers, a new shirt and a pair of slippers. Unlike his blue prison uniform, this shirt was immaculately white. The color had been chosen deliberately: the suffocating cloud of greenish vapor could be more easily distinguished against a white background.

After asking the prisoner to undress, the guard inspected the smallest corners of his anatomy. He made sure the condemned man had concealed nothing with which he might attempt to take his own life. Nothing must impede the natural course of justice.

When he had finished, the guard held out a plump hand. "Thanks, Chess, and above all, good luck for tomorrow!"

"Good luck for the rest of your life!" Chessman replied, eager to be alone again and start on the long letter to his friend Mary Crawford. The administration of the California penitentiary surrounded its prisoners' last hours with such solicitude he would have difficulty in finding a few moments to himself. The assistant warden, van Brunt, returned.

"Caryl, what would you like for your dinner?" he asked.

The question was part of the ritual of the night before an execution. Condemned people could indulge their every whim when it came to their last meal. Nine days previously, the black saxophonist, Lawrence Wade, had taken full advantage of this final privilege. He had asked for shrimp gumbo, a specialty of his native Louisiana. Two members of the prison staff had had to go into San Francisco to fetch Creole shrimps from one of the restaurants in the harbor.

"A chicken sandwich and a Coke will do me fine," answered Chessman.

Unable to bring his precious typewriter with him, he began his letter to Mary Crawford by hand, with a ballpoint pen stamped with the San Quentin crest, on a pad of lined yellow paper: "Dear Mary. It is said that the child is father to the man. Tomorrow morning, regardless of my lawyers' last efforts, the executioner will put me to death. The physical man will die.

What will become of the child? Who was this boy who, figuratively speaking, gave birth to Caryl Chessman?"

It was nearly five o'clock in the afternoon. The guard switched on the radio. It was time for the news. The prisoner drew nearer to the bars to hear better.

"For the last eighty-three minutes Caryl Chessman has been seven steps away from the gas chamber," announced the commentator before going on to explain that the California Supreme Court was still due to assemble at eight o'clock next morning, two hours before the time set for the execution, to decide upon the latest appeal brought by the condemned man's lawyers.

It was clear the newscaster believed there was no chance the Supreme Court would alter its previous vote; he concluded: "Short of a miracle, therefore, Caryl Chessman's meeting with death will take place at ten o'clock tomorrow as determined . . ."

On the previous February 18, at the same time, Chessman had listened as that same voice uttered the same words in the same dramatic tone. He calmly resumed writing his letter.

He was soon interrupted by a visit from the prison's Roman Catholic chaplain. Although he professed to be an agnostic, Chessman had always derived comfort from his meetings with Father Marens, beyond whose somewhat brusque exterior were hidden treasures of humanity. He and Chessman liked to talk politics and philosophy.

"May God bless you and grant you his mercy, Caryl," Marens said in an emotional voice as he took his leave.

Chessman received a blessing before embracing the chaplain with an uncharacteristic display of feeling. Once more his large script began to flow across the yellow page.

"It seems more like three centuries than three decades since the little curly-haired eight-year-old that I was then, counted the days to go to his ninth birthday twenty-eight days later," he confided to Mary. "Now, as far as I know, the man that little boy became has no more birthdays to look forward to."

Again a voice in the corridor interrupted him.

"Chess, your dinner!"

Caryl Chessman took the sandwich and the bottle of Coca-Cola from the guard's hands. Scarcely had he begun his last evening meal than another guard came to announce the return of Rosalie Asher. Condemned men could talk to their lawyers until midnight on the eve of their execution.

"Hi, Rosalie!" exclaimed the prisoner when she appeared beyond the bars. "You must be dead tired!"

The young woman admitted meekly that she was.

"Poor Rosalie!"

The attendant unbolted the door and the visitor came and sat beside her client on the mattress. To hide her feelings, she lit a cigarette and busied herself opening her briefcase. She still had a battle on her hands to try and win a fresh reprieve. She was going to wait for the verdict of the Supreme Court of California, due to be announced next morning between eight and nine o'clock. If the court did not reverse its decision, she and George Davis would jump in a taxi and rush to the offices of federal judge Louis Goodman, the only person with the authority to delay or defer the execution to allow for the reexamination of the fresh evidence of innocence, presented in her last appeal. It would be a dramatic race against the clock for an objective that was far from certain.

Chessman wanted to be assured his affairs were in order in case he had to go into the gas chamber: his will, his cremation, the transfer of his ashes near Hallie, his mother, in the Los Angeles cemetery where she was at rest, the disposal of his personal possessions, the destruction of certain manuscripts . . . Rosalie reassured him. Everything was in order.

Soon a guard announced the arrival of another visitor. Chessman's second lawyer, George Davis, with his small build and a skull as shiny as an egg, possessed a dynamism that made his presence felt wherever he went. Chessman had engaged this great star of the California bar at Rosalie's request. The *Argosy* journalists' revelations had so convinced him of his client's innocence that he wanted to appeal to the president of the United States. His determination and energy brought a gust of hope into the dismal antechamber. The worst was not certain. The farewells between the prisoner and his two lawyers were brief. All three, especially Rosalie, tried to diffuse the drama of a particularly cruel moment.

As soon as he found himself alone again, Chessman went back to writing his letter to Mary Crawford.

"You have asked me what could have been done to transform the rebellious, troubled adolescent that I was, full of mistrust of the world and of himself, into a useful citizen. There is no easy answer . . . But it seems to me that some of my thoughts are clear."

In several pages of firm, regular writing, he again condemned society's belief that punishment could be "a corrective measure or a cure" for criminality in young people.

"You might compare a young delinquent with a kettle full of water underneath which a fire has been lit," he explained. "The hotter the water becomes, the more steam comes out. In order to stop the steam forcing the lid off, we weight it down. The punishments we inflict only keep the lid on. We allow the pressure to increase until the inevitable explosion occurs. To be sure, young people are not kettles, but there are in them pressures (conflicts, needs, anxieties, desires, hopes, dreams) that must find an outlet. For as long as we do not know how to give these pressures a legitimate, positive outlet, we will not resolve the problem of juvenile crime.

"I am dying with the hope that one day society will have recourse to its reason and humanity rather than to its executioners and its desire to punish . . . I would like to think that no man will ever again have to experience the twelve years of hell that I have gone through," he concluded.

The arrival of yet another visitor interrupted him. It was nearly two o'clock in the morning. Ernest Pritchard, the chief warden of San Quentin, had come without an escort. Smoking a cigar, plump and jovial, his paternal air inspired trust. He was the man who, the next day, would look at his watch and tell the executioner that the time had come to drop poison into the container of acid. In his capacity as warden of the penitentiary, he had come to make sure that his illustrious prisoner's last hours were passing as serenely as possible.

"Thank you, Ernest, everything's fine," Chessman assured him. Then in a jocular tone, he added: "You smoke too much, Ernest. You'll die of lung cancer!"

The chief warden smiled. "Bah! You've got to go one way or another."

"Given the choice, better to get a good whiff of the peach-blossom smell of cyanide balls, right? It's quicker!"

The two men's laughter surprised the guards on duty nearby. Recovering his gravity, the warden laid a friendly hand on the condemned man's shoulder. Twice already Chessman had seen Pritchard's round face appear outside his cell on death row, lit up by a broad grin. On both occasions it had been to announce that the execution had been deferred. That night, despite his laughter, there was no joy discernible on the official's face. He searched for a few words of comfort.

"Hang on, Caryl! There may be news tomorrow."

"I'm ever hopeful, but I'm ready to die," Chessman declared.

The warden gave him a thumbs-up by way of encouragement and pulled on his cigar. By the time the cloud cleared, he had vanished.

At three o'clock in the morning the prisoner listened to the news.

In the slightly forced tone certain American newscasters reserved for dramatic events, the anchor announced: "There are only seven hours left to go before Caryl Chessman, the man under sentence of death, takes his seat in the gas chamber."

Chessman made a sign to the guard to turn off the radio.

Three o'clock, four o'clock, five o'clock. The night ticked onward into a new morning to the smell of stale cigar smoke. Already, far reaches of the bay were streaked with light; on the hills around San Francisco, dawn was breaking.

Caryl Chessman had fallen asleep.

Two Eggs and Bacon with Toast

It was a spring morning worthy of the day the world was created. A relentless ballet of helicopters circled in a cloudless sky. The drive leading up to the main entrance to the penitentiary was swarming with a motley crowd, giving it an artificially carnival-like atmosphere. Above the heads appeared a gallows, from which dangled a dummy representing Governor Brown. Armed with placards and signs, people had come from all over California. "Chessman must live! He has paid," proclaimed some. Others demanded: "Stop legalized murder!" "Mercy!" implored one giant banner. From the top of a stepladder a man with long curly hair harangued the assembly.

"The death penalty is inhuman!" he yelled. "It should be abolished. Chessman must not die!"

Applause greeted the orator. I recognized him. It was Marlon Brando.

Farther away, the voluble words of an individual in a gray felt hat were trying to attract attention: "Chessman must die!" he cried. "He deserves to die! I want to see him die. I want to be there where he finally pays for his crimes!"

A hostile uproar drowned his words.

A number of demonstrators had brought transistor radios with them to follow the even more frequent news bulletins. An announcer interrupted a music program to say: "The Supreme Court of California has just rejected the appeal lodged by Rosalie Asher and George Davis, Caryl Chessman's lawyers, by four votes to three. So the condemned man will be executed in one hour's time, at ten o'clock precisely."

For an instant those words resonated in the still air.

"Only fifty-eight minutes to go!" someone next to me shouted.

CARYL CHESSMAN WOKE at about eight o'clock.

"What would you like for breakfast?" asked a guard.

"Two eggs and bacon with toast, coffee with cream, and orange juice," he replied amiably.

The tray arrived less than a quarter of an hour later. Chessman ate a hearty breakfast. Then he had another cigarette and asked the guard to switch on the radio. A few bars of music preceded the news bulletin announcing the rejection of his appeal. Not a muscle of the condemned man's face moved.

He had just finished shaving when Ernest Pritchard appeared. This time the chief warden of San Quentin was accompanied by the captain of the prison guards and a man dressed in a white smock that hung almost to his ankles. Dr. Eliott Wilson was the coroner for San Marino County. He was the one who had to confirm the fatal effect of the gas and pronounce the condemned man dead. His small bag contained the various instruments of his profession: an electrode, earphones, a chronometer, a rubber strap and a roll of medical tape.

The heavy barred door grated on its hinges. The prisoner started imperceptibly at the sight of the doctor's white smock. His lips paled.

"Caryl," Pritchard declared, eager to be done with the unpleasant task, "I regret to inform you that the Supreme Court has rejected—"

Chessman cut him short. "I know," he said calmly. After a few seconds he added: "Well, Ernest, I guess this is it."

Pritchard nodded in confirmation and had Dr. Wilson enter. He stood back to make way for him, then withdrew.

"See you shortly, Caryl."

OUTSIDE, AN EVER-GROWING CROWD listened for news on their transistors. Some people were weeping. Others knelt in prayer. A newscaster announced that the condemned man's lawyer had just asked the governor to postpone the execution by one hour to enable them to submit a final petition for reprieve. This time no one seemed to believe that Caryl Chessman could be saved. The door to the penitentiary opened and I could see the tall outline of Mike van Brunt, the assistant warden. He advanced toward the crowd.

"Those of you with passes are asked to come to the guard room."

California law required that at least twelve citizens "of good repute" be present at every execution. The authorities usually had a great deal of difficulty finding witnesses for this macabre spectacle. In order to make up the requisite quorum, guards or police officers were often commandeered at the last minute. That had not been necessary for Chessman's execution. The San Quentin authorities had received several thousand letters from people who wanted to watch him being put to death, and had been forced to resort to a lottery. Fifty candidates were chosen: men and women of a variety of ages, of a wide range of backgrounds and social circumstances. There were business-men among them, government employees, some blue-collar workers, a teacher and a dentist. There was also a man in a navy-blue uniform. Officer Dick Brennam was one of the po-lice officers who had arrested Chessman after the car chase and shoot-out on Vermont Avenue. He had subsequently married Regina Johnson, one of the two victims sexually assaulted by the Red Light Bandit. He was proud to be there. For Brennam, Chessman's death would be the high point of a career totally committed to the fight against crime.

Some ten journalists, all of them American citizens, had also been authorized to be present at the execution. Among them were the prisoner's four personal guests, Mary Crawford, Pony Black, Ed Montgomery and Will Stevens. I had stayed the whole night with Mary Crawford, the *San Francisco News Call Bulletin* journalist, drinking coffee and reciting poetry to quiet our fears.

The group of witnesses and journalists formed a double line. Pony Black and Mary waved to me through their tears, showed their pink passes and proceeded through the metal-detecting se-curity gate. Those behind them did the same, under the vigilant gaze of several impeccably polite guards. The San Quentin au-thorities had made provision for each stage of operation "Chess-man Execution" as if it were an official ceremony. As usual in America, the media had been the object of particularly attentive care. Prison officials provided us with a detailed information sheet. There were several dozen American and foreign journal-ists, photographers, television cameramen and commentators in the vast prison yard that morning. In anticipation of the press con-ference that the warden would give "approximately fifteen minutes after the completion of the execution," rows of chairs and several microphones had been set out in the prison staff room.

A guard instructed the witnesses to write their names and occupations in a register. Once these formalities had been completed, a prison officer led them into the main visiting room of the penitentiary.

"Ladies and gentlemen, please be patient for just a little while longer." The guard spoke with the tone of a museum guide. "Someone will come to collect you in a minute or so."

"WOULD YOU PLEASE TAKE OFF your shirt?" Dr. Wilson asked Caryl Chessman pleasantly.

The prisoner knew the ritual. As soon as the doctor stepped into his cell, he had begun unbuttoning the white shirt he had been given on the previous evening. He presented his naked torso to the practitioner, who adjusted his glasses and ran his finger over Chessman's chest to locate the position of his heart as precisely as possible. He squirted a little foam onto the area, before shaving off the hair, then applied an electrode with a suction cup which he fixed firmly in place with two strips of surgical tape. Once the condemned man entered the gas chamber, the doctor would attach a cable to this electrode. Linked this way through the airtight walls, Wilson would be able to hear the dying man's heartbeat in his earphones.

Sixteen Cyanide Balls and a Pan of Sulfuric Acid

Execution by gas was not as simple as I had thought. Quite the opposite: it was a highly technical and complicated operation. The process had to follow more than thirty recommendations set down in a constantly updated twenty-page document.

These instructions were the result of experience acquired in the course of hundreds of executions.

The first execution by asphyxiating gas took place on February 8, 1924, in a Nevada prison. The condemned man was a Chinese American found guilty of several murders. The innovative method used to execute the prisoner was yet another demonstration of America's enterprising spirit. The idea stemmed from experiments conducted during World War I on the effects of gas on human organisms. The basic principle was very simple: it was merely a matter of making the condemned man breathe toxic fumes while confined in a hermetically sealed area. After testing various substances on animals, the American engineers finally selected cyanide, which had the property of paralyzing the respiratory enzymes responsible for carrying oxygen from the blood to the cells. Deprived of oxygen, the cells died. The brain centers were rapidly affected. Brain death generally occurred before cardiac arrest. Like California, other states had abandoned the electric chair, the gallows or the firing squad in favor of this apparently less barbarous method of execution. In the wake of World War II the horror evoked by the Nazi gas chambers induced several states to give that method up. In May of 1960 only eight states were implementing the death penalty by asphyxiation.

Obviously what the executioners dreaded most was a technical hitch. At eight o'clock prison technicians began checking the operating levers that released the cyanide into the pan of sulfuric acid placed under the chair, the valves, and the fasteners on the straps used to hold the condemned man down. As a precaution, they even sprayed an airtight sealant onto the rubber joints of the "chamber" door. In some states prisoners took part in this rehearsal. On the eve of their execution, they had to try out the chair to make sure that their size and weight were not going to pose any particular problems.

Telecommunications engineers came to test the special telephone line connected to Governor Brown's office in Sacramento. They synchronized the pendulum clock that presided over his mantelpiece to the wall clock near the gas chamber. If he had to announce a pardon or another reprieve, the governor had only to pick up the telephone and give an order to suspend the execution. It was imperative that such an order come before the balls of cyanide had been dropped into the acid. Once the poison had been released, nothing could stop the condemned man from asphyxiating. Everyone in San Quentin could recall the horrific sound of the telephone ringing as a young black man named Greg Baldwin inhaled the fatal vapors. Brown's predecessor, Governor Goodwin Knight, had called ten seconds too late.

NINE-THIRTY.

The executioner responsible for preparing the lethal solution busied himself with a dexterity born of long practice. He was the oldest of three executioners whose identity remained confidential. His work involved first weighing precisely the balls of potassium cyanide supplied by the penitentiary's technical laboratory, then putting them into two small linen bags that would be suspended over the pan of sulfuric acid underneath the condemned man's chair. When the order was given, the bags would be released from their support and fall into the acid. Next the executioner prepared the acid solution he would pour into the pan, adding two pints of distilled water to facilitate the chemical reaction. Finally he checked the airtightness of the chamber by pumping it full of compressed air. This process took less than a minute, but the distinctive whistle, like the brakes of a truck slowing down, alerted Chessman. Everything was now ready for him to be put to death.

IN TEN MINUTES IT WOULD BE ten o'clock, the fateful hour. A prison officer in an olive-green uniform entered the room where the witnesses waited.

"Ladies and gentlemen, please be so good as to line up three by three," he ordered.

Mary Crawford and Pony stiffened. So it was all over: there was no more room for hope. Led by the officer, the group marched across an exercise yard where prisoners played basketball, apparently ignorant of the drama about to take place. They came to the metal door of the building that housed the gas chamber. "Absolutely No Smoking," a notice warned. In the middle of a circular gallery the small, octagonal green-painted chamber was visible. People jostled with each other. Those eager to see Chessman die wanted a place in the front row, in front of a porthole and, if possible, in line with the chair to which he would be strapped. Pony Black and her colleague Will Stevens found themselves opposite the chair. Guards took up position at every corner of the octagon. Their backs turned to the enclosure, their role was to keep an eye on the assembled civilians, prevent any incidents and assist any spectators who felt faint.

NINE FIFTY-EIGHT.

With her short hair in disarray after a sleepless night and her eyes red from crying, attorney Rosalie Asher had just entered the San Francisco office of Judge Louis Goodman, the magistrate with the gold fillings in his teeth who presided over the U.S. Court of Appeals. She was accompanied by her colleague, George Davis. Both believed they had one last card to play. Chessman's advocate showed the judge a photograph.

"Your Honor, this is the real Red Light Bandit."

The judge examined the document. It was almost ten o'clock. Davis quickly enumerated all the reasons why Charles Terranova was the Red Light Bandit and why, by the same token, Caryl Chessman was innocent. After listening to their case, the judge thought for a moment.

"Your theory seems feasible," he said at last. "I shall study all your documents carefully and—"

Rosalie Asher interrupted. "Your Honor, Caryl Chessman may already be in the gas chamber. It's only a matter of seconds."

"In that case I shall have the execution suspended for one hour," the judge replied.

Rosalie thought her heart was going to burst. She glanced anxiously at her watch and saw the seconds racing madly. As if in a dream, she heard the judge ask his secretary:

"Miss Hickey, be so good as to get me the chief warden of San Quentin penitentiary urgently."

ONE MINUTE PAST TEN.

Ernest Pritchard had deliberately waited until a few seconds past the fateful hour. He mopped his brow and stood up. He had probably come to the most difficult moment in his career. He knew the prisoner would not put up a fight, but it was with a profound sense of dread that he approached the condemned man's cage.

Chessman was waiting, sitting quietly on his mattress. If he was afraid, he showed no sign of it.

"Caryl, I'm terribly sorry," said Pritchard. "The moment for us to part has come."

There was a lump in the warden's throat as he pronounced those last words, words that did not form part of his usual vocabulary. An expression of sympathy came over the face of the condemned man.

"I'm ready, Ernest," Chessman replied as he got up.

The two men faced each other.

"I'd like to thank you, you and your staff," said Chessman. "You've all been very straight with me." He drew breath and, this time looking the warden directly in the eye, spoke clearly and with emphasis. "I'm not the Red Light Bandit, Ernest. I hope my ordeal will help toward the abolition of the death penalty."

Pritchard nodded and stiffened abruptly.

"Let's go, Ernest," Chessman said.

In the passage two guards had unrolled a gray carpet on which the condemned man had to take his last steps. No one knew why the rules prescribed this peculiar formality, nor why the prisoner had to remove his slippers and walk barefoot to his death.

The responsibility for putting Chessman in the death chamber fell to thirty-eight-year-old Captain Juan Chicoy, a former cowboy of Mexican origin, now the captain of the San Quentin prison guard. The task of this giant of a man with the build of a football player was not always an easy one. Many prisoners resisted when it came to the point of death. Chicoy had been obliged to literally carry some to the chair. On his forearm he still bore the scar of a savage bite inflicted on him by a prisoner. Despite the fact that their relations had not always been of the most cordial kind, Chessman had often had occasion to appreciate Captain Chicoy's humanity and his efforts to temper the senseless brutality of life on death row.

"Take a big gasp, Chess!"

Captain Chicoy would have given a great deal to be anywhere else that morning. He contained his emotion with difficulty as he invited the prisoner to follow him. Chessman moved forward like an automaton. Two guards fell into step with him. No bonds restricted the hands or feet of the condemned man who impassively submitted himself to the ceremony of his death. Was he still hoping? Of whom was he thinking? Of the goddess of death he had once nicknamed "the grim reaper," who had proved to be more obstinate than his illusions? The end of his journey was only a few steps away.

Pritchard watched him. He looked so solid, so much in control of himself. Was he relieved to put an end to his interminable suffering? Arriving at the door to the gas chamber, Chessman turned his head in the direction of the chief warden. Was he waiting for news of a reprieve? Would he say a last farewell? Chessman winked at Pritchard and resumed his walk.

The time had come for him to discover in reality the scenario he had envisioned in such minute detail in his books. He could not help a slight lurching in the pit of his stomach: the chamber was probably more terrifying than anything he had imagined. First the two straight-backed metal chairs, with their straps, solidly anchored in the middle of the small octagonal chamber; then the surrounding walls painted in pale green, with the eight portholes from behind which stared dozens of eyes. "You are alone when you die but people watch you die. A ritual, ugly death devoid of meaning," he had written in *Cell 2455*. Beyond the pane of the central porthole he recognized his friends Pony Black and Will Stevens. He waved to them, then scanned the other faces, no doubt looking for Mary Crawford. The young woman had hidden herself behind the imposing body of the police officer who had arrested Chessman more than twelve years earlier. She had come because he had asked her, but she did not want to see the awful spectacle.

The ritual speeded up. Chicoy signaled to Chessman to sit down on the chair marked with the letter *B*, the one closest to the spectators. With a swift, deft movement, he lifted the condemned man's shirt and connected the electrode stuck to Chessman's chest to a slim cable linked to Dr. Wilson's headphones. Two guards hung the bags of cyanide under the chair. Securing the belts and straps that snapped and spun around to mold the victim's body to the chair took only a few seconds.

Captain Chicoy cast a last glance around to make sure that everything was in order. Before leaving, he placed his heavy cowboy hand on the condemned man's shoulder.

"Try and take a big gasp, Chess, so it's over more quickly," he said.

"How do you know?"

Chicoy did know. He had seen too many men die in this torture chamber not to know that asphyxiation by gas was swift and without excessive suffering only when the victim actively participated. If he filled his lungs with toxic gas, Chessman could lose consciousness in ten to fifteen seconds. If, on the other hand, he tried to hold his breath, the agony was prolonged. He could remain conscious—and in intense pain—for several minutes. Chicoy had seen one condemned man try to delay the effects of the gas. In all the forty-two executions in which he had been involved, it was the most horrible sight he had ever witnessed. As if the condemned man had suddenly been struck by an interminable epileptic fit, cramps and muscular contractions convulsed his body. The poor wretch had died after sixteen minutes.

Chicoy gave the prisoner a final friendly word and went out. The heavy door immediately closed. A guard screwed down the wheel lock, rendering the chamber as hermetic as a submarine hatchway. Another guard engaged the system that kept the atmospheric pressure in the gas chamber constant throughout the execution. This was crucial: the effectiveness of the poison depended upon the volume and nature of the mixture breathed.

"The dreadful, the ultimate moment has now arrived," Caryl Chessman had written, imagining his own death. "During the preparations, and while you were moving, things did not seem real. Movement made it impossible to appreciate what was happening. It was like watching a film in which some absorbing scene played at an accelerated speed drew you irresistibly into the action. You were only vaguely aware of where it was leading. But now that you are physically immobilized, what a devastating change! The film has resumed its normal speed. You can see. Each image emblazons itself on your mind. The scene develops with terrifying clarity. For a moment time seems to have stood still. Your thoughts, your perceptions divide into fragments and pierce you like as many daggers. You realize that you are going to die . . ."

Everything was ready. The chief warden had only to give the order and the pan beneath the chair would fill with the sulfuric acid. The cyanide balls would drop. Ernest Pritchard consulted his watch again. It showed exactly the same time as the wall clock. The execution was four minutes late.

FOUR MINUTES PAST TEN.

Miss Hickey, Judge Louis Goodman's secretary, struggled to get the telephone number for San Quentin. There was no listing in her telephone book, and telephone information did not answer. Exasperated, she ran to the clerk of the court's office. She finally obtained the number, hastily jotting it down on her shorthand pad. She took it straight to the judge for him to dial the number himself on his direct line. A first attempt proved abortive, as did the second. Frantic, Rosalie Asher grabbed the telephone to call San Quentin herself. Then she realized that the number the secretary had noted down was incomplete. In her haste, Miss Hickey had forgotten one digit.

FIVE MINUTES PAST TEN.

Ernest Pritchard inclined his head. With scientific precision the execution began. The guard who had prepared the bags of cyanide undid the sluice that controlled the flow of sulfuric acid and distilled water into the pan. Chessman could hear the sound of liquid running under his chair. Outside the enclosure, the room was filled with tension. Dr. Wilson donned his headphones. The condemned man's heart was beating with the regularity of a metronome at a rate of sixty beats a minute.

Pritchard looked at the telephone on the wall. If it were to ring now, the execution could still be stopped. The balls of cyanide had not yet dropped into the acid. The chamber could be decompressed, the door unlocked and the prisoner released. In a few seconds it would be too late. Once the cyanide balls dropped, the process would be irreversible. Pritchard could not know that a few miles away, in an office building in San Francisco, two lawyers and a judge were frantically trying to contact him.

One last time he consulted his watch; then, very slowly, almost reluctantly, he inclined his head again. With a sharp movement the guard lowered the lever that released the bags of poison. Chessman could hear them fall into the acid; he heard the bubbling of the resulting chemical reaction. Pony Black saw him turn his head and smile at her. He said something and she realized it was: "Say good-bye to Rosalie for me." Then he winked at her. Pony could still see the "O.K." on his lips.

It was then that the telephone rang. Pritchard rushed to pick up the receiver. His chubby, round face, usually so pink, turned white. "I'm so sorry." He let out a sigh. "The execution has begun. The cyanide balls have dropped."

Rosalie—the devoted, generous Rosalie—had lost her final sprint to save Caryl Chessman by scarcely a few seconds. The fatal vapors were already rising from the pan. A slight greenish cloud had reached his knees. Chessman started as he smelled the acrid, sickening scent of bitter almonds and peach blossom. He breathed deeply. "Suddenly your head swims," he had written. "You strain at your bonds and darkness closes in on you. You breathe in and out again. Your head aches. A sharp pain burns your chest. But head and chest pains are nothing. You are barely conscious. Your head drops back. For one brief moment you float freely. . . ." Pony Black saw a spurt of foam well from his mouth and a look of terror burn in his eyes. It seemed to her that he was looking for someone among the spectators. Chessman's gaze alighted on Will Stevens, the journalist for the *Examiner*, with whom he had devised a code to communicate his last sensations. His mouth opened like that of a fish out of water. Tears poured down his cheeks. "He's crying," observed one witness. His eyes closed and his chest swelled. His hands gripped the arms of the chair. His body was racked with convulsions, while his head began to move from left to right. That was the agreed signal. "I'm in pain and it's terrible," Chessman told his friend. He opened his eyes again. His gaze shone for an instant and then went out under the burning effect of the greenish cloud of gas that now enveloped his face. His head became still, then flopped onto his chest.

"It's finished," sighed several witnesses, relieved.

They were wrong. Dr. Wilson could still hear his heartbeat pounding against his rib cage at a rate of about forty beats per minute. He was surprised at its vigor and regularity. Several seconds elapsed. Chessman managed to raise his head. Pritchard could not take any more. He turned away from the porthole to follow the progress of the dying man's agony on the doctor's face. Soon Chessman's heart rate plummeted to less than thirty beats a minute. Pony Black was amazed at how cheeks so pale after twelve years of imprisonment could grow even paler. Dr. Wilson pressed his earphones to his ears. He was having difficulty picking up the heartbeat that was becoming less and less audible. The chest swelled for three more short, jerky inhalations and then the head fell forward again. Still the doctor thought he heard faint signs of life— then nothing. Caryl Chessman's heart had stopped. Pony saw a dribble of saliva escape his lips and flow over the collar of his shirt and the strap restraining his chest. His features relaxed into an expression of surprising peace. Even the deep furrows that ran across his forehead were suddenly erased. He looked as if he were asleep. Pony told herself that his Calvary was over at last.

Dr. Wilson stopped his chronometer. He took off his earphones and turned to the warden of the penitentiary.

"The condemned man is legally deceased," he said. "He died after nine minutes. But he lost consciousness in less than a hundred seconds."

It was the official formula.

"An ideal execution," remarked Pritchard, anxious to find something positive to say.

"Ideal," the coroner was quick to confirm.

Mike van Brunt, the assistant warden, entered the witnesses' gallery.

"Ladies and gentlemen, the execution is over," he announced. "Caryl Chessman died at fourteen minutes past ten." After a pause, he added warmly: "Ladies and gentlemen, don't forget to sign the visitors' book on the way out."

WHAT I WITNESSED THEN was astounding. The correspondents charged forward like a horde of wild buffalo to the special lines their newspapers had installed at the door to the gas chamber. In this way, America and the world received news of Chessman's death moments after it was over. Neither Pony Black nor Mary Crawford was part of this throng, of course, nor was Will Stevens, the friend to whom Caryl Chessman had made known what horrible suffering he was enduring, nor was Ed Montgomery of the *Chronicle*. The latter had turned ghastly pale. Montgomery had scarcely set foot outside when I saw him tear out the hearing aid he wore in his right ear. He wanted to hear no more the noises of this world.

ALL TRACES OF THE EXECUTION were disposed of promptly. Powerful vacuum cleaners were already expelling the lethal vapors from the death chamber into the sky. Underground pipes beneath the chair evacuated the remains of the toxic mixture. Once the small pan of acid was completely empty, several pressurized jets of water cleansed it of any dangerous substances.

This series of operations could be completed in less than thirty minutes. The executioner could then unlock the door to the chamber. He and two assistants, all wearing masks, entered the green room, released the condemned man's body and carried it to a metal table, where they undressed it and washed it down with a jet of water. They sprayed Chessman's clothes with disinfectant and packed them in a plastic bag to be incinerated. The California penitentiary administration generously provided fresh clothes for those whom it had put to death. Chessman was dressed in a white shirt and a blue linen suit with a pair of matching sandals. The deceased was then carried into an adjoining room which served as a morgue.

A long Cadillac hearse was already waiting at the door. The three men placed the body in a coffin and the vehicle drove away. I watched it slowly cross the courtyard to the imposing portal through which, twelve years earlier, a twenty-seven-year-old offender, rebelling against society, had stepped. The sentries at their posts came to attention and saluted. Journalists and photographers bowed their heads. I had difficulty holding back my tears. Soon the hearse was just a black speck at the end of the drive lined with palm trees.

Chessman had asked to be cremated. This last formality would be afforded him by the state that had executed him. Only the epitaph he wanted engraved on the urn that held his ashes would be charged to him. It was his last message: "If there is a triumphant note in what has happened, it will be that the son of Hallie Chessman died with dignity."

A BELL HAD RUNG A FEW MINUTES earlier on the floor of death row. It had set off a commotion among the prisoners. They had all been waiting feverishly either for the return of their comrade or for the telephone call confirming that the execution had taken place. The guard's voice informed them that Chessman was dead. The guard then called for a colleague and a prisoner to go and strip cell 2455 of the last vestiges of Chessman's twelve-year presence—a few personal effects, papers and books. There, stretched out beside the small Underwood typewriter, they found Prometheus. The little herring had leapt from the peanut butter jar that had been his fishbowl.

"WARDEN, THE PRESS IS WAITING for you!"

Ernest Pritchard gazed at the silver-streaked Pacific Ocean. From the rosebushes beneath his windows rose the heady scent of spring. All around him was light and beauty. He took one more puff at his cigar and, tearing himself away from his thoughts, made his way resolutely toward the conference room where the journalists were waiting for him. Television lights illuminated the room. His arrival set off a salvo of flashes.

"What were the last words Chessman said to you?" a journalist asked.

Pritchard blinked under the glare of the lights. "His last words?" he repeated with respect. "They were a message. He told me he hoped that his suffering and death would contribute one day to the abolition of capital punishment." A volley of questions burst from all the sides of the room. How had Chessman spent his last hours? Who were his last visitors? Had he seen a priest? Had he written any letters? To whom? What did he want for breakfast? Did he know that a judge had wanted to postpone his execution? Had he denied being the Red Light Bandit? Had he suggested who the individual in question might be? Was he frightened when he went into the gas chamber? Had he allowed himself to be strapped in without struggling? Did he suffer?

For over an hour the mob grilled the unfortunate warden. The interrogation was all part of the game. Finally someone asked a suitable question with which to conclude the interview.

"What about you, Ernest, are you for or against capital punishment?" a television reporter demanded.

The man who, in the months to come, would have to execute some forty condemned men hung his head.

"I'm very sorry," he apologized, "but I'm not allowed to comment on the performance of my duties."

Then, surveying the room with a touching look, he said in a resonant voice: "The death penalty is an infamy!"

4
Two Young Hounds on the Trail of History

Terror of terrors! As soon as the small black Renault poked its chrome muzzle over the horizon, the regiment broke into a panic. Even before the vehicle passed the sentry post, the men had adjusted their berets and spit-shined their laced military boots. Short as he was, Colonel Baron Norbert de Gévaudan—known as "Hm-Hm" because of the way he cleared his throat before speaking—literally terrorized his officers and men. Nothing escaped his merciless monocle, whether it was three beard hairs on a serviceman's chin, a barrel cover missing from the cannon of a tank or a cauldron of soup too thin to hold his swagger stick upright.

The regiment Hm-Hm commanded, the 501st Tank, was one of the most prestigious units in the French army. The striking force of the World War II armored division of General Philippe Leclerc, the legendary French Patton, the 501st had taken part in the fighting in North Africa and Normandy, liberated Paris and Strasbourg, crossed the Rhine and driven its way into the heart of Germany. Its motto, "Kill as many as you can," was shamelessly displayed on its flag, as well as on the badge of the black beret I was wearing. The 501st was a melting pot of semiliterate peasants, privileged individuals like me (to do one's compulsory military service in Rambouillet, twenty-five miles outside of Paris, was every young Parisian's dream) and noncommissioned officers back from Indochina, their blood riddled with malaria or burned out with *choum*, the local brew that sent people mad. With their surnames preceded by an aristocratic "de," their sticks, their hide breeches and their shiny boots, some of the officers looked like they had galloped out of a nineteenth-century cavalry unit. Most of the men were heroes. Ten years earlier, my unit commander had launched his Sherman tank against a German antitank cannon; he had been the first to reach the Eiffel Tower. The black berets of the 501st had paid a heavy toll in men for the liberation of France and its capital.

On July 14, 1954, almost ten years after the historic procession of General de Gaulle and Leclerc's liberating tanks down the Champs-Elysées, my regiment had the honor of taking part in a march along the triumphal avenue. My tank bore the mythical name "Leclerc." Atop my forty-two-ton machine, I suddenly caught sight of my mother waving to me from the corner of the rue Washington. She was weeping for joy and scattering rose petals in front of my caterpillar tracks. The 501st's participation in the military parade for Bastille Day was not just a tradition, it was a deliberate political gesture. One of our unit's permanent missions was to be ready to swoop down upon Paris in the event of a communist coup.

AFTER TWELVE MONTHS of forced marriage to my steel monster, one morning the colonel's secretary appeared at the foot of my gun turret. Hm-Hm wanted to see me at once. In the year I had spent at Rambouillet, I had not once been summoned to see the commander of my regiment. On my arrival I had, however, sent him an inscribed copy of the book that detailed the round-the-world honeymoon I had just spent with my bride.[1] The colonel had declined my gift and an orderly had returned my book, without a word of explanation.

"*Hm-hm!*"

1. *Honeymoon Around the World* (London: Secker and Warburg, 1953).

The dreaded clearing of his throat brought me to frightened attention. Colonel Baron Norbert de Gévaudan got up from his table to greet me at the door to his office. It was the first time I had been able to observe him from such close quarters and without the beret that usually covered half his face. His dyed hair, carefully plastered back with brilliantine, exuded a sweet smell. His smile revealed little rabbit's teeth.

"Hearty congratulations, my dear fellow, you've got your transfer at last! The regiment is going to lose you: I have just received notification from the War Office that you have been appointed as a translator at SHAPE."[2]

Promotion to the rank of general could not have given me a greater thrill. To abandon my grease-spotted fatigues to go and serve my last six months' service in such a prestigious institution was a gift from God.

"Thank you for the good news," I said.

Already Hm-Hm was adding ingratiatingly: "By the way, my friend, do you remember, a year ago you sent me a copy of your book *Honeymoon Around the World* with a charming inscription?"

"Indeed, sir, and allow me to take this opportunity to say that I found quite humiliating the way you sent it back to me."

Hm-Hm looked contrite. "Your indignation is entirely justified, my dear man. But I shall give you an explanation in an attempt to exonerate myself. Do you realize that traditionally the regiment recruits part of its manpower from among the farming population of the Loire Valley?"

"I don't quite see the connection . . ."

"Well, you can perhaps imagine that with every draft, the parents of those called up send me an avalanche of hams, cheeses and other delicacies to induce me to look after the welfare of their offspring. Naturally I dispatch the foodstuffs straight back to their senders. So I have come to make it a rule never to accept presents. But I would be very flattered if you would now renew the gift of your book."

Flabbergasted at the gall of the man, I confined myself to clicking my heels as I had seen it done in films. I adjusted my

2. The Supreme Headquarters of the Allied Powers in Europe.

black beret with its badge, "Kill as many as you can," gave a right-angled salute, did a regulation about-face and rushed out to say good-bye to my dear tank.[3]

A Yank's Love Story with France

A mere twelve and a half miles separated the old Rambouillet barracks of my tank regiment from the bright campus in Rocquencourt where the greatest military coalition of all time had chosen to reside. I felt as if I had landed on some other planet. I found myself in a cushioned world, populated by men and women in gold braid who seemed to be perpetually en route to some social gathering. The vast, bright office assigned to me would have suited the general manager of a bank. As soon as I arrived, the colonel in charge of the staff of translators, an Englishman with a mustache who was the spitting image of Field Marshal Montgomery, came to welcome me and briefed me on the conditions of my service. Much to my surprise, he was not particularly concerned with security regulations relating to the confidential documents I was going to have to translate, or with special instructions in case of a communist coup or a Soviet attack. He did, however, familiarize me with the times of my daily breaks. Mornings and afternoons, I could leave my work for half an hour to go for refreshments in the general staff's British canteen. Like all my "colleagues," from the topmost general to the lowliest orderly, I got in the habit of going there twice a day, hoping that the Warsaw Pact forces would not have

3. Ten years later when I was a senior reporter at *Paris Match* I would suddenly hear the familiar "*hm-hm.*" It was Colonel Baron Norbert de Gévaudan trying to engage my attention from the sidewalk opposite the magazine's office. A reflex brought me to attention. I crossed the street to greet him. He was in civilian clothing, his eternal monocle in his eye. His attitude had lost none of its haughtiness, but this time his look was full of guile.

"My dear friend, now you're the veteran!" he announced. Anticipating my surprise, he went on immediately in a tone of confidentiality. "I've left the army and I have just joined the administrative staff of *Paris Match*. I'm counting on you to give me a few tips on how to fill out my expense accounts."

the poor taste to attack SHAPE's Europe during my coffee breaks.

One morning as I was dunking a doughnut in my cup, I met a young American conscript who would one day give direction to my life. He was a tall guy with glasses and a fine open face. That morning, he was making his comrades split their sides with laughter by telling them hilarious Irish stories in an accent so authentic he might have been a patron of a Dublin pub. His name was Larry Collins. The son of a Connecticut lawyer, graduate of Yale, Collins had intended to have a career as a manager in a large commercial firm when the wicked draft fairy had obliged him to don the uniform of a G.I. Then another fairy, this time a good one, had dispatched him to Europe, and a third, even better one had assigned him to the SHAPE press office. For a young American who had known no environment other than his tranquil New England, to land all of a sudden, at Uncle Sam's expense, some twelve miles from Paris was like a tale out of *The Arabian Nights*.

I was immediately drawn to him. I invited him to spend the Christmas holiday in the picturesque village of the Alps where my wife's family had an old mansion with mullioned windows. Together we followed the procession of shepherds walking through the snow with their cows and sheep to the illuminated crèche. I recall those moments of warm conviviality with tenderness. The new environment must have been somewhat bewildering for a Yank. I made him taste the delicacies of our soil: foie gras, truffles, boletus mushrooms and even frogs' legs and snails. I introduced him to Armagnac, Sauterne wine, pear brandy, to the much-loved country wines that would wipe the taste of Coca-Cola forever from his palate. I showed him our museums, our cathedrals, our chateaux. One day I took him to Rambouillet where the colonel baron of the 501st gave us an effusive reception. The first result of our friendship was that Larry Collins fell in love with France.

One morning he appeared at the door to my office, his face drawn. Usually so bright, so optimistic, he looked completely distraught. His eyes were red behind his glasses. He had almost certainly been crying. I was worried.

"Something dreadful's happened," he informed me dolefully. "I've just been given my discharge notice. I'm going back to America the day after tomorrow."

I had a hard time stifling a laugh.

"That's awful!" I said in an effort to show my solidarity. Then I added: "In the French army when we get our discharge we toast it with champagne. Come on! We'll crack open a bottle."

I invited the whole office, including the colonel, to mark the occasion. Clinking glasses, we all wished Larry the best of luck and made him promise to come back before the following Christmas.

The day after next, I accompanied Larry to the Gare du Nord railway station. He was leaving for Bremerhaven to board a troopship destined for New York. As we walked across the platform toward the train, I suddenly gripped his arm.

"Listen," I said, "I think I've just found a family reason for you to come back to France soon. This morning my wife told me we're going to have a child. We'd like you to be its godfather."

A look of surprise followed by intense emotion passed across his face.

"Is it a boy or a girl?" he asked.

"We don't know."

"If it's a girl, what will you call her?"

"Alexandra."[4]

A FEW WEEKS AFTER HIS RETURN to the United States, Larry received an attractive offer from Procter & Gamble, the giant soap and detergent multinational corporation. The salary, working conditions and numerous perks made the offer irre-

4. Alexandra was born on November 14, 1955. She was taken to the baptismal font by her godfather, Larry Collins. Like her father and godfather, she is today a writer and the author of several best-selling books.

sistible, even if it did mean moving to Cincinnati. Warmly encouraged by his family, Larry signed the contract and mailed it special delivery on a Friday evening. It would reach the personnel manager's desk first thing on the following Monday morning. Over the weekend, an unexpected telephone call swept away any dreams of his dazzling career in soap and detergent. The United Press was offering Larry a job writing captions for the photo department of its Paris office. A meager salary, no perks and slave labor—but in Paris!

Larry waited feverishly for Monday morning to telephone Procter & Gamble. "Miss," he instructed the manager's secretary, "be so kind as to destroy my special-delivery letter without opening it. I've got a job in Paris."

Scarcely four months after taking him to the Gare du Nord, I had the pleasure of welcoming my daughter's prospective godfather at Orly Airport. In the meantime I, too, had been demobilized and had become a probationary reporter for *Paris Match*. During the next four years we never missed an opportunity to meet and deepen the precious friendship begun while we were both in uniform. Larry was rapidly promoted. United Press soon sent him to run its Rome office, then he left for the Middle East to cover the tragic events of the first Lebanese war and the Suez crisis. Soon *Newsweek* snapped him up as an outstanding journalist.

We often ran into one another on assignments. At such times our friendship had to be forgotten in the fierce competition to which our editors subjected us. On one occasion Larry locked me in my hotel room in Baghdad to prevent me from sending photos of the Iraqi revolution to *Paris Match;* he had grabbed the exclusive rights on behalf of *Newsweek*. A few weeks later I had my revenge by giving him a false timetable for the train leaving from Djibouti for Addis Ababa, a ploy that enabled me to be one of the last journalists to interview the negus of Ethiopia. The bond between us was reinforced by these strokes of deviousness, which made us realize what a force we might be if we could only combine our talents instead of using them to compete. The idea developed: why not write a book together for both French- and English-speaking readers? Larry wrote his articles in English, I wrote mine in French, but we were both practically bilingual. We could share the writing and translate each other mutually. Between us we could reach 300 million potential readers. All we had to do was find a good subject.

Fortune smiled on us in the form of a short article that originated in Germany and was published in the French daily *Le Figaro*. According to the article, documents recently discovered in the Wehrmacht archives revealed that Paris should have been completely destroyed in August 1944. "Fourteen times Adolf Hitler ordered the general he had appointed to command the defense of Paris to obliterate it," these sources maintained. Why had an order issued fourteen times not been carried out? What miracle had preserved my country's capital?

We had found our subject: Paris had been saved from Hitler's madness by the providential arrival of twenty thousand American G.I.'s and twenty thousand French soldiers, fighting shoulder-to-shoulder. The liberation of Paris was the most marvelous epic a Frenchman and an American could ever have dreamed of recounting together. All the more so since, despite our youth, we both had unforgettable memories of that historic event.

Paris Will Be Another Stalingrad

That summer of 1944, I was one of the 700,000 or 800,000 Parisian schoolchildren who waited, like our parents, for the magical day of our liberation. The Germans had occupied Paris for fifty-two months. The destruction of lines of communication and the battle raging in the whole west of France had deprived us of our usual vacation haunts. Our playgrounds were the city's parks and gardens; our beaches the ornamental fountain pools and the banks of the Seine. A large part of our day was also spent patrolling the streets and avenues on bicycles, looking for a grocery store with something to sell. To enable me to take advantage of every possible opportunity—a pound of turnips, a head of lettuce, a cauliflower that had miraculously arrived from the country—my mother had sewn a hundred-franc note into the lining of my shorts. For the last summer of occupation, Parisians were preoccupied with finding something to eat. We were hungry. That August, my mother had only been able to buy two eggs, three and a half ounces of oil and three ounces of margarine with our ration cards. Our daily allowance of black bread had fallen to less than half a pound. The meat ration had been so reduced that a songwriter claimed it could all be wrapped up in a subway ticket, provided the ticket had not been punched through.

People had converted their baths, cupboards and guest rooms into chicken coops. In the rue Jean Mermoz, where I lived with my younger sister and parents, we woke in the morning to the sound of cock crows. The toy chest in my room harbored four rabbits. To feed them, I used to go out before school and pull up a few blades of forbidden turf from the grass verges of the Champs-Elysées. The little white hen that I raised on our balcony laid her first egg on July 30, my thirteenth birthday.

Even more than our empty stomachs, it was the immediate future of their city that worried the Parisians. Whereas London, Berlin, Vienna, Budapest, Tokyo and so many other capitals were in ruins, in that fifth year of the war, France's City of Lights had emerged intact from history's most destructive conflict. Were the Germans going to put an end to this miracle by turning Paris into another Stalingrad? There were plenty of indications to warrant concern. Every day I saw some new concrete pillboxes appear. Soldiers belonging to the Todt organization and laborers dug trenches in the place where I used to play with marbles. The avenues around the Champs-Elysées bristled every day with some new antitank devices. Notices saying "Achtung minen" (Warning, Mines!) appeared. The pitiful sight of strange convoys covered with foliage making their retreat, day and night, from the Normandy front did nothing to allay our apprehension.

My father came home one evening looking distressed. A former official in the Colonial Ministry revoked by the Vichy government, he occupied a modest position at the Paris town hall. That afternoon the mayor, Pierre Taittinger, had assembled members of his staff to tell them about a meeting he had had with the new German military governor of the capital. Frantic at the discovery that the Nazis were beginning to mine the bridges over the Seine, the Frenchman in charge of the municipality had rushed to the general's headquarters at the Hôtel Meurice, to beg him to break off the operations that were putting the lives of tens of thousands of Parisians at risk. The account my father gave us of that meeting made our hair stand on end.

"Suppose, Mr. Mayor, that a gunshot is fired at one of my soldiers from one of the buildings in the avenue de l'Opéra," the German general had declared, pointing at a map of Paris. "I would burn down all the buildings in the block and shoot their occupants."

He claimed to have the means necessary for such reprisals.

"My forces," he had stated, "number more than 22,000 troops, mostly S.S., a hundred or so Tiger tanks and ninety bombers."

At this point in the meeting, the general, who suffered from asthma, suddenly had a suffocating attack. The commander led his visitor over to the balcony of his office. While the mayor waited for the Nazi to get his breath back, Pierre Taittinger had found in the spectacular scene that spread before their eyes the argument that might perhaps move the German and spare Paris.

"Generals often have the power to destroy, but rarely to preserve," he said, waving his arm in the direction of the spires of Notre Dame and the Sainte-Chapelle, the dome of the Pantheon, the latticework facade of the Louvre and the graceful silhouette of the Eiffel Tower. "Imagine that one day, it is given to you to come back as a tourist to look again at these monuments to our history and say: 'I am the one who could have destroyed all this and I saved it!'"

After a long silence, the German general, visibly moved, turned to the mayor of Paris. "You are a good advocate for your city," he began. "You have done your duty. But by the same token, I, as a German general, must do mine."

The people of Paris would only know the name of that general when they came across his signature at the bottom of the steely proclamations he had posted on the walls of their city. His name was Dietrich von Choltitz. In the mayor's circles it was said that he had been appointed to the post by the Führer himself because of his exceptional service record and his unwavering loyalty to the Nazi cause.

Hitler's envoy was eager to provide the Parisians with a show of his strength. At midday on August 14 he had his garrison troops parade through the capital. I had never seen so many armored vehicles, artillery pieces and trucks crammed with soldiers. Setting off from the Tuileries Gardens, the columns marched up the Champs-Elysées and turned into the avenue Matignon, before taking the Grands Boulevards and the avenue de l'Opéra. For hours on end I watched the incredible parade that stretched for miles and seemed as if it were never going to finish. One small detail eventually intrigued me, however. I thought I recognized the face of an officer with an unusual scar on his cheek and an iron cross around his neck. He was sitting in the gun turret of an armored vehicle marked with the number 246. Forty minutes after he had gone by for the second time, number 246 appeared before my eyes for a third time in the same spot. I felt the urge to laugh. Perhaps the German general was not quite as powerful as he wanted to have our city's chief magistrate believe.

Ever more alarmist rumors would sweep away my reassuring conjecture: massive German reinforcements were about to arrive in Paris. Other rumors announced the imminent insurgence of the Parisian Resistance. It was also alleged that the Germans were preparing to blow up the water, gas and electric utilities. Already the gas supply was no longer functioning. My mother had to cook tapioca or pasta from our meager food stores on a small portable stove that I fueled with pages of my school notebooks screwed up into balls. We were granted electricity for one or two hours a day at times that could never quite be predicted. I would rush then to the knobs of our radio set to track the magic voice of the English BBC through the thick German jamming. In anticipation of losing our water supply completely, my mother filled the bathroom tub to the brim.

One morning I bore witness to the arrival of the first of the dreaded reinforcements. Unlike the retreating columns, this unit of brand-new armored cars and guns arrived from the east. The Place Saint-Philippe-du-Roule was deserted when the leading vehicle emerged into it, occupied by an officer in the black epaulettes of the Waffen S.S. The German was obviously trying to find his way. He called out to me.

"Boy! Boy!" he cried. *"Wo ist die Brücke von Neuilly?"*

I made sure that I was all alone in the square.

"Die Brücke von Neuilly ist dort!" I replied unhesitatingly with the tiny bit of schoolboy German I knew, and pointed in the direction of the Saint-Honoré boulevard. It was the opposite direction.

"Danke sehr!" shouted the officer, before signaling his column to follow him.

I made off as fast as my legs could carry me, terrified at what I had done.[5]

ONE FINE MORNING MACHINE-GUN and cannon fire rent the summer sky. The uprising of the Paris Resistance had begun. From our fifth-floor balcony I watched the confronting hail of bullets like fireworks for the Bastille Day celebrations. On the third day we noticed a thick column of smoke hanging darkly in the sky. The Grand Palais on the Champs-Elysées was on fire. That summer, the huge building was harboring the last of Europe's great circuses still in existence after five years of war—the circus belonging to the Swede Jan Houcke. In a city

5. Twenty years later Larry Collins would recount this anecdote in a U.S. radio interview, telling his listeners that "the act of bravery performed that day by the young Parisian Dominique Lapierre enabled the Allies to enter Paris two days earlier than predicted." His exaggeration was a mark of the feeling Larry had for one who had witnessed those historical days of liberation.

that was starving, his animal cages were full of lions, tigers and panthers, his stables full of horses and elephants. This tragic situation was to provide the Parisians with an act the circus owner would never have dreamed of printing on his program. Crazed with fear by the gunfire, horses broke loose and were galloping about the burning monument. One of them managed to escape into the Champs-Elysées. Hit by a stray bullet, however, the beast keeled over and rolled in the dust.

I will never forget the scene I saw then: occupants of the apartment buildings along the avenue rushed out like vultures. Armed with knives and plates, they butchered the still-warm animal in a matter of minutes.

"Parisians, we have been liberated!"

It was the evening of Thursday the twenty-fourth of August. The electricity had suddenly been restored. I had hurled myself at our radio set. Along with hundreds of thousands of the city's inhabitants, I heard a voice cry: "Parisians, Parisians, keep listening! The tanks of the first liberators have just arrived! You are about to hear a French soldier, the first soldier to enter Paris!"

A fantastic evening, the most marvelous of my childhood, was beginning. "Parisians, we have been liberated!" cried the voice on the radio. "Spread the word! There must be rejoicing everywhere!" From up in a tank turret, a reporter, his voice breaking with emotion, quoted Victor Hugo. "Rouse yourselves!" he proclaimed. "Put shame behind you! Become the great country of France again! Become the great Paris!"

I rushed out onto the balcony of our apartment. People were pulling back their curtains, opening their shutters, falling into each other's arms, running out into the streets. On the balconies and doorsteps and at the windows, the inhabitants of the rue Jean Mermoz, which had for four years been our village, were singing the "Marseillaise" along with the radio. All over Paris similar scenes were taking place. Back on the air, the announcer asked all parish priests to ring their church bells. Throughout the occupation, by order of the Germans, the bells had remained silent. Now they were coming back to life. Within minutes the sky was resonant with the ringing of hundreds of bells. I tried to make out the bells of our parish of Saint-Philippe-du-Roule in the din, but no sound seemed to come from our church. I rushed to the telephone to call the parish priest but his line was continuously busy.

"My dear brothers and sisters," our priest declared when he climbed into the pulpit on the following Sunday, "thanks to all those who tried telephoning me on Thursday evening to ask me to ring the bells in honor of our liberation. Unfortunately our parish has neither bell tower nor bells."

With a sly grin he was quick to suggest that the collection for that first Sunday of freedom should go toward providing the church of Saint-Philippe-du-Roule with bells.

THE BATTLE between von Choltitz's soldiers and the liberators raged on throughout the morning of August 25. Paris paid a high price for its liberty. From the pillboxes built on my playgrounds came bursts of automatic gun fire. The sound of cannon fire could be heard from the direction of the Arc de Triomphe of the Place de l'Etoile and the Place de la Concorde. I waited desperately for a lull because I had promised myself that I would be the first in my family to embrace an American soldier.

Around three o'clock in the afternoon, desperately impatient, I escaped my parents' vigilance and ran toward the Champs-Elysées. I sneaked under the chestnut trees, past the Ledoyen Restaurant and the Marigny Theater. I knew every bush, every clump of flowers, every tree. There, in front of the Guignol, the children's puppet theater, almost four years earlier, on November 11, 1940, the anniversary of the armistice of World War I, I had seen a German officer kill a student shouting "Long live de Gaulle!" I was nine years old.

Suddenly I heard the rumble of Caterpillars. A tank was coming from the Invalides Bridge, its hatchways closed and its cannon pointing straight ahead. I hid myself behind a tree. It could have been a German panzer. The tank turned left and came to a halt in front of the main entrance to the Grand Palais. I started: a splendid white star adorned its armor plating. It was an American tank. From the gun turret emerged a fair-haired giant. He was bareheaded and his overalls were spattered with oil and dust. My first liberator! I shot toward this magical vision. I wanted to shout my joy at this American, to thank him, hug him. But I spoke no English. Like many Parisian schoolchildren, I had had to study German during the occupation. Too bad! I ran just the same, risking being hit by a stray bullet. It was too good an opportunity. When I reached the American tank, wonder of all wonders, I suddenly remembered that I did know at least two words in the language of Shakespeare. They were a reflection of the times in which we lived. I eyed the G.I., then shouted at him with all my might: "Corned beef!" For a second his unshaven face registered his stupefaction, immediately followed by a resounding roar of laughter. He made a sign to me to stay where I was and I saw him climb up his armored vehicle, step over the gun turret and disappear inside. Ten seconds later he reappeared, brandishing an enormous tin. "Corned beef for you!" he cried, jumping from the tank to deposit the tin in my arms. He nearly knocked me senseless with a hearty pat on the shoulder. "Very good!" he insisted, rubbing his stomach. "Yum-yum for you!" At this point a volley of bullets fired from the Grand Palais whistled past our ears. With one bound the American jumped into his tank to grab his machine gun. I called out several *mercis* to him and made off as fast as my legs would carry me.

My parents' reaction was quite the opposite of what I had imagined. In vain I gave them a detailed account of the memorable encounter with our liberator. My father suspiciously examined the tin I had brought back. He propelled me hurriedly into the bathroom, pointing to the tub full of water. "Throw your tin in there!" he ordered me. "It could be an explosive device." My poor father had his reasons: strange things had happened in Paris in those days of madness.

After two hours of this enforced bath, my tin of corned beef had not shown the slightest inclination to explode in our faces. My father therefore undertook to open it with all the precautions worthy of an artificer dismantling a 75mm shell. The result exceeded all my expectations. After four years of deprivation, I rediscovered with ecstasy a long-forgotten indisposition—indigestion.

Next day, Saturday August 26, my young Parisian eyes glimpsed the most wonderful sight they would ever see: the triumphal parade of the liberation forces along the Champs-Elysées with, at their head and marching on foot, the tall, proud figure of Charles de Gaulle, the man whose voice we had listened to for four years without ever seeing his face. Led by my parents, my hand firmly hooked in my sister's, I picked my way through the throng as far as the Place de la Concorde. A shot rang out the moment de Gaulle and his retinue entered the square. A fusillade immediately broke out on all sides. Terrified, thousands of people packed into the square lay down on top of each other. My mother pushed me and my sister under an armored car. That was when a voice in the crowd shouted: "It's the fifth column!" Unfamiliar with the meaning of the expression, which referred to undercover German infiltrators, the gunner of a Sherman tank took the idiomatic expression literally, trained his cannon at the fifth column of the Hôtel Crillon building, and fired! The column collapsed in a cloud of dust.

General de Gaulle took his place in an open car. Heedless of the bullets whistling past from all directions, he waved his long arms tirelessly at the crowd. My mother and thousands of other Parisians wept for joy. Watching the hero who had given us back our freedom and honor, I was overcome with pride. Suddenly I was no longer a child.

WEST HARTFORD, CONNECTICUT, U.S.A. On that same August 26, 1944, at around three o'clock in the afternoon, twenty Loomis High School students were waiting in their classroom for the arrival of their teacher. They were due to have their first French lesson. Fifteen-year-old Larry Collins was part of the group. It was on the pressing insistence of his father, a fervent admirer of France and its culture, that the teen had resigned himself to giving up a few hours of his summer vacation to learn the language of Victor Hugo. The war that had raged for five years in various parts of the world had done nothing to change the comfortable existence of these young Americans. They knew nothing of what it was like to be pulled out of your sleep by air-raid sirens, to scurry down into shelters dug beneath your playgrounds, to be forced to watch enemy soldiers parade down your avenues, to see a relative or a neighbor taken away by the Gestapo. They had experienced neither the acts of violence nor the fear their European comrades had. Above all, they had never known what it is to have an empty stomach. Hamburgers, french fries, ice cream and a thousand other treats we didn't even know existed had remained a part of their daily diet. Young Americans like Larry Collins had gone through the war without really even noticing it, or knowing what was at stake. Europe and Japan were so far away! And now suddenly, for some twenty of them, the tragedy that was tearing the world apart had assumed a face: that of the elderly French teacher who wore on the tip of his nose a strange kind of glasses unknown to adolescents on this side of the Atlantic: a pince-nez. The man was crying—crying out of happiness, joy, emotion. "Boys," he exclaimed, "this is the most beautiful day of my life. Paris is free!"

He explained the news he had just heard on the radio: French and American forces had entered the French capital, the German defenders had surrendered and the people of Paris had taken to the streets to acclaim their liberators.

The sight of the old man who wept for joy at the liberation of Paris made a profound impression on the students of Loomis High School. "I was never to forget it," Larry Collins was to say. "For me it was as if the war had ended that day."

Sixteen years later the former Loomis High School student of French and the ex-schoolboy from the rue Jean Mermoz joined forces to recapture that chapter of Franco-American history in a book. Sixteen years was an ideal distance from which to approach a historic event of that magnitude. Most of the witnesses were still alive, and we could still hope to make people who had kept their secrets to themselves speak out. In addition, after such a span of time, many records and documents hitherto inaccessible or unknown had become available, such as Hitler's orders to destroy Paris, which had inflamed our imaginations.

My three-room apartment on the avenue Kléber in Paris became the command post for our research. We draped the living room walls with maps of Paris on which we had marked the site of every little incident, the position of barricades and German operational bases, targets taken by the Resistance, the routes taken by the convoys retreating from Normandy, the lines of advance of German reinforcements and Allied columns. In that way we had an instant overview of the situation. My dining room, bedroom and even my bathroom were filled with piles of files and indexes, containing the various fruits of our investigations.

The previous occupants of my apartment would have been very surprised to see this flood of papers in the rooms where they had lived. My flat at 26 avenue Kléber was right opposite the former Hôtel Majestic, which, during the war, had housed the general headquarters of the German army in France. The premises had been requisitioned as accommodation for the senior officers. In the depths of the cellar a passage still connected my building to the adjoining building in the rue Lauriston, where the Gestapo used to torture its prisoners.

Those former occupants would also have been astonished to discover the identity of the old lady in the large black hat who lived on the third floor of the same 26 avenue Kléber. Every time I met her in the courtyard, coming or going in the modest

Citroën she preferred to the black chauffeur-driven Peugeot the French government placed at her disposal, she would give me a broad smile: "*Alors*, Lapierre, have you at last liberated Paris?" Coming from her, the question was not without humor. She was the widow of General Leclerc, the liberator of Paris.

Passionately interested in our research, she invited me to leaf through the documents her husband had left and their albums of souvenirs. One day my attention was drawn to a slip of paper. The general's wife told me that the piece of paper had been dropped out of a British plane in 1941. She had retrieved it from the chicken coop on her family's estate in northern France, where she had taken refuge with her six children after her husband left to join General de Gaulle in England. She did not know that on arriving in London, he had changed his name from de Hautecloque to Leclerc to prevent reprisals against his family. At dinner that evening she read her children the message that had fallen out of the sky: "A great French victory," it said. "The key African post of Koufra has surrendered to a French column commanded by Colonel Leclerc." The text went on to say that the soldiers in the unit had braved thirst and crossed nearly five hundred miles of desert to attack the enemy. "I don't know who this Colonel Leclerc is," she told her children, "but I like him: that is how your father would have acted." Ten months later she received a visit from two gendarmes and a bailiff of the Vichy government who informed her that her husband, Philippe de Hautecloque, known as Leclerc, had been stripped of his French citizenship and that all his property was confiscated.

IT WOULD TAKE US FOUR YEARS to discover almost all the secrets of that tremendous page in history, which had had as its main characters the 4 million inhabitants of Paris, their 40,000 liberators and the 20,000 German soldiers ordered to defend to their death the last capital still in the hands of their Führer during that fatal summer of 1944. Our book took four years of hard labor that had to be undertaken at night, over the weekends and during vacations, while we kept up our jobs as journalists for our respective publications. Four years to collect and dissect the memories of some 1,200 protagonists or witnesses; to find and meet 2,000 soldiers, both liberators and German defenders of the Gross Paris; to analyze and deal with nearly a ton of German, American and French records, for the most part new. Four years to reconstruct, together with the principal commanders of the Allied armies, the chiefs of the Paris insurgents, and Hitler's generals, the battle over France's capital and the untold story of the miracle that saved it.

Looking Back to a Miracle with a Nazi General

One autumn day we rang the doorbell to an apartment in a small building on the outskirts of the German spa town of Baden-Baden, just the other side of the Rhine River. The man who, nineteen years earlier, promised the mayor of Paris that he would blow up the avenue de l'Opéra and shoot all of its residents if one single bullet was fired at his soldiers was living in peaceful retirement there with his wife, Uberta, and his cat, Pumper. He had replaced the uniform jacket, Iron Cross and red-striped general's breeches we had seen in photographs with a comfortable beige tweed jacket over gray flannels. In fact, General von Choltitz looked more like a retired post office bureaucrat than a senior officer in Hitler's army.

And yet it was indeed this man, with his short legs, monocle, powerful neck and thin, bladelike lips, that Adolf Hitler had appointed to the head of the entrenched camp in Paris on August 7, 1944. His orders: defend the city to the last of his men and, in the event of failure, turn it into a "field of ruins."

Our research had shown us what importance the leader of the Third Reich attached to holding the French capital in the summer of 1944. For Hitler it was a prime strategic and sentimental stake. From 1914 to 1918 Corporal Adolf Hitler and 6

million of his comrades had fought on French soil to the magical cry of *"Nach Paris!"* Two million of them had paid for their
ambition with their lives. A generation later, as head of the
most powerful military force in Europe, after a lightning conquest, the little corporal kept his appointment with the city of
his dreams. Few Parisians had seen his black Mercedes stop at
the Trocadéro esplanade that June 24, 1940, at seven o'clock in
the morning. For a long moment the conqueror had surveyed
the glorious view stretching out before him: the Seine, the Eiffel Tower, the gardens of the Champ de Mars, the gilded dome
of Napoleon's tomb at Les Invalides and, far away to the left of
him, the spires of Notre Dame Cathedral. Four years later he
followed the invading forces' advance upon the capital of
France on the ordnance maps in his bunker. If he lost the battle of France, there would be only one battle left to fight: the
battle of Germany. To put off that dreaded moment, he clung
to Paris. The city was the axis around which the whole of
France revolved. Moreover, losing Paris would mean losing the
launching bases for the new weapons that he anticipated would
reverse the direction of the war. If Paris fell, the Allied armies
could reach Germany's gates. He had therefore decided to
make Paris a formidable spike of defense to slow the enemy
onslaught. Banging his fist on the conference table in his
bunker, he shouted at his generals: "Whoever holds Paris holds
France!"

To carry out this supremely important mission, the Wehrmacht high command had chosen an obscure lieutenant general posted on the Normandy front whose service records
revealed that he had never "questioned an order, no matter
how harsh." The son, grandson, and great-grandson of military
men schooled in the tough discipline of the Saxon cadet corps,
Dietrich von Choltitz had earned his rank under fire.

Patiently we reconstructed the career of this German general
who had rarely been troubled by the pangs of conscience.
When, on May 10, 1940, he landed at the Rotterdam airport as
head of the 16th Airborne Infantry Regiment, he had been the
first invader to penetrate the west. Faced with Dutch resistance, he had not hesitated to have the Luftwaffe raze the city

to the ground. Two years later, outside Sebastopol, he received his general's epaulettes. When the siege of the great Black Sea port began, his regiment numbered 4,800 men. By the twenty-seventh of July 1942 there were only 347 survivors left, but Choltitz, with a bullet through his arm, had taken the city. To achieve this victory, he had forced Russian prisoners to carry shells on their backs to his siege guns and charge them. Subsequently posted to the rear guard of the Army Group Center, he had become a scorched-earth specialist. On August 9, 1944, Hitler sent the forty-nine-year-old general to Paris.

Sixteen days later that officer capitulated to the Allies almost without putting up a fight and without carrying out his Führer's apocalyptic orders. Why? In order to find out, we had persuaded Choltitz to receive us in his Baden-Baden retreat.

A POLITE BUT CHILLY RECEPTION awaited us in the small living room cluttered with rustic furniture inherited from the family castle in Silesia. Frau Uberta von Choltitz, a plump lady with gray hair worn in a bun, had prepared coffee and a few sweets. But the general's closed, almost hostile face did not augur well for our visit. The pall cast by the Nuremberg trials lingered over Germany at the beginning of the sixties, and few of Hitler's former officers allowed themselves to be drawn into the game of confidences. In any case, Choltitz suffered, he assured us, from a very bad memory. He had only a very vague recollection of the brief days he spent in Paris.

We were not prepared to be put off. We had come armed with everything it might take to jolt the memory of the most inveterate amnesiac, an entire suitcase bursting with papers: ordnance maps, copies of orders from the Führer's bunker and from the various headquarters for the war in the west, transcripts of most of the telephone communications he had received or made in his command post at the Hôtel Meurice, minutes of military meetings, battle plans, programs for the destruction of Paris, etc., etc.

We had even brought him a surprising bit of paper I had found with his former secretary in Munich. It was a bill from a Parisian tailor made out to him for the purchase of a thick woolen overcoat. It was dated August 16, 1944. The reasons for this acquisition intrigued us. Why had the commander of the Gross Paris bought himself a winter coat in the middle of summer—a summer that I remembered as being stiflingly hot—when he had been ordered to defend Paris to his last man and to die there among the ruins?

Choltitz surveyed the bill with suspicion.

"Nein, nein, nein!" he grumbled, shaking his head energetically. "I never bought that coat."

There was an awkward silence. Then we saw Frau Uberta get up and quietly leave the room. She reappeared a moment later carrying a threadbare civilian overcoat. I unbuttoned the garment and opened it. Sewn on the inside pocket was the label of Knize's tailors, 84 avenue des Champs-Elysées, and under it, the general's name and the date, 16 August 1944, had been hand-stitched.

Large beads of sweat were forming on Choltitz's forehead. He was having difficulty breathing. He stood up and went over to the window and opened it to get some fresh air. Several times he filled his lungs. Then in a whisper he said: "I thought it would probably be very cold the following winter in the prisoner-of-war camp where I would see the war out."

THE EPISODE WITH THE COAT and the flood of military papers we spread over the tables, sideboard and carpet of the living room worked like an electric shock. The general had recovered his memory, and the idea of again donning his boots as commander of the Gross Paris for us seemed suddenly to delight him. Our interview could begin. We had prepared for this opportunity with the meticulousness of two judges presiding over the trial of the century. Our interview was to last sixteen days, longer than our host had spent in Paris.

Among the whirlwind of events the general had been through during those fateful hours, none seemed more decisive than his meeting with the leader of Nazi Germany on August 7, 1944, two days before he took command of the Parisian stronghold. Our research had convinced us that that encounter had significantly influenced his behavior in Paris. It might even have been the cause of the miracle that induced Choltitz to spare the capital. Larry, whose experience with *Newsweek* had made him a master interviewer, opened the discussion.

"General, when you met Hitler on August 7, 1944, at his headquarters in Rastenburg, it was the second time you had been in the presence of the leader of Nazi Germany. The first occasion, according to our sources, was one year earlier, on the Russian front, at a lunch on the banks of the Dnieper. For a Wehrmacht general to sit opposite the Führer at lunch was an extraordinary privilege. What memories do you have of that first meeting?"

Choltitz's eyes began to sparkle. He seemed to be caught up in the question-and-answer game. He began:

"One thing struck me initially: the infectious optimism the Führer exuded despite his nervous twitching. The way he described the situation, his assurances and predictions electrified us. By the time we got to the dessert, everyone at the meal was convinced Germany was going to win the war."

"Your posting one year later to the Normandy front enabled you to compare the reality with the promises Hitler had made you," I remarked.

Choltitz sighed. "In Normandy I realized that Germany had lost the war."

"When you got to Rastenburg on August 7 to meet the Führer again," Larry intervened, "the advance guard of the Red Army was less than sixty miles away. What state of mind were you in?"

Choltitz closed his eyes as if to sort out his ideas. Finally, after a long silence, he said: "I believed in Germany's historic mission. I was ready to let the Führer inject me with confidence again. For me that meeting was a kind of pilgrimage from which I hoped to emerge with new strength, reassured and convinced there was still a chance of changing the outcome of the war.

"Hitler, I remember, was standing behind a simple wooden desk. The man I saw before me then was not the one I had glimpsed a year earlier. He had turned into an old man. His face was grayish, his features drawn. His prominent eyes were lusterless and his shoulders sagged. I even noticed that his left hand was trembling and that he was trying to conceal the tremble with his right. But what shocked me most of all was his voice. It was no more than a weak murmur. One year earlier that voice had captivated me.

"Hitler began by giving me a lecture on the history of National Socialism. He recalled the circumstances in which he had created the Nazi Party and sang the praises of the perfect tool he had turned it into, to lead the German people to the historic destiny that was theirs. Then, speaking more strongly and clearly, he predicted that victory was to come, because of the new weapons that were going to reverse the course of the war. Then he changed the subject abruptly to touch upon the attempt to kill him on July 20, when he had nearly lost his life. He raised his hand in my direction in a way that was almost menacing and roared: 'Herr General! Do you realize that dozens of generals are dangling on the end of a rope at this very moment because they wanted to put a stop to my work? But no one can stop me fulfilling my destiny, which is to lead the German people to victory.'"

Choltitz seemed caught up in the spell of that scene. He had begun to imitate Hitler's voice and mannerisms.

"Spittle flowed from the corner of his mouth. It was quite a sight. He leapt up like a jack-in-the-box, waved his arms about, sank into his armchair, and then his expression took on a ferocious glare. On and on he railed against the clique of Prussian generals who had tried to get rid of him. Then he calmed down. After a long silence, he at last looked up at me. After all, I had traveled halfway across Europe for this interview. On my way out of the bunker, I jotted down in my notebook the precise orders he gave me then. I've reread them so often, I know them by heart. He said to me: 'You will go to Paris, Herr General. To Paris where the only fighting going on is for the best seats in the officers' mess. What an insult to our soldiers in Normandy who are putting up the biggest fight in history! You will therefore begin, Herr General, by sorting all that out. Then you will make Paris a frontline city and you will see that it becomes the terror of any backsliders and defectors. To that end, I have appointed you commander in chief of the Gross Paris, and your powers will be the most extensive any general in charge of a garrison has ever had. I am granting you all the prerogatives of a commander of a besieged fortress.'

"He gave me to understand that difficult days lay ahead for Paris and that I might be given ruthless orders. He expected blind obedience of me. 'You will put down any attempt at rebellion on the part of the civilian population,' he added. 'You will stamp out without pity any act of terrorism, any attempt at sabotage against our armed forces. Rest assured, Herr General, that in this you will receive from me all the support you need.'

"I have never forgotten the cruel, almost inhuman look that accompanied those last words. I had come to Rastenburg to be galvanized by a leader. I had found a sick man. I was deeply disappointed."

Choltitz had uttered those last words with an almost painful emphasis. I looked at his temples shaven Prussian style, and imagined him wearing his general's cap with its eagle and swastika, his Iron Cross on his chest, a revolver at his waist, threatening the mayor of Paris with a bloodbath if the slightest incident were to occur. Onto his hard face I superimposed my father's, the day he informed us that the new German general sent by Hitler would not hesitate to slaughter us at the first shot fired at his soldiers. It was hard to believe that those tragic moments were separated by only nineteen years from this sincere and warm encounter in a middle-class sitting-room that smelled so pleasantly of fresh wax.

After leaving Hitler's bunker, Choltitz had stopped at Baden-Baden to embrace his wife and children—Maria-Angelika and Anna-Barbara, who were fourteen and eight at the time, and Timo, who had been born four months earlier.

"I told myself it might be the last time I saw them," he admitted.

Quite apart from the uncertainty of the outcome of his new posting, the general was in the grip of a particular worry that day. On the train that had brought him away from the Führer's bunker, he had met a high-ranking Nazi official. Reichsleiter Robert Ley had just had Hitler sign a new law which determined that the wives and children of German officers would be held responsible in case their husbands and fathers did not fulfill their duties. In some cases, they could be condemned to death and executed.

OUR RESEARCH HAD INDICATED that the sixteen days and sixteen nights General von Choltitz spent in Paris had been a nightmare. Responsibility for a besieged fortress inhabited by 4 million civilians was an assignment very different from leading an army in the field. No military academy, no frontline command, had prepared the Prussian officer for a task both civil and military with infinite ramifications. His primary duty was to guarantee the safety of his troops, but in a city on the verge of insurrection this was a singularly complex and delicate obligation. Should he carry out the threats he had made to the mayor of Paris at the risk of provoking a general uprising? Should he sign a truce with the "terrorists"? Should he accept the Luftwaffe's offer to wipe out the whole of northern Paris from the Le Bourget airport? Should he do as Hitler demanded and blow up the forty-five bridges spanning the Seine in and around Paris' industrial sites, the electricity, gas and water works and public buildings? Should he continue to reinforce the capital's defenses with a view to making a desperate stand like at Stalingrad? Should he ask for the urgent dispatch of massive reinforcements?

These queries were overshadowed by one supreme question, the one Choltitz had been asking himself ever since his meeting with Hitler: could the defense and destruction of the

French capital change the course of the war? The Prussian general knew that the answer was no. Nevertheless, he must do his duty and carry out the orders he received. Unless ... Unless the Allies were to arrive so quickly that they beat his own reinforcements, thus preventing him from carrying out his mission.

On the evening of August 23 the general received a telegram from the Führer's GHQ marked "Extremely urgent." It reiterated Hitler's strict instructions: "Paris must not fall into enemy hands or if it does, he must find there nothing but a field of ruins."

Curiously the message failed to provide Choltitz with the only piece of information that would help him to prevent the fall of Paris: namely, that two S.S. armored divisions, the 26th and 27th Panzer, recalled from Holland and Denmark, were on their way to the French capital. No one thought to inform him, either, that Karl, the giant mortar he had used to wipe out Sebastopol, had reached the Soissons area and that it would be in Paris the day after next.

Unaware of the imminent arrival of these reinforcements, von Choltitz saw only one way out of the impasse: he must speed the Allies' arrival in Paris. He picked up his telephone and asked Raoul Nordling, the Swedish consul, to come and see him immediately. For several days the diplomat had been actively working to prevent Paris from becoming a battlefield.

"The consul had difficulty concealing his surprise when I suggested he go and find the Allies, to tell them to make an immediate move toward Paris," Choltitz told us with a sly look.

Accompanying his visitor back to the door, the German general took his hand. "Be quick, Mr. Nordling!" he had urged. "You have twenty-four hours, possibly forty-eight. After that I can't guarantee what will happen here."

Struck by a heart attack just as he was about to cross the front lines, Raoul Nordling asked his brother Rolf to take his place, armed with a pass from the commander of the Gross Paris. The following evening, after a fantastic rush, the first liberating tanks reached the Place de l'Hôtel de Ville, hailed by the sound of bells ringing all over Paris.

Choltitz was dining with members of his general staff on the first floor of the Hôtel Meurice when he heard the sound of the bells.

"I saw a flicker of surprise on several faces," he told us. "Irritated, I asked whether anyone present had expected the outcome to be different. 'You seem amazed. But what did you seriously expect? In all the years you've been carrying on here in your own little dreamworld, what have you really known about the war? Don't you know what has happened to Germany in Russia and Normandy?' I let loose my indignation. 'Gentlemen, let me tell you what the good life in Paris appears to have kept from you: Germany has lost this war and we have lost it with her.'

"Those words put an abrupt stop to the artificial gaiety of our farewell dinner," Choltitz went on. "So I withdrew to my office and telephoned Army Group B, to which the Paris garrison was directly answerable. I had just received confirmation that the Allied advanced guard had that very instant entered the center of Paris. I knew that at dawn, behind that advanced guard, the main body of enemy troops would appear. At the other end of the line I recognized the voice of General Hans Speidel, chief of staff and a former philosophy professor.

" 'Good evening, Speidel,' I said to him, 'I've got a surprise for you, so please listen.' I took the receiver over to the window that was open wide to the night air filled with the sound of bell-ringing. 'Can you hear that?' I asked impatiently.

" 'Yes,' he replied, 'they're bells, aren't they?'

" 'Indeed, Herr General, they are the bells of Paris ringing at full volume to tell people the Allies have arrived.'

"I sensed an awkward silence. Speidel was not a fanatic. He, too, knew that the destruction of Paris could not change the outcome of the war. I informed him nevertheless that I had, as instructed, completed the preparation work for the destruction of the bridges, railway stations, water, gas and electric utilities and buildings occupied by the German army.

"I asked him whether he had any last order to give me. Speidel replied that he had not.

" 'In that case, my dear Speidel, it only remains for me to say good-bye to you,' I said. 'Permit me to entrust my wife and children in Baden-Baden to your protection.'

" 'You can count on me,' Speidel assured me. He seemed very moved."

The next morning, executing the orders of the commander of the Gross Paris, the various German strongpoints outside and inside Paris put up a fierce resistance to the progress of the Allied columns.

"I had no intention of surrendering the city without a fight," Choltitz declared. "That would have been against my honor as a soldier. But I wanted to avoid pointless destruction and the loss of civilian lives. In any case, the chips were down. My only concern was that my soldiers should fall into the hands of regular soldiers and not in those of the insurgents."

THE SURRENDER, ON THE AFTERNOON of August 25, 1944, of General von Choltitz and all the forces under his command silenced the noise of battle on the streets of Paris. It did not, however, free the city from the threat of Hitler's destructive madness. The next day, August 26, as General de Gaulle's triumphal parade along the Champs-Elysées was beginning, General Jodl, the Führer's chief of staff, telephoned Field Marshal Model, commander in chief of the western front, at his headquarters in Margival, sixty miles to the east of Paris. He wanted to personally pass on Hitler's order to start bombing Paris immediately with the V1 and V2 rockets the Germans had positioned in the north of France and in Belgium.

As luck would have it, the implacable Marshal Model was not there. His deputy, General Hans Speidel, to whom Choltitz had spoken the night before his surrender, answered. Speidel assured Jodl that he would relay the Führer's instructions to Marshal Model as soon as he got back. Considering such ruthless bombing to be pointless now that Paris had fallen, Speidel never did pass on Hitler's order to his superior, thus saving the capital from a dreadful massacre. One week later Speidel was arrested by the Gestapo.

AFTER FOUR YEARS OF HARD WORK, the book was finished. All that remained was to find a good title. Luckily, the man who gave it to us would never claim royalties. The title came from Hitler himself. The question he had asked was revealed to me by General Walter Warlimont, former deputy chief of staff of the Wehrmacht, over a glass of Scotch in his home near Munich. Warlimont had taken part in all the Führer's daily conferences at his Wolf's Lair in Rastenburg during that summer of 1944. Each night, before going to bed, he recorded the day's events in his diary. He had kept the green leather-bound notebook in a corner of his library. Under the entry marked August 25, 1944, I read: "1500 hours, first strategy meeting. An officer gave an operations report for Army Group B for the half day. He announced that the Allied forces had reached the very center of Paris where they are attacking our defenses with their artillery and infantry. The Führer went into one of his usual rages. He turned to General Jodl and thundered that for a week he had continuously been giving orders that the French capital should be defended to the last man. He repeated that the loss of Paris could lead to the rupture of the entire Seine River front. He shook with fury. He shouted that he had given the necessary orders for the city to be wiped out. Had those orders been carried out? Then he banged the table violently and yelled: *'Brennt Paris?'* " Is Paris burning?

This terrible question was to become the title of our book.

"Merde! They're back."

First in France, then in the United States, *Is Paris Burning?* became an instant best-seller. The book was subsequently translated and published in some thirty countries, reaching a global print run of about 5 million copies.

Two years after the French publication, we invited the former commander of the Gross Paris to return to the city Hitler had ordered him to reduce to a "field of ruins" and defend to his death. The most moving moment of this return visit took place on the balcony of the Hôtel Meurice, outside the office Choltitz once occupied. After having recalled the scene that had occurred on that same balcony when the capital's mayor, Pierre Taittinger, begged him not to destroy Paris, I showed the general the glorious view spread out before us.

"One day," Larry told him, "history will acknowledge you spared all these treasures for the glory of humanity."

General Dietrich von Choltitz died a few months after his journey, without seeing the star-studded film based on *Is Paris Burning?* that director René Clément shot in the streets of Paris. His character, portrayed by the German actor Gert Fröbe, seemed almost more real to us than Choltitz had in the flesh. Throughout a whole summer, Clément's cameras roamed about the capital, filming the book's most striking scenes in their actual setting. To spare Parisians too much inconvenience, the film was shot in the early hours of the morning. The Place de la Concorde where Yves Montand's Sherman tank was to ram a German panzer was closed to traffic for several mornings.

Undertaking to film *Is Paris Burning?* in the streets of the capital was one of the foolhardiest challenges in the history of cinema. I shall never forget the very first scene Clément filmed. It was around six o'clock in the morning and German soldiers, helmeted, armed with grenades and submachine guns, were bringing cases of dynamite to mine Napoleon's tomb under the dome of Les Invalides. Satisfied with this first sequence, Clément suggested the actors go for a beer or a coffee in Le Vauban café located just opposite the monument. The bewildered face of the waitress behind the counter when she saw all those Nazi soldiers enter her establishment, put their submachine guns on the counter and, in a Parisian accent, order a glass of red wine or a cup of coffee will remain forever engraved upon my memory.

A few moments later, when those same "Germans" returned to the location where they were filming, I witnessed an even stranger scene. At the sight of all these Nazis in the middle of the avenue, a Parisian postman, peddling past on his bicycle, shouted at the top of his voice, "*Merde!* They're back!" before falling on the pavement, overwhelmed by emotion.

The world premiere of *Is Paris Burning?* was held at a gala event at the Palais de Chaillot, in the presence of all the actors and nearly all the characters they represented. Atop the Eiffel Tower illuminated by tricolored floodlights, pop singer Mireille Mathieu sang "Paris en Colère," the popular song of Paris's uprising set to the film score composed by Maurice Jarre. For the tens of thousands of Parisians crowding the Champ de Mars, the bridge over the Seine and the Trocadéro esplanade, the capital put on a sumptuous fireworks display. Seated in a box next to the heroes of the great epic story we had written, Larry and I were like two schoolboys at a prize-giving ceremony.

5

A Dance of Death with the Black Bulls of Spain

"You're going to have to grow a beard like Papa Hemingway and get used to smoking a cigar," Larry Collins informed me as he handed me a telegram that had just arrived from the United States. "*Reader's Digest* is suggesting we go to Spain to write an article about a Spaniard even more famous than General Franco. How do you fancy a story on bullfighter El Cordobés?"

It was too good to be true. Spain was my Garden of the Hesperides. I had visited there ever since I was twenty, bewitched by its many wonders. A large part of my family had fallen under the country's spell. My only sister, Bernadette, had married there at the age of eighteen. On their retirement, my parents had settled in Madrid near their grandchildren, Xavier and Carlos. I could speak Spanish reasonably enough and had, for a long time, been following the political and economic development of a country where I carried out numerous assignments for *Paris Match*. I had even been an involuntary guest in a Guardia Civil cell when I was caught sneaking onto the grounds of a hunting lodge in the Sierra de Córdoba, where King Baudouin of Belgium and Queen Fabiola were having their secret honeymoon. True, my knowledge of tauromachy was limited, but that did not mean I did not feel the flame of an authentic *afición* burning in my heart. The *Reader's Digest* offer was thus a real source of delight, all the more thrilling for the fact that it presented Larry and me with the opportunity to continue our fruitful literary collaboration, even if it was limited to writing an article profiling a single character.

Several evenings later, on a frosty night, a taxi from Córdoba deposited us outside the entrance to an estate surrounded by cork oaks and wild olive trees. The iron gate sported the emblem of the master of the house: a flat-brimmed Andalusian hat and the name of the former urchin whose success this luxurious dwelling now symbolized—Hacienda Manuel Benítez El Cordobés.

Huddled around a fire they had lit a few yards from the gate, three young boys were writing with a piece of coal on a strip of cloth one of them had torn off his shirt. They were half starved. Scattered around them were the cups from the acorns that were their only food. Having finished their inscription, they carefully knotted each corner of the piece of linen to the black bars of the gate. "Manolo," said the message, "we congratulate you on your success in Mexico. We want to experience glory like you. Give us a chance to practice in your ring." They were *maletillas*, apprentice bullfighters. One of them, Antonio Carbello, was the son of a shepherd and the last of a family of sixteen children, of whom only five were still alive. The puny lad next to him, the fourth son of a blind beggar, had been almost crippled by a beating at the hands of the Guardia Civil. The third boy had been abandoned at birth outside the door to a convent in Huelva. A spark of hope flickered in their eyes when they saw the gate open to let us in.

We were taken to the living room, where twenty or so admirers formed a circle around a tall, ungainly fellow with long, tousled hair, dressed in a checked shirt and a pair of jeans over Andalusian boots. He was dancing and clapping his hands in front of a stunning dark-haired girl who was partnering him by tapping her feet and waving her arms gracefully. His rough voice was singing out the heart-rending tones of a *cante hondo*, the tragic song of the Andalusian soul. We did not dare draw any closer for fear of disturbing the magic of the duo. Every now and then the master of the house interrupted to administer a robust slap to the shoulder of one of the guests, strum a few chords on a guitar, drink beer straight from the bottle or break into laughter. El Cordobés was in life what he was in the ring: an unpredictable, instinctive being, as much an animal as the wild bulls he fought.

As soon as he saw us he came rushing over. Larry was escorted by an interpreter, a charming young English girl. With the face of an Italian Madonna she immediately aroused the matador's interest. With a broad, boyish grin he invited her to dance. Blushing with pride and pleasure, the girl allowed herself to be led away. Soon the room resounded with the frenzied pounding of the dancers' feet as onlookers clapped in time. The audience, made up exclusively of gentlemen in dark suits smoking fat cigars, was unusual: they were breeders of bulls, bullfight organizers and ring owners. The boy dancing before them was the hero of a new golden age that was making their fortune. Never before in Spain had people spent so much money on bullfights. A thousand *corridas* were being advertised for the forthcoming year alone. Three bullfight critics, a stout captain from the Guardia Civil and a florid young churchman in a black cassock completed the small group of courtiers. Padre Juan Arroyo was also a talented guitarist. It was through his music that he had come to know El Cordobés. One day as the matador was putting on his suit of lights before a *corrida*, the priest had burst into his hotel room with his guitar and sung him a ballad he had composed in his honor. Entitled "The Smile of El Cordobés," the song had become a hit. Since then, Padre Arroyo's relationship with the bullfighter had little to do with religion. The priest was El Cordobés's private tutor: Spain's most celebrated matador could neither read nor write.

The evening lasted forever. Beer, wine and whiskey flowed freely. The master of the house exhibited an insatiable capacity for drink, laughter, playing the guitar, singing and dancing. His joie de vivre, exuberance and spontaneity delighted his guests. Our young English interpreter was in seventh heaven. She knew she was experiencing what millions of young Spanish girls dreamed of. Suddenly El Cordobés left her to get his latest toy, a gun which he took down from a rack on the wall. He had each one of us examine it, then opened the breech and caressed the steel in a state of ecstasy. The weapon bearing the prestigious trademark of Purdey & Purdey had just arrived from London, but it was only a modest plaything compared to the toys we would discover beyond the adjacent dining room, a large room with walls decorated with stuffed bulls' heads.

The servants had piled the table high with chorizo sausages, Serrano ham, Manchego cheese, omelets, prawn and squid fritters and all kinds of pastries. In the immoderate dimensions of this mountain of food, one could see the reaction of a starving urchin for whom wealth meant first a full stomach. Legend had it that El Cordobés had squandered the proceeds of his first torero's fee on buying a whole ham, just so that he could carve himself a slice at any hour of the night or day.

Suddenly all the chandeliers in the room went out as the double curtains hanging at the far end of the dining room slid back. Powerful lights beamed through the darkness, illuminating yet another compensation for his poverty. After filling his belly, El Cordobés spent his first fees on a blatant symbol of his success, a little Renault car. Five years later he had a stable of automobiles. Through the glass we saw a royal-blue Jaguar convertible, a fat gray Mercedes sedan and a white Alpine sports car. At the back of the garage, two trestles supported the gleaming bodywork of a Chris Craft speedboat. The garage had been built next to the dining room so that at every meal the master of the house could contemplate these symbols of his success at leisure.

There were other surprises in store. The matador pressed a button and one of the room's glass bays slid open. In front of the floodlit swimming pool there appeared a sublime dapple-gray stallion. Held on a leading rein by a *vaquero*, it pawed the ground with pleasure. This magnificent specimen of Andalusian stock was a recent addition to El Cordobés's stable to help round up the bulls he bred. His name was Amor de Dios and he did not walk—he danced. Every tread of his hooves provoked noisy expressions of enthusiasm from our host, who clapped his hands in time to his horse's hoofbeats. The Andalusian in man and beast communicated in the same wild incantation.

MANUEL BENÍTEZ EL CORDOBÉS had been born in Palma del
Río, a small Andalusian town on the banks of the Guadalquivir,
between Córdoba and Seville. His father, a farm laborer, leased
his services to the local landowners. In the Benítez home they
ate their fill only twice a year: when the oranges were picked
and when the olives were harvested. For El Cordobés's parents, the birth of their fourth child, at the beginning of May
1936, could not have been less opportune. Like so many other
towns and villages in Spain, socialist Palma was in the throes of
an insurrection against the established order. There was a succession of strikes and looting, which forced a number of
landowners to flee. To feed themselves, the Palmenos resorted
to the ultimate crime: they slaughtered the wild bulls from the
national fiesta's most prestigious breeding ranches, killing even
the *sementales*, the animals kept for breeding, whose genes had
perpetuated the bravery and nobility of the stock for centuries.
That spring of 1936, the smell of grilled meat spread as far as
the town's most wretched hovels. Three months later, returning in the wake of General Franco's soldiers, the landowners
took their revenge. The civil war had just broken out. Palma
del Río became the setting for bloody massacres. Here, as elsewhere, began years of fear, poverty and hunger. At the beginning of 1939 privation took little Manuel's mother. Shortly
afterward, his father succumbed to the poor treatment he had
received in a Franco labor camp. The Benítezes' story was that
of millions of other Spanish families.

Like many other young men, the lad from Palma knew only
one way to a better life: the Spanish way of courage and death,
confronting the horns of the wild bulls. For years he had wandered the streets, his *maletilla* bundle on his back, looking for
an *oportunidad*, a chance to practice with calves and learn the
rough rules of bullfighting on the end of their horns. On foot,
clinging to the backs of trucks or on the buffers of trains, he had
crossed Spain, going from breeding place to breeding place,

from city to city, sleeping in fields, stations, work sites; living on stolen fruit, plants, acorns and scraps. The doors remained closed to the teenager in rags. In desperation one day he had leapt into the Madrid bullring in the middle of a *corrida*, in front of 25,000 spectators, hoping to show his courage. His crazy gesture nearly cost him his life and landed him in prison. Years went by before a small *corrida* organized by his village priest enabled him to take a tentative revenge. Too poor to rent a suit of lights, he fought the bulls in his vagabond's rags. He emerged from the arena borne on the shoulders of the crowd, brandishing the ears and tails of the monsters he had killed. There was still a long way for the former orange thief to go before he attained the glory of the great rings. His meeting with a shellfish-seller-turned-bullfighter-manager would enable him to achieve that glory. Raphael Sánchez, better known as El Pipo, believed that a bullfighter could be launched like a brand of detergent. He decided to exploit the spontaneous courage of the young Andalusian, with the firm intention of turning him into Spain's best-paid matador as quickly as possible. El Pipo began by changing the young man's name. From then on his protégé would be called El Cordobés, the man from Córdoba, as a tribute to the city that had given the fiesta such gods as Belmonte and Manolete.

"On Sunday I have a meeting with death."

El Pipo first set about making a name for El Cordobés in Andalusia. He pawned his wife's jewels, rented arenas, organized fight upon fight, did the rounds of the breeders to choose the most "accommodating" bulls, had the tips of their horns filed down to reduce the accuracy of their blows, rigged the draw, bought off journalists. El Pipo wrote their articles himself, plastered the walls with posters bearing a photograph of the young Benítez and advertising slogans that proclaimed: "Come and see me on Sunday. I have a meeting with death." He flooded the newspapers with publicity, and himself handed out the ears, tails and hooves of the bulls that are the trophies of the truly magnificent bullfights.

One summer was all it took for this magician to launch his phenomenon. The timing could not have been better. With his disregard for tradition, his refusal to obey the rules and his wild, improvised, spontaneous way of taking on the bulls, El Cordobés, the son of the poor laborer who had died as a consequence of the civil war, brought a wind of revolt to the sands of the bullrings comparable to that which was sweeping the country. The sword he brandished signaled changes that would affect not only the art of bullfighting but the future of Spain.

Twenty years of Franco's dictatorship had stranded the country in a medieval past. By the mid-fifties its road network was scarcely more developed than Yugoslavia's. Nearly one in three Spaniards could neither read nor write. The number of cars amounted to only 250,000, one for every 120 inhabitants, in comparison with France's one car for every 11 people. The country's industry did not produce refrigerators, washing machines, television sets, any of the household appliances that filled the shop windows of other European countries. Spain was living in rigorous, voluntary isolation. No foreigner could enter without a visa; no Spaniard could leave without special permission from the police. Yet 3 million Spanish people—one in every ten citizens—had abandoned their homes to go and seek better living conditions elsewhere.

El Cordobés's eruption onto the Spanish scene at the beginning of the sixties coincided with the advent of a new era. Spain was beginning to shake off the chains of a rigid and archaic system. The annual invasion of 15 million foreign tourists had destroyed the myth of Spanish isolation and at the same time sown the seeds of an irreversible economic and social revolution. The Spain of El Cordobés had discovered neon, television, Coca-Cola, American aid dollars and industrialization. Skyscrapers rose out of the lunar aridity of Castile, and in the depths of the countryside, the backfiring of small cars forever replaced the antiquated creaking of donkey carts. Like an outbreak of fever, a string of seaside resorts with modern buildings, luxury hotels, bars and nightclubs with such sacrilegious

names as Broadway, Soho and Pigalle would from then on line
the once-deserted shores. The Spain of the flamenco, of pilgrimages and mantillas, the noble and beautiful Spain celebrated by Hemingway and Montherlant, was being wiped out
by a rising tide of modernity. Its youth, thirsty for life, turned
their backs on the events of the past and dreamed of shaking
off the tyranny of official obscurantism. Young people wore
blue jeans, Bardot-style bikinis and Beatles long hair. They
chewed gum, straddled scooters, danced the jerk, read Sartre
and repudiated the sexual taboos of their elders.

For millions of Spanish people seeking a better life, no personality could better incarnate this transformation than the
young Andalusian who, through courage and passion, had overcome both hunger and poverty.

A NEW INVENTION would spread his myth right across the Iberian Peninsula to the very humblest of its villages. El Cordobés
was the first bullfighter to enjoy the blessings of television. I
was in Madrid for the first great *corrida* of the San Isidro *feria*,
where the name of the former urchin of Palma del Río was displayed in banner headlines. The event would be televised live
on the country's only channel. Twenty million Spaniards could
thrill together at their idol's prowess. The colossal number of
people watching probably exceeded that of all the spectators of
all the bullfights in the history of the *fiesta brava*. Life in Spain
came to an abrupt halt. Madrid was a ghost town. Shops had
drawn their iron shutters, news vendors shut up their stalls,
movie theaters closed their doors. Even the beggars and the
blind men selling tickets for the national lottery had disappeared. Two hours before the fateful *cinco de la tarde*—the
faithful five o'clock hour—the people of Madrid, like people
all over Spain, positioned themselves in front of the small
screen. Bars and cafés with a television set were invaded by
noisy, happy crowds who had paid up to a hundred pesetas for
the right to sit on a stool to watch the bullfight. Calle Serrano,

calle García de Paredes, on the Castellana, in the residential area, the suave voice of Lozano Sevilla, Spanish television's most popular bullfight commentator, resounded from every story. In the working-class district where crowds gathered outside the cafés a similar atmosphere prevailed. Everyone wanted to see the vagabond-turned-millionaire enter the arena. For that was what made El Cordobés a myth: no matter what the experts might think of his art, he was the bullfighter of the people, a people who had never been able to buy tickets for a fight but who, thanks to television, could now dream of better tomorrows watching their idol. Thousands of families had acquired their first television set for the occasion. Educational establishments, factories, large stores, banks and offices closed early to enable their pupils or employees to watch the broadcast. The newspapers announced that the head of state would tune in as well. Comfortably installed in front of his set in one of the boudoirs of his Pardo Palace near Madrid, General Franco would not miss watching the triumph of the only Spaniard whose fame exceeded his own.

FROM THE *CALLEJÓN*, the passageway around the arena—at the level of the sand, the bulls, the horses, the noises and the smells—the spectacle grips you with a power no spectator in the tiered seats can experience. Here, I felt, danger, fear, courage, emotion and death are tangible, the threat of tragedy is ever-present. It was as if I were in the ring itself.

The first bull shot out of the *toril* like a bullet. After observing it for a minute, El Cordobés advanced to meet it. He wanted to goad it into the center of the ring, the point where the bullfighter was farthest away from any possible help. Five yards away from the beast he stopped, opened his arms and summoned it. His gesture marked the beginning of a spectacular ballet of movements punctuated by raucous calls to the bull. Flicking the cape over the animal's head with a jerk of his wrist, rolling it around him with a dancer's volta or holding the cape behind his hips, he lured the animal into a whirlwind of such daring passes that man and bull seemed to merge with one another. Twenty-five thousand voices marked the timing of each encounter with a storm of *olés*. But what people were waiting for was the placing of the *banderillas*, the six short arrows to be lodged behind the bull's neck. Usually matadors left the execution of this graceful sequence to the *banderilleros* in their *cuadrilla*, their team. El Cordobés, on the contrary, never missed the opportunity to display the full range of his talent. He seized the two *banderillas* held out by one of his *peones* and made a provocative show of them to the public. Then he went through the sequence that had contributed so greatly to his reputation as a man who danced with death: breaking the sticks in two on the edge of the *barrera* that bordered the ring, he kept hold of just two pencil-size pieces. His face lit by a brilliant smile, he ran toward the spot where the beast was waiting for him. Five or six yards from the horns he halted. A rumble of fear rose from the stands. El Cordobés had thrown himself to his knees on the sand. Could a matador face any challenge more dangerous than planting half-*banderillas* while kneeling? The slightest deviation in the trajectory of the animal and its horn could pierce his eye or mouth, smash his skull, puncture his lungs. Wounds like that were fatal. No surgeon could stop the hemorrhaging of a lung slashed by the twisting horn of a bull.

Spectators held their breath as if the slightest movement of air might trigger a tragedy. El Cordobés raised his arms with the sticks between his fingertips, threw out his chest and cried: *"Venga toro!"* The animal hesitated, then, abruptly, he charged. For a lightning interval I thought the beast would skewer the man. But a *peón* waved a piece of cape over the *barrera*, diverting the bull's attention for a split second. As the horns whistled past his head, Manuel Benítez planted his half-*banderillas* in the animal's neck. With one movement the entire arena got to its feet. People yelled, waved, stamped their feet. A beam of happiness lit up the matador's face. Slowly he stood up again, wiped the sweat from his forehead with the back of his hand and thanked his *banderillero* with a wink. Then he held out his arms to his public, who were applauding him, throwing flowers, hats, footwear, bags, flasks of wine. People were hysterical. Even the bull seemed stunned. The ringing of a trumpet then announced the third and final *tercio*, that of the kill. The previous year, during his *alternativa* ceremony—the official confirmation of his status as a matador—El Cordobés had deliberately sought to silence the controversy surrounding the quality of his art by giving the demanding and knowledgeable Madrid public a sober *faena* performance reduced to its essentials, without any unnecessary embellishments. One year later, confronted with this pugnacious and very noble bull, he wanted to show this same public the full range of his abilities and his courage. It was by getting closer to the horns than any other bullfighter that El Cordobés had become *número uno*.

With his hair in disarray, his face transfigured by a cheery grin, he walked forward for the final confrontation. Freezing twenty yards from the animal, he spread out the red cloth of his *muleta* and called it. The beast took off with a furious bound. While it was in midcharge, he spun around gracefully to finish his half-circle at the precise moment the animal was passing him. The movement lasted no more than a second and had given the entire arena goose bumps. Excited by the audacity of this fresh challenge, El Cordobés let himself go. As if in a rage, he ran to catch the bull again, shook his red rag right under its frothing muzzle and pricked it with his sword to provoke a charge. Here was the meeting of two monsters. Hypnotized by the cloth brushing the sand, the bull charged, went past, turned and charged again. Each time it passed, the animal drew closer, confining the matador to an ever more constricted circle. For seconds on end he remained thus imprisoned by the mortal onslaught, just barely keeping his balance by clutching at the animal's bleeding backbone. Faced with this wild demon, stomachs contorted with cramps, spines tingled with cold sweat. The *plaza* thrilled, shouted, wept for joy, sharing in the anger, love and savage instinct of a man who was even more primitive than the animal he was fighting. There were unbearable moments like the one when he threw himself to his knees in front of the animal, making it pass to the right, then to the left, level with his chest or his head. Changing hands, he presented his *muleta* at every possible angle, in front of the bull, behind, beside him, from far away and close, so close that people screamed with terror. At any moment I expected to see the horns run him through. Each time, he evaded the charge, and smiling, took up his stand in front of the bull, which had stopped to get its breath back. This respite would last only a few seconds. A series of left-handed passes brought the spectators to their feet in a wave of enthusiasm punctuated with *olés*. He finished with a pass that forced the animal to scrape its horns along his chest. Smiling with sparkling white teeth, his suit of lights red with the blood of his adversary, he raised his sword and *muleta* in the direction of the crowd. A storm shook the *plaza*. Once more they stood in one concerted movement, stamping their feet, applauding, shouting. The band launched into a *paso doble*. Three minutes later, the bull fell, struck down with a single blow of the sword. A deluge of hats, shoes, bags, flowers and cushions rained down upon the sand. Admirers and detractors, united in the same enthusiastic fever, paid tribute to raw courage.

EL CORDOBÉS'S BRAVERY took its toll. Our hero's body was covered with over four and a half feet of scars. The Spanish, French and South American *plaza* surgeons had given him transfusions of thirty-nine pints of blood. Four times—in Valencia, Barcelona, Granada and Madrid—he had been given the last rites. The previous year, during his *alternativa*, and his first fight to be televised live, 20 million spectators watched as the bull, Impulsivo, left him half-dead on the sand. On the *ramblas* in Barcelona, under the arcades of Salamanca's Plaza Mayor, in the cafés of Seville, an anxious Spain sat about listening to the radio. In Córdoba the churches were filled with the faithful who had come to pray to the Madonna on his behalf. The Carmelite chapel overflowed with men and women reciting the rosary in front of the picture of Jesus falling beneath the weight of the cross on the way to Golgotha, a fetish for Cordoban bullfighters. In Lima, Caracas and Mexico, radio stations interrupted their programs to bring news of the injured idol.

A little before midnight word had gone around the bullfighters' clinic in Madrid: *El Cordobés está muerto* (El Cordobés is dead.) Plunged for a moment into a stupor, Spain exploded with joy when the news was proved false. The photo of El Cordobés on the sand, fending off the horns of the bull about to kill him, appeared on the front pages of papers throughout Spain. Publications far removed from the bullfighting world, the *New York Times*, the *Times* of London, *Le Monde* of Paris and the *Tokyo Mainichi*, carried the story. An impressive crowd mounted guard for days outside the clinic. Visitors brought miraculous medals, remedies they had concocted, formulae to dispel the evil eye, cakes, fruit, chickens. The telephone switchboard was flooded with calls. Two young French girls, who had caught a plane to Madrid just to be nearer their idol, volunteered to serve as switchboard operators. Telegrams—some addressed simply to "El Cordobés, Spain"—poured in by the thousands. They came from actresses, waiters, political leaders, workmen, ecclesiastical dignitaries. One of them was signed by the man whose Guardia Civil had once hounded the little orange thief through the orchards around Palma del Río: Francisco Franco.

Fortunately he recovered, and not all of his injuries were so serious. But his style condemned El Cordobés to be ceaselessly scooped up, knocked about, tossed in the air and trampled upon. His desire to be the best was so strong that during one fight, he delivered the sword thrust and then forgot to let go of his sword. The bull tossed its head and people were treated to the extraordinary sight of Manuel Benítez rotating like a wheel in the air, his hand still gripping the sword that was buried to the hilt in the animal's neck. The bull fell down dead. El Cordobés's incredible pirouette had dislocated his shoulder. Condemned to three weeks of immobility, he withdrew to his estate near Córdoba.

While Larry was reconstructing the civil war in Andalusia, I would meet El Cordobés each morning to talk to him about his childhood, his family and his arduous path to fame; about fear, courage and death. His enforced rest gave me my only opportunity to keep him within reach of my notebook for an hour or two. No notion was more alien to him than that of an appointment, a date or a timetable. He was quite capable of suddenly jumping on a horse and galloping off with his *vaqueros* in search of some stray bull calf. Or he would take a gun and go off shooting birds. Then again, he might call for bread and sausage. A servant would run off and fetch it, only to find when she got back that her master had disappeared. He could well have driven off in his Mercedes to Córdoba to have another floor added to the hotel he was building. One night after an entire evening spent dancing the flamenco in a nightclub in Córdoba, he invited me to get in his Alpine sports car and we tore off to Madrid because he wanted to eat a potato omelet with his sister Encarna.

It was a terrifying journey. The bends succeeded each other like a roller-coaster ride at an amusement park. The tires screeched as they tore at the asphalt. Every tree seemed destined to be our coffin. Singing at the top of his voice, Manuel would let go of the steering wheel to give me hearty slaps on the thigh. *"Tranquilo, Dominique, tranquilo!"* he laughed as I cursed *Reader's Digest,* the bulls, Spain. At last, ninety-five miles later, he stopped, exhausted, in the square of a sleeping village. We got out of the car and stretched out side by side next to the fountain. Within minutes we had both sunk into a deep sleep. When the first rays of sunshine caressed my cheeks an hour or two later, I opened my eyes. I could hardly believe what I saw. The local residents, their faces transfigured, had silently formed a circle around us. For the poor people of that village lost in the sierra, the sleeping body of the god of the fiesta in their village square was as miraculous an apparition as that of the Virgin Mary to the children of Lourdes.

ONE MORNING I FOUND MANUEL in a state of rapture on the balcony to his room. A group of wild bulls had come close to the fencing. The cousin of the monster that had almost torn out his shoulder was probably among them. El Cordobés's face was furrowed with suffering, but his passion transcended any pain: "*Dominique, mira que bonito el número 14!*" (Look how beautiful number 14 is!). He described the animal with an ecstatic voice: the perfect symmetry of the horns, the small head, the enormous mass of muscles enveloping the neck, the glossy spine, the powerful curve of the rump. At that moment I understood one of El Cordobés's secrets. "To be a bullfighter, you have first to be a bull," he explained. In that instinctive communion between man and beast lay the secret of his success.

Inspired by the matador and ever concerned about authenticity, Larry and I decided to take on a bull ourselves. After all, how could we write about fear if we had never experienced it? A friend who was a breeder lent us a cape and released a stout young calf onto the sand of his private ring. To ensure there was a survivor to record the experience, we decided to toss a coin to see who would face the beast. Alas, fortune chose me. Though not much bigger than a French poodle, the ferocity, power and agility of the little monster dispelled all the courage I had mustered in a matter of seconds. I had scarcely unfolded the scarlet cloth before a stomach-high locomotive seemed to tear past me. The rush of air alone nearly made me lose my balance. Fortunately there was no bullfighting reporter there, but I might have liked an Olympic timekeeper about; he would have awarded me a gold medal for the hundred-meter sprint, so swift was my flight before that diminutive but murderous creature. I had no need of a second charge to understand what El Cordobés had been unable to explain to me. No duel demands more real courage than a man on foot against a wild bull.

I WAS ABOUT TO EXPERIENCE the most frenetic season in the whole history of bullfighting. That year, 1965, El Cordobés took part in 175 fights, a number unequaled by any other matador. I had the good fortune to accompany him on part of that infernal whirl. One afternoon we were in Málaga, the next day in Bilbao and the day after that in Algeciras, almost back where we had started two days previously. The *cuadrilla,* his staff, slept in a fat Mercedes with folding seats that hauled from one end of Spain to the other, and even as far as France. On its roof were trunks decorated with representations of the matador, packed with capes, *muletas,* swords and suits of lights in every conceivable color.

El Cordobés himself traveled about in his private plane, a twin-engine Piper Aztec he had bought for $100,000, on which he had had his name painted in gold letters. To pilot this flying Rolls-Royce, he had been quick to entice a young colonel from the Spanish air force. Hiring a pilot was a totally theoretical precaution. Much to the terror of his passengers, Manuel took the controls immediately after takeoff, with the same impulsiveness he showed at the wheel of his Alpine or his Jaguar, or when he knelt in the sand with his back to a bull. Listening to the aircraft's radio revealed that his fame had as much impact in the sky as on the ground. He had only to ask permission to land and the flight controllers would chase away any other aircraft. They might well be jumbo jets that had just crossed the Atlantic with hundreds of passengers on board. It didn't matter. In Spain the god Cordobés took priority. One day all the fire engines at the Madrid airport rushed out to surround the small plane to give him an aubade with their hoses, like the fireboats in the port of New York greeting Lindbergh on his return from Europe. On another occasion the airport staff provided a triumphal escort for the man who gave the whole of Spain goose bumps every time he fought a *corrida.*

"How can men circle around the earth?"

The article commissioned by *Reader's Digest* had slowly assumed the dimensions of a book. We had gone to Andalusia for three weeks. Two years later we were still there. The destiny of this Spaniard who had shaken off the shackles of hunger and poverty by choosing a path to success that Spain alone could offer, a way that passed via the horns of wild bulls, had mesmerized us. We had the material for a major historical account. In his character, in the history of the village where he was born, in the destinies of his sisters, of the fat owner of the Palma café, of the Guardia Civil sergeant, of the parish priest Don Carlos, of the large landowner Don Felix and of a hundred other associates, there lay a vast fresco of Spain's last generation for us to paint. Thirty years after being born into the horrors of the civil war, a new generation instigated an economic and social revolution unique in the country's history.

We called our book *Or I'll Dress You in Mourning*, a title we borrowed from the hero himself. The first evening young Manuel Benítez put on a suit of lights to earn a few pesetas, his sister Angelita threw herself, weeping, into the arms of the boy she had raised and implored him not to risk losing his life to the horns of a wild bull. "Don't cry, Angelita," he replied calmly, "this evening I shall either buy you a house, or I'll dress you in mourning." Angelita invited us to visit the magnificent house in the heart of Palma del Río that he had given her. But every time he went onto the sands of the *plaza*, the poor woman knelt before the statue of the Virgin Mary to beg the mother of Jesus to spare her from ever having to wear mourning for her little brother.

ONE NIGHT AT THE END of that crazy season of 175 bullfights, Manuel Benítez woke up with a start. He had had a nightmare: the horn of an enormous black bull had pierced him right through his body. As on the evening of his Madrid *alternativa*, El Cordobés suddenly felt his life "slipping away through the gaping hole of the wound." He woke his driver, jumped into one of his cars, made for Córdoba and called his manager in Madrid to say that he was giving up the gamble of the arena.

Four days later, like a long funeral cortege, a string of black limousines stopped outside the entrance to his property. Out of each of the cars stepped an emperor of the bullfighting world. There was the director of the Madrid *plazas;* the men in charge of the Seville, Córdoba and Barcelona rings; bullfighting impresarios—in short, all those threatened with ruin by the matador's nightmare. When his retirement was announced, hundreds of spectators rushed to the Maestranza bullring in Seville to get their money back for tickets to the next *feria.* The owner of the largest hotel in the seaside resort of Castellón de la Plana declared that without Cordobés there would be "no *feria* and no tourists." A well-known economist calculated that the matador's retirement would deprive the hotels, taxi drivers, ticket touts, restaurant owners and a host of other businesses several million dollars. The bullring directors would lose nearly $10 million for the fights in which the *torero* would not take part.

Manuel Benítez received his visitors dressed in a casual shirt, standing under a bust of Manolete, one of his illustrious predecessors killed by a bull, and a statuette of the philosopher Seneca, another famous Cordoban. For nearly an hour, the potentates begged the matador to change his mind and save the *fiesta* from disaster. Manuel was weak enough to allow himself to be convinced. He returned to the infernal whirlwind of the *toros* and the capricious crowds. But something in him had changed.

On the rare occasions El Cordobés came home, Larry and I accompanied him to one appointment he would not miss for the world. No mistress, no flamenco dancer, no bull breeder awaited him. A priest was there to receive him: Padre Juan Arroyo, whom we had met, guitar in hand, the night we arrived in Córdoba. Since the day El Cordobés had cried out to the priest in despair, "Padre, make a man of me," the priest's humble living room in Córdoba had served as a classroom. Manuel Benítez came there to learn "to be a man."

I watched, always with extreme emotion, as the hand that had slain over a thousand bulls copied into a schoolboy's exercise book the simple words written out by the priest: "*Yo soy Manuel Benítez*" (I am Manuel Benítez). "*Me gusta mucho torear*" (I like bullfighting very much). Learning to write his name had taken patient practice. To make room for the young billionaire's whole signature at the bottom of his checks, the bank of Córdoba had had to double the size of his checkbooks.

Sometimes by way of reward, Padre Arroyo would supplement writing practice with a French lesson. The illiterate Andalusian was fascinated with the French language. To keep within the scope of his pupil's concerns, the churchman had chosen the most everyday words. The first page of his exercise book began with *Bonjour* and went on to *Mademoiselle*.

The reading lesson also had its own distinctive features. Padre Arroyo preferred to encourage Manuel Benítez to decipher handwritten texts rather than printed ones. Practical demands dictated this choice: the bullfighter needed to read the contracts drawn up in his name, in which the financial clauses were invariably written by hand.

More scholarly subjects completed the famous matador's education. In a large volume in his library, entitled *Thoughts and Maxims*, Padre Arroyo found the reflections that spoke to his pupil's imagination and reason. One day it would be Pythagoras's advice: "Do not allow your body to become the tomb of your soul." Another, it would be philosopher Auguste Comte's assertion that "to live for others is not just a rigorous duty, but a source of happiness." Yet another, a thought from Kant: "Friendship is the beauty of virtue." The man who had for so long known nothing of the world into which he had been born but the unspeakable poverty of his people, the beatings of the Guardia Civil, prison bars and the concrete jungle of Spain's cities, and who now, hardened but victorious, lived in a universe of rapaciousness and flattery, opened wide his eyes and sought to understand strange words relating to happiness, virtue and the soul. Using simple imagery, the priest would explain them to him. To watch a man cloaked in fame and fortune discover the underlying meaning of existence in this way was a poignant experience. Spain's greatest bullfighter went from discovery to discovery. One day, intrigued by pictures he had seen on television, he asked: "Padre, I don't understand this astronaut business. How can men circle around the earth?"

The churchman fetched a globe from his study. Showing his pupil the seas that Christopher Columbus, Vasco da Gama and so many other Iberian navigators had plowed, he spun the orb around in Manuel's hands. As his fingers caressed the continents explored by his forefathers five centuries previously, El Cordobés realized he was in the throes of discovering a mystery. *"Fenomenal, fenomenal, fenomenal . . ,"* he repeated, enraptured. Until that moment, the world's most famous matador had not known that the earth was round.

NO MAN IS MORE ALONE than a god of the arena. And yet the company of endless crowds is part of the legend that surrounds him. It is the drug that constantly reminds him of his importance and popularity. There was no door in Spain through which Manuel Benítez could not pass. Duchesses begged him to grace their balls, film stars' publicity agents implored him to dedicate a *toro* to their star so she could ride on the back of his fame. Braving the barbs of American animal rights activists, one day he dedicated a kill to Jackie Kennedy. He was invited to London, Paris, Rome. Everywhere he went he was greeted with joy and respect. He never felt completely at ease, however, except in the rocky spaces of his estate where he roamed about without a jacket or tie. Only there could he escape the embarrassments of the high life; once, during the San Sebastian film festival, he had been obliged to ask the lovely starlet sitting next to him to cut up his fish because he did not know how to use his cutlery.

Martine, a pretty dark-haired young woman from the south of France, succeeded in doing what El Cordobés's sister Angelita— with all her nightmares—could not. At the end of the 1970 season the wild god of the Spanish bullrings dropped another bombshell into the bullfighting world by announcing his definitive retirement. The idol pursued by hordes of female admirers had succumbed to the charm and quiet determination of this French girl who would wrest him from the bulls' horns. Manuel and Martine set up home together in the heart of the Cordoban sierra, on a new estate planted with several thousand olive trees, in the middle of immense pastures that harbored hundreds of wild bulls. For five years, scorning the institution of marriage, they lived together and had several children. Finally, after the bishop of Córdoba officially refused to baptize their last-born, they married. The papers gave the news front-page coverage. Thousands of aficionados and humble villagers from the area came rushing to the celebration organized by the newlyweds.

Nevertheless, nostalgia for the bullrings continued to haunt Spain's former idol. Shocked by the terrorist acts that plunged the country into mourning during the last years of General Franco's dictatorship, El Cordobés announced that he wanted to give a *corrida* for the widows and orphans of police officers who were victims of terrorism. The painful memory of the execution ordered by Franco of five young Basques accused of killing policemen was too fresh in everyone's mind. His proposal caused a scandal. The matador was threatened with death and the abduction of his children. The press reported that he and a squad of bodyguards had gone into hiding on his estate. He was photographed with a leg in a plaster cast, and a press release announced that a horseback riding accident had forced him to cancel the *corrida*.

Manuel Benítez El Cordobés, now in his sixties, has lost none of his dashing charm and warm conviviality. After a tentative attempt at a new career in singing and musical comedy, he finally retired with his wife and children to the land of his birth, surrounded by his bulls and his olive trees. Our meetings are always occasions on which to recall, in a flood of beer and *vino tinto*, the unforgettable events of the extravagant *temporadas* of the sixties.

Franco's death at dawn on November 20, 1975, heralded the birth of a new Spain. And yet, a quarter of a century later, famished-looking boys in rags, carrying their dreams in a bundle on the end of an old sword, continue to rove the roads of a country now intersected by freeways and high-speed trains. In most cases, their dreams of glory will fade without their ever having crossed the threshold of an arena. But one day perhaps a new god will emerge from their ranks—more gifted, more intrepid and more daring than all the current stars of the *fiesta brava*—to give Spain a new idol.

6

The Modest Man Who Saved Israel

The queen of cities appeared suddenly before me, set in its lunar landscape like a "bride come down from heaven."[1] My taxi driver had given me a lavish gift when he offered to take me straight to the top of the Mount of Olives. There in front of me, in a profusion of cupolas, minarets, bell towers and terraces, in a maze of narrow streets and secret passageways, lay the Old City of Jerusalem, capital of Abraham, David and Solomon; city of John, Mary and Jesus; conquest of Godefroy de Bouillon, Saladin, Allenby's British forces, Abdallah's Jordanian legionnaires and Moshe Dayan's paratroopers.

I blessed my good fortune. I arrived on a Friday, as crowds of men in kaffiyehs and women in long embroidered Palestinian robes were leaving the mosques in the Haram enclosure, their devotions to Allah completed. The penetrating call of the muezzins from high up in the minarets soon fell silent. As the sun disappeared behind the chain of Judean hills that barred the horizon, the skies above the ancient city began to resound with the raucous lament of the Jewish shofars heralding the beginning of the Sabbath. Two hours later, as dusk fell, it was time for the Christian churches to set all the bells ringing out the Angelus. My first encounter with Jerusalem was in its glorification of God. And yet what sacrifices had been inflicted

1. Saint John, Revelation.

upon that city in the name of God, in the course of its long history!

I had just seen evidence of its recent violent past on the narrow road that climbed up to its defensive walls from Tel Aviv. In the strait pass through the hills, on the hard shoulders of the road lay the wrecks of dozens of burned-out trucks. Some were decorated with flowers, others with inscriptions in Hebrew, yet others with commemorative plaques. I asked my driver about the significance of this scrap-metal Calvary on the road to Jerusalem. My question seemed to shock him. Had I not heard about the tragedy that had occurred here in the spring of 1948? He stopped his taxi behind the remains of one of the trucks and, in a voice full of respect, told me what had happened.

In the spring of 1948, some weeks before the birth of the State of Israel, Jerusalem found itself besieged by the Palestinian Arab leader Abd el-Kader el-Husseini and his partisans. Deprived of water and food, the 100,000 Jewish inhabitants were on the point of surrender. To prevent this tragedy, David Ben-Gurion, then leader of the Jewish community in Palestine, had requisitioned all available trucks and transport vehicles to take water and provisions to a population at death's door. During the night of March 23–24, 1948, a convoy of three hundred trucks, driven by immigrants who had only just arrived from Europe, had made a dash for Jerusalem. Warned by their lookouts, Abd el-Kader's partisans descended on the long convoy, massacring the drivers and burning or pillaging the vital foodstuffs they were carrying. It was a night of fire, bloodshed and horror. Not one ounce of food, not one pint of water, reached the Jews in Jerusalem. The remains that had littered the roadsides ever since served as a reminder of those terrible days when the future Jewish state was nearly wiped out before it had been born.

My taxi driver's account and the magical sight of the holy city caught my imagination. There was no doubt in my mind: this was where Larry and I should set our next literary collaboration.

The idea fired my partner with such enthusiasm that he left behind the masons who were building him a small house just behind the Great Pine of Saint-Tropez. He jumped on the first plane he could get and joined me in Jerusalem. The book, we agreed, would tell the epic story of the birth of the state of Israel. Jerusalem would be the core of our story. We knew our research would be long, arduous and complex because of the passions and the hatreds that embittered that part of the world. But what an adventure it would be to take up the challenge!

THIS CHALLENGE BEGAN in a somewhat unusual setting. Shortly after the Six-Day War of June 1967, the magnificent Jerusalem home of Israeli couple Miles and Guita Sherover generously hosted the country's elite. Their dining-room table, renowned for the refinement of its Chinese cuisine, gathered politicians, military leaders, financial and industrial wizards, representatives of the artistic, literary and religious intelligentsia and important foreign visitors. Going to the Sherovers was always an exciting experience. There I met Vivian Herzog, who in 1948 had been chief of staff of the famous 7th Brigade, charged by Ben-Gurion with opening up the road to Jerusalem whatever the price; Ezer Weizman, who, from the cockpit of Israel's first fighter plane, had shot at the Egyptian columns heading for Tel Aviv; and Moshe Dayan, who was still glowing from his recent conquest of the Old City of Jerusalem at the head of his paratroopers, and who in 1948 had captured the two great Arab cities of Lydda and Ramlah. The eminent archaeologist Yigael Yadin, an expert on the Dead Sea Scrolls, was also a frequent guest at the Sherovers' home. Twenty years earlier, when Yadin was still a young officer in the Haganah, Palestine's secret Jewish army, he had one day received an order from Ben-Gurion to prevent the fall of Jerusalem. In the course of a heated confrontation, he had refused to obey the aging leader's orders to deploy all his forces to save the ancient city. That evening, there were other threats to deal with. Egyptians were at the gates of Tel Aviv and the Syrians were bearing down from the north. "I was born in Jerusalem," Yadin had shouted at Ben-Gurion. "My wife is in Jerusalem. My father and mother are in Jerusalem. Everything that makes you attached to Jerusalem makes me even more so. But this evening we need all our forces to take on even greater dangers than those threatening Jerusalem." At those words the elderly leader had sunk his neck into his shoulders, drawn himself up in his chair and, looking Yadin straight in the eyes, repeated his order clearly and unequivocally: "You will prevent the fall of Jerusalem."

Among those who dined regularly at the Sherovers' was also a reserved gentleman of Austrian origin in his mid-fifties whose blue eyes sparkled with intelligence. Although his name was relatively unknown to the Israeli public, Ehud Avriel was one of the founding fathers of the State of Israel. When I met him, he had just returned from a long spell in Africa where he had set up special links between his country and the African continent. Prime Minister Golda Meir had recently appointed him ambassador to Rome, an official posting that was the pretext for another: that of secretly reactivating the flow of Jewish immigrants from Europe to Israel. The prime minister's choice of Avriel to carry out this assignment was scarcely surprising. This discreet man had been responsible for two epic tasks crucial to the birth and survival of the Jewish state: the clandestine mass immigration of European Jews to Israel and the purchase of the first arms that had saved the country.

We were instantly drawn to each other. He invited me to share the austere hospitality at Neoth Mordechai, his kibbutz in Upper Galilee, where in 1938 his own life as an immigrant from Austria had begun. For thirty-five years this community of apple growers and sandal makers, nestled among the eucalyptus trees within range of Syrian guns, had been the home base of this indefatigable fighter for Israel. He and his wife, Hannah, a robust Viennese woman and the mother of his three children, had helped to create it. Foiling the vigilance of the British police, they had one night set up the first barrack huts and, later, with a handful of European immigrants and a few donkeys, drained the surrounding snake-and-mosquito-infested marshlands.

His phenomenal memory, his attention to detail and his talent as a raconteur were such a treat that our work sessions went on as a feast for days and nights on end.

EHUD AVRIEL'S EXTRAORDINARY life epic had begun on a glittering spring day in 1938. That day, March 13, Vienna, his birthplace, was celebrating. Windows, rooftops, trees, streetlamps—all were coated with people. A riot of streamers, flags and banners spattered the old gray facades of the historic city with red and black. Among all these decorations there appeared a new symbol, an enormous black spider: the swastika. That day the Austrian capital was celebrating the arrival of Hitler's troops, the first stage of the Nazi conquest of Europe.

From the living room of his family home on the Marcus Aurelius Strasse, twenty-year-old Avriel watched as tanks covered with flowers, and soldiers with steel helmets and heavy uniforms with black crosses, filed past. Born in an old merchant family totally assimilated into urbane Viennese society, he was finishing his law studies. He wanted to be a lawyer. But deep down, in his heart of hearts, he intended to build his future a long way from Vienna. For three years he had been actively involved with a Zionist organization that ran agricultural schools in Austria where young Austrian Jews were taught how to work the land with a view to going on to Palestine. Neither he nor his parents had ever visited the Promised Land. Their only physical link with it was the scent of an *etrog*, the jasmine-scented Jaffa lemon that the Palestinian Jews use to celebrate the harvest festival of Sukkot each autumn. In Avriel's home some traveling friend always brought back an *etrog*. The fruit was a powerful evocation of a distant, unknown place that was yet so familiar to them, a place made all the more desirable by the cries of "One people, one nation, one Führer!" that resounded relentlessly through the streets of Vienna that morning.

It was not long before young Ehud and the 220,000 Austrian

Jews discovered the fate reserved for them by the men in black from the Gestapo's Central Department for Jewish Affairs. Nazi-controlled newspapers proclaimed that, like Germany, the latest addition to the Third Reich was "to be swiftly rid of the Jewish vermin infesting it." With arrests, beatings, the pillaging of Jewish-owned shops, imprisonment, expulsion and all kinds of humiliation, the arsenal of Hitler's terror poured down on a community totally unprepared for such punishment. Overnight, the foreign consulates in Vienna were besieged with thousands of terrorized families desperate for visas. Only a privileged few found a safe haven. As to openly taking the road to Palestine, it was out of the question. The British authorities administering the country strictly enforced the prevailing immigration quotas. These quotas were set twice a year. Under pressure from its Arab allies, London had reduced the number to an almost token gesture. In 1935, the year in which the Nuremberg race laws were adopted, the British had granted only 61,854 immigration certificates. Since then the number had steadily decreased. In 1938 fewer than forty thousand Jews were given official permission to enter Palestine. The day Hitler took control of Austria, the Jewish Agency's safe contained only sixteen authorizations to enter Palestine for the entire Jewish population of Austria.

This unbearable situation was to alter many a life, including that of young Avriel. Since the British were refusing to allow Nazi-persecuted Jews to enter Palestine, immigration by clandestine channels had to be organized at once. The leaders of the Haganah went into action. They laid the foundation for an underground network to transport as many people as possible. Somewhat prosaically, they baptized this network Institution for Parallel Immigration, in Hebrew, *Mossad*. The Mossad's activities would subsequently extend to all kinds of activities relating to the protection of the Jewish people. It would embody the Jewish capacity to survive.

The modest room on Marcus Aurelius Strasse from which Avriel and his Zionist comrades coordinated the recruitment for the agricultural schools became a hive of industry. The Haganah leaders chose Vienna as the capital for their new clandestine immigration operations. Ehud became the youngest member of the organization. He and his friends knew they had to work quickly. But suddenly, there was a glimmer of hope. On March 22, 1938, nine days after the Nazi occupation of Vienna, the president of the United States, Franklin Roosevelt, proposed that an international conference of thirty-three nations, including France, Great Britain and Italy, be held to determine a common policy to help political refugees driven out of Germany and Austria. Hitler responded that he sincerely hoped "the countries taking pity on the plight of these criminals would be able to turn their compassion into practical aid." He was prepared, he announced, "to ship out all this vermin himself, even on first-class liners."

The conference, which opened on July 6, 1938, under the paneled ceiling of the ballroom in the Royal Hotel at Evian-les-Bains, the peaceful French spa on the edge of Lake Geneva, made young Avriel realize at once that the Jews could only look to themselves for their survival. No Jewish leader had been invited to Evian to speak for those actually suffering persecution. The solution most likely to resolve the refugees' predicament—their unrestricted immigration to Palestine—had been ruled out in advance. The United States and Britain had agreed to exclude it from the debate. This blow was all the more terrible for the fact that not one country expressed the intention of opening its borders to the victims of Hitler's madness. The Australian representative made clear that his country "did not wish to introduce a racial problem to its territories, when to date it had been spared such a curse." New Zealand could not see how it could lift the current restrictions. As for Great Britain, it confined itself to informing the conference that the British Empire had no lands at its disposal capable of taking in large numbers of Jewish refugees. Even the name of Palestine was carefully excluded from its delegate's speech. A handful of countries declared that in case of dire necessity, they would take in a few farmers. Others refused to let certain professionals immigrate. For fear of creating an intellectual proletariat likely to worry the ruling class, Peru was categorically opposed to the immigration of doctors and lawyers. Other

South American countries excluded tradespeople as well as intellectuals.

Argentina and France pointed to past acts of solidarity to excuse them from making any others. Only Holland and Denmark undertook to widen their frontiers. In all this self-interest there was, however, one minor miracle. The Dominican Republic announced that it would take 100,000 refugees. This generous gesture might have given rise to others. But it was not to be. The United States merely announced that it would for the first time honor the annual legal quota of immigrants from Germany and Austria: 27,370 people. This ludicrous figure showed just how determined the United States was to ignore the gravity, urgency and magnitude of the problem. Beyond the 500,000 German and Austrian Jews loomed the plight of 7 or 8 million Polish, Romanian, Hungarian, Czech, Bulgarian and Russian Jews whom Hitler's imperialism was soon to threaten.

The German government found its own way of commenting on the gathering at Evian. Goebbels, minister for propaganda, declared that Evian had shown "the danger world Jewry represented, thus justifying Germany's policy toward the Jews." In the audience sat an unknown young woman in a peasant's head scarf. She had come specially from Jerusalem to plead the Jewish cause on behalf of the Jewish Agency. She was not given the opportunity to address the conference. When a journalist asked her what desire this conference had inspired in her, she replied: "The desire that by the time I die my people will no longer need the sympathy of the world." Her name was Golda Meir.

Face-to-Face with the Devil

Ehud Avriel and the Mossad team returned from Evian convinced that the Jews' only chance was a clandestine, mass exodus to Palestine. For that they must find ships. Agents were hurriedly dispatched to the Romanian and Bulgarian ports on the Black Sea, to the Turkish coast and to Greece. They had to act discreetly to avoid alerting British secret agents, and with discernment to uncover the innumerable fraudulent dealers attracted to such operations. Small boats would have a better chance than liners of fooling British surveillance. On the other hand, lots of comings and goings were also likely to attract attention. Remembering that Christopher Columbus had discovered America aboard a forty-nine-ton caravel, Avriel opted for a secret voyage involving modest numbers. On June 12, 1938, sixty-six young Austrians landed safely in David's Creek, south of Haifa. Spurred on by this success, Avriel and his companions spotted a boat of bigger capacity in the Greek port of Piraeus. An old tub of Russian origin, the *Attrato* was capable of transporting six hundred passengers. The operation promised to be difficult, since immigrants would have to be brought clandestinely across several of the Balkan states to reach their port of embarkation. They all needed a transit visa to cross Hungary, Yugoslavia, Romania and Greece. These documents were only granted upon production of a passport duly stamped with an entry visa for the country of destination. Since Palestine had been excluded, they had to find an obliging alternative country. Their search took months. In the end it was not for the land of the Prophets and Judges that the passengers on the *Attrato* would officially set sail, but for Mexico.

Thanks to this boat and several others, thousands of Jews escaped Nazi terror. The numbers were still insignificant, however, and the Germans grew more and more impatient to drive all Jews out of Reich territory. For young Avriel this impatience meant being summoned one day to Vienna's Central Department for Jewish Affairs. Thirty years later he would still feel goose bumps remembering the horror of that dreadful visit.

"Baron Louis de Rothschild's palace, where the Nazis had their offices, was dimly lit," he told me, drawing nervously at a cigarette. "Most of its precious furnishings had been stolen by the conquerors. Here and there a painting or tapestry overlooked in the pillaging gave the place the atmosphere of an abandoned museum. Boards and placards had been nailed to the ancient wall paneling. An S.S. guard led me along endless corridors to the office of the senior officer who had summoned me. He was wearing a black uniform and boots that gleamed like mirrors. He was standing, waiting at the far end of the room, one foot on a chair and a whip in his hand. It was Adolf Eichmann.

" 'Come closer!' he barked as I approached him. 'Closer!' Then he roared: 'Now, three paces back!'

"The crack of his whip rent the air like a bullet. I realized he had drawn a boundary between us. He sat down at his desk and I saw a grimace deform the rather fine features of his face. Again he barked: 'Progress is too slow! You're not working fast enough!'

"There followed a storm of recriminations. Why had we sent so few people along the Danube to the Black Sea? And so few people via Yugoslavia to the Adriatic and Palestine? Why hadn't we made the British and Americans take more Jews? Didn't we realize that the German government had had enough of Jews? That it was high time the Reich was purged of its vermin?

" 'We're doing everything we can,' I protested apprehensively, explaining that it was becoming more and more difficult to find boats because of mounting international tension, and because they had to sail under the greatest secrecy for fear of the British boarding them.

" 'Excuses!' yelped Eichmann, cracking his whip. If we were taking it slowly it was because we only wanted to take young people. Well, young people had no money and that was why we lacked resources. We should be taking the rich as well, even if they were sick or old. Eichmann said he refused to have his time wasted while we indulged our whims.

"I tried to make the brute understand that the only criterion dictating the choice of immigrants was the difficulty of the journey. Once they got near the shore, they had to jump into the sea and swim quite fast to avoid the British patrol boats.

" 'Nonsense!' interrupted Eichmann, visibly exasperated that an inferior human being like me had dared to answer him back. 'Make the old and the sick jump into the sea as well. That's an order!'

"The Nazi leader cracked his whip again under Baron Louis de Rothschild's crystal chandelier. The interview was over."

THIS MEETING WITH ONE of the future organizers of the Final
Solution would leave a lifelong impression on the young Jewish militant. Paradoxically, during those months preceding
World War II and the beginning of the Holocaust, Eichmann
proved to be a cooperative partner to the Mossad. His inter-
ventions with the Balkan consulates made it easier to obtain
transit visas. Thousand of German and Austrian Jews were able
to reach their embarkation ports. True, they did not all reach
their destination. The British hardened their attitude relentlessly. In a white paper published on May 17, 1939, London announced the end of all legal Jewish immigration to Palestine
and prohibited Jews already living there from buying further
Arab land. David Ben-Gurion, leader of the Palestinian Jewish
community, replied that "only bayonets would stop Jewish immigration." It was a declaration of war. All the kibbutzim, all
the Jewish settlements scattered along the coast of Palestine,
received the order to be prepared, weapons at the ready, to
meet boats bringing in illegal immigrants under cover of night.

On September 2, 1939, a rust bucket known as the *Tiger Hill*
reached Tel Aviv with fourteen hundred Jews from Romania.
The British coast guards opened fire. The three women and
one man who fell that day on the deck of the *Tiger Hill* were the
first casualties of the war that had broken out a few hours earlier between England and France and Nazi Germany. Some
weeks later, the British intercepted another boat off Istanbul
which they took to Haifa under escort. The announcement that
all of its passengers would be deported to Paraguay unleashed
an immediate revolt throughout Jewish Palestine. Strikes
broke out. The Haganah responded by blowing up several
British military installations. As a result of the violence, the
British renounced their plans to deport the immigrants, and, instead, interned them in camps around Haifa. Thereafter other
boats tried to run the blockade after weeks of nightmarish wan-
dering about on the high seas. One thousand people nearly

died of thirst on board a hulk designed to carry sixty passengers. They were captured and Haganah commandos blew up the boat before it got under way. The result: more than three hundred dead.

Many other tragedies were to cast a shadow over the efforts of Avriel and his companions to save several thousand Jews from the extermination that awaited them in their native countries. Many of the ships were in such a pitiful state that they could not withstand the storms of the Black and Marmara Seas. The *Salvador* went down with 107 women and 66 children, the *Struma* with 769 Romanian refugees. Fortunately there were numerous successes to balance these setbacks. Every time a boat managed to off-load its passengers in the Promised Land, the coded message "The tents have arrived safely" was sent across war-torn Europe to the impatient ears of the team in Vienna. As the hostilities gradually encompassed more countries, it became more and more difficult to arrange these departures. Under pressure from the British, who threatened to suspend their oil purchases, the Romanians closed their borders to Jews trying to reach Mossad boats in the Black Sea ports. In Yugoslavia a convoy of eleven hundred refugees was blocked by ice when the Danube froze over. They were transferred to a camp at the small river port of Sabac, near Belgrade, to spend the winter there, awaiting a thaw and their reembarkation. On April 7, 1941, the Nazi invaders of Yugoslavia emptied their machine guns into the camp. Not one single person survived.

Avriel and his companions had to abandon their headquarters in Vienna and withdraw to Istanbul. The illegal shipments started up more effectively than ever. The names *Maritza, Morina, Bulbul, Mekfure* and of so many other ships would feature prominently in the epic of Jewish immigration to Palestine.

"We spent a large portion of our time immersed in reading the Psalms, praising the Lord who held his children's fate in his hands," Avriel told me, recalling the anxious waiting that followed the departure of each embarkation.

Soon, they bought up a whole flotilla of fishing boats. These trawlers could carry about a hundred passengers and were small enough not to show up on the radar screens of the British patrol boats. They would reach preordained points at the Palestinian coast by night. There, teams of kibbutznikim waited, up to their waists in water, to help the passengers reach land. Afterward, trucks would take them to local kibbutzim and settlements. By the time the British patrols arrived at the settlements, it was no longer possible to distinguish the new arrivals from the others.

A Very Special Russian Prince

The end of the war brought a radical change in Avriel's activities. In Vienna and later Istanbul he and his companions had fought to snatch the Jews from the gas chambers. Their mission had been strictly humanitarian. With the restoration of peace, their mission became political. Jews had to be allowed to come to Palestine not simply because they had nowhere else to go but because they needed to increase the Jewish population of the country and show the British that the right of the Jews to return to their land was not a matter for negotiation.

"From now on we have only one adversary: His Britannic Majesty's government," Ben-Gurion announced. Visionary that he was, the Jewish leader was already envisaging the birth of a sovereign, independent Hebrew state. But for this state to be viable, masses of European Jews would have to be brought to join their Jewish Palestinian brothers.

In December 1945 Ben-Gurion gathered Avriel and his companions together in a small room in the Claridge Hotel in Paris. Avriel recited the elderly leader's words as if they were a verse from the Bible.

"I have called this meeting as a matter of urgency because we're going to have to act very fast, and on a very wide front," he explained. "We need to get tens of thousands of survivors of the Holocaust out to Palestine. We need to create new kibbutzim in the desert and on the borders, and we need people to build them. Those who escaped the gas chambers will be the workforce for this task."

The little man had paused to think. This was always a sign that what he was about to say was crucial. His expression was particularly somber.

"We must give the immigrants some military training before they arrive in Palestine," he declared, emphasizing his words. "This training will be easier to carry out in Europe than over there where the British government is still hostile. After that, we must get hold of the arms we're going to need to defend ourselves when the inevitable confrontation comes. The time for major battles and major decisions has come. Are you ready to assume your responsibilities?"

As usual, Ben-Gurion's question was purely rhetorical. He was not expecting any answer.

FRANCE BECAME THE CENTER for the new operation ordered by the Jewish leader. It was a logical choice: the Zionist cause could count on plenty of supporters in influential French circles, including the government. As for the general public, repelled by Hitler's atrocities, it did not begrudge the escapees of Hitler's genocide its sympathies. Avriel therefore moved to Paris, together with several of his companions. They rented a small apartment at 53 rue de Ponthieu, a few steps away from the Champs-Elysées, which became the general headquarters for the Mossad in Europe. Such was the French authorities' goodwill that the Jews did not want to embarrass their hosts in any way, especially when it came to relations with their British allies. All transit operations through France and regroupment in camps near ports of embarkation must be made to look like legitimate immigration to some country other than Palestine. To this end they had to obtain authentic immigration visas for the countries in question. This monumental challenge would test Avriel's ingenuity to the full.

At cocktail time the bar of Paris's Claridge Hotel became a watering hole for a wide variety of wildlife. Avriel made a point of stopping there every day in the hope of making a valuable

new contact or catching up with a former work associate. One
day his constancy was rewarded with a hearty slap on the back.

"Isn't your first name Ehud?" asked a big fellow with a
strong Austrian accent.

Avriel recognized one of the Viennese Jews he had wrested
from Eichmann's grasp in August 1938 by supplying him with
an immigration certificate for Palestine. The man clasped his
benefactor to his chest.

"What can I do for you?" the Austrian inquired effusively.

"I need three thousand immigration visas," Avriel replied.

"For which country?"

"It doesn't matter."

The man didn't look at all surprised. "Leave it to me."

The very next day the Austrian introduced Avriel to a Russian prince, who happened to be the special envoy to Europe
of the sovereign of an African country. In biblical times the
country in question had enjoyed close relations with the Jewish people. Obtaining three thousand visas from Negus Haile
Selassie of Ethiopia seemed, therefore, a feasible objective.
Ethiopia needed craftsmen, skilled laborers and tradespeople
to rebuild an economy devastated by the war. Volunteers from
the displaced-persons camps would quite conceivably find a
warm welcome there. The Russian prince promised to put the
idea to the emperor. He had no doubt he would agree. The
proposition seemed highly attractive, but there was one slight
hiccup. For all his sympathy for Ethiopia, Avriel had no intention of sending his immigrants to rebuild the land of the Queen
of Sheba. From lunches at Maxim's to dinner dances at Mon-
seigneur's, the Russian prince kept his interlocutor on tenter-
hooks for several weeks. Had the prince been too optimistic?
Had Avriel's offer of one dollar per visa been considered insuf-
ficient? At the Mossad HQ everyone began to give up hope.

It was at this point that a carefully wrapped cardboard box arrived at 53 rue de Ponthieu. It contained one hundred blank
sheets of paper with the letterhead of the Ethiopian legation in
Paris, together with a collection of official stamps. Each sheet
had space for some thirty names. It was the miraculous open
sesame for which Avriel and his companions had been so des-

perately waiting. Three thousand refugees would be able to go through France quite legally, without Great Britain being able to accuse its ally of any wrongdoing. Ethiopia was not Palestine.

A few precious unused sheets remained in a drawer in Ehud Avriel's desk. Two years later they would do his country a crucial service.

GALVANIZED INTO ACTION by the messianic appeal of their elderly leader, the Mossad's envoys multiplied their efforts. From Romania to French Languedoc, along more than 1,850 miles of coastline, not one port, not one shipyard, not one inlet, eluded their search. Finding suitable boats became an obsession. The dearth of vessels did not mean they had no resounding successes. On April 4, 1946, 1,014 refugees from several displaced-persons camps boarded the *Fede*, an old tub bought by the Mossad, anchored in the Italian port of La Spezia.

The professed objective of the voyage, a cruise to Sardinia, was not sufficient to allay the suspicions of British Intelligence agents on watch in the Mediterranean port. Royal Navy patrol boats immediately blocked the exit channel of La Spezia while British officers climbed aboard and ordered the passengers to evacuate the boat. To the cheers of the Italian dockers whose sympathies lay with the illegal passengers on the *Fede*, the Mossad representative responded by hoisting the Zionist flag. The Jews rejected the British offer to intern the passengers provisionally in a camp while they waited for London to grant them valid immigration certificates. The Mossad was quick to take advantage of the incident to muster world opinion by organizing press conferences and demonstrations of support on the spot. The gateway to the La Spezia harbor was renamed Port of Zion. Telegrams were dispatched by the ship's radio to Stalin, Truman and Attlee. On Easter Sunday local Jewish families came to serve meals on the deck of the boat profusely decorated with Jewish and Italian flags. An Italian police officer who had been arrested and released by the British was carried triumphantly up to the bridge.

After a month the passengers, still immobilized on their floating prison, began a hunger strike and announced that ten of them would commit suicide every day. Two posters appeared on each of the pillars at the entrance to the port. One recorded the hours the hunger strike had been going on; the other the number of passengers who had lost consciousness for lack of food. As the two figures mounted, the crowd thronging the iron gates became more and more threatening toward the British soldiers who were isolating the port. Dockers in Genoa stopped working out of solidarity. In Jerusalem the leaders of the Jewish Agency began their own hunger strike, declaring they would keep it up until the boat was released and all its passengers arrived in Palestine.

The British finally gave in. They announced that all the occupants of the rebel ship would be issued with a certificate to emigrate legally to Palestine. The confrontation had lasted thirty-three days. So that the survivors of this harsh ordeal could travel in better conditions, the Mossad chartered a second vessel which took half the survivors of the *Fede* on board. The two boats received a triumphant welcome in Haifa. They would make the same crossing four months later, but this time clandestinely, with 1,846 illegal immigrants.

The British government decided to make the Jews pay for its humiliation at La Spezia. On the Sabbath day of June 29, 1946, paratroopers supported by police units launched an assault on the seat of the Jewish Agency in Jerusalem and on forty-nine towns and kibbutzim in the main settlement areas. The operation was intended to put a stop to the Zionist immigration venture by arresting Haganah's leaders and seizing all the Jews' arms and ammunition, legal and illegal. Warned in time, the Haganah leaders went underground and most of the arms depots changed hiding places. A month after the raid, the Irgun, one of the Jewish terrorist organizations, blew up the King David Hotel in Jerusalem that housed the general headquarters of the British forces. The explosion claimed ninety-one lives.

Ten Thousand Rifles to Save Israel

The escalation of violence soon became irreversible. The odyssey of Jewish immigration to Palestine reached a peak of horror when the 4,554 passengers of an old American passenger ship renamed the *Exodus*, which had left the French port of Sète on July 10, 1947, were forcibly returned to displaced-persons camps.

"But on that occasion time was on our side," Ehud Avriel would recall. "The inevitable day when Britain would have to give up its mandate was imminent."

It came on Saturday November 29, 1947, only five months after the tragedy of the *Exodus*.

Assembled in what had once been a skating rink in a New York suburb, United Nations representatives voted, by thirty-three to thirteen with ten abstentions, to divide Palestine into a Jewish state and an Arab state. This double birth was to take place on May 15, 1948, seven months later. The visionary leader of the Palestinian Jewish community was to act immediately on that historic decision. A few hours earlier, an old gray Ford sedan had pulled up outside the same small house on the kibbutz in Upper Galilee where I was listening to Ehud Avriel's account. After long months of living abroad, the Mossad fighter had just rejoined his wife, Hannah, and their one-year-old daughter. "Go and wash and change your clothes," the driver of the Ford announced. "I'm taking you to Jerusalem. The old man wants to see you."

Three hours later Avriel entered a vast book-lined room on the second floor of the Jewish Agency building in Jerusalem. Seated behind a desk piled high with files and papers, David Ben-Gurion was waiting for him. With even more gravity than at their last meeting in Paris, the Jewish leader explained to him that the survival of the future State of Israel would depend on the success of the mission he was about to assign to him.

"Listen carefully," he instructed. "War is going to break out in less than six months. The Arabs are getting ready for it. Five regular armies are going to invade us the minute the last British soldier leaves next May 15. But, even before that invasion, an Arab uprising is going to reduce this country to blood and gunfire."

Ben-Gurion informed his visitor that he was sending him back to Europe, where his experience would help with Israel's most crucial objective: the purchase of arms.

"We've got to change our tactics radically," he explained. "We don't have time any longer to wait for four pathetic guns hidden in tractor tires to arrive in Haifa. You have a million dollars at your disposal at the Union of Swiss Banks in Geneva to buy armaments in large numbers."

Taking out of his pocket a carefully folded piece of paper on which there were six lines of typing, he added: "Here's a list of our immediate needs."

Avriel read: "Ten thousand rifles, one million rounds of ammunition, one thousand submachine guns, five hundred machine guns." When he looked up again, Ben-Gurion was holding out a second piece of paper. It was a letter.

"There's a Jewish businessman in Paris by the name of Klinger who claims he can get this merchandise for us," he went on. "You must go and see him at once." The Jewish leader stood up and walked around his desk. He placed his hand on the young militant's shoulder. "Ehud, you've got to send us those ten thousand rifles."

TWO DAYS LATER Ehud Avriel took off from Palestine's Lydda airport on board Swissair Flight 442, destination Geneva and Paris. He carried only a toothbrush, a black leather-bound Bible and the copy of *Faust* his wife had given him when they got married. In his jacket pocket was a Palestinian passport in the name of George Alexander Uberhale, financial director of the public works company of Solel Boneh.

By a surprising coincidence Avriel was not the only passenger on that plane vested with a special mission. A few rows behind him sat a young Syrian captain in civilian clothes. Adbul Aziz Kerine belonged to the Ministry of Defense in Damascus.

The Arab was traveling to Prague to confirm a similar order for ten thousand rifles, one thousand submachine guns and two hundred machine guns with one of the principal European arms manufacturers, Zbrojovka Brno in Czechoslovakia. By World War II standards, the purchase order was modest enough, but it represented twice the number of weapons in all the Haganah arms factories put together.

EHUD AVRIEL'S FIRST DAY in Paris began with a series of setbacks. That evening he felt as if all the arms dealers in Europe had passed through his room in the Hôtel California on the rue de Berri. All of the offers, including Klinger's, had proved to be unacceptable. Avriel's last hope rested with the elegant visitor sitting opposite him with a cigar in his mouth. In tones that betrayed a certain shame, Robert Adam, a Romanian Jew and the director of a small import-export business in Paris, told Avriel how in 1943 he had succeeded in getting into Palestine in a small sailing boat but had not stayed. The Promised Land had seemed too exiguous to him at the time and the prevailing living conditions too spartan.

"I'm too fond of the good life," he admitted. "I like horses, I like women. So as soon as the war was over I came to live in Paris. If I hadn't been so demanding, I would still be in Palestine. And it might have been me that Ben-Gurion sent looking for arms instead of you."

To Avriel's surprise, the man revealed that he had been an agent in Romania for one of the biggest arms manufacturers in Europe and that he had kept in touch with its management.

"They'll sell us everything we need," he affirmed, taking two catalogs out of his briefcase.

Adam went on to say that the purchase of the goods would, however, be subject to one single important condition. The manufacturer could not deal with just any individual, but only with the accredited representative of a sovereign state. As the

Jewish state would not officially exist for nearly six months, Avriel would have to provide credentials from another country.

Ben-Gurion's envoy thought for a moment. He picked up the telephone and asked for a file to be brought to him from a drawer in his old office in the rue de Ponthieu. The dossier contained the unused sheets of official notepaper from the Ethiopian legation in Paris. A smile of complicity spread over his visitor's face. They were just what was needed for the transaction. Adam pulled two envelopes from his pocket and offered one to Avriel. The Romanian had thought of everything: inside were two airline tickets for the town where the arms manufacturer was located.

While Avriel rejoiced in his good fortune, more than 1,250 miles away another traveler was also congratulating himself on the success of his European mission. The Syrian captain Abdul Aziz Kerine emerged from a large modern apartment house in Prague where he had just closed a satisfactory deal. There, at the company headquarters of Zbrojovka Brno, 20 Belchrido Avenue, he had signed an initial agreement for ten thousand Mauser E-18 rifles and a hundred MG-34 machine guns. He had even arranged for their delivery to Damascus.

Before he began his evening meal, Ehud Avriel put his toothbrush, his Old Testament and the copy of *Faust* back in his briefcase. Next morning he, too, had an appointment in Prague, at 20 Belchrido Avenue.

BEN-GURION WOULD HAVE every reason to be satisfied. In less than an hour his special envoy in Czechoslovakia purchased the ten thousand rifles, one million rounds of ammunition and the machine guns and submachine guns requested. With the notepaper from the Ethiopian legation, Avriel managed to obtain all the necessary international export and transit licenses without mishap. Now all he had to do was find a boat prepared to break through the British blockade to take the whole lot to Palestine. Most maritime insurance was underwritten in London, and companies prepared to cover a boat with Haifa as its destination were few and far between. To avoid placing his precious purchases in jeopardy, Avriel might have to store them in Europe until the official birth of the State of Israel. But could the state survive that long? Ben-Gurion showed his impatience in an avalanche of telegrams, demanding the immediate dispatch of the first rifles. After several weeks of searching, Avriel eventually discovered, in the Yugoslavian port of Rijeka, a coaster by the name of *Nora*, prepared to take on some of the arms. To divert the attention of the British customs officers on arrival, he covered the armaments with a hundred tons of onions in various stages of decay. His hope was that the smell of the cargo would keep His Majesty's representatives at bay.

Those light weapons made it possible for the Haganah forces to resist the Palestinian Arabs' attacks. But what good would they be against tanks, cannons and the airpower of the Arab regular armies whose intervention Ben-Gurion anticipated the day the British moved out of Palestine? Avriel received a fresh flood of telegrams pressing him this time to buy heavy weapons, tanks, cannons and even planes. But with what funds? Vast sums of money were needed. At least $25 to $30 million to start with. Where was that kind of money to be found?

ONE MORNING EHUD AVRIEL drove me in his old Fiat to see the woman who had actually managed to raise this fortune. She lived in an unpretentious two-room apartment in a working-class district in West Jerusalem. Only the two large American cars, bristling with aerials and filled with plainclothes bodyguards keeping watch in the street, pointed to the importance of this person. The ardent young militant who, at the Evian conference thirty years previously, had expressed the desire that she would live to see the day when her people would no longer need "the world's sympathy" was now prime minister of Israel. Golda Meir's seventy years sat lightly upon her. She received us in her kitchen, the walls of which were lined with a collection of saucepans that sparkled like sunlight.

"Breakfast is ready!" she announced in her gruff authoritative voice well known to journalists.

In front of each of us, she placed a bowl of coffee and a plate of delicious-smelling fritters. There was no sign of any servants: on the Sabbath the *mamma* of Israel reigned alone over her private domain. The idea of escaping in the company of her old accomplice into an account of past achievements so delighted her that she forgot to stub out one cigarette before lighting another. Avriel contributed to this smoking frenzy, which meant that I had to take my notes blindly through a cloud of smoke.

Fifty Million Dollars for the Messenger from Jerusalem

"Finding the money to buy the arms we needed to survive was absolutely vital," she began, looking me right in the eye. "One evening in January 1948 I was summoned, along with all the leaders of the Jewish Agency, to listen to a report from our treasurer, Eliezier Kaplan, who had just returned almost empty-handed from a fund-raising visit to the United States. The American Jewish community, which had for so long been the main support for the Zionist movement, was growing tired of our appeals. Kaplan told us we couldn't expect more than $5 million from the United States in the months to come. His report came as a dreadful blow. We knew that to equip an army capable of resisting the tanks, cannons and planes of the Arab regular armies, we would need at least five or six times the sum our treasurer was forecasting. Ben-Gurion announced he would leave at once for the United States to try and convince the Americans of the gravity of the situation.

"Thinking of the days when I used to beg in the streets of Denver for the Zionist cause, I asked to speak. I offered to go to the United States in Ben-Gurion's place."

"How did he react?" I inquired.

Golda Meir had a giggle. "He went quite red. He hated being interrupted. He said the matter was crucial and that he was the one who should resolve it. With the support of several of my colleagues, I asked that the motion be put to a vote. Two days later I was the one to go.

"I left in such a hurry that I didn't even have time to go to Jerusalem to pick up a suitcase and some clothes. I landed in New York in a freezing cold. All I had with me was a light dress and my handbag. I'd gone to America to try and raise millions of dollars and I had just one ten-dollar bill in my purse. A customs official asked me with some surprise how I thought I was going to live in the United States with so little money. I told him I had family there. And next day, shaking with nerves, I found myself face-to-face with the elite of that family on a platform in the ballroom of a large hotel in Chicago."

"Who were those people?" I asked.

"Most of the big financiers from the American Jewish community were there. They'd come from the forty-eight states to discuss an economic and social aid program for needy Jews in Europe and America. The most astonishing thing was that my being there at the same time as their gathering was pure coincidence."

"You must have been dead nervous," I ventured.

"You bet!" confirmed Golda Meir, crunching into a fritter. "I hadn't been back to the United States for several years, and on my previous travels my audiences had been made up exclusively of fervent Zionists who generally shared my socialist ideals. Those people in Chicago represented a broad spectrum of American Jewish opinion. My New York friends had urged me to avoid this confrontation because most of the delegates were indifferent, even hostile, to the cause I represented. They were already overrun with requests for funds for their American charities, for hospitals, synagogues, cultural centers, etc." Golda Meir stopped to cast a mischievous glance in Avriel's direction. "As Kaplan, our treasurer, had reported, all these people were fed up with foreign requests, especially from the Palestinian Jews. But I had stood my ground, and, although the program for the day had already been set, I had announced my arrival in Chicago. I waited quietly for my name to be called and then climbed onto the platform."

"Did you have notes?"

"Not a single one. I just wanted to speak from the heart . . ."

LARRY AND I HAD FOUND the word-for-word transcript of the speech Golda Meir made, that January evening in 1948, to an audience of Jews unfavorably disposed to the cause she stood for. Her polemic was a moving piece of purple prose.

"My friends! You must believe me when I say that I haven't come to the United States with the sole intention of preventing 700,000 Jews from being wiped off the surface of the globe," Golda had begun. "Over the last few years the Jews have lost 6 million of their people, and it would be very presumptuous of us to remind Jews from all over the world that today the lives of a few hundred thousand of their brothers are in danger. But if those 700,000 Jews do disappear, there can be no doubt that during the centuries to come, there will be no more Jewish people, no Jewish nation. It will be the end to all our hopes. In a few months' time, a Jewish state is to be born in Palestine. We are fighting for its birth. We know we have to pay for that and shed our blood. The best of us will fall, that's for sure. But what is equally sure is that our spirit, no matter how many invaders we must face, will not founder."

After informing her listeners that the Arab invaders would attack with artillery and armored divisions, she had cried out:

"Against such weapons, sooner or later there will be no cause for courage because we shall have ceased to exist. Unless we manage to buy heavy weapons in time, to enable us to take on the Arab artillery. That is why I am here: I have come to ask American Jews for $30 million to buy arms.

"You must know, my friends, that we are living in a very short-term present," she had concluded. "When I say that we need this sum at once, it doesn't mean next month or in two months' time. It means now! It is not up to you to decide whether or not we should pursue this combat. We shall fight. Jerusalem's Grand Mufti will never induce the Palestinian Jewish community to wave a white flag. But it is up to you to decide who will claim the victory, us or the Mufti."

THE EMOTION GOLDA MEIR experienced as she sank onto her chair after that difficult confrontation was still perceptible twenty years later. She shook her head several times and looked long at Avriel. Her small dark eyes were moist.

"I was exhausted," she said slowly. "A heavy silence had fallen over the auditorium, and for a moment I thought I had failed. Then the entire audience got to its feet and broke into a thunder of applause. The platform was stormed by the first delegates coming to tell me how much money they could give. By the end of the meeting, over a million dollars had been collected. For the first time in the history of Zionist fund-raising, the money was made immediately available. Delegates called their bankers and arranged loans in their own names for the sums they thought they could collect later from their communities. By the end of that incredible afternoon, I was able to telegraph Ben-Gurion that I was sure I could raise the $30 million we needed.

"Amazed at this success, the American Zionist leaders urged me then to go all over America. Accompanied by Henry Morgenthau, Roosevelt's former secretary of the treasury, and by a group of financiers, I went on pilgrimage from town to town. Wherever I repeated my appeal, I was fortunate enough to rouse the same spontaneous enthusiasm as in Chicago. Everywhere I went the Jewish community responded to my pleas with the same generosity. Every evening I sent a telegram to Tel Aviv with the total amount raised during the day."

"Did you ever have a moment of doubt?" I asked, concerned.

"Yes, once. It was in Palm Beach, Florida. Seeing all the jewels and the furs on the elegant guests assembled in front of the platform, catching sight of the moon's reflection on the sea through the bay windows of the dining room, I thought suddenly of the Haganah soldiers shivering in the cold of the hills of Judea. Then I felt tears in my eyes. I told myself those people had no desire to hear talk of war and death in Palestine. But I was wrong. By the end of the evening, overwhelmed by what I had told them, those elegant Palm Beach dinner guests had donated one and a half million dollars, enough to buy every Haganah soldier a coat."

HAVING ARRIVED IN NEW YORK with a ten-dollar bill, Golda Meir had left five weeks later with $50 million. The figure was ten times what the treasurer Kaplan had hoped for and nearly twice the objective Ben-Gurion had set himself. It exceeded all the oil revenues raised in the year 1947 by Saudi Arabia, the largest oil producer in the Middle East. Ben-Gurion went to meet the messenger from Jerusalem at the Lydda airport on her return. No one could appreciate better than he the magnitude of the success she had achieved and its importance for the Zionist cause.

"The day the history of the Jewish state will be written," he declared solemnly, "it will be said that it is to a woman it owes its existence."

THE DAY AFTER each of Golda Meir's American speeches, a small piece of pink paper with the Zivnostenka Banka heading arrived for the occupant of room 121 in the Hotel Alcron in Prague. The paper announced the transfer of the money collected during the previous day's gathering. Ehud Avriel was now in a position to acquire the tanks, cannons and airplanes that Ben-Gurion was asking for. He soon became Czechoslovakia's best arms and ammunition customer.

To transport this cargo, Avriel succeeded in persuading his Czech friends to let him use an airfield close to the small town of Zatec in the Sudeten Highlands area, recently liberated from the German occupying forces. It was not long before this modest airfield and its few hangars were turned into a proper air base for planes of all origins and sizes. The Haganah emissaries bought them from suppliers of military surplus from World War II, dispersed throughout Europe and America. One of these aircraft, an old DC-4 from Le Bourget Airport in Paris, would transport the first Messerschmidt 109 fighter Avriel had purchased with the dollars raised by Golda. It took several hours of effort to get the Messerschmidt fuselage into the belly of the DC-4. Then the bays were packed with bombs and machine-gun belts so that this first fighter painted with the Star of David could go into action immediately on arrival. Every night the Egyptian air force had bombarded Tel Aviv without encountering any opposition. A bomb dropped on the bus station had just killed forty-one people.

IN THE SPRING OF 1949 an armistice drawn up on the island of Rhodes at the instigation of the United Nations, between Israel, Egypt, Jordan, Lebanon and Syria, put an end to the conflict the Israelis called their "war of independence." The young nation had survived the combined assault of five Arab armies and paid heavily for its victory. Approximately six thousand of its citizens had laid down their lives for the birth of the new state. The modest man who had contributed so much to this victory had returned to Israel six months earlier. No government delegation, no band or guard of honor, turned up at Lydda airport, renamed Lod, to welcome him. Ehud Avriel took a *sherout*, a communal taxi, to Upper Galilee. He returned to his Neoth Mordechai kibbutz where his wife, Hannah, and their daughters were waiting for him in their small prefabricated home among the jacaranda blossoms. That evening, the whole community gathered in the cafeteria for a party in honor of their hero. Then, as was the custom, they offered him a new job on the kibbutz. The man who had bought the equipment for an entire army would be responsible for looking after the maintenance of the rifles used to defend the community.

His return to the fold was only temporary. The State of Israel still needed Ehud Avriel's services. Czechoslovakia, the country that had sold him the arms to ensure the survival of the Jews, soon saw him return in the role of ambassador, a strategic position that meant that he would witness the Soviet Union's first armed coup in a European country. Five years later it was the Knesset's—the Israeli parliament's—turn to welcome as a member the man to whom so many Jews owed their homeland. But the assembly's gilded cage was ill suited to one more used to the challenge of the undercover world than to the oratorical niceties of a praetorium. Avriel was next assigned to Ghana, then the Congo, Liberia, Rome and Chicago. In the mid-seventies this last posting was more important than any ministerial position in the Jerusalem government. The American Midwest was full of young American Jews returning from Vietnam who could be persuaded to emigrate to Israel. This was to be his last crusade.

One night in April 1980, when he was taking a few days of rest with my wife and me in our Saint-Tropez home, he had a cardiac episode after dinner. I immediately called a cardiologist and spent the night at his bedside. The next morning everything had returned to normal. Five months later, during a talk he was giving in Jerusalem on the diaspora of American Jews, he suffered a massive heart attack. He died within minutes.

Since then, my wife and I go regularly to visit his grave in the small cemetery on his kibbutz in Upper Galilee. He lies in the shade of a cluster of tall eucalyptus trees. He may have planted those trees himself in 1938 to drain the malaria-infested marshland around the makeshift huts that housed the first settlers. His tombstone bears only his name, the dates of his birth and of his death, in Hebrew and Roman script. No inscription recalls that beneath that mossy slab lies one of Israel's noblest figures.

7

"They've Murdered Preferido!"

A generous truce proposed by his children had put an end to the boundary war my Saint-Tropez neighbor Cuissard had declared on me. On the site of my seller's wood cabin I had built a small Provence country house. To pay for this construction, I had squeezed an advance of several months' salary out of my editors at *Paris Match*. Built facing the Great Pine, the house was made up of three small rooms. Thanks to the success of each of the books I was to write with Larry Collins, that initial construction would be subject to various extensions. One day there would be a dining room named "Is Paris Burning?"; a living room, "O Jerusalem"; a master bedroom with a terrace, "Freedom at Midnight"; and even a swimming pool, "The Fifth Horseman."

Despite its fame, in the beginning of the sixties the Saint-Tropez peninsula was, like many other rural areas in France, still remarkably backward. I had to prostrate myself lower than the ground itself before the local electricity board manager in order to have some light in the house.

"I can only supply you with one single kilowatt," the official warned me, as he had me sign my contract.

"One single kilowatt?" I repeated, disconcerted.

"That means you'll have to unplug the refrigerator and put out all the lights when you want to watch television," he explained.

The telephone line, acquired with similar suffering, ran from pine to pine into a primitive instrument that I had last seen in the films of the thirties. To obtain a number, you had to call an operator by cranking a handle. The slightest mistral wind could condemn us to total isolation.

THE WINTER LARRY AND I WROTE *Is Paris Burning?* we received invaluable assistance from my neighbor Antoine Navaro. This vine-grower bibliophile was our first reader. Every Saturday when he got back from market, he would bring us a demijohn of his rosé and, in exchange, we would hand him the pages we had written during the week. On Mondays, at aperitif time, he would come again, seat himself solemnly beneath the Great Pine and impart his observations to us.

Our community was soon enlarged by a new member. Our local newspaper, *Nice Matin*, announced one day that the abattoir of a nearby village was about to slaughter a batch of horses bought in Spain for meat. I rushed over and discovered among the doomed animals a splendid chestnut mare, one whose right thigh was branded with an *E* surmounted by a crown, the mark of the royal Spanish stud farm. For the price of the butcher's meat, I snatched her away from the executioner's pistol. In honor of the great parasol pine beneath which she would live, I christened her "Pinecone" and took her home.

My attempts to saddle her proved to be fruitless. She rejected all contacts. As soon as I brought my foot near the stirrup, she would let out a cry and throw herself sideways. I whispered in vain a thousand sweet words to her and gorged her on fresh carrots. She repelled my advances, flattened her ears and tried to bite me. One morning, totally disheartened, I resolved to take her back to the abattoir. Did she sense my decision? For a miracle promptly happened. The same horse that reared up every time I approached her suddenly presented me with a back to mount that was as motionless as a statue. This mysterious change marked the beginning of a wonderful love story that was to last for more than twenty-five years. That morning, I had scarcely made contact with her flanks before my Andalusian mare set off at a trot, then a gallop, skimming over the uneven ground like a gazelle. I was in a flying armchair. Alas, I was too inexperienced a horseman to take full advantage of the creature who could dance, paw the ground, change feet and back up like a dressage star. Our partnership was to be based on considerations other than my skill as a horseman.

Every morning before writing the first line of the day, we would take off at a gallop into the hills above the house. It was the magical moment when the motionless, almost silent countryside receives the gift of daylight. The sky would gradually brighten with a hint of pink. Then suddenly the red disc would rise out of the sea onto the horizon, and we would both fill our lungs with the invigorating air of the wilderness surrounding us. I savored those sumptuous winter moments. Whereas elsewhere it was a time of the year synonymous with decline, sadness and grayness, here winter burst forth like a revival of nature. The curl of the parasol pines, the dark green candles of the cypresses, the silver shimmer of the olive trees, were more distinct than at the height of summer. Using paths worn by the cork pickers and wild boar hunters, sheep trails and waterways, Pinecone and I explored ever-different corners of the countryside. The dense, bushy undergrowth would sometimes impede our progress, but my mare's agility made the most daring acrobatics possible. It was hard to believe that scarcely two and a half miles from the resort of Saint-Tropez there flourished a natural world so wild that my horse and I would sometimes lose our way. In the course of these explorations I discovered the picturesque villages that, on hill after hill, encircled the peninsula with a string of strongholds. The high houses huddling behind the ramparts of Ramatuelle, Gassin and Grimaud bore witness to the fact that this peninsula had once been a land beset by dangers.

In the vineyards peasants burned bundles of vine shoots, spreading the sweet smell of incense over the countryside. The only birds that dared to show themselves during that hunting season were magpies. They had been stuffing themselves with berries and grapes since the autumn, and with their black and white plumage they looked like plump nuns. My rides would often end at the ruins of an ancient olive oil mill just above the red-tiled roofs of Saint-Tropez. From this observation point I was presented with one of the world's most beautiful views: the spread of the village below with its glazed church steeple, the small harbor with its confusion of masts and, beyond it, moiréed by the winter light, the calm waters of the bay dotted with white sails. On the far shore I could see the red and white mosaic of the Sainte-Maxime houses and behind them, streaking the horizon with a whitish line, the snowy fleece on the first foothills of the Alps.

Contemplating these wonders on horseback increased my happiness. Pinecone shared my feelings. Generally so twitchy, she would freeze into an equestrian statue, allowing me to gather my thoughts in a constantly renewed prayer of thanksgiving. Afterward we would return at a walk, reins loose, both intoxicated by joy. She would then clamber back down to the house with all the agility of a wild Alpine sheep. And I would close my eyes and pray that our rides would never come to an end.

LARRY SUGGESTED WE SHOULD let this exceptional mare have a foal. The idea captured my imagination. I wanted to find the finest Spanish or Portuguese stallion in the neighborhood to be the father. I called all the breeders and stud farms I knew—to no avail. In one place they offered me an American quarter horse, in another an Appaloosa, in another a Lippizaner and in another a French saddle horse. It was then that a rider friend told me about a Portuguese stallion he had noticed near the seaport of Fréjus, in a paddock on the banks of a canal behind the warehouse of a supermarket. He thought the horse belonged to one of the employees. I jumped in my car.

It was one of those melancholy equinoctial days when the

fog, rain and cold strip the peninsula and the coast of all their magic. I crawled along behind a procession of trucks, railing about the black fumes issuing from their poorly maintained diesel engines, fuming at our editors for wanting chapters from us before they had even been written, cursing the whole world. My arrival at the warehouse could not have been more ill timed. Disaster had just struck. As a result of some mysterious tremor, a mountain of jam pots had fallen over onto a mountain of toilet-paper rolls. The result was spectacular. The huge warehouse was awash in a sticky tide of jam and pink paper. Wearing boots up to their waist, the employees floundered through this magma, trying to sweep it out with brooms. One of them was a small man with olive complexion, thin and wiry like a *banderillero* from a Spanish *corrida*. His name was Raymond Andreani. It was he who owned the horse. I introduced myself and told him the reason for my visit. He let out a long, modulated whistle.

"You want Preferido to cover your mare?" he repeated in tones of extreme reverence, as if I had asked the Centaur of classical mythology to do me the honor of impregnating my humble mare.

"If Preferido is the Portuguese stallion I've been told about, that's exactly what I've come here to ask you," I replied respectfully.

The small man's olive cheeks turned purple. "Preferido has never yet granted his favors," he declared, "and I shall need references for your mare."

I told him about my love affair with Pinecone. He seemed touched.

"All right," he said, "but first you must meet my horse."

He signaled to me to follow him. Drowning my depression in the sea of sticky pink muck that surrounded us, I trod in his steps. We arrived at a door that opened out onto a narrow canal. To our left, propped against the warehouse, was a cabin made out of rough and rickety planks. It had no window and its only door was fastened with a piece of wire. Undoing the wire, Andreani swung it open. What I saw then in the darkness will remain with me always.

A prehistoric monster! A mass of muscle, flesh and bone, startling in his power and beauty. His dark chestnut coat was so shiny that it reflected every tiny ray of light. A thick, dark mane enveloped his bull-like neck and withers. Woven into long tresses, his tail hair hung down to the ground in majestic volutes. Most surprising of all was the apparent calm of this mythological powerhouse whose least quiver could have shattered the plank enclosure that contained him. His master seemed to share an astonishing understanding with the horse, who responded to Andreani's series of whistles with a thunderous neighing. Andreani slipped inside, passed under his belly and caressed the two enormous bags that dangled between his thighs. Then he went around the animal, patting him lovingly all over, before planting his lips on his muzzle. The stallion accepted these attentions with greedy pleasure. There were other surprises yet to come.

The supermarket employee had more than just a grocery store mystique flowing through his veins. He led me along the canal to the old trailer where he lived. He asked me to wait and disappeared inside. A few minutes later he emerged, completely transformed. He had swapped his working overalls for a white shirt with embroidered cuffs, a vest, a short, closely fitting jacket and a pair of gray-striped breeches over Andalusian boots with spurs. A large sombrero with a rounded brim and a chin strap, like those worn by the *vaqueros* that herd wild bulls, completed his outfit.

Then began a long and meticulous grooming of the horse, who succumbed to Andreani's attentions with a voluptuous motionlessness, allowing the man to currycomb and brush even his most intimate parts. Then Andreani placed an Andalusian saddle with inlaid decorations on the horse's back. The touch of the saddle girth made Preferido tremble with impatience. Before mounting him, Andreani walked the horse over to the other side of the warehouse. I followed them. There, on the raised ground between the canal and the building, I came upon a scene that was totally surreal: a small arena had been formed out of railway ties set in the ground. Nearby was parked an old battered Peugeot. Taking a cassette out of his pocket, Andreani put it in a player in the dashboard. At once the frenzied sound of a *paso doble* rang out. Drawn by the music, dozens of youngsters were already running out of the nearby houses to come and perch on the railway ties. It was not quite the *cinco de la tarde* of Spain's prestigious bullrings, but the young people of the neighborhood knew that every evening the *rejoneador*[1] from the supermarket would provide them with an unusual spectacle.

Arming himself with a short lance, Andreani mounted his stallion and made a majestic entrance into his improvised arena. At a signal from him, one of the spectators opened the door to an area fenced off with planks that served as a bull's pen. Then I saw a young black bull appear like those I had seen in the wide-open spaces of Andalusia. The beast launched itself at the horse and his rider. The ring was so small that I thought collision was inevitable. But with a prod of his spur, the rider snatched his mount away from the animal's horns. Excited by the duel, the music and the shouting, bull and horse now chased each other around in ever more constricted circles. Andreani slowed down, accelerated, changed trajectory, obliging the horse to perform acrobatic pirouettes that challenged the man's ability to balance. It was breathtaking. With his nostrils dilated and his breast, neck, withers and flanks dripping with foam, Preferido displayed his wild strength in elegant arabesques that delighted the young onlookers. The game went on until the last tremolo of the *paso doble* as man, horse and bull came to a halt, exhausted. The horseman and his mount left the ring with a few short, graceful steps. What a pity Goya wasn't there to immortalize those few magic moments on canvas.

I WAS IN A HURRY to bring Pinecone to this mythical stallion. But the abrupt change of environment traumatized her so much that for several days she literally starved herself. She re-

1. *Rejoneador:* a matador mounted on horseback.

pelled all her suitor's advances, lashing out viciously with kicks that made deep cuts in the stallion's breast. She had to be un-shod and have her hindquarters held down every time he pre-sented himself. Fortunately Preferido was not put off by her bad temper. Patiently he renewed his attempts. In the end Pinecone succumbed to his seduction and I was able to take her home. Eleven months later she gave me a delicate cinder-colored little foal. In honor of her phenomenal father, I chris-tened her Preferida, "the Preferred One."

A few days after her birth, I heard an unexpected voice sob-bing on the telephone. It was Raymond Andreani. He had called to tell me that Preferido had been murdered. One morn-ing he had found him standing rigidly in the small paddock where he ran loose during summer afternoons and nights. An-dreani immediately thought the horse had suffered a stroke. He called the vet and did not leave his horse for one minute, nursing him like a child, with infusions, poultices, antibiotic in-jections and enemas. Blood, saliva and urine tests revealed no specific disease. Preferido was dying for some unknown reason. His master put up a cot in his shed. The stallion's agony went on for four days and three nights. On the morning of the fourth day the powerful horse who had toyed with the horns of a mighty bull lay down on his side and breathed his last. Out of his mind with grief, Andreani had an autopsy performed. It was discovered that the animal had been killed by a .22 rifle round lodged in his spleen. The bullet's entry point was so small that it had gone unnoticed. The few drops of dried blood on his coat could have passed for an ordinary horsefly bite.

"Dominique, they've murdered Preferido," repeated poor Raymond through his tears.

I immediately offered to give him the young foal sired by his beloved horse. In her he might find again the magic qualities he had so passionately loved in Preferido. Raymond declined my offer. No other horse could ever replace the magnificent an-imal that every evening had given a handful of admiring chil-dren from a small Provence port a taste of the *fiesta brava*.

8

"Grandma, What's France Like?"

"Dominique, pack your bags. You're going to Algeria!" my editor in chief declared. "De Gaulle is due to spend two days in Kabylia. According to my informants, terrorists from either the OAS or the FLN are going to try and assassinate him. Stick to him like a louse, right through the journey. Take a camera. If anything does happen, it'll be more use to you than a pen."

That tragic spring of 1962 Algeria was a cauldron of hatred and violence. On one side, the French extremist groups of the OAS (Organisation Armée Secrète) were waging a bloody struggle to sabotage de Gaulle's plan to grant Algeria independence. On the other side, Algerian partisans of the FLN (Front de Libération Nationale) were intensifying their war against the century-old French presence.

As always, my editor in chief expressed himself without much soul-searching. To him crises, tragedies, catastrophes, were opportunities to offer readers of the magazine spectacular coverage. It should be said that he had been through the mill himself. Although he never talked about his experience, he was a survivor of the Nazi camps. A young member of the Resistance arrested at the age of nineteen by the Gestapo, he had spent two years digging a tunnel through the mountains of Czechoslovakia. All his comrades had died of exhaustion or S.S. beatings. He had survived. My editor in chief was a hero. At thirty-four he wore the rosette of a commander of the Légion d'Honneur. His orders were not to be questioned. In short, he could send us wherever he liked.

That was how I came to find myself in the great square in Tizi-Ouzou, a small town in the province of Kabylia about eighty miles from Algiers, pressed next to General de Gaulle, who was trying to clear a way through the multitude of people surrounding him. Muslims of the region had turned up en masse to hear the general speak about his plans for Algeria's coming independence. His legendary kepi stood out in the crowd. The roofs, terraces and trees were draped with tight clusters of people chanting his name. Solemn, dignified, visibly moved, he was tirelessly shaking the innumerable hands outstretched toward him. In the midst of that sea of humanity, killing him would be easy. His escorts had been jostled to the four corners of the square. Anyone could fire from one of the terraces, creep up on him and stab him in the back or shoot him point-blank with a revolver. With my hands poised over the button of my Leica, I used my knees, hips and elbows to stay as close to him as I possibly could.

Surrounded by all those people, I could not help thinking of an almost identical scene a German navy officer had described to me while Larry Collins and I were researching *Is Paris Burning?* It was the day Paris was liberated. Lieutenant Commander Harry Leithold of the Kriegsmarine was defending the naval ministry in the Place de la Concorde. Suddenly from a window he had seen a large black open vehicle emerge into the square. Seated in the backseat was a French general in a kepi. Leithold reached for his gun. Just as he was about to pull the trigger, dozens of civilians surged off the sidewalks and surrounded the car and its passenger. Taken aback, the German had put down his weapon. A few hours later he was taken prisoner. Two years later, in a photo in a magazine he recognized the French general he had almost killed that day. It was Charles de Gaulle.

Now, eighteen years after Paris's liberation, in this Algerian square, another gunman might have the same man in his crosshairs. As ordered, I stuck to him "like a louse." I was so close, in fact, that a movement of the crowd thrust me in front of him. De Gaulle shook my hand. He was shaking everyone's hand.

Fort-National, another of Kabylia's towns, was the second stop in his triumphal journey. For de Gaulle there followed the same enthusiastic welcome, the same immersion in the crowds and, for me, the same worried glances at the terraces. At that point, I was hustled toward him for a second time. I apologized. Too late. He had already taken my hand and stepped forward to shake others. Two hours later we arrived at Michelet, the last stop on his tour of Kabylia. With my finger still poised over the button of my camera, I was more than prepared for any eventuality. Suddenly there was a surge in the crowd. An irresistible force propelled me for a third time in front of France's imperious leader. Once again his hand reached out to mine. But he stopped in midmovement and gave me a furious look: "Oh no! Not you again!"

My EDITOR IN CHIEF'S informants had been wrong. No one had tried to assassinate the president of the French Republic during his Algerian visit. But it was merely a matter of time: many killers were waiting in the shadows. A few months after that journey, 8 million Algerians voted for independence. In the eyes of the million people of French origin for whom Algeria was an integral part of France, this vote was a tragedy. Forced by the FLN insurgents to choose "between a suitcase and a coffin," terrorized by French fanatics in the OAS, the French population of Algeria was forced to flee, in most instances leaving everything they had behind them. One morning I found myself on a quay in the port of Algiers for *Paris Match*, as fifteen hundred refugees struggled to board a boat bound for France.

It was a pitiful sight. Beyond the coils of barbed wire blocking the entrance to the rue Figeac, I noticed, above the human sea, the head of a tiny girl topped by a white hat. She was perched on the shoulders of her father, a bearded giant of a man. Her name was Nathalie Tisson and she was six years old. Tossed and pulled about by the crowd, she was crying. There were thousands of people all around her, all trying to squeeze into the narrow bottleneck guarded by the police, thousands who had come to the port in the hope of boarding the large white ship for Marseille that was moored a mere three hundred yards away. A police officer repeated: "Women and children first." One man shouted: "I've got four children!" "I've got six!" a woman replied. Then I heard her calling: "René! René! Where are you?" Somewhere another voice wailed: "We've come from Tizi-Ouzou. We were shot at on the way. This is the second time we've tried to embark! Sir, I beg you, let us pass. We won't be able to come back anymore!"

On her father's shoulders Nathalie wore an expression of despair. Bent over in the throng, her mother was pulling two enormous suitcases. The Tissons were teachers. Nathalie's father managed to edge forward a few inches. Next to him, an elderly gentleman in a black felt hat with a Légion d'Honneur rosette in his buttonhole said: "Last Thursday, more than two thousand people were unable to go on board." His remark brought an expression of anguish to all those who heard it. A young girl half strangled by the straps of a rucksack remarked angrily: "In Paris, they'd rather we were crushed to death here than turned up there." Sharp ripples ran through the crowd. Someone called: "Jacqueline! Jacqueline! Don't lose sight of me!" In the group that had just passed through the customs gate were the Tissons and the elderly gentleman with the Légion d'Honneur. The latter had scarcely pushed his way through the narrow entrance to the quay when he turned around, his face flooded with sudden joy, and began shouting through cupped hands: "Long live de Gaulle! At last now I'm free to shout 'Long live de Gaulle!'" Had he shouted such a sentiment in the streets of Algiers, he would have been shot by the OAS.

Crushed by misery and fatigue, the crowd around him did not react. That day the Fort-de-France quay was like a game preserve in which the animals waited for the authorities to check their authorization to leave. The ground was strewn with hundreds of suitcases, reinforced cardboard boxes, wooden trunks, moleskin cases, roughly tied with string or straps. They contained the only belongings the fifteen hundred candidates for the voyage had been able to bring away with them.

Seated on her suitcase, an old lady in a veiled black hat waited for a policeman to call her number. The numbers had not been handed out in sequence, and thus sometimes the last to arrive got through first. She was holding the hand of a little girl clutching a doll. They were the only members of the Guilloud family who would board that morning. The others were still behind the barbed-wire barrier. The Guillouds had lived in Boufarik since 1830, when the first colonizing ship landed on Algerian soil. "Grandma," asked little Josette, "what's France like?"

Beyond the wooden barriers of the enclosure reserved for fourth-class passengers, people jostled against each other. "Let us sit down," one woman begged. Another woman boxed her small boy's ears because he was swinging on a tent bracing wire. Every five minutes a naval captain armed with a bullhorn uttered appeasing words: "Ladies and gentlemen, don't worry. You are now sure of boarding. Proceed to the various controls for the embarkation formalities!" Supported on a sailor's arm, the elderly Madame Marceau, widow of the former chief warden of Algiers prison, tried to gather up her suitcases. She had sworn never to leave Algeria, but her daughter had forced her to go. There was no one waiting for Madame Marceau in France apart from her two sons killed in World War II, who had been buried near Reims.

Ten-thirty. Couillaud, the vessel's sublieutenant, looked at his watch and gave the order: "Let's go!" At once, Lavoine, André and Suznik of the fourth mine-clearance diving squad, jumped into the dark water. For twenty minutes the three men, equipped with scuba gear and flashlights, inspected the hull of the *Ville de Marseille* inch by inch, to make sure French OAS saboteurs had not planted any plastic explosives. In the coach that served as shuttle between the Fort-de-France quay and the loading dock, a woman was knitting. In front of her, another had a handkerchief clenched between her fingers: "My carpets . . . I've left all my carpets behind," she moaned. In the corridor a man in a cap and shirtsleeves, squatting on a small metal box, rolled a cigarette. He was Dédé, the mechanic from the Majestic Garage in the rue Thiers. He had taken his toolbox with him when he left.

At the entrance to the ship there was total congestion. A father let out a cry: "Martine!" Jupin, the *Ville de Marseille*'s second-in-command, rushed over. He caught hold of little Martine just as she was about to fall into the water. In front of the "4th class" notice, a young woman with blond hair wiped her sunglasses. Her face was puffy from crying.

"Panic has broken out between Orléansville and Algiers," she explained to the sailor helping her carry her two suitcases. "The trains are being attacked. Everyone's running away. There aren't any more troops inland . . ."

In the arms of a little girl with long braids, a fat cat meowed lugubriously. Her little brother was crying: he had jammed his foot in a railing. A sailor came to his rescue. A helicopter was describing circles above the *Ville de Marseille*. On board a naval captain watched the embarkation process through binoculars. The mine-clearance divers had not found any explosives on the hull, but a mortar shot or bazooka could still be fired from the heights of the city. And up there, where white apartment houses rose out of islets of greenery, was the Belcourt district, an OAS citadel.

Eleven-thirty. The Tissons reached the ship's gangway. Nathalie was still on her father's shoulders. He was sweating large beads of perspiration. Next to the Tissons, a squat little man in a green peaked cap read a newspaper as he waited patiently for his turn. He was the warden for the Gardimaou National Forest. A little earlier he had confided to the Tissons: "I'm leaving because the local authorities for Saint-Arnaud told the Muslim population they could graze their herds in *my* forest. I'd just reforested a hundred acres. In a year that place will be desert . . ."

Supported by a police officer and a sailor, Madame Marceau boarded the ship. Inside, like all the other passengers, she would hand over 6,300 francs, about twenty dollars, to pay for her fourth-class journey into exile. Behind Madame Marceau, a bare-headed woman led a German shepherd named Darling. She seemed totally confused. Of the policeman checking the embarkation cards she asked timidly: "I'm to report to the Villejuif cancer hospital near Paris, what should I do?"

1,524 . . . 1,525 . . . 1,526 . . . A hardware merchant from Cherchell, his wife and their son were the last three passengers on the ship that morning. Monsieur Mossi fiddled nervously with the key to the brand-new Simca automobile he had left behind the barbed wire in the rue Figeac.

It was midday. The ship was full. Embarkation had taken five hours. Suddenly a military truck covered with a tarpaulin burst onto the quay. A civilian with a crewcut jumped to the ground and held a parley with the police. These last passengers, five Arab harki families, had not been expected. The harkis were those Arabs who had chosen to fight on the side of France. In independent Algeria, they would be massacred. The Frenchman in civilian clothes, a former army officer for Arab affairs, was trying to save them. A gangway was put back in position. With haggard eyes and the look of hunted animals, some twenty men, women and children were hurriedly swallowed up into the flanks of the rescue ship.

Twice the siren blew. Pulled by two tugboats, the *Ville de Marseille* turned on its own length. On the quay the red-bereted driver of the truck that had brought the harkis moved slowly off, then suddenly sounded his horn. *Ti-ti-ti—ta—ta*, the rallying cry of French Algeria. On one of the tugs two sailors responded by unfurling the tricolor flag inscribed with the letters *OAS*. From poop to prow, on the port side, the crowds had lined up in closed ranks to take a last look at Algiers. Warm and luminous, gleaming white, one of the world's most beautiful postcard scenes passed slowly before our eyes. Every now and then the sun would catch the windshield of a car traveling along the coast road. Clinging to a safety rail on which French soldiers sent to fight in Algeria against the Arab rebellion had carved "Let's go home!," a woman sobbed: "Marcel, Marcel . . ." She was beside herself. Marcel was her husband, a petty official with the central government which sat in the imposing concrete and glass rectangle rising up, there, just opposite, like a high-sided ship anchored in the heart of the city. The woman's husband had disappeared three days previously. Whether he had been taken away by the French of the OAS or the Arabs of the FLN she did not know. Yesterday the *fatma*, the Arab maid, had come to tell her that the order had been given to slit her three children's throats. The poor woman had been frantic. She had filled their small home with provisions in case Marcel should return and had fled with the children. Her cries were heartbreaking. "Marcel! My poor Marcel!"

At the very back of the ship, beneath the softly fluttering tricolor flag, a boy was weeping. He might have been fifteen, but the tears pouring down his streaked face made him look like an old man. Through his anguish, he gazed at the Casbah, the Arab quarter of the city, with its confusion of houses and alleyways on the side of the hill. On the right, he recognized among the trees the ocher walls of his *lycée*, the Bugeaud *lycée*, where there were no pupils or teachers anymore. Farther on, at the end of the rue Mizon, stood a tall building slightly askew: his house. To the right, almost at the water's edge, under a white stone next to other white stones in the Saint-Eugène cemetery, lay his father and mother. Four years previously they had both died in a terrorist attack.

A little girl placed a maternal hand upon the boy's shoulder. Her father was a bookkeeper for a grain business and her mother a switchboard operator at the Hôtel Aletti, Algiers's luxury hotel in happier days. Although they were on board with their six children, there was no one in France awaiting the Simonneau family.

Leaning on the railings of the upper deck, the Tissons watched as the cupolas of Notre-Dame-d'Afrique disappeared in the pink light. Behind them, squatting on some ropes, her face hidden in a white handkerchief, old Madame Guilloud sobbed under her black hat. On his bridge Commander Latil shook his head sadly: "Poor people," he sighed. Then he added: "This is the Exodus I'm in charge of today." Only yesterday, there had been dancing on the *Ville de Marseille*, people had thronged the great lounge in first class to play lotto or miniature horse racing. For many French residents of Algeria, the *Ville de Marseille* was the happy host of the first days of their summer vacation. That evening the boat's musicians had been canceled. There would be no horse racing, no film, no dancing on the deck.

On board I met up again with a young lawyer with whom I had made the outward journey. He had rushed to the High Court Building in Algiers where he had been due to plead a case, but at the Algiers Law Courts there were no more plaintiffs, no clerk of the court and no roll. When the judge called his case, the young lawyer heard someone announce that his client had been murdered on the previous day. All he could do was climb back on board ship. He was devastated.

In the distance Algiers was now nothing but a whitish patch on the blue of the sea. Tired to death by that terrible day, each passenger had improvised a place among the jumble of suitcases, packages and bundles. Children played hide-and-seek in the gangways. A Muslim woman breast-fed her baby. An old man switched on his transistor radio. Deck B was immediately filled with a raucous voice: de Gaulle was speaking in Bordeaux. A woman rushed over, snatched the transistor out of the old gentleman's hands and threw it into the sea.

During the afternoon the sea rose and the beautiful Algiers sunshine gave way to a grayish mist. Between decks a woman fainted for the second time since that morning. She had heart problems. Everyone knew Madame Marti, the grocer in Bab-el-Oued. Since setting sail she had not stopped telling her neighbors her life story and her misfortunes. They knew that her husband had disappeared. When she collapsed against the porthole, a small man with a mustache rushed to her side: "I'm a doctor," he said, "leave it to me!"

Dr. Lauta, the ship's doctor, rushed over with a syringe. Lauta was all over the place handing out seasickness tablets, giving injections, relieving the countless problems of the pitiful cargo. On the previous voyage he had delivered a baby.

The two doctors transported the plump Madame Marti onto the deck and gave her an injection. That evening I found them having a tête-à-tête over a beer in the first-class bar. The doctor from Algeria stared into his glass. In a monotonous voice he told his colleague from the mother country:

"I had a quarter of an hour in which to leave. That was yesterday . . . yes, only yesterday. A Muslim came and warned me. 'Don't go out,' he said, 'they're lying in wait for you.' I barricaded the door and said to my wife: 'Pack a case quickly. We're leaving.' We went out by the back door and scrambled away from the village. At the first turn a band of Muslims armed with billhooks, knives and axes stopped us. We thought they were going to slaughter us but an old patient of mine recognized me. He said: 'It's the doc. Let him pass!' The younger ones threatened us but we could escape."

Next day, their eyes heavy with tiredness, the passengers on the *Ville de Marseille* gathered up their luggage and went on deck. One young boy, accustomed to life in a city where after 8:00 P.M. people still in the street would be shot on sight, asked: "Daddy, is there also a curfew in France?" At the sight of the French coast, I saw a worried expression on many faces, replacing the anxiety of the previous day. The teenager from the Bugeaud secondary school had dried his tears but he still looked sad. Standing on the forward deck, the Tissons, the Rossis, the Simonneaus and many others wondered what fate lay in store for them. Leaning on the port railing of A deck, old Madame Guilloud watched Marseille drawing closer. She nodded her head slightly and said: "I'll go back."

ON THE QUAY AT MARSEILLE there was no band, no loudspeakers and no welcoming banners, no official or local delegations, no teams of medical and social workers except for a small and completely overwhelmed Red Cross unit, to greet the returning citizens. No provision had been made to distribute food, drink or milk for the children. The municipality had sent neither porters nor volunteers to help the old and weak carry their suitcases or bundles off the boat. No communal transport was available to take the arrivals to the railroad station or airport.

No central accommodation had been created to take in and act as a transit point for those with least funds. The 1,526 repatriated people on the *Ville de Marseille* who arrived on French soil were met with total indifference. Soon, one million others would make the voyage in almost the same circumstances.

As I carved my way through the pitiful mob, I felt tears of shame flowing down my cheeks. My thirty years suddenly weighed down upon me like centuries. My journey in the company of those castaways concluded with the discovery that my country, always so quick to extol humanitarian values, always so keen to champion human rights, could fail to provide the most basic generosity.

9

A Kamikaze in the Holy Land

The man had not thought twice about crossing the Atlantic in his private jet to meet us in Paris. Larry and I were, he maintained, his "favorite authors" and for that reason he had a book idea to put to us. Pointing to his gold Cartier cigarette case, he spoke in a heavy German accent: "Let's imagine that Gaddafi manages to manufacture an H-bomb this size, or even a little larger, that he gets it to New York and sends a letter to the president of the United States, telling him he will detonate it if Israel does not withdraw within forty-eight hours from East Jerusalem and the Arab territories occupied in 1967."

Our interlocutor watched for our reaction and gave us a beguiling smile.

"You're the only ones who could tell the story of what would happen if such a letter were to turn up at the White House one fine morning. This, boys, is the subject for your next book!"

At fifty-four Charlie Bluhdorn was president of Gulf & Western, a conglomerate of several dozen companies that Wall Street valued at $4 billion. In the bosom of his empire this magnate had two companies, which he treated like his mistresses. One was Paramount, which had just broken box-office records with *The Godfather* and *Love Story*. The other was Simon & Schuster, the large New York publishing house that had published all our books in the United States since *Is Paris Burning?*

The scenario this captain of industry who turned over millions of dollars a day in sugar, zinc, paper pulp and automobile parts was presenting us struck us as brilliant. He was offering us the opportunity to embark on one of those extensive research projects we were so fond of. Charlie Bluhdorn's original idea would develop, four years later, into one of our favorite books, *The Fifth Horseman*.

This was new territory for our duo. All our "four-handed" books to date had been historical accounts based on actual facts. Bluhdorn's scenario provided us with the additional possibility of using a political reality to develop and test an original hypothesis. Was it likely that Gaddafi could get hold of a nuclear bomb? Was it realistic to imagine that he could plant it in New York and detonate it there? Was it possible to neutralize it before it was too late? Could a city like New York be evacuated? Could the Israelis be made to give up the Arab occupied territories? There were so many questions for which we would have to find precise and detailed answers, real historian's answers. To start with, was the idea of the nuclear blackmailing of a city like New York a mere flight of fancy or, on the contrary, a very real possibility?

A high-ranking FBI agent whom Larry had known at Yale was to provide us with the answer. President Gerald Ford had been through just such an experience in 1974, also in connection with the Mideast conflict. A group of Palestinians had threatened to set off an atomic bomb in the heart of Boston if eleven of their comrades were not released from Israeli prisons. For several hours Ford considered evacuating Massachusetts's largest city. Fortunately the blackmailers were arrested and their threat proved to be a hoax, but thereafter fifty similar incidents were to send the FBI into a state of turmoil. Half a mile from the White House, on the corner of Pennsylvania Avenue and Tenth Street, the sixth floor of the FBI's fortresslike building harbored a nuclear emergency department created as a consequence of the 1974 threats, at a time when the FBI decided to give the possibility of atomic blackmail absolute priority.

This revelation set us on the trail of one of the most secret organizations in the United States, a group of scientists and technicians kept on alert day and night by the Department of Energy's emergency operations center. This center was housed in an underground blockhouse in Maryland, twenty-five miles from Washington. It was one of numerous secret command posts from which America could be governed in the event of nuclear war. The organization in question was officially known by the acronym NEST: Nuclear Explosives Search Teams. Thanks to their ultrasensitive neutron and gamma ray detectors, combined with their highly sophisticated techniques, in theory these teams could detect the presence of any nuclear device. Six times, unbeknownst to the local population, they had beleaguered the streets of an American city to hunt down a bomb.

In a small mud-walled house in New Mexico, Larry Collins managed to unearth the man who had set up these teams. A six-foot-seven-inch giant with a swarthy face, wearing cowboy hat, boots, checked shirt and a Navajo amulet around his neck, he looked as if he had stepped out of an advertisement for Marlboro cigarettes. Fifty-two-year-old Bill Booth was an atomic physicist. With his help we were able to realistically reconstruct NEST's detection of an imaginary H-bomb hidden in a deserted warehouse in the heart of Manhattan. Our real challenge as writers was persuading our readers that such a scenario was likely, convincing them that that bomb could be planted in New York, ready to kill 6 million people. We then had to show our audience that an Arab head of state such as Gaddafi could, because of his oil riches, get hold of a nuclear device, or failing that, have one built somewhere in the desert in his own country, then send it to the American devil, ally of the Jews. Unlike Israel, India and South Africa, who had pursued their nuclear arms programs in total secrecy, Gaddafi had never tried to conceal his determination to equip his country with atomic weapons. The West had always ridiculed his ambitions, portraying him as a fanatical adventurer incapable of actually carrying out such an enterprise.

Our research was to show that his efforts had come within a hair's breadth of succeeding.

WHO WAS THIS MAN to whom we had decided to attribute such diabolical intentions? One day Collins's connections in the CIA arcana and the reputation for reliability our books enjoyed brought us an unexpected answer. It took the form of an eighteen-page booklet with a white cover bearing the pale blue crest of the CIA and the label "Confidential." It was entitled "Study of the Personality and Political Behavior of Muammar Gaddafi."

This study was part of a secret program carried out by the CIA since the end of the fifties. Its objective was to shed light on the most intimate details of the personality and character of a number of international political leaders in order to anticipate their reactions in event of a crisis or conflict. Castro, Nasser, de Gaulle, Khrushchev, Brezhnev, Mao Tse-tung, the Shah of Iran, Khomeini and many other heads of state had thus been screened by experts. The studies of the personalities of Castro and Khrushchev had been of decisive help to John F. Kennedy during the Cuban missile crisis of October 1962.

Each profile was the product of considerable financial and technical input. Every aspect of the subject had been examined. What had influenced his life, what major trauma he had undergone, how he had reacted to extreme situations, what particular defense mechanisms he had used. Specialists had traveled all over the world to verify a detail or explore a character facet. Did so-and-so masturbate? Did he drink? Did he like pepper on his food? Did he go to church? How did he react in periods of stress? Was he suffering from an Oedipus complex? Did he like boys? Girls? Both? What were his sexual fantasies? How big was his penis? Did he have sadistic or masochistic tendencies? A CIA agent had even gone into Cuba clandestinely to question a prostitute with whom Castro had relations when he was a student.

The cover of the Gaddafi folder bore a portrait of the man; as usual the Arab leader wore that disconcerting look of his, as if he were about to bite. We were itching to meet this intriguing person. In the past we had almost invariably come by our most interesting material during encounters with the main characters of our books. Heads of government or state had given generously of their time. Eisenhower, Ben-Gurion, Golda Meir, Indira Gandhi, Mountbatten had all answered our questions in detail.

This time, however, we felt unable to tell Gaddafi the exact reason we wanted to meet him, so we sent a young and talented Franco-Spanish ethnologist to Libya in our place, to bring back all the particulars we needed for our story. Xavier Moro fell in love with the country and its inhabitants. He came back with a wealth of information, including the fact that every evening the young dictator left his quarters in his official residence in Bab Azzira, in the suburbs of his capital, to spend the night in a Bedouin tent erected in the courtyard near the little herd of she-camels that provided him with his only daily drink.[1]

"Better let the pot cool down."

America's largest city, headquarters of the United Nations, the cathedral of skyscrapers, the world temple of finance, art and entertainment, the beacon of the triumphant West, taken hostage by an Arab dictator ruling over a desert inhabited by scarcely 3 million people! Our research indicated that in such a scenario, the authorities' primary concern would be to enter into dialogue with Colonel Gaddafi to dissuade him from car-

---

1. When our book *The Fifth Horseman* came out in the bookshops, two German journalists from *Stern* magazine rushed to Tripoli to ask Colonel Gaddafi what he thought of the scenario of nuclear blackmail Lapierre and Collins had attributed to him. Gaddafi had not yet been informed of the publication of the book.

"What happens in this scenario?" he inquired, visibly intrigued.

The two journalists told him how he took the city of New York hostage and threatened to explode an H-bomb there if the United States did not force the Israelis to evacuate East Jerusalem and the occupied territories.

Gaddafi assumed a mysterious air before declaring: "In any case, if ever that were to happen, it would be your fault because you gave me the idea."

rying out his deadly threat. Holding a dialogue with terrorists is always a difficult and dangerous undertaking. A single word, a single sentence, badly interpreted can result in catastrophe. We discovered that to minimize this risk, the CIA and the FBI had engaged several psychiatrists specializing in the psychology of hostage takers and terrorists in general. We learned that the leading expert in this field was a fifty-six-year-old Dutch doctor living in The Hague. All the Western police used Hendrick Loden as a kind of "Dr. Terrorism." The son of an inspector of prisons in Amsterdam, as a child, Loden had accompanied his father on his visits to detainees. His contact with the prison population had awakened in him a precocious interest in the psychology of the criminal mind. Financing his medical studies by guiding tourists through the museums and around the canals of his hometown, he had become a psychiatrist, specializing in criminology. It was he who had resolved some of the most universally interesting hostage situations to occur in Holland in the mid-seventies, notably the abduction of the French ambassador to The Hague by the Palestinians, the taking hostage of a choir that had gone to sing a Christmas service in a prison and the attack on two passenger trains by Moluccan terrorists. Dr. Loden was a strong-backed, rosy-cheeked little man, reminiscent of a burgermeister painted by Frans Hals. He received me in one of those narrow brick houses in The Hague that nestle tightly up against each other.

"I've studied your scenario and your CIA report on Gaddafi," he informed me in Dutch-accented English. "After sending his letter to the president of the United States, your colonel would probably be in a state of psychological arousal, that is to say in full paranoid delirium. He can see his objectives within reach: liquidating Israel, becoming the uncontested leader of the Arabs, dictating terms for the world's oil market. To enter into negotiations with him at this point would be a fatal mistake. It would be better to let the pot cool down before taking the lid off to see what's inside!"

Loden filled my coffee cup.

"You know, in a situation of this kind, the first moments are always the most dangerous. At the outset the anxiety quotient of the terrorist is very high. He is often in a state of hysteria that can drive him to commit the irreparable. He must be given oxygen, helped to get his breath back, allowed to express his opinions and his grievances. That's why the first thing to do would be to establish a radio or telephone link with him. His voice absolutely must be heard. That's essential."

The doctor continued: "For me, a man's voice is an indispensable way into his psychological makeup, the thing that enables me to understand his character, the modulation of his emotions, and eventually predict his behavior."

In all hostage situations Dr. Loden recorded all conversations with the terrorists, then listened to the tape again and again, picking out the slightest alteration in tone, elocution or vocabulary.

"Who should speak to him?" I asked. "The president, I suppose . . ."

"Under no circumstances!" the psychiatrist protested vehemently. "The president is the only person who can grant him what he's asking for—at least, that's what he believes. So he should be the last person to have contact with him." Loden swallowed a mouthful of coffee. "The object is to gain time, the time the police need to find the bomb. How are you going to draw things out and get a postponement of the ultimatum if you bring the supreme authority into play at the beginning of negotiations?"

I was finding what he had to say more and more absorbing.

"That's why I always recommend placing a negotiator between the terrorist and the authorities. If the terrorist formulates a pressing demand, the negotiator can then pretend he must refer to those who have the power to give him what he wants. Time is always on the side of the authorities. As the hours pass, terrorists show themselves to be less and less sure of themselves, more and more vulnerable. Let's hope that's the case in your scenario!"

"What kind of person should the negotiator be?" I asked.

"Someone mature, calm, who knows how to listen and draw him out of any possible silences. On the whole a sort of fatherly figure, such as Nasser was for him in his youth. In short, someone who will win his trust. His tactic will be to get this message

through to Gaddafi: 'I sympathize with you and with your objectives. I want to help you to achieve them.'

"You should start by telling Gaddafi he's right. That not only
are his grievances against Israel legitimate but that the United
States is ready to help him find a reasonable solution."

"All right, Doctor, but all this presupposes Gaddafi is willing
to talk to this negotiator," I observed.

"He'd talk. The excellent study you gave me to read shows
that quite clearly. The poor little desert Bedouin ridiculed by
his schoolmates wants to become a hero in the eyes of all the
Arabs by imposing his will on the most powerful man in the
world, the president of the United States. Believe me, he'd talk.

"Clearly Gaddafi's desire to be the 'justiciary' for his Arab
brothers is the fundamental reason for what he's doing. At the
same time, there is another imperative driving him: the disdain
in which the West holds him. He knows the Americans, the
British, the French and even the Russians think he's a lunatic.
He wants to force the West to respect him, to take account of
his wishes, to allow him to fulfill his grandiose dream. And to
prove that he's not as mad as people think, he's ready to see
things through to the bitter end, to destroy everything."

I was fascinated by the way in which this Dutchman had become caught up in our scenario.

"What might drive a man like Gaddafi to this kind of blackmail? Power mania?" I asked.

The psychiatrist closed his eyes for a second. "Personally I
share the opinion expressed by the CIA report. He's not mad at
all."

"So why would he organize such a maniacal plot?"

"On the basis of what I've read, the dominant trait in his personality is a taste for solitude. He was a loner as a child, at
school, then at military college in England. As head of state he
is still a loner. Now, solitude is dangerous. The more a man is
turned in upon himself, the more likely he is to become dangerous. Terrorists are generally isolated individuals, marginals,
outsiders, who rally around an ideal, a cause. Ill at ease with
themselves, they're driven to act. Violence is their way of as-
serting themselves in the eyes of the world. The more Gaddafi

feels his isolation growing in relation to the other Arab nations, the greater the gulf dividing him from the world community, the more obsessive the need to act and prove to the world that he exists would become. He's made himself the champion of the Palestinians. He's convinced their cause is well founded. And now, having taken New York hostage, he thinks he's God the Father, ready, beyond all concepts of good and evil, to dispense justice himself!"

"If the man is such a megalomaniac, why waste all that time trying to talk to him?" I asked.

"You shouldn't try and reason with him. On the contrary you would have to try and convince him of the need to grant you a delay, in the same way that I always try and convince a terrorist of the need to free his hostages. Often, with time, the unreal world in which the terrorist evolves disintegrates around him. Reality takes over and his defense mechanisms break down. At that juncture a terrorist is ready to die, to commit suicide in a spectacular fashion. The risk of his taking his hostages with him is therefore enormous. In that case, I wouldn't put much money on the lives of your New Yorkers. On the other hand, the blessed opportunity might arise to take the terrorist by the hand—so to speak—and lead him away from danger. So you have to try and convince him he's a hero, a hero who has been constrained to submit honorably to superior strength."

"And you think that a Gaddafi could be manipulated like that?"

"It's to be hoped so. That's all. But the situation would offer little alternative. Clearly you're dealing with a personality suffering from a power psychosis, from slight but in no way chronic paranoia. That type of subject generally has difficulty mastering difficult situations. You should therefore confront him with a whole range of secondary problems, try and divert his attention from the bombing with a host of practical, unimportant questions related to the manner in which his requirements should be met. You know my 'chicken or hamburger' theory?"

I said that I did. The psychiatrist's idea was to take the terrorists' minds off their primary preoccupation by forcing them to deal with an uninterrupted stream of questions and problems that bore no relation to the situation. The example he invariably cited was the way one should respond to a terrorist asking for food. "What would you like? Chicken or a hamburger? Wing or drumstick? Well done or rare? Mustard or ketchup? With or without bread? Broiled or grilled? With what seasoning? Pickles? Would you like onions with your meat? Raw or fried?" The Dutch doctor had added numerous finishing touches to this basic technique. He made sure, for example, that the food was always sent on proper plates, with proper cutlery and proper glasses. This precaution, he claimed, subtly introduced an element of civilization into relations between the police and the terrorists. It also introduced an idea of fragility that obliged the terrorists to be careful. A porcelain plate or a glass can break. Similarly a hostage's life is fragile. Furthermore, whenever possible, he would ask the terrorists to do the washing up before sending the dishes back. That led them gradually to carrying out orders. Distracting a hostage taker from his obsessions with such a barrage of questions often made it possible to calm him down, put him in touch with reality and ultimately make him more malleable.

Dr. Loden gave a protracted sigh before concluding:

"The trouble is that Gaddafi wouldn't be an ordinary terrorist."

Some Very Bloodthirsty Butterfly Collectors

Every year more than eight thousand vessels unload their cargoes in the port of New York. It is quite impossible to keep an effective check on their merchandise, so unloading a container with a nuclear device in it on a Brooklyn or Jersey City pier would be child's play. Finding a hiding place for the device would be just as easy. The lower part of Manhattan is full of warehouses and garages for rent. Once his bomb was in position, however, how would Gaddafi set it off? By radio signal from his HQ in Tripoli? From a hiding place in his desert?

From a ship at sea? Or would he entrust its firing to a person, to a kamikaze, for example, who would come and press the detonator at the appointed time? Our research showed there would be no difficulty in finding a volunteer for a suicide mission of this kind. In the 1970s the training camps for the war against Israel were filled to bursting point with fanatics prepared to lay down their lives. In Lebanon the camps even included quite a number of foreigners. The most determined belonged to a small, extreme left-wing Japanese political group that called itself the Japanese Red Army. On May 30, 1972, three of its members had garnered fame through tragedy when, using hand grenades and automatic weapons, they massacred thirty-two passengers from an Air France plane that had just landed at Lod, Israel's international airport. Two of the Japanese terrorists perished in the slaughter, but the third, a twenty-four-year-old botany student called Kozo Okamoto, had been captured alive.

Why had this young Japanese from a respectable middle-class family traveled halfway across the world to become a killer in the service of a cause that had nothing to do with his country's history, culture or concerns? Why would he or any of his companions be willing to press the detonator for Gaddafi's H-bomb, hidden in the heart of New York?

This question was to take me into Israel's most closely guarded building, Ramla top-security prison, in which the Hebrew state locked up its most dangerous enemies. For eight years Kozo Okamoto had been serving a life sentence in a cell that had harbored the Nazi leader who had planned the extermination of Europe's Jews, Adolf Eichmann. Apart from the occasional visit from an official from the Japanese embassy in Tel Aviv, the terrorist was living in total isolation. No journalist, no historian, had ever been able to reconstruct with him his terrorist itinerary.

Purely on the off-chance of being granted an interview, I submitted a request to visit him to the Israeli authorities. Banking on my good luck, I feverishly prepared our meeting. I had a whole list of questions translated into Japanese and learned them by heart. Then, hoping to establish a friendly rapport between us, I wrote to his parents to tell them about my possible visit to Ramla, and in response I received messages of encouragement and affection which they asked me to relay to their son. Finally, from a grocery shop that sold Oriental specialties in Tel Aviv, I managed to get hold of a whole range of Chinese and Japanese delicacies likely to liven up the Japanese prisoner's diet for a few days. Now all I needed was the miraculous authorization.

I was on the point of returning to France when a telephone call invited me to present myself at the prison gate. I ran to the nearest tobacco shop to buy a pack of Pall Mall, Okamoto's favorite cigarettes, and rushed to Ramla. It was the first time I had been to a prison since my meetings with Caryl Chessman at San Quentin's death row twenty years earlier. After a thorough search, the head warden did me the honor of escorting me in person through the numerous yards overcrowded with Palestinian prisoners, to the top-security block where Israel detained its VIP guests. Before I had time to register what was happening, my guide pushed me into a spacious cell and, like the door to a lions' cage when a tamer enters, the lock clanged behind me.

I made out then, at the far end of the room, a tiny, motionless shape perched on the edge of his cot, like a stuffed sparrow. As I approached, I first noticed his hands. His nails were long and curved like claws. I said good day in Japanese. Surprised, Okamoto stood up and turned to look at me. "Good day," he repeated, accompanying his words with a slight hissing noise and bowing ceremonially, Japanese style.

"I'll go get you some coffee," the chief warden announced. Drawing closer to me, he added in a whisper: "Be careful: that little rat knows a karate blow that can kill you in a flash."

He had scarcely uttered these words than he unbolted the door and left. I was alone with the Japanese, who had quietly resumed his place on the edge of his mattress. I went and sat next to him. From close up, his nails looked just like small daggers. As I looked at him I thought with horror of all the innocent people whose deaths this man, now imprisoned, could cause, of all those who might be taken hostage in a plane, school or church so that this apparently insignificant individual could have his freedom. Yet he seemed so puny, frail and generally inoffensive, I could not imagine him having the strength to kill anyone, even with a secret karate chop.

He listened to me, gazing through small eyes that were incredulous but appreciative. It was a good sign. That was when I saw death looming before me. Okamoto's right arm had shot like a saber into the air. In a flash I deduced it was going to hit me on the nape of my neck or the trachea. I had no time to move away before his hand was on me. But I felt no impact. The Japanese did not want to kill me. Like a bird of prey, he had seized the pack of Pall Mall poking out of my shirt pocket. He opened it with his nails and blithely lit a cigarette. The chief warden returned shortly afterward with two cups and a pot exuding the reassuring aroma of coffee. Then he withdrew again, leaving us under the discreet surveillance of the guards in the corridor.

I went directly for one of the key questions for our book.

"Kozo, if your leaders had ever ordered you to press the detonator for an H-bomb meant to kill 6 million inhabitants of New York, to make the Israelis get out of East Jerusalem and the Arab occupied territories, would you have carried out that order?"

The Japanese emitted a series of grunts. He stiffened.

"I am a soldier. Soldiers carry out orders," he replied.

"But you're Japanese. The Jewish-Arab conflict doesn't concern you. Neither you nor your country."

A glimmer of reproach passed across his tiny eyes. "I am a revolutionary militant! The revolution knows no frontiers."

A revolutionary militant! I had searched in vain through this Japanese's revolutionary past without managing to work out how a young man with an apparently timid and reserved personality, brought up with the principles and traditions of a respectable family, and passionately interested in his botanical studies, had managed to stray into the ranks of an organization of desperate leftists like the Japanese Red Army. Did the example of his much-admired elder brother explain his commitment? Or were there hidden reasons?

I came straight out with the question. It earned me a sequence of throat clearings and an embarrassed smile. Then, letting his head drop backward, with his eyes tightly closed, eventually he said: "Possibly the fact that I was unlucky in love."

I pressed him to explain.

"First I loved the girl next door," he said sadly, "but she ran away on the morning of our engagement. Later, at university, I fell in love with another student. She shared my passion for flowers and plants. But our relationship ended in a total fiasco." He sighed deeply. This time his small eyes were wide open. "At the time, the Japanese Red Army seemed to me like a less demanding lover."

I grasped this opportunity to ask him whether the Red Army still represented his political ideals. The question provoked a grin.

"Of course!" he said with sudden anger.

"Do you ever think about the airport tragedy?" I asked after a moment.

"I think about it every day."

"And eight years afterward what do you feel about what happened that evening?"

He blew a series of fresh smoke rings with his Pall Mall. Then in a very slow voice he said: "In my capacity as a revolutionary militant my duty was to agree to fight the war. The unfortunate thing is that the war affected women and children too."

I asked him then his point of view not as a militant but simply as a human being. He remained silent for a long while. I saw his Adam's apple rise and fall nervously in his throat, a sign of intense emotion. Finally he said: "Excuse me, but words cannot express what I feel."

"Kozo," I said familiarly, gesturing to the walls and the bars, "if you ever get out of prison, what will be the first thing you'll do?"

The Japanese mustered a broad smile. The question had touched a nerve.

"I shall go around the world expressing my regrets to the Jewish and Puerto Rican people," he said solemnly.

His response made me pity him. It called for further explanation. A terrifying chapter of my research was about to begin.

THE REVOLUTIONARY MYSTIQUE that had precipitated the student Kozo Okamoto into the turbidity of Palestinian terrorism had been born out of the great struggles that had set the Japanese campuses ablaze at the end of the sixties. Convinced their demonstrations would do nothing to change Japanese society, a number of communist students decided to take direct action. In search of absolute justice, they opted for violence as their argument in a debate they believed had become bogged down, and regrouped under the title of "Japanese Red Army." This group was mostly made up of students, but there were also doctors, engineers and even businessmen among them.

One of the leaders of this terrorist avatar of the students' movement was an enigmatic young woman whose face was framed by long sleek hair. Fusako Shinegobu was the daughter of an extreme right-wing lawyer. No task in the service of the cause could put her off. As a student at the Meiji University in Tokyo, she had not hesitated to work as an evening barmaid in a topless cabaret to fill the movement's coffers. "Every caress from a client is one more bowl of rice for my comrades," she used to say. Fusako had been arrested several times in connection with violent incidents, including the day of rioting that in May 1969 brought bloodshed to Tokyo. Two years later the young woman and eight of her comrades proclaimed the official birth of the Japanese Red Army. They hijacked a Japan Airlines Boeing 747 with three hundred passengers on board and forced it to land in Pyongyang, the capital of North Korea.

This exploit fired the imagination of millions of Japanese persuaded that only radical action could force Prime Minister Sato's ultraconservative and corrupt government to stand down, and change the rigid, archaic structures of Japanese society. Hailed as heroes by a whole section of the public, the nine pirates became part of the romantic mythology of the samurai overnight.

The founders of the movement would learn a lesson from the Pyongyang incident. Since revolution was not yet possible in Japan, they must fight on the international battlefield to purge not just the archipelago but the whole world of its rottenness. Thus the revolution would become international before it could be Japanese.

It was not long before this message reached the ears of the Christian Arab doctor who led the Popular Front for the Liberation of Palestine (PFLP), one of the most extremist and fanatical of the Palestinian resistance movements. The philosophy of action of the small Japanese group provided Dr. George Habache with an unexpected opportunity to internationalize his terrorist action against the Hebrew state. At once he dispatched his right-hand man, Bassam Tawfiq Sherif, to Pyongyang with orders to rally the hijackers to the PFLP cause.

Young Fusako and her comrades did not have to be asked twice before accepting the Palestinian emissary's invitation. They caught a plane to Lebanon. The trip was almost a honeymoon for the young Japanese terrorist who, in Pyongyang, had just married one of her companions, the electronics student Tekishi Okudeira. Once in the Lebanese capital, her prime concern was to arrange for her group's cooperation with the PFLP. Press correspondents in Beirut would find in their mail a manifesto typed on a sheet of paper with no heading or address. Many of them tossed it in the wastepaper basket. Some, more perceptive, added it to their files relating to Mideast terrorism. "The Japanese Red Army wishes to consolidate a revolutionary alliance with the PFLP against the imperialists of the world," the document stated. "It is committing itself to intensifying and speeding up international revolutionary violence to combat the Israeli enemy, in cooperation with the Palestinian terrorist organization. We accuse the Japanese government of pretending to be neutral in the Mideast conflict when it is secretly helping the Israelis against the Arabs."

The young Japanese woman then obtained a subsidy to make a film about Palestinian resistance and the activities of the PFLP. It was called *The Japanese Red Army and the PFLP—A Declaration of War on the World*. This surprising report was shown in Japan to many extremist left-wing groups, notably in the universities. One such showing took place in a classroom belonging to the agronomy department of the faculty of Kagoshima, in the south of the island of Kyushu. In the audience was a boy of twenty-two with crew-cut hair, a frail, timid look and features that were almost feminine. His only known passion was hunting butterflies.

Kozo Okamoto was the youngest of five children of a retired schoolmaster in the small city of Kagoshima. The Red Army and its revolutionary ideology were not unknown to him: his elder brother, Takeshi, belonged to the Pyongyang commando. He professed unlimited admiration for this big brother who had urged him to join the ranks of the movement. But avenging the Palestinians and fighting for the elimination of Israel seemed objectives very far removed from the preoccupations of a future forestry engineer in his native Japan. In any case, he still had vivid memories of a film that portrayed the situation of the Jews not as villains but as victims. Without water or food, crammed into the holds and decks of an old tub called the *Exodus*, several thousand survivors of Hitler's gas chambers had fought for freedom, trying to return to the land from which the PFLP now wanted to drive them away. His brother's repeated appeals did not, however, leave him unmoved. Like many other young Japanese who wanted to escape the frenzied Americanization of their society, Kozo Okamoto had turned to his country's familiar myths. He had devoured works extolling the cult of the warrior, the cult of suicide in the service of an ideal and some of the acts of rebellion that had occurred in the country's recent history. He had been particularly influenced by the message of one young intellectual whose spectacular suicide by the sword two years earlier had traumatized millions of his compatriots.

Although at the opposite end of the political spectrum to the leftist Red Army, the right-wing writer Yukio Mishima had also extolled that supreme virtue the Japanese call *makoto*, meaning "sincerity, authenticity, integrity." His books denounced corruption, spiritual emptiness, obsession with material wealth and oblivion of the makoto and of the other virtues rooted in the Japanese soul. *The Sea of Fertility*, his final tetralogy, summed up his thinking. "To know and not act is not enough," he wrote, "and in order to act there is no need of any guarantee of success. It is enough to have the soul of a *heishi*, the soul of a warrior." Before committing suicide, the writer had appealed to the disillusioned officers and soldiers in the new Japanese army. "Our ancestors' country now finds itself plummeted into a spiritual abyss," he warned them. "It has repudiated its fundamental values and lost its national spirit. And we have stood by with our arms folded, watching as the Japanese themselves profane our traditions."

Like so many of his fellow countrymen, Kozo Okamoto had been deeply affected by this moving farewell. And now, two years later, his elder brother was offering him the opportunity to prove that he, too, had the soul of a *heishi*. How could he decline such an invitation? He signed a commitment to join the movement. At the beginning of February 1972 he received a visit from a PFLP agent who handed him several hundred dollars and a plane ticket for Beirut via Vancouver, Montreal, New York, Paris and Rome. He would not know his mission until he reached his destination.

KOZO OKAMATO TOOK OFF from Tokyo on February 29, 1972. In Paris he visited Notre Dame Cathedral before the nostalgic aroma of shrimp in ginger coming from the Japanese restaurants lured him into the alleyways of the Latin Quarter. In Rome he toured the Forum, then sampled the charms of an African prostitute in the via Appia. If his fellow terrorists had known about this display of worldly weakness, the apprentice samurai might have been executed. The leaders of the Japanese Red Army did not take virtue lightly. Bloody purges had just been carried out on a group of militants who had gone astray in the Siberian cold of the mountains of central Japan.

Accused of halfheartedness and deviationism, fourteen of them had been tortured and executed, some of the young women simply for the fact that they had put on makeup, worn earrings or flirted with a companion. The discovery of their mutilated bodies had horrified the Japanese public and lost the Red Army's revolutionary ideal a number of sympathizers.

Fusako met Okamoto in person at Beirut airport. She had taken command of the operational cell the Red Army had set up in the Lebanese capital. She directed the traveler to a minibus where two other Japanese were waiting. One, the electronics student, Tekishi Okudeira, was Fusako's husband. The other, Yasuda Yakushi, was taking a course in architecture at the University of Kyoto. All three had been allocated to the same training unit and the same action group. Their destination was a vast area closed off behind barbed wire some miles outside Baalbek. This was the most important Arab military training camp for the Near and Middle East, where Israel's enemies of all nationalities and backgrounds came to learn the latest guerrilla warfare and terrorist techniques. The camp was commanded by one of the great figures in the PFLP, the terrorist Abu Hija, who counted among his achievements the 1969 attack in Zurich on an El Al plane. His team included Russian, Czech and Algerian instructors, experts on weapons and demolition using explosives. Like a Hollywood film studio, the camp was divided into several sections in which railway lines, bridges, houses, water towers and electrical transformers—anything that might become a target for destruction—had been built. The chief attraction among these constructions was sheltered beneath a vast hangar. It consisted of the pilot's cockpit and fuselage of a Boeing 727 reconstructed down to the very last dial and switch.

Neither the samurai of feudal Japan nor the pilots of World War II had been subjected to the intense physical and military exercise program that awaited the Japanese volunteers. With four hours of gymnastics a day, commando training and sabotage operations under real fire, instruction in handling automatic weapons and throwing grenades, and repeated courses of indoctrination—in the space of a few weeks Abu Hija's students were transformed into relentless killing machines. This did not mean that the three Japanese were any less committed to the cult of Japanese values. Every evening, after letting loose their last round of fire at a dummy sporting a Star of David, they would rediscover their poetic souls and their love of nature. Swapping their Kalashnikovs for bamboo sticks, they went off in pursuit of butterflies across the scorched country-side. In the absence of nets, they tied the checkered kaffiyeh they used as headdresses onto the end of their bamboo sticks. Then, when darkness cloaked the plain, they would sit down on a stone to study the celestial vault and its myriad stars. These were, Okamoto would tell me, "really ecstatic moments during which each of us could meditate like a *haiku* poet on the ephemeral character of the life of the butterfly."

One evening as they were contemplating the sky with spe-cial concentration, a childhood memory came to Okamoto's mind. In his country, parents often told their children that when they died they would go up into the sky to become a star. He remembered his mother promising him that he would be-come a star in the constellation Orion.

"We must all three become stars in Orion," he suddenly an-nounced to his comrades.

The idea appealed to them greatly. Okudeira, Fusako's hus-band, however, was concerned.

"Do you think the people we're going to kill will also be-come stars?" he asked.

"Certainly," replied Okamoto. "A fair number of them, at any rate. Don't worry: there will be lots of stars in the sky and the revolutionary war will be a constant source of new ones."

AFTER EIGHTY DAYS of rigorous training, the three Japanese were at last informed of the nature of their mission. It was to be an act of blatant terrorism, its sole object to kill and spread ter-ror. The commando would first go to Frankfurt where mem-bers of the Baader-Meinhof terrorist group would provide them with new passports and false identities. Then they would travel to Rome to collect sports bags that concealed the automatic weapons, ammunition and grenades they would need for their mission. All they had to do then was catch the first commercial airplane to Lod, Israel's international airport, close to Tel Aviv. Once there, they would collect their bags from the conveyor belt at baggage claim. As soon as they were in possession of their weapons, they would open fire on the passengers. It was a suicide operation in the purest Japanese tradition. Under no circumstances were the kamikazes to fall into the hands of the Israelis alive. They were to perish with their victims, directing the last round of fire at their own heads. The order came from Fusako herself. In her revolutionary madness the young woman did not hesitate to sacrifice the man she had just married.

ON MAY 22 THE TRIO TOOK OFF from Beirut for Frankfurt, where a member of the Baader-Meinhof group was waiting for them with new passports. From then on, Kozo Okamoto was known as Daisuke Namba.

They left Frankfurt on board a Simplon Express train which deposited them in Rome at one o'clock in the morning on Friday May 26. A taxi took them to the Anglo-American Hotel, not far from the Piazza di Spagna, where their local contact had booked two rooms for them.

AT TEN O'CLOCK ON THAT SAME MAY 26 a black Mercedes, stripped of its diplomatic plates for security reasons, rolled up at the entrance to the French Foreign Office in the Quai d'Orsay in Paris. Inside was the Israeli ambassador to France. A former member of the Mossad secret service, Asher Ben Natan cultivated the art of intelligence-gathering as if it were a religion. He had an appointment with Hervé Alphand, the ministry's secretary-general, to pass on an urgent message. His government actually wanted to ask the French authorities to drastically step up security measures on all Air France flights to Israel.

"We have good reason to believe the Palestinian guerrillas are on the point of taking violent action against Israel," the ambassador warned.

He explained that "a suspect terrorist organization is preparing to introduce arms and explosives into Israel in luggage traveling in the holds of aircraft destined for the Hebrew state."

Alphand was eager to reassure his visitor. He was in a position to tell him that, as far as France was concerned, Israel's fears were unjustified. He refrained from providing any explanation for this assurance. It was, however, well founded. Alphand knew that as a token of gratitude for its pro-Arab politics, his government had received a solemn guarantee that Palestinian terrorism would not use Air France planes in its fight against Israel.

AS SOON AS THE ROME offices opened on that same May 26, the three Japanese went to the American Express agency to change the wad of dollars they had brought from Beirut into Italian lire and buy air tickets for Tel Aviv. The first available flight was with Air France on Tuesday May 30 at 8:05 P.M.

Shortly afterward they received an order to check into the Scaligera boardinghouse on the via Nazionale, where they would receive the packages they were expecting. The establishment was occupied almost exclusively by Arab clients. Even the breakfast menu was written in the language of Muhammad. They had no sooner checked into their room than there came a knock on the door. A messenger delivered three zip-up sports bags. Each contained a Czech V-258 7.62-caliber submachine gun, about thirty magazines and twenty Soviet F1 grenades the size of oranges, laid out in a box. Enough to carry out a massacre.

On that same Tuesday, just before 5:00 P.M., they climbed into a taxi headed for Fiumicino Airport. The check-in formalities for the Air France flight from Rome to Tel Aviv took only a matter of moments. The hostess paid no particular attention to the luggage belonging to the three passengers who looked like sportsmen off to some competition. The bags disappeared on the conveyor belt, their labels bearing the initials of Israel's international airport. The three men then passed without hindrance through the metal detector gate, showed their brand-new passports at the border police control and sat down at gate number 44. At Fiumicino, Air France had its passengers boarded by an Italian company that specialized in this kind of service. They never examined the contents of checked-in baggage unless an airline asked them to. Air France had not made any request of this kind for its flight AF-132 on that thirtieth of May. Their negligence was all the more surprising because, two days earlier, a Lebanese woman passenger on one of the airline's flights to Beirut had been picked up at a metal detector gate in possession of two large-caliber revolvers, one hidden under her armpit, the other attached to her thigh. She claimed she was taking the weapons to her father so he could defend himself against the wolves that ran rampant over the Lebanese mountain where he lived. The police later suspected that she had been assigned to test the sensitivity of the metal detector.

The computer had allocated the three Japanese seats in the same row at the back of the Boeing 727. Shortly after takeoff, Okamoto sank into deep meditation. He reflected upon his imminent death. He pictured the sophisticated ceremony surrounding the death of the samurai of historic Japan. At the end of the previous century, a number of knights had committed suicide by plunging their swords into their bellies, to show their opposition to the Westernization of their country. In memory of the storm that in the year 1281 sent the invading Mongol vessels to the bottom of the sea, thus saving Japan from catastrophe, these defenders of orthodoxy had given their

movement the romantic name of Divine Wind. To put an end
to the hecatomb of suicides, the government of the time had
been obliged to ban the possession of swords. But the sacrifices
of the knights of the Divine Wind had forever glorified the
myth of suicide in the Japanese imagination. At the end of
World War II, as the specter of defeat loomed large, this myth
induced thousands of young pilots to offer their lives in their
turn. As his plane bore him to a similar destiny, Okamoto felt
he was heir to the knights of the Divine Wind. In Japanese this
poetic concept was known as *kamikaze*.

The arrival of a flight attendant with the meal trays brought
the young man back down to a more prosaic reality. He hesitated. Was it appropriate in the circumstances to lower himself
to taking earthly food? Did the moral code of the samurai have
anything to say on the subject? Okamoto recalled that, one day
in 1877, a knight from Kyushu, his native island, had considered this very point before his own suicide. Finally he decided
to eat a generous lunch, at the risk of presenting the repugnant
spectacle of his entrails spewing out his meal when he punc-
tured his stomach.

"We all three summoned up our courage and shared our last
meal," Okamoto would admit to me, "and we even washed it
down with a beer."

A few minutes later Okamoto got up and headed for the toilets at the back of the plane. While he was urinating a bizarre
anecdote came to his mind. It was an episode from the 1905
Russo-Japanese War. During the decisive naval battle in which
the two enemy fleets confronted each other, the Japanese commander in chief, Admiral Togo, directed operations from the
bridge of his cruiser, the *Mikasa*. At a moment of great danger,
the admiral's second-in-command wanted to check his leader's
state of mind. He slid his hand furtively between the admiral's
legs and found to his relief that his testicles were hanging as
normally as ever. The admiral was manifestly calm. Reassured,
the officer promptly returned to his post. Okamoto noted with
shame that his own testicles were not hanging the way those of
the admiral's had. Nervousness had retracted and hardened
them like small hazelnuts about to burst.

A Journey to Hell

The lights of Tel Aviv soon appeared beneath the wings. In response to instructions, issued in three different languages, the
passengers returned to their seats. Okamoto recognized one of
the languages as English and knew that on an Air France flight
another must be French. What about the third? Out of courtesy
to the sixty-eight Spanish-speaking Puerto Ricans in economy
class that evening, the hostess had repeated the landing instructions in Spanish. These passengers had come straight
from the Caribbean island for a ten-day visit to the main sanctuaries in the Holy Land. They were sugarcane and tobacco
planters, businessmen, civil servants, white-collar workers, students and retired people. The oldest was seventy-two; the
youngest fourteen. Their guide was an athletic-looking secondary school teacher of twenty-eight, who was a leading light
in the island's Baptist community. José Muñoz had already
been on pilgrimage to Jerusalem twice and had sworn to show
his young wife, Nilda, and his friends the holy sites. All were
united in the same worship of Christ, the same craving to see
where the Messiah had spent his earthly life, the same impatience to set foot in the Holy Land.

The plane flew over the orange orchards bordering the coastline and described a large circle in the air. With their faces
pressed to the windows, José Vega, aged thirty-six, and his
young wife, Vastiliza, gazed enraptured at the darkness studded with lights. José was the minister at the Methodist church
in Arecibo, Puerto Rico's second-largest city. Below his white
collar, in the left pocket of his shirt, was the small prayer book
he had read every day for the last twelve years. Was it not in
this part of Palestine that Saint Peter cursed Aeneas, the lame
man? Here that Saint Paul stopped off on the road to
Jerusalem? Here again, that Saint George was born and that his
martyred remains lay? Here that the wise men of Israel had at
one time set up their yeshivas, that the Roman legions had
camped and that Richard the Lion-Hearted's crusaders had regrouped before mounting their attack on Judea?

A few seats behind them, thirty-year-old Juan Padilla and his

wife, Carmen, both members of the Church of the Disciples of
Christ, were also scouring the darkness. Devotees of biblical
history, they told themselves the plane must surely be passing
over the valley of Sorek, where Delilah was born and where
Samson's foxes set fire to the Philistines' crops with their burning tails. Juan Larroy, a bearded insurance representative of
twenty-eight, wondered to himself if Lod airport had not been
built on the plain where Joshua stopped the sun. Juan had not
made this journey solely for religious reasons. He was secretly
in love; the object of his passion, a striking young woman with
green eyes, was sitting in the seat next to him. Her name was
Carmen Crespo. This journey to the Holy Land was a gift from
her parents: Carmen had just celebrated her twentieth birthday. When Juan Larroy found out about her birthday, he had
rushed to book himself a ticket too. He meant to declare his
love for her in Jerusalem.

The landing was greeted with applause and cheers. Then all
the pilgrims sang the well-known hymn in praise of Jerusalem,
"Ciudad de Dios." As soon as the doors opened, the marvelous
scent of orange blossoms filled the plane. The night was fra-
grant with it. Teacher Matilda Guzman paused on the steps to
take a deep breath. "It was as if we were arriving in paradise on
earth," student Sonia Ortiz would say. Kozo Okamoto himself
was amazed. Eighty days of inhuman training had not blunted
his love of nature. He filled his lungs. Then, pushed by
Okudeira, pretty Fusako's husband, he shot down the rear
steps as fast as he could. The three Japanese were the first to
reach the arrivals terminal and presented themselves immediately at the police control. Before making for the baggage claim
to wait for their bags, the Japanese went and locked themselves
in the toilets, as they had been instructed in Beirut. They took
out the two pages of their passports bearing their names and
photographs and tore them into several dozen small pieces,
which they flushed down the toilet. Whatever happened, even
their false identity must remain unknown to the Israelis.

It was 10:25 P.M. No one noticed the three Asians who had
taken up their positions on the far side of the luggage carousel
to wait for the arrival of their bags. They did not have to wait

long. The first pieces of luggage to come out were those belonging to the passengers who had boarded in Rome. The three bags full of arms followed in single file. Okamoto and his comrades rushed at them. Like automatons, they went through the motions they had repeated so often at the Baalbek camp: they undid the zippers, grabbed hold of the automatic weapons and magazines and stuffed their pockets full of grenades. The unusual group attracted the attention of several passengers. Engineer Medina thought to himself that the young men were playing some kind of joke. Scientist Aaron Kamir from the Weizman Institute in Rehovot thought they were actors there to make a film. Vastiliza Vega, the Methodist minister's wife, actually realized that the submachine guns were not toys. "They're going to kill us!" she cried. Those were her last words. One of the terrorists had jumped onto the framework of the conveyor belt and opened fire point-blank. Hit in the head, the young Puerto Rican woman fell to the ground. The bullet that should have lodged itself in her husband's heart was miraculously deflected by the small prayer book that rarely left the pocket of his shirt.

All hell had broken loose. The Japanese tossed their grenades over the surrounding heads, aimed their gunfire at the groups of people waiting for their suitcases and continued firing as bodies fell like bowling pins. The cries and groans, the noise of the explosions, the smell of powder and sulfur—in less than a minute the baggage claim area looked like a scene from the Apocalypse. Juan Larroy, the Puerto Rican insurance representative, would never declare his love to his beloved. Carmen had been torn to shreds by the first burst of gunfire. The student Sonia Ortiz should have suffered the same fate. But on leaving the police control, she had gone to the ladies' room to touch up her hair. When she heard the gunfire and explosions she remarked to herself in surprise: "Goodness, they're welcoming us with fireworks like they do in San Juan." Then several screaming and blood-spattered passengers burst into the room seeking refuge. Thinking they were being followed by the killers, some set their backs against the door while others collapsed to their knees and prayed. God seemed to have abandoned the terminal of Lod airport. Twenty-two-year-old Olga Navedo had been about to take a photograph of a group of friends when the shooting started. Instinctively she had thrown herself flat on her stomach. Bodies fell on top of her, forming a shield. Grenade blasts had wounded her exposed feet and ankles. As soon as she could extricate herself, she started to crawl toward the exit at the far end of the terminal. Suddenly a strange object caught her eye. It was a foot in a shoe, a foot belonging to her Aunt Luz, who lay dead beside her in a pool of blood.

By a reflex action Cristina Matos, who had come to the Holy Land to fulfill her promise to bury her husband's ashes on the Mount of Olives, had protected her face with her handbag. After a moment she felt warm liquid on her fingers and realized she was bleeding profusely. The bullet that should have hit her straight in the head had gone through her hand before lodging itself in her powder compact.

The Japanese were leaping about from one side of the terminal to the other, firing frenziedly. It was as if they were trying to kill themselves even as they destroyed their victims. A burst of bullets in fact hit Yasuda, the architecture student from Kyoto, who had rashly moved in front of his companions. He let out a roar before toppling forward, dead. Almost out of his mind, Fusako's husband put down his submachine gun and took two grenades out of his pocket to avenge his comrade. To get a better aim, he climbed onto the edge of the conveyor belt, but a sudden jolt of the machinery made him lose his balance. In the process of righting himself he let go of one of the projectiles. The grenade exploded and blew his head off. Okamoto was left on his own. Climbing over the corpses of his comrades, he made a dash for the glass partition behind which the panic-stricken families and friends of the passengers were waiting. He emptied two magazines. The glass shattered under a constellation of gunfire. People collapsed, screaming. The Japanese returned to his starting point, took a fresh supply of grenades out of his bag and stuffed them into his pockets, jumped onto the baggage conveyor and left by the hatchway through which the luggage arrived. Seeing a plane that was just lining itself up on the tarmac, he opened fire on the cockpit and threw two grenades at the engines.

From a hiding place behind a container, El Al engineer Nahum Zaiton had witnessed the attack. When the terrorist came level with him, he hurled himself at the Japanese and rolled him to the ground. Police and soldiers came running from all sides. As a guard rushed at Okamoto, the young man turned the barrel of his submachine gun to his chest and pulled the trigger. The gun went "click." The magazine was empty. Next he tried to take the pin out of a grenade in his pocket, but the lightning intervention of another police officer prevented him. The *heishi* warrior had failed. He would not enter the paradise of the knights of the Divine Wind. He had not succeeded in committing suicide.

The massacre had lasted less than three minutes. One hundred and thirty-eight cartridge cases would be found on the ground. George Habache and the widowed Fusako could congratulate themselves: they had struck Israel right in the heart. Their butchery had killed thirty-two people and injured seventy-two, some very seriously. Some survivors would have legs amputated, others would remain disfigured; yet others would be permanently blind.

As the country's main international civil airport, Lod was subject to constant surveillance. Within minutes, security forces had closed off the whole sector and occupied sensitive targets such as the control tower, the fuel depot and the telecommunications center. General Rehavan Zeevi, a forty-six-year-old colossus, arrived on the scene very swiftly. Zeevi commanded the central Israeli military region which included the airport, but he was better known in the army for his nickname, Gandhi, because of a collection of poems the Mahatma's ideal of nonviolence had inspired him to write. The apocalyptic vision that awaited him that night was a brutal negation of that ideal.

The tangled bodies of the dead and dying, groans and cries

for help in every language from the living, the unbearable
stench of blood and burning, the scattered clouds of smoke
from the explosions, the suitcases torn to pieces—all the ingredients of horror came together in that Israeli airport building.
Unaware that two of the assassins were dead and the third captured, passenger Alejandro Rivera was still convinced he would
die in that slaughterhouse. He wanted, at all costs, to get away.
His wife and he had taken cover behind a soda machine. Taking advantage of the smoke screen emitted by a grenade that
had fallen in front of their hiding place, Alejandro grabbed his
wife and ran for the exit. Arriving outside miraculously un-
scathed, the Riveras dived straight into a taxi.

"The Saint George Hotel in Jerusalem, quickly!" Alejandro
cried.

Seeing the Israeli police trying to protect the last terrorist
from the furious crowd, another Puerto Rican passenger
thought he was going to be lynched. The son of Caribbean Indians, with his jet-black hair, prominent cheekbones and slit
eyes, he looked distinctly Asian.

When the first Israeli soldiers appeared, Regina Filiciano, a
retired schoolteacher from San Juan, was panic-stricken. She
thought they were more terrorists coming to finish off the survivors. Deciding not to wait to find out, she fled toward the
exit. "My old legs bore me along like a winged horse," she
would say. While she was running a Psalm came into her head.
"A thousand may fall at your side, ten thousand at your right
hand, but you will be spared," she recited with fervor.

THE ARMY HAD TAKEN control of the airport and temporarily interrupted air traffic. General Zeevi, alias Gandhi, was in a
hurry. He was conscious of being responsible for the lives of
thousands of passengers due to arrive at or depart from Lod airport over the next few hours. The massacre in the baggage
claim area might only be a prelude to other more extensive and
murderous acts of terror. The only way to prevent further

tragedy was to induce the only survivor of the commando unit to talk. But the frail young man with the downcast eyes brought before the Israeli general did not look at all like his idea of a terrorist. He had withdrawn into a sepulchral silence, and the only document found on him, a Japanese passport, contained neither photograph nor any indication of his civilian status. Zeevi had the Japanese ambassador to Tel Aviv awakened, to get him to send an interpreter urgently. Then he had Okamoto taken to baggage claim where doctors and nurses were caring for the wounded. Suddenly the Japanese caught sight of the headless body of his comrade Okudeira. The horrific vision broke him. He collapsed, moaning. A little farther on, he recognized the body of Yasuda, his chest perforated by his own comrades' bullets. All three were wearing the same belt with a gilded buckle, a fact that Zeevi saw as confirmation that they belonged to the same commando group.

Back in the office being used as the general's command station, Okamoto no longer showed any sign of emotion. With his head hung, his eyes closed and a face that was set and totally devoid of expression, the terrorist remained obstinately mute. Several hours elapsed. Air traffic was flowing again. Apart from the marks of impact on the walls and glass screens, the baggage claim area looked much as it usually did. The general and his officers were desperately trying to interrogate their prisoner. The interpreter did his best. But neither entreaties nor threats could get him to utter a sound. Suddenly, after six hours, there was an unexpected breakthrough. Emerging abruptly from his torpor, Okamoto made a sign that he wanted a pencil and a piece of paper. "I request that I be taken outside and executed, or else be allowed to commit suicide," he wrote carefully. The general saw this as an opportunity to strike a deal. He asked his officers to leave and remained alone with the prisoner and the interpreter. Seizing the enormous Colt revolver hanging from his waist, he placed it on the table in front of him. With a slowness designed to underline the significance of the gesture, he released the cylinder and removed the bullets one by one. When the small metallic container was completely empty, he chambered a single round. Afterward he put the magazine back in its housing. He then flourished the revolver under the eyes of the Japanese, who had followed his every move with rapt attention.

"In exchange for a complete and honest confession, I'll give you this revolver and the bullet in it to commit suicide," he announced.

"Offering him that deal was like waving a magic wand," General Zeevi was to say. Okamoto instantly snapped out of his apathy. Convinced he had betrayed his Divine Wind idols by escaping death, he now thought he would be able to rejoin them and die like a *heishi* warrior. Zeevi stipulated that Okamoto begin his written confession with a solemn pledge that he would not use the weapon against anyone other than himself. Simultaneously translated, the Japanese prisoner's answers allayed the general's fears. No other terrorist acts against the airport were in the process of execution or even preparation. Zeevi was immediately able to reassure Prime Minister Golda Meir and her minister of transport, Shimon Peres, who had come rushing to the scene of the disaster area after visiting the wounded in various hospital emergency rooms, and were now waiting in a nearby room.

Soon Okamoto's confession extended to nine long paragraphs. It provided valuable information, particularly with regard to what had motivated the three Japanese to become kamikazes for the Palestinians. But it did not reveal all the secrets of the tragedy. What was more, Zeevi exposed several lies in Okamoto's story, which released him from having to honor the contract he had made with the prisoner. When Okamoto had finished, Zeevi put his Colt back in its holster and handed the terrorist over to the police.

"A crime to which no name has yet been given"

Other than Egypt and Syria, where the Israeli airport massacre was applauded by political leaders and many journalists, the tragedy stunned the whole world. That the killers were citizens of a country unconnected with the Israeli-Palestinian conflict and their victims were innocent tourists equally uninvolved in the Mideast drama made the Lod tragedy particularly odious. One of the first Japanese reactions came from Okamoto's father. In a letter to the Israeli ambassador to Tokyo, the former schoolmaster expressed his consternation at what his son had done. "For forty years I believed I had devoted myself loyally to the education of our young people," he wrote. "I see that I have been mistaken. I beg you to punish my son without delay by condemning him to death."

Naturally, in Israel itself outrage was at its peak. The whole of the Knesset rose to observe a minute of silence as a tribute to "the innocent dead." Her voice choked with anger, Golda Meir condemned "the Arabs who are so lacking in courage themselves that they are obliged to recruit foreigners to do their dirty work." She demanded an international air boycott of Lebanon and bluntly castigated "the state that harbors and encourages the planning of such crimes."

Israel locked Kozo Okamoto away in the maximum-security cell in Ramla prison that had been specially fitted out for the most famous prisoner tried within its frontiers, the Nazi leader Adolf Eichmann. Okamoto was chained and stripped of any clothing or item he might use to kill himself. Army units were brought in to reinforce the prison guards. The country was resolved to take advantage of the general emotion to try the surviving coauthor of the dreadful slaughter very quickly. Opinion was divided as to the punishment he warranted. A large proportion of the population thought the Japanese deserved to die. Israel did have the death penalty. Its application was governed by the law relating to Nazi war crimes and by an exceptional ruling instituted under the British Mandate to deal with terrorist offenses. The ultimate punishment could therefore be invoked in the case of the Japanese prisoner. Other than in Eichmann's case, the death sentence had been passed only three times since the birth of the state, in all three instances against Arab terrorists. For security reasons, however, in each instance, capital punishment had been commuted to life imprisonment. The risk of creating martyrs or provoking reprisals had seemed too great.

The trial opened on July 12, 1972, under the blinding glare of television lights and surrounded by exceptional security. Neither the implacable charge read by the colonel presiding over the trial, nor the poignant roll call of the names of the thirty-two people who died on the fatal night, nor the description of the mutilation suffered by the injured, nor the display of prosecution exhibits (automatic weapons, grenade fragments, etc.) provoked the slightest reaction on the Japanese prisoner's face. All this commotion was no concern of his. He looked so vacant, in fact, that the policeman to whom he was shackled had to shake his arm constantly to make him follow the proceedings. But appearances were deceptive. Since death had insulted him by rejecting him, he would have his revenge by turning his trial into a useful propaganda exercise. The very first time Okamoto met with his defense counsel, his lawyer realized he would receive no cooperation from his client. Convinced that only a lunatic could commit so heinous a crime, lawyer Max Kritzman told the tribunal he was going to plead insanity; instantly Okamoto snapped out of his false torpor and leapt about like a fiend. Fists clenched and eyes blazing, he burst out: "I am of perfectly sound mind! I assume on my own behalf and on behalf of my comrades full responsibility for the events that took place at the airport. I reject my defense counsel's claim that I should undergo psychiatric tests."

Kritzman cast about for another way to save his client's neck. Since inquiries had been unable to certify Okamoto's exact age, Kritzman assured the judges that the accused's very youthful appearance suggested he was considerably younger than twenty-one, which meant that he should be referred to a juvenile court. Again, his Japanese client reacted violently.

"I'm twenty-four. I was born on February 25, 1948!" he shouted in a voice as staccato as the report of his automatic weapon he had wielded the evening of the tragedy.

The Israeli lawyer persisted with his impossible task. "My client is a strange person with bizarre ideas," he pleaded. "To condemn him to death would make a martyr of him. Hanging him would not be in the interests of either Israel or the world.

We have today the opportunity to demonstrate our generosity and magnanimity."

To the outrage of a large section of Israeli opinion and the stupefaction of observers, especially the Japanese diplomats and press correspondents, the prosecution promptly opted for a similar magnanimous line.

"The moral perversion of the accused and his associates requires us to call upon our own strength to restrain ourselves from asking, even in this dreadful case, for the full rigor of the law," declared the prosecuting colonel in his indictment, before concluding: "I know, gentlemen, that what I am asking of you goes beyond the bounds of human generosity. It would be inconceivable to ask for such moderation on another occasion. But we hope that there will not be another occasion."

Paradoxically the accused's aggressive comments inclined the tribunal to clemency. When a judge asked Okamoto why "Japanese soldiers" had carried out the attack, and not Arab terrorists, Okamoto replied: "Our action in conjunction with the Arabs is just a means to move our organization onto the international scene. Tomorrow the Red Army will spread the revolutionary war throughout the world."

To another judge who expressed his revulsion at the thirty-two deaths at Lod, the Japanese explained calmly that "war always involves massacres and destruction." In his final statement he made several references to Vietnam, "whose people wept for the world," and to the American Black Panthers, who were "marking out the route for a worldwide revolution." Curiously enough, out of the ninety minutes it took to deliver this carefully prepared statement, there was no mention of the Arab-Israeli conflict for which he and his comrades had been prepared to lay down their lives.

Kozo Okamoto escaped Adolf Eichmann's lot. He was condemned to life imprisonment. His judges considered that, unlike the Nazi leader, he had not expressed destructive impulses against the Jews as a people, but against human society in general, by an undertaking designed to change the world's social structures. In a country as organized as Japan, the president of the tribunal explained, he and his comrades had had little chance of realizing their ambitions. They had therefore turned to foreign political and military groups likely to provide them with the springboard they needed for their goal of "spreading," in the accused's own words, "the revolutionary war throughout the world." It was not a question of genocide—the elimination of a people—but of a new and bigger crime to which no name has yet been given.

The Japanese stood at attention listening to the tribunal's reasons without the slightest display of emotion. When it came to the announcement of the verdict, however, Okamoto suddenly discovered that he was being robbed of the death he believed he warranted. Yelping like an injured animal, he threw himself to the ground, sobbing.

DESPITE KOZO OKAMOTO'S incarceration behind the walls of Ramla's prison, the Japanese terrorist continued making headlines. Throughout the Arab world he became a sort of idolized martyr of the Arab-Israeli conflict. On the bodies of the fedayeen killed trying to infiltrate themselves into Israel, authorities found leaflets demanding his immediate release.

THE JAPANESE RED ARMY based in Lebanon continued to be very active. Fusako Shinegobu, the movement's *passionaria* who had unhesitatingly sacrificed her young husband in the Lod massacre, sent a letter to the *Asahi Shimbun*, the biggest Tokyo daily, informing the world that a Japanese commando was planning a spectacular terrorist attack to snatch their fellow countryman from his Israeli jailers. The management of IATA, the International Air Transport Association, received several messages threatening reprisals in many of the world's airports if the Israelis refused to release their prisoner.

Kept in ignorance of all the activity he was inspiring, the prisoner spent solitary but studious days in his spacious cell. As soon as he had been locked up he had asked for books to learn Hebrew and make a start on English, along with works about the Jewish religion. For a while his progress in the language of the Prophets and the language of Shakespeare remained somewhat halting, but it was not long before his passionate interest in Judaism gave rise to considerable alarm among his guards. One morning they came upon their prisoner bleeding profusely from an intimate part of his anatomy. Okamoto had tried to perform the symbolic act that through the spilling of blood, sanctifies the alliance of the Jewish people with the God Jehovah. He had tried to circumcise himself with nail clippers but had only succeeded in wounding himself. He was taken to the infirmary, where he duly underwent a proper circumcision, this time at the hands of a Jewish doctor.

In 1976 the Ramla stronghold received yet another prisoner of note. Sentenced to twelve years' imprisonment for smuggling weapons in the trunk of his diplomatic Mercedes, Monsignor Hilarion Capucci, archbishop of Jerusalem, was locked up in a cell close to the Japanese prisoner's. Their unexpected cohabitation gave the circumcised kamikaze an opportunity to discover the rites of another religion that had sprung to life in Palestine, a land so rich in spirituality and so close to God. The prelate also helped to further his young neighbor's knowledge of English and encouraged him to work in one of the prison workshops. The fingers that had triggered the deadly rounds of fire set to work weaving camouflage cloth for the Israeli army. Okamoto's choice of occupation was probably not entirely accidental, the art of dissimulation being one of the cardinal virtues of the heroes of the kabuki theater he admired so much. In any case a mysterious voice put a swift end to his weaving. The prisoner told his jailers one morning that, during the night, the Messiah had ordered him to stop all manual work and devote himself exclusively to the study of psalms in praise of him.

On May 20, 1985, nearly thirteen years after being sentenced to life imprisonment, Kozo Okamoto was abruptly removed from the cell where I had met him. His guards had him climb into a bus parked in the prison courtyard. It was full of Arab prisoners. Arranged by Austrian Chancellor Bruno Kreisky after twelve hundred hours of secret negotiations, the exchange of three Israeli soldiers for some 4,600 Palestinians and Lebanese detained by Israel had just begun. Naturally Kozo Okamoto's name was on the lists presented by the leaders of the Palestinian Liberation Popular Front, one of the principal participants in the negotiations. A few moments later the Japanese walked impassively through the same airport terminal that in May 1972 he and his comrades had turned into a human abattoir. He was placed on board a plane bound for Geneva, where he was transferred onto a special Boeing 747 sent by Libyan dictator Muammar Gaddafi. Thousands of enthusiastic Libyans waving olive branches were waiting for the Japanese and his 394 Arab comrades on their arrival in Tripoli. Under the lenses of the entire world's television cameras, Ahmed Jibril, head of the Action Branch of the PFLP and principal organizer of Arab terrorist activities in the world, clasped the former botany student in his arms.

Okamoto's release brought the Israeli government plaintive protestations from the Japanese minister for foreign affairs, Shintaro Abe. On behalf of his government, he regretted a gesture that in his view could only encourage international terrorism. Anxious to preserve their good relations with Tokyo, the Israelis apologized: setting Okamoto free had been the sine qua non condition of the release of three of their soldiers held by the Syrians.

The Japanese Red Army leaders based in Beirut decided to send the Japanese away, at least provisionally. They feared an action against him from the Jerusalem secret services. They begged China and North Korea to take him, but neither of those two countries would agree to give the former terrorist asylum. As for Japan, the government made it clear that Kozo Okamoto would be arrested immediately and brought before a special tribunal if he ever set foot in Japan. In the absence of a better destination, it was eventually in Damascus, which was already serving as a refuge for several major Nazi war criminals and a number of terrorists, that the coauthor of the Lod killings came to hide. He lived there, relatively forgotten, for several years. Then he returned to Lebanon to go into definitive retirement.

Alerted to his presence by the Israeli secret service, the Japanese government at once put pressure on Lebanon to arrest the refugee, along with the handful of former Japanese Red Army terrorists still at large in the area. Tokyo had no qualms about "buying" these arrests.

During a visit to the Japanese capital, a high official in one of Beirut's intelligence services allowed himself to be persuaded, in exchange for hard cash, to pick up Okamoto and four of his former comrades and have them indicted at once. The trial opened in Beirut on June 9, 1997. Some thirty Lebanese and Palestinian organizations, among them Hezbollah and the Lebanese branch of the Ba'th Party in power in Damascus, rose against the indictment of these militants of the "Palestinian just cause." No fewer than 136 Syrian and Libyan lawyers came forward to defend them. In a collective communiqué the defense lawyers described Okamoto as "an Arab hero" and "a strategist who had understood the oneness of the struggle against Israel." While waiting for a judgment which seemed unlikely to be passed for months or even years, Okamoto and his comrades announced that they would kill themselves if Lebanon decided to extradite them to Japan.

At the end of May 1997, on the occasion of the twenty-fifth anniversary of the killings at Tel Aviv airport, the white-haired former botany student and retired terrorist ordered flowers and cakes to be delivered to his cell.

10

"I Shall Pin You to the Spot"

"Monsieur Dominique Lapierre? The doctor would like to speak to you."

I knew at once. My Parisian urologist's secretary never expressed herself so formally. Her tone that morning confirmed what I had been so dreading.

Propelled by some mysterious stroke of intuition, my wife, Dominique, had forced me to consult a doctor. She was concerned about my general state of health. An abdominal ultrasound carried out at the Saint-Tropez clinic, together with a specific blood test, had revealed some slight anomalies relating to my prostate, a small gland beneath the bladder, the function and indeed the existence of which is a mystery to most men.

I had only heard about this organ through a most unlikely stroke of fortune. A former British general in the Indian army whom I interviewed for my book *Freedom at Midnight* had told me how he had nearly died under fire from Pathan warriors because of his prostate. Like many other British officers who had served in India, he had retired to Kashmir. When, in the aftermath of independence, fighting broke out in the province, all those elderly British gentlemen had had to be evacuated by bus. Their exodus had been dangerously retarded because the vehicles were constantly obliged to stop to allow the men to attend to an urgent call of nature. Age had dilated their prostates to a point where they were pressing on their bladders. I had sympathized with their affliction, never imagining that one day it would hit me.

The urologist in Saint-Tropez had tried to be reassuring. Every man over fifty was likely to have prostate problems, he told me. In the vast majority of cases, straightforward treatment with medication or a minor surgical operation was enough to solve the problem. In any case, the prostate was not a vital organ. Its sole function was to secrete the whitish liquid that dilutes sperm and facilitates ejaculation.

In Paris an eminent specialist had used needles to take several samples of tissue. We had then returned to Saint-Tropez to await the verdict from the pathology lab. For a week I jumped every time the telephone rang. Finally the call I had been waiting for came.

"I've just received the laboratory report," began the practitioner. "It's not very good. Two out of three of the biopsies show the presence of an adenocarcinoma."

"Of an adeno—?"

"A cancerous tumor."

"*Merde!*"

"But we appear to be dealing with a primary tumor," he was quick to add. "It isn't a metastasis of some other tumor elsewhere. What's more, it is clearly discrete and only of grade 2+2. That means it's not very aggressive. So it's less likely to spread its cancerous cells to other organs. We shall do further tests to check."

"Doctor, is my life in danger?"

There was a silence at the other end of the line. Then the reassuring voice was back: "Don't worry, my dear Monsieur Lapierre. Medicine has plenty of ammunition to throw at this kind of cancer."

The way his answer was formulated only half appeased me.

"Are you thinking of surgery?"

"Surgery, but also radiation therapy and chemotherapy. My initial reaction is probably to opt for surgery. But we'll decide when we've seen the results of the next tests."

This "we" comforted me: the doctor was involving himself with my ordeal. I rushed to the library to get my old Larousse

In three days, this condemned man will be executed

My meeting with the condemned man Caryl Chessman on death row in California's San Quentin Penitentiary was one of the most upsetting experiences of my early career. Chessman had been sentenced to the death penalty for theft, kidnapping and sexual assault, three crimes that could warrant this punishment if committed simultaneously. Chessman, who never ceased to protest his innocence, had succeeded in postponing his execution for twelve years. I managed to see him six times in the last fourteen days of his fight to escape the gas chamber. In this photo I am showing him a telegram from my editor in chief at *Paris Match*, announcing that a hundred thousand French people had signed a petition for clemency.

Going back in history with the commander of the Gross Paris regiment and Spain's most famous matador

My meeting with the American Larry Collins (on the left in the above photograph) gave rise to a stimulating and fruitful literary partnership. Our first book, *Is Paris Burning?*, reconstructed the dramatic events of the liberation of Paris. Among the twelve hundred witnesses we interviewed, we found General Dietrich von Choltitz (photographed below in the company of his wife, Uberta, and their two daughters), whom Hitler had assigned to defend and then destroy Paris.

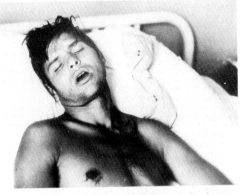

. . . *Or I'll Dress You in Mourning* took us to Spain on the trail of El Cordobés, the famous matador who was born into the horrors of the Civil War and became a billionaire. His audacity and courage—and his terrible injuries—made him the idol of a new Spain that craved freedom.

Moving encounters with the founders of Israel

Research for our book *O Jerusalem* brought us to Israel and all over the Middle East. With the help of Ehud Avriel (top left), Larry and I reconstructed the fantastic epic of the purchase of arms that, in 1948, enabled the Jewish state to survive the initial attacks of the Arab army. Golda Meir (top right), then Prime Minister, told us how she raised in the United States the thirty million dollars needed to finance these arms acquisitions. At four o'clock on May 14, 1948, beneath a large portrait of Theodor Herzl in a museum in Tel Aviv, David Ben-Gurion proclaimed the birth of the state of Israel.

A Japanese who came from the other side of the world to sow terror in Israel

Kozo Okamoto, aged twenty-three, a botany student at the University of Kagoshima, joined the ranks of the Japanese Red Army to "purge his country, and then the whole world, of its rottenness." Since revolution was not yet possible in Japan, it had to be exported. The Palestinian cause provided an ideal field of action. On his arrival in Lebanon, Okamoto was subjected to intensive terrorist training. On May 30, 1972, together with two comrades, the Japanese machine-gunned a group of pilgrims arriving from Puerto Rico in the luggage hall of Tel Aviv airport. Twenty-six were killed and twenty injured. The only survivor of the commando unit, Okamoto was interrogated by the Israeli General Zeevi, who offered him the opportunity to commit suicide in exchange for a full confession. When Zeevi did not honor the deal, the Japanese was tried and condemned to life imprisonment. I was granted exceptional permission to question Okamoto in his cell. That meeting gave me one of the biggest frights of my life.

Two idealists: one who wanted to protect wild life, another who sought to break the chains of tyranny

My meetings with Raphaël Matta, the "Saint Francis of the elephants," and with the Portuguese Henrique Galvào were unforgettable. Matta (photographed here in the thick of the bush with his children) was the chief warden of the Bouna game reserve in the northern Ivory Coast. On his arrival he recorded forty thousand antelopes, four hundred hippopotamuses, about a hundred elephants and some sixty lions. Two years later, half of that animal population had disappeared from the reserve, slaughtered by poachers and white hunters. To save the survivors, Matta, weapons in hand, decided to go underground and defend them. He was killed before he was able to carry out his plan.

To protest against the tyranny of Portuguese dictator Antonio de Oliveira Salazar and Spain's General Francisco Franco, Captain Enrique Galvào and a commando unit of twenty-five revolutionaries seized the flower of the Portuguese commercial fleet, the *Santa Maria*, with its full crew and 630 passengers on board. Hunted down by American, British, Spanish and Portuguese warships, the liner was unable to reach its destination of Angola. The adventure ended in the port of Recife, where it was my turn to "kidnap" the pirate captain to get his exclusive story. The intrepid photographer Charles Bonnay (seen here with me on the deck of the *Santa Maria*) actually parachuted onto the hostage liner to get the story.

The lovely old cars that propelled me along the highway to adventure

My sixth birthday present was a Torpedo pedal-car—my first opportunity to experience that magical feeling of wrapping my hands around a steering wheel. My adventures in it were confined to driving at top speed along the sea wall on the beach at Châtelaillon, near La Rochelle.

On my fourteenth birthday my mother gave me a real car, a 1923 Nash convertible. Alas, I had to wait two years before I was allowed to drive it. To curb my impatience, every day after school, I repaired a bit of my car. When at last I passed my driving test I set out to explore Louisiana. To pay for gasoline, I repainted letter boxes along the route.

COMBAT
L. JOURNAL DE PARIS ¶ ◀   **VENDREDI 31 AOUT**

29.000 francs les 8.000 kilomètres   Dominique Lapierre, dont les lecteurs de COMBAT connaissent déjà les aventures sur le continent américain (« Un dollar les mille kilomètres »), a achevé hier matin le raid Paris-Ankara et retour. Il a parcouru, en compagnie de son coéquipier Dominique Frémy, près de 8.000 kilomètres à bord d'un antique « Amilcar », en réalisant la performance de ne dépenser que 29.000 francs au cours de son voyage

Voici les deux héros du raid photographiés à leur arrivée place de l'Etoile

I found my third car in a junkyard near Paris: a 1927 6 CV Amilcar. The day after my final exams, I set off with my friend Dominique Frémy on a three-thousand-mile drive from Paris to Ankara. We were so heavily loaded that we had to drive hundreds of miles in reverse—a gear more powerful than first.

It was near Lafayette College in Pennsylvania, where I was a student, that for thirty dollars I purchased this 1938 Chrysler convertible. On the evening of my wedding day, I set out with my new bride, Aliette, for a 4,500-mile honeymoon across the United States and Mexico. Here we are in front of the famous Aztec sun pyramid, thirty miles from Mexico City.

Across the USSR in a Simca, and from Bombay to Ramatuelle in a Rolls-Royce: twenty-five thousand miles of dreaming, apprehension and joy

In 1956 the Soviet authorities opened a chink in the Iron Curtain to allow the Simca Marly I was driving with my friend, the photographer Jean-Pierre Pedrazzini, and our wives, to enter. This was a first. Never before had a private car containing foreign tourists been allowed to travel freely about the USSR. The state of the roads, the dreadful quality of the gasoline and the absence of bridges (the auto is pictured crossing a river in the Caucusus Mountains) often made our journey a nightmare. But the magnificent welcome the Russian people gave us wherever we went made up for the difficulties of the journey: In the center photograph an Armenian man, Georges Manoukian, kisses the French flag.

A Rolls-Royce in the open desert of Afghanistan! This was the climax of my road adventures. The car, which I had bought from the largest second-hand Rolls dealer in the world, behaved like a queen: one single flat tire and a thousand admiring salutations through all the 6,364 miles from Bombay to the entrance to the Great Pine in Ramatuelle.

In the footsteps of India's Great Soul, the last Viceroy, and the princes of the *Arabian Nights*

Reconstructing the story of the end of one of the world's great colonial empires and the subsequent freedom of four hundred million people was the literary adventure that took Larry and me to India. Lord Mountbatten opened up his archives for us and even came to my home to hand-deliver his testimony.

Twenty-eight years earlier, in the garden of his residence in New Delhi, the last Viceroy of India and his wife, Edwina, had posed for a photo with Gandhi, the elderly leader who forced the British to leave. With their departure, the 565 maharajahs (pictured below is Bupinder Singh of Patiala) lost their greatest support. After renouncing their privileges, the princes of India had to abandon their sovereignty and drop their states into the basket of Indian independence.

In Calcutta with the children who are the light of the world, and their savior from the West

By introducing me to some of this planet's most underprivileged children and the extraordinary man who saves them, India turned my life upside down. The Englishman James Stevens (top) picks up the children of lepers in the slums of Calcutta and houses them in a spacious home called Resurrection, where they are given medical care, clothing, food and education. Entry into this oasis of hope begins with a plate full of rice, lentils and chicken (above left). Every day mothers with leprosy (above right) come and beg James to take their children. Since 1981 Resurrection Home has been entirely dependent for funding on my royalties and my readers' donations.

Extraordinary triumphs are experienced each day by the staff at Resurrection Home. Next to twelve-year-old Kishore, one of the brightest residents of the home, is his leprous mother, whom my wife, Dominique, clasps in her arms (top photo). This mutilated and prematurely aged woman is not yet thirty. Because she was not treated in time, her disease has been aggravated with irreversible lesions. If it is caught in time, leprosy can be cured in a year. Mealtimes are a sacred part of the day. Before eating, the children sing grace. Plenty of healthy, high-protein food is needed to put the children back on their feet after living in the poverty of the slums.

Saints from abroad who came to bring hope

Mother Teresa (seen above in her home for the dying in Calcutta) and the Swiss doctor Gaston Grandjean (seen at right during a consultation)—the first famous, the other practically unknown—have struggled for years among the poorest of the poor to help them in their misfortune and give them cause to hope. In the slum I christened The City of Joy, their crusade has inspired thousands of people who are now giving themselves selflessly and with love, in the service of their less fortunate brothers. It was a great joy for me to be able to take Gaston to the Vatican. The head of the Roman Catholic Church and the humblest servant of the poor met to talk about the ideals of sharing and justice.

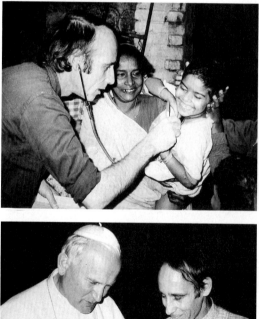

A joyous reunion with our little Indian brothers

These children have been cured of the many diseases afflicting them (leprosy, tuberculosis, intestinal infections) by the staff at our dispensary in Bankra. A school has been created to provide them with a normal education.

The school and dispensary existed only for the duration of the shooting of the film *The City of Joy* by director Roland Joffé. After the filming, the materials for the set were salvaged and reused by the occupants of the neighboring slum.

A victory over fear and poverty

These children, originally from the very poor villages in the Belari region, fifty miles from Calcutta, are now cared for, fed, dressed and educated thanks to Shukesi, an admirable young nurse whose dispensary treats six hundred sick and injured people every day. The smiles that bring a luminous beauty and happiness to the drabness of the setting are proof that there is a way out of crippling poverty. Tomorrow these children will learn a trade. Then they in their turn will be able to help their families. It may well be but a drop in the ocean of need, but as Mother Teresa often said, the ocean is made up of "drops of water."

medical reference book and carried it out to the Great Pine. For thirty years I had soothed my fears and my anger in the shade of this lord among trees. It had become my friend and protector. Today I had come to confide my feelings of outrage. At fifty-eight I felt young, active, full of plans for the future. I hadn't smoked a cigarette for thirty years, I didn't drink, I didn't go in for any kind of excess. I led a healthy existence, far from the pollution, noise and stress of urban life. I was a husband, a father, a friend, an author, who had everything he could wish for. I was sure that every single one of my cells shared in this balance and happiness. So why had some of them suddenly risen up and turned me into a cancer patient?

I searched feverishly through my medical dictionary for the word "prostate." The entry devoted to the small gland was scarcely heartening. It could double, even triple, in size after the age of sixty. Its location, deep in a densely vascular area, at the intersection of the urinary and sexual functions, combined with the number and variety of its possible disorders, ranging from simple inflammations to malignant tumors, or disabling enlargements like those that had affected the elderly Britons of Kashmir, meant that the prostate is a problematic organ. The development of all these afflictions involved hemorrhaging, abscesses, retention, incontinence and infections that are often extremely severe. In the case of cancer, the entry described violent pains between the anus and the genitals, along the thighs and in the sciatic nerve. The dictionary stressed that it is a serious cancer because of the likelihood of its spreading locally to the bladder, the cell tissue of the renal pelvis, the rectum and urethra, and farther afield in the form of bone, pulmonary, brain and hepatic metastases. None of the treatments seemed exactly anodyne. I read words that made my hair stand on end: "incontinence," "impotence," "castration." Because the prostate is a genital organ, it is sensitive to the effects of male hormones. If the latter are suppressed, the activity of the gland is reduced and, by the same token, its various pathologies. These treatments could prolong the life of patients by months, even years, but often at very great cost.

Ever attentive to my fears, my wife reminded me that the

Paris specialist had expressed a preference for surgical removal of the tumor. But the dictionary had no epithets sinister enough to describe this option. This dangerous, major operation required "considerable experience in the detachment of the lower part of the bladder, and very careful hemostatic treatment, often difficult to carry out in subjects whose adipose tissue is too developed." In order to be operable, the tumor "must not be too large that its removal does not cause perforation of the bladder, the healing of which would be impossible." After other equally optimistic insights, the book concluded that "the immediate and long-term consequences must not be disregarded." These consequences were far from rosy: what man in the prime of his life would happily accept the possibility of never again sampling the joys of lovemaking, or seeing his urine end up in a plastic pouch suspended from his waist?

My feelings of rebellion went on for a substantial part of that fateful day, until at last my survival instinct regained the upper hand. I saddled up my mare, Pinecone, and galloped off into the hills. This sensitive Andalusian horse I had wrested from the abattoirs still shared with me the happiest and most beneficent cooperation. For twenty years she had been my daily yoga. On her back, at a gentle trot, with my eyes lost in the greenery, I had resolved most of my writing problems, found the solution to my personal worries, dreamed up the wildest adventures and ceaselessly given thanks to God for the gift of all his benefits.

It was one of those luminous, transparent September evenings. The reddening of the vines cloaked the peninsula in scarlet. Purged of its summer stickiness, the crisp air stung my face. From the undergrowth and scrub rose the scent of mushrooms and wild lavender. At the top of a slight slope, I caught the ever-magical view of the bay of Saint-Tropez, the legendary little harbor and its confusion of boats and red tiles, nestling at the water's edge under the walls of its citadel. Spurred on by the beauty of it, I began to rail at the nasty little creatures eating into me. "No, no, no, you're not going to win!" I raged. "No, you're not going to move anywhere else in my body. I shall pin you to the spot, then root you out and obliterate you."

Childish as my outburst was, it brought relief. I returned home, my serenity restored, and firmly resolved to fight.

DESPITE THE EARLY MORNING hour—half past seven—the waiting room for the radiology department of the large Parisian hospital was already full. At least thirty people were lined up in the chairs ranged along the pale green partition walls. There were about the same number of men as women. Most were over fifty but some were younger. Like me, all were suffering from cancer. The bone scan of our skeletons was going to tell us whether our cancer had spread and if we had any chance of conquering our disease. I was amazed to see so little anxiety on people's faces, so much calmness in their bearing. Some were placidly reading the paper or leafing through the old magazines that littered the tables; others chatted cheerily with the relative or friend who had come with them. One woman was knitting a pullover. An elderly couple sat holding hands. On his jacket the man wore the red button of his Légion d'Honneur. A shapely young woman in jeans and a leather jacket was happily listening to rock music her Walkman pounded into her ears through her frizzy hair. A little farther on, with a stooping back and a thin neck emerging from the collar of his black smock with its small cross, a priest was reading his breviary. Next to him, a large black man in sneakers was filing his nails and chewing gum. A plump little lady had placed a large black vinyl bag on her lap. She nodded to me in greeting and then undid the zipper. I saw the head of a cat emerge.

"He doesn't like being left on his own," she apologized. "Ever since I've been ill, he meows his heart out if I leave him."

She ran a hand over its coat and the animal began to purr. Soon all eyes were on this unusual presence.

Indeed, this sample of suffering humanity was a model of tranquil stoicism. A nurse appeared.

"Monsieur Perrin!" she called.

The elderly gentleman fondly holding his wife's hand got up. Soon it was my turn. Before each patient could have the bone scan, he or she had to be injected with an iodine-based contrast liquid which would deposit itself on the different parts of the skeleton. As soon as the needle went into my arm, I felt a burning wave flood my body. I was sent back to the waiting room. The examination proper would take place in an hour's time. I was glad to get back to my fellow sufferers. Monsieur Perrin had taken hold of his wife's hand again. The lady with the cat had managed to quiet the animal's desperate meowing. The priest's lips had resumed reciting of the sacred litany for a day that liturgy would classify as ordinary but was so very far from ordinary for our small assembly of castaways.

The young woman with the rock music, Monsieur Perrin, the large black man in his sneakers and all the others went one by one for their test. Before doing so, the lady with the cat entrusted her bag and her animal to me.

"Stroke him," she directed me. "He'll give you good energies too."

I obeyed with a smile and felt immediate relief as my hand strayed over the little ball of fur. The cat must not have been entirely oblivious to my attentions for it started licking my fingers vigorously. It was not without regret that I saw its mistress return. The contact had brought me a certain peace.

A FEMALE TECHNICIAN who smelled of stale cigarette smoke had me lie down in my underpants on a radiology table. At once automatic cameras began to move about over my body.

"Hold your breath! Breathe! Turn over!"

The sharp, impersonal orders came at me like the voice of a robot in a science fiction film. The control screens lit up, went out, clicked. The technician pressed buttons, manipulated handles, controlled the slide of the cameras. I tried to read a reaction on her face.

"You'll be called in half an hour," was all she said after I had dressed.

I rushed to the cafeteria to down a coffee and some bread and jam. Other patients in my group had had the same idea. Quite spontaneously they had sat together. Two hours of waiting side by side for a life-or-death verdict inevitably creates bonds. The young woman with the Walkman had offered the priest a croissant, and Madame Perrin had given the little cat a scrap of ham. Surprisingly enough, these people continued to put up a show of absolute placidity. Afraid of missing my name when it was called, I got up. Everyone else followed. The ensuing minutes will remain the most unbearable of my life. The young woman with the Walkman was called, then the priest, then the black man. In my heart I wished each one a warm "good luck." People came out more or less quickly from the doctor's room. The priest was in there for a long time, which I took to be a bad sign. At last I heard a voice calling: "Monsieur Lapierre!"

The radiologist was a little man with graying hair, seated behind a desk strewn with photographs depicting the human body. Each related to one of the patients there that morning. As I watched the doctor sort through those documents to find mine, I felt as if I sat before a fortune-teller preparing to read my cards. I tried to make out some sign, some emotion, on his face. Calmly the radiologist showed me the results of my bone scan.

"Look, Monsieur Lapierre, everything is perfect! Not the smallest black speck. No metastases in the bones."

I wanted to yell, to tear this man out of his chair and hug and kiss him. His name, written on his white smock, will remain forever engraved upon my memory. You have my gratitude forever, Monsieur Perez. May you be forever blessed. It was then that my eye fell upon another photograph on the table. The rendering of the body was covered in black dots. They were everywhere: all around the bladder, along the back, neck, shoulders. Even the skull was affected. Dr. Perez shook his head sadly.

"General metastases in the bones," he let slip with a sigh. "A very sad case. No hope at all. A woman of forty-eight."

I read the name: Antoinette Dupeyron.

After a few more effusions, I hurried away from the doctor and his office. I wanted to get out into the fresh air. As I crossed the corridor on my way to the exit, I heard a nurse call out "Madame Dupeyron!" I turned instinctively to look back at the waiting room. The lady with the cat had gotten to her feet.

My wife, Dominique, was waiting for me at the hospital exit: younger, livelier, prettier than ever, with her hair cut short, Chinese style, and her large dark eyes full of love. She instantly read the joy written all over my face and threw herself into my arms. I smothered her lips, her neck, her cheeks, wet with tears, with kisses. People stopped to look at us. We walked away with our arms around each other's waist, in such a perfect state of communion of heart and mind that words were unnecessary. We wanted to laugh, to cry, to pray. And most of all to thank God and the supportive circle of friends who had held us in their prayers, for this marvelous new beginning, for our unmitigated happiness. I greedily breathed in the smell of the damp leaves of the chestnut trees. Passersby, cars, shop windows, pigeons, all danced about us in celebration. Ecstatically I savored the confirmation of my presence among the living. That morning had been the toughest of my life. More intensely than any of the war experiences in my career as a journalist, it had brought me in contact with the narrow boundary between life and death, hope and despair. I had been lucky.

The major Parisian hospital where my cancer had been diagnosed had made no provision for supplying its patients with information or helping them to help themselves. The urology department had no brochure, not the smallest leaflet, to instruct a man with prostate cancer about the nature of his illness, about how to treat it or how those around him could support him. This oversight both surprised and outraged me. Research in the United States for my book *Beyond Love* had shown me what tremendous efforts the American health organizations make to provide cancer victims with information. Whether it was a question of the early detection of all kinds of tumors, the respective merits of different types of treatment, the means of combating the side effects of chemotherapy, suitable diet, participation in therapeutic trials, coping with relapses, psychological support or a hundred other pertinent questions—everything, absolutely everything, a patient and his family might wish or need to know was explained in as many brochures as there were types of cancer. Here in France there was nothing.

And yet the cancer from which I was suffering affects twenty thousand Frenchmen every year. It is the most common cancer in men after that of the lung. With some eight thousand deaths, prostate cancer claims more victims in France than road accidents. Like so many other patients, I could only turn to my doctor to satisfy my craving for information. I shall never forget his extreme humanity, the way he listened, the infinite patience with which he answered all my questions, his readiness, above all, to make my distress his own and steer me toward the treatment that would give me the best chance of a cure. How many victims of cancer have been so fortunate? I knew that in cancer hospitals the choice of treatment depended on what day you happened to turn up. On Mondays, for instance, you were likely to be treated by chemotherapy, Tuesdays by radiation therapy, on Wednesdays by surgery, and so on. This technique made it possible to compare the relative merits of different treatments and draw up statistics for the benefit of future patients. Woe betide you if you turned up on the day of a treatment that proved ineffective!

My doctor presented me with four different approaches. Surprising as it might seem, first and foremost, I could do nothing at all. In other words, I could forget about my cancer. My type of tumor, I was told, sometimes developed very slowly. Even taking into account the fact that I was still young, I had a good chance of dying of something else. It would be enough to monitor the tumor and make sure the malignant cells remained quietly ensconced within my prostate. This was not so much a case of trying to cure it but of "waiting and seeing." The advantage of this approach was that it spared a frail patient the possibly pointless trauma of extensive or radical treatment. The disadvantage was that it left the cancer in situ and risked the escape of malignant cells into other parts of the body.

"Do many of your patients dare to take that risk?" I asked.

My doctor burst into ribald laughter. "All those for whom life without sexual intercourse is no life!"

His answer was no joke. It pinpointed the particular tragedy of the cancer that had affected me. Ever since reading my medical dictionary under the parasol pine, I had known that the prostate was seated at the very center of man's most sacred function. Around the small genital organ clustered the testicles, the seminal glands, the ejaculatory ducts and, reigning supreme over all this equipment, the erectile nerves. Could one treat the prostate, remove it even, without definitively damaging the accessories indispensable to virility?

The three forms of therapy most apt to save my life involved a strong risk of castration. With chemotherapy that risk became a certainty: the hormones given in order to stop the evolution of the tumor automatically produced a chemical castration. Fortunately I did not qualify for this aggressive form of treatment, reserved for cases where the cancer had exceeded the boundaries of the prostate and invaded other organs. But the two other possible treatments were still no picnic. Radiation therapy might well destroy most cancerous cells, but it overlooked others and often caused severe damage to neighboring organs, including the bladder and those celebrated erectile nerves. How many men had been rendered incontinent and impotent for the rest of their lives by X rays! Surgery was the third option, and it was in this direction that my doctor had pushed me. The absence of any metastases and the limited spread of my tumor made me an ideal candidate for an operation that in urologists' jargon is referred to as a radical prostatectomy. Once my two and a half ounces of cancerous prostate had been removed with a scalpel, I would be cured. It was, he assured me, "an option for life." Life! Life with a capital *L*. Yes, a hundred times yes, a thousand times yes, Doctor.

"I can't give you a 100 percent guarantee that the operation will preserve your sexuality," my doctor admitted gravely. "That depends on a number of factors which vary according to the individual patient. Notably the size of the prostate, the thickness of the fatty tissue surrounding it. The greater the gland's increase in size as a result of the disease, the more difficult it is to extract. It also depends on examination of the ganglia during the operation. If they've been affected, then the cutting has to be more extensive, in which case the erectile nerves have to be sacrificed in the patient's own interests."

As I listened to him, I looked at his hands. I'd imagined that a surgeon would need long, supple fingers, like a pianist. My surgeon's hands were quite the opposite. They were more like a woodcutter's solid hands. Although they were not as I imagined, they inspired confidence.

In the late 1980s, radical prostatectomy preserving the sexual and urinary functions was still a very new operation. It was only carried out by a small minority of urologists.

"Doctor, may I ask how many operations of this kind you've performed to date?" I asked.

"About forty," he replied, not in the least disconcerted by my curiosity.

"All of them preserving the erectile nerves?"

"Admittedly no. Preservation was only possible in the case of sixteen or seventeen patients."

"Sixteen or seventeen!" I repeated, dismayed at the modesty of such proportions.

"How long does the operation last?" was my next worry.

"Between three and three and a half hours. Usually with very ordinary aftercare. A day and a night in the recovery room, and the day after that you'll be trotting about the corridor of the hospital."

HIS THIN BLACK MUSTACHE and tiny twinkling eyes gave him the misleading appearance of the actor Groucho Marx. Professor Sam Broder, aged forty-one, was one of America's leading lights in the fight against cancer. I had met him some months earlier in his laboratory in Bethesda, near Washington, D.C., where he was experimenting on antiviral substances to combat living AIDS viruses. These procedures were so dangerous that he had made me sign a disclaimer absolving him from responsibility "in the event of my contamination by HIV during the course of my visit." Our immediate liking for each other resulted in a meeting that lasted into the evening in the attractive cottage he shared with his charming lawyer wife. There, over a bottle of his favorite Gewürztraminer, I had been able to reconstruct for my book *Beyond Love* Sam Broder's long, arduous struggle against cancer and AIDS. His personal courage in handling the retrovirus that causes AIDS had eventually challenged the apathy of the pharmaceutical laboratories. It was thanks to this extraordinary little man that the first drug to counter the scourge had seen the light of day. The U.S. government had just rewarded him by appointing him director of the National Cancer Institute. I dialed his telephone number. When he answered I told him what was happening to me and appealed to him for advice.

"Sam, I've got two questions. First, who's the best American specialist for total removal of the prostate? Second, can you put in a word and get him to agree to operate on me?"

"No problem, boy! Cheer up! I'll call you back in ten minutes."

Exactly ten minutes later Broder was back on the line. He told me that the greatest American specialist was a man by the name of Patrick Walsh. He was a surgeon at the Johns Hopkins hospital in Baltimore. He had perfected an operation that guaranteed, in 80 percent of men under sixty, the conservation of the erectile nerves. He was willing to operate on me. But he did not think I would be justified in traveling to Baltimore because he had two exceptional disciples in France who had performed at least as many operations as he, using his technique to preserve the erectile nerves. Their names were Pierre Léandri and Georges Rossignol. They had a unique advantage in that they operated together, four-handed.

"One is right-handed and the other left," boomed Broder. "Which means they can take out a prostate in just over an hour. A record!"

Just over an hour! That was almost three times shorter than the time my Parisian surgeon would need. I called him at once.

"Doctor, do you know Léandri and Rossignol?"

"Certainly! I went to Toulouse to see them operate. First-rate! The best in the world along with Walsh," he replied un-hesitatingly. "People come from all over Europe and even America and Asia to attend their symposia and follow their op-erations in person. You'll see: the most likable is the one with the drooping eyelids, but they're both remarkable."

He gave me the name of their clinic. The idea of these "scalpel duettists" (as they were sometimes known) was most alluring. After all, I had experienced myself the invaluable ad-vantages of working in a twosome.

That same evening, I telephoned the Saint Jean du Langue-doc clinic in Toulouse. To my astonishment, the switchboard operator put me straight through to Dr. Pierre Léandri.

"Dear Monsieur Lapierre, tomorrow, Saturday, I shall be at home all afternoon. Here's my private number. Telephone me at three-thirty, and we can chat for as long as you like. Mean-while whatever you do, don't worry. Your case is quite routine. There's no need to be concerned."

I emerged from the phone booth, walking on air.

Next day, when I called Dr. Léandri's home address, a little girl answered the phone and said in a delightful southern French accent: "I'll get my daddy for you."

We talked for an hour and a half. The surgeon's voice was composed, dependable, comforting in its rhythm and intona-tion.

"Yes, at your age surgery is the option that will give you an almost 100 percent guarantee of a cure . . . No, there is no risk of your ending up with an artificial bladder suspended from your waist . . . Yes, you have every chance of keeping your sex-ual function . . . Yes, the operation can wait for a few days . . ."

THE SAINT JEAN DU LANGUEDOC clinic, at the northwestern extremity of Toulouse, looked to me like a kind of Hilton Hotel whose staff would have stepped out of a provincial family guesthouse. A pretty blond receptionist took me straight to Pierre Léandri's office. Neither he nor his colleague, Rossignol, had come back up from the operating wing as yet. The only decoration adorning the little room with its beige wallpaper was the diploma awarded to Léandri by the American Urology Association "for services rendered to his specialty." America made its presence felt elsewhere in the room with a pile of the *American Journal of Urology* and a series of illustrated brochures from the Johns Hopkins hospital in Baltimore reporting the operation results of Professor Walsh after five hundred radical prostatectomies. On a table lay a tract in English in which Léandri and Rossignol described their new technique of automatic suture in the replacement of cancerous bladders.

The two men who entered the little office were striking for their rather timid, self-effacing air. With his curly fair locks and his round rosy face, Georges Rossignol, aged forty-four, looked like a Rubens cherub. By contrast, doleful eyes under heavy eyelids gave Pierre Léandri, also forty-four, a hangdog expression. They talked so simply and reassuringly that all anxiety was banished on the spot. That first meeting was to go on for nearly three days, time for me to forget my cancer and again become a journalist caught up in a sensational success story.

No fairy godmother had waved her magic wand over Georges Rossignol's cradle; he was born into the sizable family of a minor police official in Albi, in southwestern France. Without the encouragement of the local family doctor, young Georges would never have dreamed of a medical career. The studies were far too costly. A providential job as a delivery driver resolved his problems. Studying by night, driving by day, Rossignol passed his exams and successfully got through his resident medical internship. His compulsory military service sent him into the blood and thunder of African Chad. There, with bodies riddled with bullets and shrapnel, he learned about the pathology of warfare. On his return to France, a period spent with a urologist from Le Havre helped him to a further discovery: urology was no longer just the surgical equivalent of plumbing. New techniques were now making it possible to achieve hitherto inconceivable feats such as kidney transplants. What was more, because the kidneys, bladder and prostate were frequently attacked by malignant tumors, urology had also become a means to important cancer research. The young man from Albi had been captivated by a discipline in which surgery and research were closely combined.

Pierre Léandri had had an easier start. The son of a French doctor settled in Algeria, he had been brought up in a medical environment and had quite naturally been drawn to study medicine. Surgery had attracted him from the start "because you can achieve instant results," he explained. Like Rossignol, he had performed his first operations while doing his military service. In Guadeloupe, where he was stationed, he had a unique opportunity to deal with all kinds of surgical emergencies, even multiple injuries: open fractures of the thigh, burst spleens, crushed rib cages.

A stroke of good fortune ordained that these two apprentice surgeons should meet over the same operating table at the university hospital in Toulouse. Together they then tried to make their way through the labyrinth of university competition. But urology posts were rare and much sought after, and the rigid laws of established elitism difficult to get around. From their very first meeting Léandri was astounded by Rossignol's surgical skill, by the ease and sureness of his movements and the way he got straight to the essentials. It gave him an idea. Since a university hospital career seemed closed to them both, why not combine their talents privately to form a team of top-grade specialists? As luck would have it, a urologist surgeon was looking for a partner for a clinic he wanted to set up in Toulouse and turn into a top European urological center. Léandri immediately jumped at the opportunity with the idea of bringing in his friend Rossignol as soon as possible. More than ever the two men were convinced that four-handed surgery could alter the prognosis for certain acute conditions. One such condition was cancer of the bladder.

At that time the complete removal of a bladder with a malignant tumor was considered so mutilating that most urologists preferred to try to reduce and eventually neutralize the tumor by means of chemotherapy. In most cases these treatments were only palliative and the incidence of recurrence with a worsening of the condition was very high. By the time it became apparent that only radical surgery could possibly save a patient's life, it was generally too late. Few European urologists dared resort to this kind of operation. Those who did would put off suggesting it for as long as possible, knowing the mutilation it entailed. Yet any delay reduced the chances of saving the patient.

One day in 1978, Léandri read a report in the *Journal Français d'Urologie,* the French urologists' journal, in which a surgeon by the name of Maurice Camey explained how he removed bladders with cancerous tumors and replaced them with a new bladder made out of a piece of intestine. With this technique he could restore normal urinary function in his patients, thus assuring them of entirely satisfactory continence both day and night. He even managed, in certain cases, to preserve their sexual function. This was something quite revolutionary. The Americans had recognized the surgeon's brilliance for a long time. In France, where Camey was a challenge to the Parisian urological establishment's prevailing dogma, he was regarded as a slightly unhinged eccentric. For twenty years he had been crying in the wilderness. There was another reason for this ostracism. The operation Maurice Camey had perfected was so delicate and difficult that he was the only one who could perform it successfully. The few colleagues who actually tried it recorded only disasters. And in surgery, for any new technique to be regarded as valid, it must be capable of duplication.

Léandri and Rossignol decided to take up the challenge. They were by this time working together in the Saint Jean du Languedoc clinic in Toulouse. They hurried to Paris to observe one of Camey's operations: ten hours of a spectacular acrobatic feat that could save several hundred lives a year. Enthusiastic converts, the two friends were convinced that they had found in this operation the perfect justification for their partnership. Had not nature foreseen precisely this by making them complementary: one right-handed and the other left?

The first removal and replacement of the bladder the "duettists" tried was performed on a fifty-eight-year-old Toulouse photographer. Although the operation took eight hours, it immediately confirmed the supremacy of their four-handed performance.

"The fact that we were the same age and had the same medical standing kept any personal complications at bay," Rossignol was to tell me. "We regarded each other as equals, which made it possible for us to take turns in directing the operation, to check on each other constantly, to take up the relay when the other person felt he wasn't getting anywhere or in a moment of tiredness. A surgeon cannot operate and watch himself operate at the same time. We felt right away that we could each be the other's critical mirror."

In a few operations they reduced the duration of Camey's procedures from ten hours to six, then to four and finally to two and a half.

Since replacing the bladder automatically implied the removal of the prostate, the Toulouse duettists also began removing cancerous prostates. Their first patient was a retired postman of the southern town of Auch. His operation took three and a half hours and required a transfusion of three pints of blood. The man recovered his normal urinary function, but the operation deprived him of his sexuality forever. Nearly two years would elapse before, in 1985, an article in the *American Journal of Urology* revealed to the two men in Toulouse that a surgeon from Baltimore had perfected a technique for the total removal of the prostate that would safeguard sexual function. In a paper abundantly illustrated with color plates, Professor Patrick Walsh explained how he had managed to modify his dissection procedures to avoid touching the minute, almost invisible fascicles of erectile nerves which enveloped the prostate gland. The article raised a general outcry in traditional urology circles, not only in France but also in America, where many specialists of considerable standing accused the author of irresponsible behavior.

Léandri and Rossignol realized at once that this development had toppled the last argument of those opposed to ablation of the prostate. If it were possible, almost certainly, to preserve the patient's virility, surgery was the best course of treatment for anyone like me, who had been fortunate enough to benefit from early detection of his cancer. Rossignol flew to New York to meet Walsh, who was showing a fifteen-minute film about his technique at a medical convention. The Frenchman was profoundly impressed by this great Irish-American not much older than he was himself. Rossignol promptly invited Walsh to operate in Toulouse in front of an assembly of European colleagues specially convened for the occasion.

But Léandri and Rossignol did not wait for the American master's visit to try out his technique. In September 1985 they operated on a Toulouse police officer.

"He was a very passionate man," Rossignol told me, "who came to us, saying: 'I'm quite willing for you to operate, but only on the condition I'll be able to screw *like before.*'"

The operation was a great success, even if the policeman had to be patient for a year before he could have normal erections.

The two surgeons refined their technique very quickly until they had cut their operating time from three hours to less than an hour and a quarter.

THE OCCASION OF MY SURGERY was almost a celebration! My wife's unlimited and wonderfully loving ingenuity managed to transform the somewhat sinister necessity of the removal of a malignant tumor into a pleasant diversion. Three weeks after my meeting with the Toulouse surgeons, she packed our car with books, familiar objects and all the other accessories conducive to my comfort in the clinic and swept me off on a fantastic drive from Saint-Tropez to Toulouse. She had alerted all our closest friends along the way, and our journey turned into a happy succession of gastronomic interludes. I'll never forget that autumn cavalcade through the luminescent pine forests of Provence, the bloodred sea of Languedoc vineyards and the golden sunflower fields carpeting the rich plains of Sardagne. How beautiful, opulent and peaceful France seemed to me then! I savored the magical appearance of each village, the harmony of the vales and plains, with all the greed of one who wondered whether he would ever see such marvels again. True, I felt serene, confident, sure of winning, but how could I help remembering every now and then that the ultimate destination of this enchanted journey was . . . an operating table. I felt so well, so young, so strong. That was the paradox of this cancer. It was consuming me insidiously without inflicting, at least at first, the slightest pain or handicap. So much so that I wondered whether my illness was actually real and whether I was really justified in risking so much on account of a few unruly cells.

I expected to receive several visitors on my arrival at the clinic, but definitely not the bright young woman who was first to knock on the door to room 229. She was not a doctor or a laboratory assistant; nor was she a nurse. The small folder she brought me contained no social security forms or test results; in fact it held no papers of any kind relating to my health or my forthcoming operation. Yet what it did contain was very much part of the special treatment the establishment provided to boost its patients' morale and speed up their recovery. It held the various menus I would have the opportunity to sample during my stay. The sight of some of the specialties on offer, such as "raviolis with foie gras in truffle sauce" or "rib of veal in a boletus crust," made me start. My visitor was amused at my surprise.

"What did you expect, my dear sir? You've chosen to have your operation in our gastronomic southwest of France," she declared, "and in the southwest we treat our patients first and foremost with the good things our land has to offer!"

Her explanation was typical of the quality of provincial life which no big city could ever offer. I was to discover that most of the doctors, nurses and staff who looked after me lived in the surrounding countryside, just a few minutes away from their workplace. Many of them came to work by bicycle or even on foot. The good humor and accessibility of the entire team were a reflection of their happy living conditions.

ONE OF MY NEIGHBORS was an Englishman with dyed hair whose jollity and quaint use of the French language delighted the nurses. Sixty-eight-year-old Jim Conrad was a former major in the British army who had retired to the Côte d'Azur after serving for nearly half a century in all four corners of the empire. When I learned that he had spent time in India during the war as an ADC to the general in command of the Calcutta sector, I went scrambling to his door to meet him. The appearance of the Messiah could not have had more of an impact on the charming occupant of room 228. His face lit up when I mentioned my name.

"You are . . . you're the author of this famous . . ." he stammered with emotion.

Without finishing his sentence, he pulled a box of books from under his bed and dug out an old English copy of *Freedom at Midnight*. Brandishing the work like a trophy, he repeated, "This is my Bible, really, this book is my Bible."

Major Conrad then had me sit down, took out two glasses which he filled to the brim with cognac and launched into an inexhaustible account of his years in India. He had known Mountbatten, Nehru and even Mahatma Gandhi, whom he had escorted during the independence riots through a burning Calcutta. He had kept several small photograph albums from this past life, which remained his constant companions. He let me leaf through the pages: Jim with the horse that won the Calcutta Queen's Cup, Jim in front of the Taj Mahal, Jim in the middle of a group of Gurkha soldiers in the Khyber Pass, Jim dancing the fox-trot with a charming lady at the Gymkhana Club in Lahore. He married this British woman after India's independence, but they divorced when he expressed his intention of retiring to the Côte d'Azur.

"I had labored too long in the sun to end my days in my wife's Welsh mists," he guffawed.

He had set up home in the foothills of Grasse and placed a personal ad in the lonely-hearts column of a local newspaper. Georgette, a former pastry shop owner who had just lost her husband, took the bait. "It was love at first sight." Georgette turned up at Jim's with her suitcase. To celebrate the first anniversary of their idyll, he decided to take her on a round-the-world tour. They should have left two months earlier, but a few days before their departure, Jim had discovered traces of blood in his urine. The urologist in Grasse had asked him to take some tests. The results of his prostate tests were thirty times higher than they should have been. The doctor made the wise decision to send the Englishman to Toulouse, where Léandri and Rossignol diagnosed a prostatic malignancy. Next day they opened him up and took out his prostate. Twenty-four hours later the retired army officer was sauntering about the corridor like a young man, urine bottles in hand. In a week's time Georgette would come and collect him to take him back to Grasse and, a month later, they would fly off to Istanbul on the first leg of their round-the-world honeymoon.

Tragically, before leaving the clinic, Jim Conrad was to receive a piece of heartbreaking news. The pathology reports on the tissue extracted by the surgeons in the course of the operation had revealed that his ganglia and his seminal vesicles had also been invaded by the malignant cells, evidence that his tumor had escaped from its original home to contaminate other neighboring organs. The only way to stop it from spreading further was to perform a radical castration. This surgical procedure consisted of cutting into the patient's testicles to extract the substance that produces the male hormones guilty, in this case, of promoting the proliferation of the cancer. The surgeons had replaced the substance with a ball of silicone. Appearances had been preserved. But the charming British gentleman, who was so kindly entertaining me, would no longer be able to prove his virility to his pastry shop inamorata.

I UNDERWENT MY OPERATION one sunlit autumn morning. A few hours beforehand the clinic postman brought me a letter covered with stamps showing the face of Mahatma Gandhi. It had come from Calcutta. Much to my surprise, I found inside a handwritten letter from Mother Teresa. For several days the newspapers had been reporting that the saint of the poor was fighting for her life in a clinic in Bengal's capital, where a cardiologist flown in from Rome had just implanted a pacemaker in her chest to stimulate her flagging heart. "Dear Dominique Lapierre," she wrote in her large round handwriting, "at the same time Jesus' gift of sharing his Passion comes to both of us. My prayer and that of our Sisters and our Poor will be with you for the success of your operation and your recovery."

I did not know how Mother Teresa had heard about the ordeal that lay ahead of me that day in Toulouse. Deeply touched, I taped the little sheet of paper on the windowpane of my room. When the nurses came to take me down to the operating room, I read it again, and, certain that the prayers of my Indian brothers and sisters would guide the surgeons' hands, I stretched out on the gurney with my mind at rest. A plastic bracelet bearing my name encircled my wrist. On the back of the label, Dominique had written, "I love you. See you very soon." The two nurses deposited me on the operating table and I saw above me the masked faces of the surgeons. The anesthetist took my arm and I felt the prick of the needle as it entered my skin. It was then that something extraordinary happened. I heard a voice ringing in my ears. Solemn, powerful, inspired, it was singing the verses of a hymn. It was the voice of Ranjit, a young quadriplegic who lived in the home we supported in Jalpaiguri in the foothills of the Himalayas. Ranjit had been stricken with polio at birth. His parents had abandoned him. A French priest had picked him out of a gutter one day. He spent his life confined to a litter and would never be able to walk. Although a Hindu, he went to his benefactor's

Mass each Sunday along with his friends who were also handicapped.

The home in which Ranjit lived was a haven of compassion
and love in the midst of the most dreadful need. Dominique
and I had assumed responsibility for financing it. On the Sunday we met, Ranjit sang out what sounded like a prayer of
thanksgiving with gusto. It had seemed quite impossible that
such resonant tones could issue from his wretched, rachitic
chest covered with its shriveled skin. His miraculous voice had
remained with me ever since. And now, just as I was about to
go to sleep, at the most crucial moment of my life, it brought
me the hopeful prayer of a little Indian brother who was so
much stronger than his affliction.

FOUR DAYS AFTER THE OPERATION, an exuberant young woman
with a mass of frizzy hair burst into my room with an unusual
present. Dr. Lucienne Gabay-Torbiera was one of the two
pathologists at the clinic. Throughout my operation she had
taken samples to check the limits of the tumor and make sure
that the tissue surrounding my prostate was unaffected. The
comprehensive tests she had just completed confirmed the initial results on all counts.

"You no longer have cancer. You're cured!" she trumpeted,
shaking both my hands in hers.

I took her in my arms and kissed her. Rossignol and Léandri
appeared next, accompanied by their delightful surgical nurse,
who had been born in Armenia. Jim Conrad arrived also, brandishing a bottle of cognac. It was party time. At this point the
frizzy-haired pathologist extracted a color photograph from her
bag.

"I thought you might like to keep this picture," she said with
a wink.

Viewed as a whole, the photograph appeared to be a kind of
Indian shawl printed with hundreds of small decorative patterns. Closer examination revealed, however, that these motifs

came in different shapes and sizes according to whether they were on the left or the right of the picture. On the left was a clearly defined collection of interlacing pale pink shapes, which reminded me of oranges or pears. Then abruptly, as if separated by some barrier I could not see, the cells became a hideous, anarchic, inconsistent jumble of small black balls and rods. The sight left me stunned. After the surgery I had just been through, the photograph raised one fundamental question. What emotional shock, what physical trauma, was responsible for causing so serious a disruption of my cells?

I am frustrated with myself that I have not yet found the answer to this crucial question. But at least I had the good fortune to learn, one day in October 1994, five years after my operation, that I had joined the statistics of patients who had conquered cancer.[1]

---

[1] The joy of this victory was overshadowed by legal proceedings brought against my two surgeons following a complaint made by a Toulouse businessman. Accused of having operated unnecessarily on patients, Léandri and Rossignol have been taken to court. Today the team whose prowess had earned the admiration of urologists all over Europe and even America has been broken up. The battle against cancer has lost its four-handed duo.

11

"What Does It Matter, Beautiful African Elephant, If I Water Your Land with My Blood?"

A cobra's bite could not have had more effect. Raphaël tore about in all directions, spitting out unintelligible words, holding his face in his hands, shivering with excitement. Finally he came to a halt in front of me. His dark eyes flashed so intensely at me that I recoiled. Rubbing nervously at the short beard that framed his ascetic face, he looked like a monk painted by Zurbarán.

"If what you say is right," he began in a doleful voice that contrasted strongly with his agitation, "we'd have to call it the *rhinoceros Lapierrensis.*"

Thirty-five-year-old Raphaël Matta, chief warden of the Bouna game reserve—two million acres in the north of Africa's Ivory Coast—froze suddenly at the thought of this unlikely hypothesis. Rhinoceroses in his reserve? Impossible. They had totally disappeared from this part of Africa a century ago, possibly even two. To make quite sure, he had dredged the memories of the village elders and gone all through the vernacular dialects looking for any word, root of a word or expression referring to the animal. He had beaten his way into the most obscure recesses of the bush and never found the faintest indication of the presence of the mythical monster. And now some journalist had come bursting into his camp in the middle of the night to bring him news that was enough to drive him demented. I was very sorry to have inflicted such a shock on a man who had just welcomed me like a brother into the very heart of his kingdom. But I was so convinced of the rightness of what I had observed that I ventured to insist.

"I can assure you the animal I spotted in the undergrowth near the Comoé River this afternoon had a large horn on its forehead."

"How far away from it were you?" asked Raphaël.

"About fifty yards."

"What position was the animal in?"

"Full profile."

"What size?"

"Hippopotamus size."

Raphaël dug a notebook and pencil feverishly out of his pocket. "Draw me what you saw," he ordered.

I am no artist but I did my best. Obviously I emphasized the pointed dagger-shaped protrusion that had made such an impression on me. Raphaël picked up the hurricane lamp to shed more light on my pencil lines. Delicate insects were singeing their wings on the globe. In the glow I noticed two children and a blond woman, asleep beneath the meshing of a mosquito net. The camp was a curious glory hole of unusual objects. There were cooking utensils, a butane gas stove, tins of food, a typewriter, scattered files, a rifle, shelves covered with books. On the corner of a garden table straggled some glasses, a bottle of pastis and a book with a surprising title for such a setting: *The Life of Plato.*

Raphaël fingered my sketch distractedly. He was sweating profusely. I sensed he was torn between his convictions and an irrational desire to believe what I was saying.

"Could you find your way back to the place where you saw your rhinoceros?" he growled.

What could I say? I had no experience of the bush. To me all the trees, thickets and clearings seemed to merge into one big jumble of vegetation. All I knew was that I had seen "my" rhinoceros to the left of the track, a few yards away from a trail worn by hippos going down to the river. Poor Raphaël. They were pitiful enough directions.

"Let's go!" he exclaimed, grabbing his lamp.

He gripped me by the arm and led me over to his dilapidated Jeep. The engine was misfiring on one cylinder. Its hiccuping punctuated the darkness with a bizarre noise that silenced the birds. We went down in the direction of the river. I stared into the shadows, trying to find the hippos' trail. Raphaël's long hands kneaded the steering wheel so nervously the vehicle seemed likely to lurch into the ravine at any minute. A herd of gazelles appeared in our headlights, then the phosphorescent eyes of a family of jackals. We drove for about two to two and a half miles (how was one supposed to tell exactly?). Then, suddenly, Raphaël stopped. There before us was the river, dappled by the moon's reflection. We could hear the grunting of a group of hippos, frolicking a few yards away.

"Do you recognize anything?" Raphaël asked me, jumping out of the Jeep.

Silly question! In broad daylight it would have been difficult enough. But at night! And what was more. . . how could I put it? This dark natural world with its confusion of wildlife noises, the risk of putting my foot on a scorpion or a snake, stepping under a panther perched up in a tree or coming face-to-face with a buffalo or a lion . . . All I knew about the jungle was that a surprised animal is always a dangerous one. But I tried to put a brave face on it. Yes, that was definitely the hippo trail I had seen. As excited as a pack hound, Raphaël nosed about in all directions. Not one square inch escaped the swinging halo of his lamp. His experience as a tracker meant that he could identify for certain the spoor of a hyena, antelope or deer. Some mysterious, invisible animal, crouching in the jungle, protested loudly at our presence. The night began to resonate with the furious barking of a horde of monkeys, then the threatening grunting of a troop of hippopotami.

Raphaël remained unperturbed by this clamorous outburst. A war injury had left him almost deaf.

"Where are your rhinoceros tracks? Where the hell are they?" he stormed.

I looked for them with a keenness that was as desperate as his. Suddenly, he gave a shout.

"There they are!"

But his exultation lasted only a few seconds, the time it took him to realize that the imprints were in fact those of a very large wild boar whose tusks seen in profile in the half-light of the undergrowth could look the very image of a rhinoceros horn.

I had missed my opportunity to go down in the great book of the jungle. There was no such animal as the *rhinoceros Lapierrensis*.

"THE SAINT FRANCIS of the elephants," "the angel of the savanna," a fanatic, a misanthrope, a maniac obsessed with wildlife protection—the man I had discovered in the far reaches of that reserve had accumulated the most contradictory epithets. One thing was certain, however: the Morel of *The Roots of Heaven* actually existed in flesh and blood. Like the character in Romain Gary's novel, with unshakable commitment he was defending a handful of elephants under threat of extinction from poachers and white hunters in the swamps and forests of his reserve.

Yet Raphaël Matta's remarkable destiny had begun in the flattest banality of a comfortable position in the import-export business in Paris. Christiane, his lovely young fair-haired, green-eyed wife, used to dress the cream of international elegance at Christian Dior's. She had given him two children, Martine and Germinal. The Matta family seemed set to have a carefree and peaceful existence, until a brief advertisement in an agricultural journal turned everything upside down. The Ivory Coast government was looking for a warden for a game reserve on the borders of the Upper Volta and Ghana. The salary offered was derisory: about sixty dollars a month with a simple native hut as the only accommodation. Matta was hooked. He called Christiane at Dior's. "Darling, we're leaving for Africa!"

Two months later the Mattas disembarked at Abidjan with two suitcases. On the back of the letter hiring him, Raphaël had scribbled a few words he had come across one day in a book by Professor Roger Heim: "The deliberate destruction of an African giraffe or a New Caledonian kagu, in that it compromises the very survival of such species, is, philosophically and scientifically, possibly as serious as the murder of a man and as irreparable as the slashing of a picture by Raphael. It wipes out a piece of the past forever."

But who—apart from a few fanatics—cared about that past? Who was interested in knowing that over the last two thousand years, hundreds of species of mammals had disappeared; that the nineteenth century alone had exterminated seventy of them; that in the last fifty years, forty had been made extinct; and that now, worldwide, six hundred more were on the way out? When he reported to his superior in Abidjan, Raphaël was given only one piece of advice by way of encouragement:

"Be understanding. Turn a blind eye if necessary. Above all, don't make waves!"

Raphaël, Christiane and their children clambered into an old Forest Department Jeep and set off on the five hundred miles of mottled red rock track to the small town of Bouna. On the way they looked out for any survivors of the prodigious herd of elephants and buffalo that, less than a century before, had still inhabited the vast plains and forests of the Ivory Coast. But the landscape was bare.

On reaching their destination they took possession of the thatched hut that was to house them, a dilapidated shack where snakes, scorpions and bats had chosen to make their home. Never mind, their dream was taking shape. Before falling asleep for their first African night, they went out and surveyed their domain by the light of the stars: an endless ocean of trees and bush where the only inhabitants were the occupants of a fetishist village; an expanse almost as large as the state of Vermont; a disturbing, hostile world devoid of any road, where some of the big game left from the earliest ages still roamed the bush.

By virtue of the government order that had decreed it a "total reserve," hunting and fishing were forbidden in this vast territory, as was agricultural, forestry and mining development. No one was allowed to enter it, move about in it or camp in it without the written permission of the responsible authority. Soon after his arrival, Matta discovered that the local tribe of Lobis, the formidable hunters who supplied all the region's markets including those of Ghana and the upper Volta with cured meat, had set up their camps in his beautiful reserve. Night and day, come the dry season or the downpours of the seasonal apocalypse, they plundered the reserve. At night they put acetylene lamps with large gilded reflectors on their foreheads. The superstitious natives in the region had nicknamed them "golden-eyed Cyclops." But, worst of all, the Lobis were also voters. To win their vote, the local French administration generously granted them hunting permits. Some eight thousand officially sanctioned and ten thousand clandestine guns were passing from hand to hand.

The white killers were not far behind. Every weekend they arrived from Abidjan and other French African capitals, armed with licenses obtained directly from the governor's office. The colonel in charge of game regulation for the Ivory Coast had consumed forty thousand dollars—over forty years of the chief warden's salary—by building a sumptuous lodge for tourists. Officially it was supposed to provide important visitors and curious tourists with the thrill of a night in the bush, complete with lions' roaring and the passing of a family of elephants at cocktail time. In reality the lodge served as a base camp for the Sunday hunters with their blunderbusses.

THE VERY DAY AFTER his arrival, Raphaël plunged into his reserve. He was within reach of the goal he had long been nurturing in his imagination and his reading: that of protecting the wildlife threatened by humanity's destructive folly. There was so much to be done: the approximately 350-mile perimeter of the protected area had to be marked out with "Warning: No Entry" notices, trails had to be cleared, watchtowers and surveillance posts built, a team of wardens recruited and motivated. A scope of ambitions that a pathetically small budget promised to leave as unfulfilled dreams. But, above all, he needed to win over the fierce Lobi poachers who traditionally enjoyed the right to kill his animals. Was it possible to change the habits of stone age men who never came out of their huts without arming themselves with a bow, a quiver crammed full of poisoned arrows, a club in the shape of a pointed beak, a machete and a small wooden three-legged stool more often used as a bludgeon than a seat? Could he persuade them to accept the white man's extravagant idea of turning their traditional hunting ground into a reserve from which their bows and arrows were banned? Matta refused even to ask himself the question. He was in a hurry. His animals were being slaughtered with every passing day.

He introduced a whole succession of unpopular measures: he prohibited hunting, clearing the undergrowth, cultivation and lighting fires. He prohibited anyone from coming to draw water in the reserve, from collecting honey from wild bees, uprooting plants and even gathering dead wood. He even went so far as to decree that all the inhabitants living in the protected territory would be expelled, which would oblige them to abandon their fields and their ancestors' tombs. The neighborhood elders lost no time in comparing the new warden to the cruelest soldiers of the colonial invasion.

To second him, Matta had the good fortune to find a tall Baulé black man reputed to be the best tracker for six hundred miles around. Rémi Sogli was a former adjutant in colonial troops of the French army. He was to become guide, accomplice and brother to the small white man in his perilous and frantic crusade. Sogli recruited a dozen wardens. To give them a certain presence, Matta put topees on their heads and bought them, at his own expense, uniforms worthy of those worn by their colleagues in British Kenya and the Belgian Congo. Making deeper incursions into the savanna each day with his little troop, he undertook to make an inventory of the animals entrusted to his protection. His tacit understanding with the bush animals drove him to all kinds of acts of boldness. One day he photographed a family of elephants from less than ten yards away. On another he dared to snatch an antelope's thigh from a lion's jaws. Fortunately the beast was full and made off grumbling. He bathed with his children in the Comoé, the river that ran through the reserve, among the crocodiles and the hippopotami. He was never armed.

"If I were to carry a gun when I was with the animals, even if I never used it, the spell would immediately be broken because

I would be conscious of committing an act of betrayal," he told me.

After a few weeks, he sent a report to the Abidjan Forest Department authorities, with the results of his long and tiring expeditions. He had counted forty thousand bovines of all kinds, four hundred hippopotami, a hundred or so elephants and some sixty lions. It was a heritage he had sworn to himself he would safeguard down to the last baby elephant, even at the cost of his life. With his binoculars constantly trained on the horizon, he lived in a perpetual state of alert. At the least sound of gunfire echoing through the vastness of the bush, at the slightest wisp of smoke rising from a clearing, as soon as a vulture began to soar over the treetops, he went on the warpath. His endurance, despite his thinness, the malaria that sapped his strength and the amebic dysentery that contorted his stomach, together with his tremendous sense of direction in a hostile jungle where the sun shone directly overhead, earned him the admiration of the natives, who soon nicknamed the diminutive Frenchman *Kongo Massa*—King of the Bush. He was a king whose hide, for political reasons, was less valuable in the eyes of the authorities than that of the poacher voters and the white Sunday pillagers. One day he returned from an exhausting manhunt in the swamps to find a letter from Abidjan advising him that in the high circles of power "the reserve would not be considered worth much if there were to be victims on the side of the poachers."

But for the defender of the elephants, a poacher's or a white hunter's life was of little importance compared with that of an antelope, a giraffe or a hippopotamus. He hoped with all his soul that when the day came for an independent black government to take over from the colonial administration, its primary concern would be to protect the unique but fragile riches its wildlife represented. "The oldest companions of our dreams are being murdered," he would lament day after day, "without any public campaign coming to their rescue." His raids on the poachers became real war expeditions. Yet his equipment was derisory. He had no radio link. His only means of transport was an old truck he was forced to abandon when it ran out of roads suitable for motor vehicles. Anyone else but this gutsy white man would have taken flight. With his wardens, his cook and a few bearers (all former poachers he had inculcated with his mystical vision), escorted by his faithful Sogli, he tracked the enemy relentlessly. As soon as contact was made, battle commenced. For these confrontations, Matta had no reservations about arming himself with the rifle he refused to carry when with the animals. His small party would bear down upon the hunters' camps like Arab horsemen, set fire to the camp, seize any meat, ivory and weapons, and capture and chain up the offenders. Of course things did not always go according to plan. Sometimes the odds were so heavily stacked against them that it was better not to attack. Sometimes, too, after three days' pursuit, they had to retreat because the road had degenerated into a crocodile-infested swamp. At yet other times, Matta would find himself on the receiving end of a particularly well-aimed blow from a poacher's club. But he would always fight back. One night he shot at several forehead lamps intended to attract game. On another occasion his wardens threw a dozen Lobis into the waters of the Comoé infested with hippopotami and crocodiles.

FRUSTRATED AT MY FAILURE to enhance his sanctuary with a *rhinoceros Lapierrensis*, I begged Raphaël to allow me to accompany him on one of his punitive raids on the poachers. It was a terrifying experience. As we were making our way along the riverbank, the stout leader of a pack of dog-faced baboons, perched on the surrounding rocks, jumped down to the ground and reared up ten yards in front of us, barking furiously. I beat a frantic retreat. We were unarmed. This angry monkey could have torn us to pieces in an instant. I could see teeth as long as daggers protruding from under his pendulous lips. Matta restrained me.

"Whatever you do, don't move! He's come to mark his territory and assert his sexual supremacy. We've intruded on his home ground. He looks upon us as male competitors."

Not feeling any particular attraction to the female monkeys,

I half turned around. But the King of the Bush knew the animals' code of good manners. There could be no question of leaving without making one's apologies. He let out several hisses. The baboon stopped barking. Then, visibly reassured, he responded with a series of satisfied grunts. After a moment that seemed like an eternity to me, he turned on his heels with a thrust of his loins and lolloped off back to rejoin his own kind on the rock.

All Raphaël had brought by way of provisions was a sausage, a packet of rusks, a kilo of sugar and some lemons. We did not even have a portable filter to purify the water from the backwaters, which was all we had to drink. The operation proved to be hard-going in bush that had turned into an impenetrable cesspool with the beginning of the rainy season. No matter! Matta's irresistible spirit drew us on regardless. A subtle complicity had grown up between our leader and each member of his little troop.

After three days of walking, the bush offered us a lavish gift which banished at a stroke all the misery of mosquitoes and leeches, infected swamp water and gnawing hunger. By the magnificent light of the tail end of a storm, we were presented with the birth of an elephant. A herd of some twenty heads had gathered around the parturient mother lying on her side. The labor went on for two hours accompanied by a sharp trumpeting which made the forest tremble like cathedral windows at the sound of a great organ. As soon as the baby elephant emerged from its mother's womb, two animals came over to help it to stand up. According to Raphaël, they were the father and the herd's midwife. Wedging the newborn baby between their flanks, they guided it gently down to a little beach beside the river. After beating the water furiously with their trunks to drive away the crocodiles, they then proceeded to spray the baby to wash off any bits of placenta left on him. Afterward they took the young elephant back to the herd. Its mother and the other females waved their ears and their trunks about. A final salvo of trumpeting shook the forest and then silence fell once more. Heaven had planted another of its roots in man's earth.

"Oh my beautiful Africa," Matta scribbled in his logbook that night, "your magic makes every pore of my skin tingle in an ecstasy of happiness and pride!"

"A poachers' camp!"

Christopher Columbus's cry of "Land!" was probably no more triumphant. We went rushing. But the spot appeared deserted. The infallible Sogli rapidly read all the signs. The camp had actually been moved near to the place where some big animal had fallen. An hour at the double and we landed right on it. We immediately surrounded it and the attack passed off smoothly without a single blow being exchanged. The spoils were six poachers who were instantly chained up and turned into bearers, half a ton of meat, partly dried, two forehead lamps, a load of flour, a quantity of bows and poisoned arrows and half a dozen guns. They were locally manufactured makeshift firearms made out of a steel tube clumsily mounted on a butt. They had to be loaded with powder and ball down the barrel. Matta said they claimed as many victims from among the poachers as they did among game. A sinister trophy lay hidden that day under a pile of branches a few dozen yards away. It was the remains of a splendid male elephant, about thirty years old, with tusks each weighing about 110 pounds. The sight of this lost gem so distressed us we could hardly hold back our tears. I could see the rage in Raphaël's feverish expression, and an even more ferocious determination to put an end to this animal genocide. It was a fight to the death he would have to launch, a holy war worthy of the love for Africa that burned inside him.

After a nightmarish night of battling with the mosquitoes and a tornado that battered the two patched old tents that the gentleman in charge of game regulation refused to replace, we were once more on the warpath. In the space of two hours, four camps were set alight, and twenty Lobis and considerable booty captured. The poachers fled in all directions as the sound of the tom-tom signaled our presence. With nothing but four lumps of sugar and three quinine and aspirin tablets in our stomachs, we at last turned back: thirty miles through mud and mist, in tropical squalls, across swamps teeming with leeches and jungle full of snakes, scorpions and tarantulas as hairy as apes. For all the wild trumpeting of its elephants and the roaring of its lions, the Kongo Massa's African paradise seemed more like hell to me that day.

Matta was triumphant. The spoils from our expedition had reached record levels: eleven camps destroyed, twenty-one prisoners, twelve guns, six lots of white weapons, eight forehead lamps, two pairs of ivory tusks and 8,646 pounds of meat taken. Even the most optimistic victory report, however, could not conceal the worrying reality.

"The elephants can breathe again," sighed the Kongo Massa as he accompanied me to the taxi that was to take me back to Abidjan, "but for how long? We can't have any more operations for a month; my cashbox is empty."

As we shook hands warmly, he added in an undertone: "I've decided to risk everything to alert world opinion."

Those sibylline words were the last my friend, the king of the elephants, said to me.

That evening, Raphaël Matta dispatched a new report to the Abidjan Forest Department authorities. With a sinking heart he asked them to strike from the inventory he had drawn up two years earlier, 40 elephants, 150 hippopotami and 5,000 wild bovines whose bleeding carcasses had been dried on the wooden riddles in the clearings of his reserve. That was a quarter of the total strength meticulously recorded on his arrival. The figures showed that, for all his desperate efforts, he was losing the battle.

Bows and Poisoned Arrows Against the Kongo Massa

A few weeks after my visit, the Ivory Coast began an election campaign. Matta wrote me that he had received an order from his superiors to stop all his professional activities and turn a blind eye to the pillaging that was going on in his reserve. Acting in direct contravention of these instructions, he continued to mount antipoaching operations, the magnitude and results of which instilled fear even into the governor's entourage. "You have no right to let your staff run such risks," the director of the Forest Department telegraphed him. Outside his hut, Matta found leaflets inviting the electorate to vote for the cocoa planters because they would "blow up the reserve." Others proclaimed: "You have been robbed of your land. Have your revenge on the wardens by intercepting their supply trucks." Soon Raphaël's children were deprived of fresh food and milk sent from Abidjan. During that time, any poachers arrested were sentenced to derisory punishments, and their weapons, sold at public auction, were simply bought back by other poachers. Matta tried to answer blow for blow. When a chief administrator made out a scathing report against the reserve, he counterattacked publicly: "I caught the signatory of that report red-handed, hunting inside the protected area." Nearly every day letters went out from the small post office at Bouna addressed to everyone, anywhere in the world, for whom the slaughter of a crested crane or a wild elephant was an irreparable crime. They were desperate appeals, begging that an international authority finally be set up to save what could still be saved, a kind of world parliament for the protection of wildlife. But these alarm calls met only with fine words and telegrams of encouragement.

In the bush, the massacring of the elephants went on. Christiane Matta, little Martine and her brother, Germinal, the lizards hiding in the straw roof of the hut and the dozens of ephemera that whirled around the oil lamp were daily witnesses to Raphaël's despair. He did not conceal his tears at humanity's lack of understanding. Soon despair would drive him to the most dramatic decision of his life. Having been refused the full powers he had requested to guarantee his elephants' survival, he went and joined them in the bush to defend them, weapons in hand. He took to the maquis like Morel in *The Roots of Heaven*. In an ultimatum to the director of the Forest Department, he wrote: "Everyone knows it is no longer possible to evict me from Bouna without resorting to bayonets and that the consequences of such an act would be extreme. I am all-powerful because my faith can move mountains and because I am honest. The reserve and I are one and the same. Woe betide anyone who gets in my way."

The dice were cast: he was going to install himself in the heart of the reserve, clear it of poachers, set fire to their haunts and the villages where their weapons were manufactured and where they recruited their bearers. One by one he was going to break the links in the meat and ivory trading chain. If he was killed, arrested, thrown in prison in the process, it did not matter. His rebellion on behalf of the animals would get the audience he wanted, the rostrum he lacked. And if that rostrum turned out to be the accused's stand of a tribunal, so much the better. He had his case for the defense ready. The product of five years of struggle, humiliation, setbacks and all kinds of scandal, it was over 250 explosive pages long. Either by design or possibly simply by carelessness, Matta had this report typed out by none other than the wife of the French commander of the local sector. She was the only one with a typewriter that could do several copies at a time. This imprudent act was prematurely to seal the fate of the Saint Francis of the elephants. For the authorities would know all about the extravagant project he had set in motion.

Along with his closest friends, I received a letter announcing that his masterstroke was imminent.

"I've hidden two trucks crammed with provisions, arms and ammunition in the bush," he informed us. "Volunteers have placed themselves at my disposal to take up arms with me to defend the elephants, regardless of the consequences."

A few days into the new year, a fight broke out between the

Lobis from a village situated on the edge of the reserve and
traders from another tribe, the Dioulas. The incident arose in a
particularly explosive context. The Lobis in the area were in a
state of seething excitement. For two months they had been celebrating the *dyoro*, the grand initiation ceremony which came
around every seven years in their tribal calendar. In the past, in
order to progress from being a child to an adult, every young
Lobi had had to prove his virility and courage by killing a man.
French colonization had put an end to this practice. These days
the young Lobis confined themselves to killing an animal in the
reserve. But every evening when they gathered together, they
heard the elders talk of legendary times when each man earned
his adulthood by killing a member of a rival tribe with his arrows.

Throughout the *dyoro*, which went on for three months, Lobi
country became a no-man's-land into which it was dangerous to
venture. Rites and ceremonies went on there in secret. Boys and
girls were taken by the elders to the banks of the Comoé, the
river-god, for a weeklong period of meditation, at the end of which
they changed their civil status. A lock of their hair, symbolizing
their identity as a child, was buried in the mud of the river. The
witch doctor gave them a new name. The young initiated then returned to their village chanting and shooting arrows at any
members of other tribes they met along the way.

But no prohibition could prevent the Dioula traders from selling their wares, even at the risk of stringent punishment. Knowing that the Lobis loved sunglasses, glass bead necklaces and
old military uniforms, several of them had infringed the *dyoro*
taboo and gone onto their neighbors' lands. The punishment
their audacity incurred exceeded the usual level of violence.
They went and complained to the native head of the district,
who appealed to the French administrator of the sector. The latter summoned Raphaël Matta. Had he suddenly seen an opportunity to get rid of the author of the inflammatory report his
wife had typed out? The assignment was well outside Matta's
field of duty but he was directed to go to the village of Timba
Ouré and settle the dispute between the Dioulas and the Lobis.
The administrator must have known to what dangers he was
exposing his fellow countryman, the Lobis having many times

threatened to settle the score with the "white witch doctor" who had been hot on their trail for five years.

Accompanied by his faithful Sogli and several of his Dioula wardens, Raphaël turned up outside the first dried-mud *soukha-las* of Timba Ouré. At once the Lobi warriors, armed with bows and clubs, and with their quivers full of poisoned arrows slung over their shoulders, formed a circle around the intruder. In a few words translated by Sogli, Raphaël urged the ferocious warriors to stop attacking the Dioula traders. Then, with his usual temerity, he dared to ask them to lay their bows and arrows down at their feet, as a sign of reconciliation with their neighbors. It seemed an insane request. A Lobi hunter's bow is his most sacred possession, the symbol of his virility, a mark of his identity. It is decorated and colored differently according to the clan, age and status of its owner within the tribe. Whether he is using it to kill a long-tailed rat or a six-ton elephant, or to fish blindly in the murky waters of the swamps, a Lobi is never separated from his bow. Death itself only renders communion with his weapon closer. For the three days during which his mortal remains are exposed to view, his bow remains with a Lobi's body.

That day, the Kongo Massa was to succeed in severing this mystical link that death itself could not rupture. Impressed by the courageous little white man's exhortation, the Lobis acceded. They laid their weapons down at their feet. But Raphaël would not have time to savor his victory. Instead of keeping quiet, his Dioula wardens rushed over and grabbed the Lobis' bows and arrows, a sacrilegious act for which the Lobis immediately held the Frenchman responsible.

"The Kongo Massa has betrayed us!" yelled one of them. "He's giving our weapons to the Dioulas!"

They all then hurled themselves at the white man. Sogli saw his boss aim his 5.5 mm. rifle into the air and heard him shout: "I'm warning you once! Twice! . . ."

As far as the best tracker in Africa was concerned, such formalities were pointless. The Lobis were savages. They did not care about warnings. Sogli dragged his boss away, but as they tried to find the path by which they had come, they both lost their way. Borne down upon by their assailants, who were coming at them from all directions, they jumped into a backwater and made for the opposite bank. The Lobis, who had recovered their weapons, directed a shower of arrows at the fugitives. Six of them hit Raphaël, one in the back, which entered his lung, one in the arm, one in the thigh and three in the buttocks. The Frenchman collapsed. The Lobis pounced on him and clubbed him several times. One of them even persisted with an ax. But the poison from the arrows had already done its work. It was January, only a few weeks after the harvest of the venomous plant with which the Lobis smeared their arrows and which was invariably fatal when it was fresh. The King of the Bush had gone to join his elephants in paradise.

THREE DAYS LATER RAPHAËL MATTA'S body was committed to the earth on the banks of the Comoé River, at the same spot where he used to bathe with his children among the animals of the jungle. On the small stele his family and friends had made were engraved the words of an epitaph found in his wallet on the day he died. Years earlier, all alone in the depths of his bush, he had written:

"Beautiful wild elephant, accept from the most faithful of your friends heartfelt wishes for peace and prosperity for you, your offspring and every one of your magnificent race. And what does it matter if one day I water the prestigious land of Africa with my blood for your sake? You are worth it."

THE TRIAL OF THE TWELVE Lobi warriors accused of murdering the elephants' protector took place fourteen months after this tragedy, within the confines of the criminal court in Abidjan. The youngest of them was sixteen. They had all been sent by their village chief to give themselves up to the police and answer to a charge for which their whole tribe carried responsibility.

Seated in the front row, dressed in black, Christiane Matta listened with sad dignity to the account of Raphaël's martyrdom. On a table in front of her were the weapons of another era that had taken her husband's life: twisted poisoned arrows, still bloodstained and still with shreds of his shirt attached to them; the club in the shape of an eagle's beak that had shattered his skull; the flint ax that had split open his chest. She had asked her lawyer to tell the court that Raphaël Matta would have come before his aggressors without hatred. The four African jurors seated next to the three European magistrates tried to take into account the customs, secular rites and superstitions at the root of the tragedy. Even though the European prosecutor only called for one death penalty, the African jurors granted two. The two condemned men greeted their sentence with a smile. They knew that, by their deaths, in the eyes of their tribe, they would become greater heroes than their victim, the Kongo Massa. After three years' detention, they were pardoned by the new president of the Ivory Coast.

The major absentees from the Abidjan trial were those for whom Raphaël Matta had laid down his life: the elephants. I am ashamed to say that neither I nor any other of his friends or admirers went to speak on their behalf. Yet Matta's fears proved to be cruelly well founded. After his death the poachers and Sunday hunters returned en masse to the reserve. The herds he had been prepared to defend at rifle point were decimated by ivory traffickers. The problem was not unique to the Ivory Coast but spread throughout the whole of Africa. Between 1979 and 1989 more than 700,000 elephants were slaughtered. In the year 1985 Japan alone bought seventy-five tons of ivory.

Raphaël Matta did not, however, die in vain. In 1977 the Washington Convention for international trade in species of wild fauna and flora under threat of extinction entered elephants on the list of protected species. One hundred and two countries ratified this decision. Unfortunately it was not strictly applied in those countries that were most affected. Fraudulently obtained firearms licenses and poaching continued to favor the mass export of white gold. It was not until October 17, 1989, thirty years after Raphaël Matta's sacrifice, that the ivory trade was definitively banned. Hunting and killing of animals were regulated. Most European countries, the United States and Japan stopped purchasing ivory.

This decision made it possible to curb the decline in the number of pachyderms, reduced from approximately 2.5 million to less than 600,000 heads during the previous twenty years. Since then the number of elephants has stabilized. But the last convention for international trade in threatened species (CITTS), held in June 1997 in Harare, the capital of Zimbabwe, dealt a new blow to the elephants' cause. After ten days of stormy debate, the convention voted for a partial lifting of the ban on the ivory trade. Although subject to certain conditions, this reconsideration of the embargo was a bitter defeat for those defending the animals' cause.

"The ban on ivory trade is much too recent to have given the elephant population time to recover," lamented the French minister for the environment. "The vote that has just taken place is a signal for ivory trading to be resumed all over Africa."

In reality that trade had never stopped altogether. There has always been a black market for white gold. Every year, in the six central African countries participating in the Forestry Ecosystem project alone, more than a thousand elephants are killed by poachers.

"Poaching has assumed alarming proportions in Gabon, Cameroon and the Central African Republic," declared an official for the project in November 1996, adding that in the Congo the situation was catastrophic.

Alas, the disappearance of the elephants is only one among innumerable animal tragedies now threatening the planet. According to the most recent estimate, 5,205 known species are in danger of becoming extinct before the year 2050. They constitute 25 percent of the world's mammals, 11 percent of its birds, 20 percent of its reptiles, 24 percent of its amphibians and 34 percent of its fish. The world needs new generations of men like Raphaël Matta.

12

A Thousand Dreams along the World's Great Highways

IT WAS THE MOST BEAUTIFUL sight a six-year-old boy enamored of beautiful automobiles could behold. As soon as the first ray of daylight filtered under the door, I would tiptoe out of my bedroom—in order not to wake my mother—and make for the foot of the garden at a run. I wanted to be the first to see, touch, feel the two marvels that had arrived from Paris during the night. They belonged to my uncles, and both were American. The more beautiful was a Hupmobile convertible painted in two shades of blue. In honor of her sheer streamlined grace, my uncle had christened her "Celestial." Two large chrome headlights framed her sparkling radiator grilles, surmounted by a silver mascot representing a bird about to take flight. Under each headlight was the long trumpet of a sonorous horn. The sound of that double trumpet was so powerful that I could recognize it from miles away. An elegant cover built into the front right fender and painted in the same colors as the car held the spare tire. Running boards under each door made it easy to climb in. They served as pedestals for me during my long and solitary admiration sessions.

For Celestial was even more beautiful inside than out. First because of the smell, a sweet, penetrating smell of soft, fresh leather. Then because of the richness of the dashboard, which harbored, among a multitude of mysterious dials and switches, a radio and an ashtray. The numbers on the speedometer went

up to 100 mph, faster, I was certain, than the La Rochelle–
Bordeaux express trains that flashed past the end of the garden
at lightning speed four times a day. It was above all, however,
the back of that car that made it a magic vehicle in my eyes. A
handle opened up a kind of box whereupon a small bench and
backrest appeared, large enough for two people. A small step
on the bumper and another on the upper part of the fender
gave access to this open seat exposed to all the elements.
Known in the United States as a "rumble seat" and in Britain
as a "dicky," this marvel was called a "spider" in France.

My other uncle's pale green Chevrolet convertible was
equipped with a similar spider. On Sundays the two cars took
the entire family to High Mass. My cousins, my sister and I
were allowed to sit in the spiders. It was the greatest treat of
our summer vacation. Passing through the village, along the
main boulevard to the church, our small caravan did not go unnoticed: two such fine cars in succession were no ordinary sight
in the streets of Châtelaillon in 1937. A small seaside town on
the shores of the Atlantic, seven and a half miles south of La
Rochelle, it was a family beach resort. My grandparents had
bought a villa there in the 1900s. Comfort and amenities were
somewhat basic in the house, but the bathing off the vast
stretch of fine sand and the feasts of grilled mussels and sar-
dines under the arbor made up for the lack of bathrooms and
the brick partitions as thin as cigarette paper that separated the
rooms. In all events, to me Châtelaillon was heaven on earth:
even though my family lived in Paris, it was there, in my parents' bedroom, that I was born one July Sunday.

After Mass, we proudly took our places in the spiders of the
Hupmobile and the Chevrolet, under the admiring gazes of the
portly Father Poupard and the vacationers. Then the cars
would go back through the village and come to a halt outside
the pastry shop next to the post office, where my mother would
buy the traditional Sunday Saint-Honoré cake, dripping with
cream. At our uncles' invitation, my cousins, sister and I would
scramble down from our respective spiders and explore the
shop next door which sold beach items. On the first Sunday of
summer vacation, the two cars would return to the villa

bristling with shrimp nets, their spiders full of baskets, sandals, inflatable crocodiles and rafts for us to play with on the beach. After parking the two cars at the foot of the garden, my uncles would lock them carefully. It was a sad moment—a whole week now separated me from my next drive.

When I was a small boy, life rarely presented me with the excitement of getting into an automobile. My parents did not and would never own one. Not only because my father's salary as a professor at the Political Science Institute of Paris would not permit such a purchase but also, and above all, because the idea of sitting behind a steering wheel driving a vehicle with all kinds of pedals was as unimaginable to him as helming a racing yacht around Cape Horn. My father was an intellectual. Books were the only things that excited him.

The war put an end to my spider rides through my birthplace. My uncles carefully hid their American beauties away for fear the French military and later the Germans might be tempted to seize them.

Like all the other beaches of the Atlantic coast, Châtelaillon was declared a "prohibited zone" at the very beginning of the German occupation. Barbed wire, bunkers and minefields replaced summer residents' tents on the long stretches of fine sand. My mother set about finding somewhere else for us to spend the summer. A relative of hers at Dormans, a large market town in the heart of champagne country, some sixty miles east of Paris on the banks of the Marne, put her in touch with a family who took children as boarders for the summer. The time spent with that family was to be a highlight of my childhood.

Adrien and Emilienne Cazé were professional secondhand dealers and ragpickers. They lived in a large house, the rooms of which were crammed to the ceiling with furniture, clothes, crockery and kitchen utensils. In the barn were heaped dozens of bed springs, mattresses, stacks of eiderdowns, blankets, sheets and a variety of linen. The basement was a real Ali Baba's cave full of bicycles, old motorbikes, carts, farming implements and trunks. Every object bore a label on which a series of letters was written in ink or chalk. Each letter was

derived from the code word Adrien Cazé used to remind himself how much he had paid for the item in question. It took me
several summers to break his code and work out the magic
word. It was CATHERINUS. The *C* stood for the number 1, *A*
the number 2 and so on. The last letter, *S*, meant zero. It was
as simple as it was infallible.

Adrien Cazé was known for miles around. At his place you
could find all the things that could no longer be bought in the
shops the war had emptied. Every Saturday he would cycle to
the auction sales rooms in Epernay, or sometimes farther afield,
to Reims, Château-Thierry and even Châlons-sur-Marne. He
might buy anything from a boiler for washing clothes to a superb Louis XVI dining room suite in speckled mahogany. One
day he fell for something of scarcely any market value given
the times in which we were living. Yet his acquisition was to
become a refuge for me in times of trouble and of joy, my secret garden as a small boy. It was a four-door Citroën open
tourer, from a model year long before my birth. The spiderwebs that draped the smallest of its recesses betrayed its prolonged immobility. Its carpeting, seat upholstery and door trim
had provided nourishment for generations of mice. All that was
left of its roof was a pair of wooden hoops in which colonies of
worms now made their home. Despite the ravages of time, the
car still had a proud look about it, with its black fins, double-
bladed bumpers, long dark blue bodywork with white stripes,
the chrome grilles on the sides of its hood and the pretty lamps
on either side of the windshield. The speedometer dial showed
an astronomical 61,600 miles, nearly a quarter of the distance
from the earth to the moon.

For the first time in my brief life, I had the good fortune to
sit behind a proper steering wheel. It mattered not that the seat
springs stripped of their stuffing dug painfully into my buttocks, for I was enthralled. Of course none of the instruments
worked. The large horn button did not unleash any sonorous
musical sequence, the headlight switches on the dashboard
produced no light, the engine push button no life beneath the
hood. My ragpicker's tourer had lost his soul. In vain I crouched
down to depress the pedals, fiddled with the buttons, played

with the gearshift; its engine remained as motionless as an Egyptian mummy in a sarcophagus. Its refusal to come to life did not in any way discourage me. Every day I came religiously to install myself in the mythical vessel. I imagined high-speed races along the highways of the world. I made engine noises with my lips and simulated terrifying acceleration, then abrupt deceleration, and finally the harrowing screech of tires braking on the asphalt.

Often Adrien Cazé would entrust the supervision of the shop to his wife, Emilienne, and join me. Seated in our old wreck, half submerged beneath the bric-a-brac that filled the garage, we were like two castaways struggling in the waves. The old man and the little boy would then indulge the same taste for adventure and fantasy. Suddenly the walls would melt away, darkness would become light, and space would open up before our triumphant hood. Adrien taught me how to change gears, maneuver the pedals, steer tightly around imaginary bends. Those static journeys in the chaos of that garage would remain my most treasured memories of escape.

I saw with despair the coming end of that magical summer vacation. The winter that followed was one of the coldest France had experienced for a century. Our apartment in the rue Jean Mermoz near the Champs-Elysées was situated on the top floor, just under the roof. It was a glacier. The brief flame my father lit at dinnertime in the dining room stove just about created the illusion of a waft of heat. As soon as we had consumed our last mouthful we would go swiftly off to bed. Against my mother's instructions, I got in the habit of slipping into bed fully dressed. This strategy made getting up in the cold less painful next morning. I would curl up at the foot of the bed and pull the sheets and blankets over my head so that just enough air could get in between the pillows for me to breathe. With a very small bedside lamp, I could light up this quilted lair and immerse myself in the latest book I had borrowed from my school library. Of course those books had nothing to do with my school curriculum. They were always adventure stories, tales of war or travel, the lives of pioneers or explorers. Those night-time vigils were unforgettably happy. Snuggled up comfortably in my warm nest beneath my blankets, I would turn the pages and travel through a thousand dreams. Forgotten was the cold that gnawed insidiously at hearts and bodies, forgotten were those slight pangs of hunger that continued to contort the stomach even after meals, forgotten were the shrill whistles of the civil defense patrols at a ray of light spilling through some window. Forgotten at last was that atmosphere of foreboding, that latent fear that affected even us children. From the depths of my bed I implored the god of war to divert the Allied planes away from Paris and not let any air-raid alert force me out of my enchanted refuge.

One of the books to brighten my evenings that winter was an account of the fantastic long-distance motor run that two French Boy Scouts, Guy de Larigaudie and Roger Drapier, had completed just before the war. Never before had a motorcar managed to go overland from Paris to Saigon in Vietnam, across the Ganges and the Brahmaputra Deltas. What those two young men had accomplished on their own initiative, without any official backing, purely and simply for love of adventure, was an exploit comparable to Lindbergh's crossing of the Atlantic or Livingstone's journey on the Congo. Since a new car was out of their financial reach, they had managed the run in an old Ford convertible which already had 43,500 miles on the clock. As a tribute to the name of their sisters in the scout movement, they christened their car "Jeannette."

"What boy, what adolescent, has not harbored in his imagination a dream of setting out on such a great journey?" inquired Larigaudie in the foreword to his book *La Route aux Aventures—Paris–Saigon en Automobile* (The Road to Adventure—Paris–Saigon by Car), before promptly providing the answer. "It was good that two young men were able to fulfill the wishes of countless others. That is why we set out and the success of our expedition was important, precisely because we felt we were making the dreams of several thousand boys come true."

Paris, Istanbul, Jerusalem, Damascus, the deserts of Syria and Iraq, the high plateaus of Afghanistan, the great highway across India . . . That icy winter, I traveled with Larigaudie and Drapier on board their Jeannette. I heard her springs groan on the dreadful Turkish roads, I felt the glacial wind from the peaks of the Hindu Kush burning my pallid cheeks, I trickled the bitter coffee of the Bedouins of Palmyra down my throat, I straddled a Pathan warrior's spirited stallion for a sprint, I donned my dinner jacket to dine with the viceroy of India on the lawns of his *Thousand and One Nights* palace in New Delhi. I, a little schoolboy in my first year at Sainte-Marie junior school, would escape each night from occupied France to roam the world in the trunk of a valiant open tourer, even more beautiful, more real and more adventurous than the one that sat in the garage of my secondhand dealer/ragpicker. Night after night, while my schoolmates were sleeping like little angels, I would jump aboard a Jeannette loaded down with cans of water and gasoline, to cross the eighteen hundred miles of the Syrian desert. I traversed the high, brigand-infested Afghan plateaus, I penetrated deep into the jungles of Orissa in pursuit of wild animals, I found myself in the hell of the Burmese mountain range. Larigaudie recounted:

The roads are atrocious. Jeannette is suffering, straining, adopting astonishing positions and improbable angles. All the bodywork is groaning. The gearbox housing bangs constantly with the stones that hit it. A tree stump literally scrapes it. We travel almost all the time with our wheels balanced on the edge of a slope. The wheels spin and we fall back on the rear axle. The support beams that hold the running boards are twisted. The steel brackets supporting the boards break. The clutch is subject to frightening knocks. Scree-covered bends, dropping sheer to fifteen to eighteen hundred feet, become more frequent. We have to use planks to create bridges to get the car across the collapsing sand.

We tie the car to tree trunks on the side of the mountain and proceed with two wheels over the edge. We pull, push, heave, sometimes driving standing up on the running board so that we can jump off in time if Jeannette slides into the abyss. The most exhausting thing is possibly having continually to empty the vehicle to lighten it, then reload it after each obstacle, only to start again a hundred yards farther on.

Half-naked, in baking temperatures, in the middle of this hallucinating jungle, we work away like convicts with our hearts full of anxiety and our willpower stretched to the utmost.

Night is going to fall. We want to pitch camp. But we are worried about the presence of tigers and wild elephants. Going over a sandy overhang that breaks away, the car slides. Only the security ropes tied to a tree save it. We try to go forward but the ground gives way beneath the levers and the jack. After two hours of effort the situation has become more than critical. If the cables break, Jeannette is lost.

Then a caravan of six small bullock carts, narrow, light, high on their wheels, made out of a simple bamboo framework, turns up. One of the drivers has just been carried off by a tiger. With the help of the four others and the caravan leader we extricate the car. It has taken us a whole day to cover seven kilometers.

Larigaudie and Drapier became my models, my masters, my idols, and their Jeannette the mythical vehicle of all my dreams. The three of them had broken the chains of monotony to pursue their taste for adventure to the ends of the earth. I read and reread the account of that Paris–Saigon journey until I knew every line by heart. There was always one of their adventures dancing about in my head, to a point where my classwork began to suffer. I drew Jeannette in every conceivable position on my school notebooks and roughed out the itineraries for my own future travels. That Paris–Saigon car journey had shown me the way. I was quite sure that one day I, too, would be able to play the game of my life on the maps of the world at the steering wheel of a car.

A Magus Mechanic

That day was to come more quickly than ever I could have imagined. At the end of the war my father was appointed French consul general to New Orleans. Unable to find a ship going straight to the great Mississippi port, we were obliged to go via New York. This was a bonus that was to present me with one of the most powerful emotional experiences of my life: to suddenly discover at fourteen, after five years of Nazi tyranny, of fear, of hunger, of darkness, the magic sight that had inspired happiness and hope in so many millions of people—first the green-draped form of the Statue of Liberty, then the illuminated towers of the Manhattan skyline appearing through the mist! The arrival of our tiny cargo boat coincided with that of the huge liner the *Queen Mary*, repatriating thirty thousand G.I.'s from Europe. Dozens of fireboats, sirens blaring, encircled the prestigious ship with a fairy-tale coronet of water jets. Rambunctious orchestras played jazz tunes and military marches on all the decks. People were singing, laughing, crying. It was enough to make me delirious. A few hours later our cockleshell came alongside a pier on 57th Street, between the tragic remains of the burned out *Normandie* ocean liner and another troopship. The sounds of New York assailed our ears with the din of horns, engines and strident activity.

A Dominican priest, a friend of my parents, was waiting for us on the pier with a yellow cab as long as a railway car. The worthy churchman had some difficulty recognizing his prewar friends. And with good reason! Tough months of German occupation and twenty-five days on a furious sea must have changed our appearance. My mother had packed some of our things in cardboard boxes and bundles roughly tied up with string. My father wore an old suit turned inside out. I was wearing shorts better suited to a little boy. As for our feet, they were shod in wood-soled shoes that clomped like clogs. But what did it matter! There was New York with its dazzling panorama of skyscrapers puncturing the sky with a million stars. As we got off the boat, I recalled a sentence from a book by Scott Fitzgerald that an American aunt had loaned me during the occupation. "Discovering New York was like grasping a crazy picture of the beauty and mystery of the world." That crazy picture hit us as soon as we left the docks. The constant sounds of horns, engines and elevated trains; the succession of giant advertisements proclaiming what you should see, eat, drink, smoke, how you should safeguard your health, move about, entertain yourself and dress; the stream of yellow cabs, cars, trucks; the shop windows brimming over with turkeys, chickens, and suckling pigs roasting on spits; the illuminated announcements that ran across the facades in a thousand colors . . . I found myself bewildered, dazzled, blinded, intoxicated. That feeling of inebriation lasted through my first American night. The French consulate in New York had put us up in a hotel on the corner of Broadway and 46th Street. The only trouble was that the windows of the first eight floors of the establishment were covered by a giant advertisement for Camel cigarettes. Circles of vapor like smoke rings from a cigarette came out of the mouth of a sixty-foot man. The effect was spectacular. No one in the dense crowd milling around Times Square could escape that advertisement, but who would ever have suspected that behind it, in a room spattered with an uninterrupted volley of yellow, red, blue and green lights, a young French boy was trying to sleep his first American night?

A whirlwind of eating, shopping and sights. Nothing could stop our indefatigable white-robed Dominican guide. He was mad about New York and had got it into his head that he would make us share his passion.

It was in New York that I left my childhood behind me: I said good-bye to the shorts I had worn to play marbles in the Champs-Elysées gardens. At Macy's, the big department store on 34th Street that had provided the setting for so many films, my mother bought me my first suit with long trousers. In welcoming me, America turned me into an adult and was soon to confirm this unforgettable passage. I had scarcely climbed off the train in New Orleans when I learned a glorious piece of news: in Louisiana you only had to be fourteen to qualify for a license to drive a car.

"When you're sixteen, we'll see!" my mother announced, determined to curb my irrational passion for automobiles.

To help me swallow her bitter decision, she resorted to a truly diabolical subterfuge. She offered me a car. But not any car. A car that did not move. Sure enough, the engine of the dilapidated jalopy she had someone tow into the garage of our residence one day had no distributor, an absolutely vital electrical part. I suspected my mother of having had it removed to make sure that her gift ran no risk of decamping with her son at the controls. It was a 1925 Nash coupé, a make much prized for its speed by the alcohol traffickers during Prohibition, as old as the Citroën tourer of my young boy's vacation in champagne country. To my mother, its age was a guarantee there was no likelihood of my finding the missing part. She underestimated my persistence. Every afternoon when I came out of school, I would do the rounds of the city's junkyards in the hope of unearthing from under the piles of scrap metal a hood like that of my poor amputated Nash. But America had manufactured so many different models and makes in the course of the past twenty years! I wrote hundreds of letters to wreckers around the country.

In the meantime, I went several times a day to speak to my car to reassure her that she would soon be out of her torpor, that she would splutter, then purr, then roar like an animal awakening. In my imagination I could already hear the magic voice that would burst forth from that long hood, I could already feel the impatient bodywork throbbing. I sat at the wheel, moved the pedals, turned the headlights on and off, made the horn grunt her hoarse voice. Through the windshield I could already see the Louisiana countryside flying by, past bayous teeming with alligators, long alleys lined with hundred-year-old oaks leading to old colonnaded cotton plantation houses, forests of derricks pumping oil. Beyond Louisiana lay Texas, Arizona, California. Beyond that was the whole of the rest of America, an entire continent that my worn tires were going to discover. In my mind I had already worked out how I was going to finance my American automobile adventures. I was going to cram the trunk full of cans of paint and repaint all the mailboxes along my route. With only ten mailboxes a day at two dollars apiece, I would be able to cover my gas and subsistence costs. The jackpot!

I offered two schoolmates at the Jesuit high school where my parents had enrolled me the opportunity to help with the restoration work of the car in exchange for a future ticket for adventure aboard the old Nash. Their enthusiasm spurred me on. Every afternoon when school let out, and again on Saturdays and Sundays, the courtyard to the French consul general's residence became a bustling repair workshop. We cut the roof off the car with a metal saw to turn it into a convertible, stripped the doors to repair the toothed rack for the window winders and bolted steel plates on the floor to cover the holes. To meet the petty costs of this patching-up process, I decided to do what many Americans of my age did: find an after-school job, the first job of my life!

I took the tram on Saint Charles Avenue and went downtown to offer the *New Orleans Item*, the principal local evening paper, my services as a paperboy. They were accepted, and a few days later I was assigned to a route that took in 150 subscribers living in a loop of the Mississippi. Deliveries began at three o'clock in the afternoon, just when I got out of school. First I had to report to the local warehouse, count out the papers, roll them into a cone so that they could be thrown from my bicycle basket, and mark off the customers' names and addresses. On Saturdays, apart from making the deliveries, I had to collect payment for the subscriptions. The job required method, speed, probity and a good measure of resourcefulness, because many of the houses and streets along the Mississippi bore neither number nor name. I threw myself into the venture with such enthusiasm that the French paperboy was soon famous throughout the neighborhood. Customers would sometimes stop me along the way to offer me a chocolate bar, ice cream or a pack of chewing gum. One black matron showed me a small notebook of poems she had written in French.

One day the paper I tossed onto steps or under porches with all the precision of an Olympic discus thrower published my photo on the front page. Having learned that I was the French consul's son, a journalist from the *New Orleans Item* had devoted a dithyrambic article to my crusade to get the old Nash going again so that I could drive across America.

The article brought me several letters of encouragement, and one afternoon while at the warehouse, I received a visit from a large black man in grease-spotted overalls who talked in a husky Louis Armstrong voice.

"Mr. Dominique," he said with a touching air of commiseration, "my name is Eddy and I've just read the sad story about your poor Nash in the newspaper. As a mechanic, my heart bled. That's why I've come to tell you I might be able to find a way of adapting a distributor from another make to fit your car and get it on the road."

He had taken my breath away. Had I understood him properly? A Balthazar in overalls had come to offer me a magus's gift more precious than gold, frankincense or myrrh: getting the old heart of my Nash going again. I fell into the arms of my benefactor. I waited until my father had taken my mother away on a consular tour in Texas to prize my car out of its paralysis and have it towed to the garage of this heaven-sent mechanic.

Every evening, after tossing my last newspaper on the doorsteps of my last subscriber, I would rush to Eddy's shop in the black neighborhood near New Orleans's main cemetery. His garage was a hangar smelling of discarded oil, cluttered up with used parts, cans and old tires. Several ramshackle vehicles almost as old as my Nash were also awaiting resurrection there. Eddy went from one to the other with all the gravity of a surgeon operating on several patients at once. An engine would suddenly show signs of life, give a choleric backfiring, then a slight spluttering punctuated with misfiring and finally an expiring rattle. Eddy did not always succeed in resurrecting his patients first time around.

This Sherlock Holmes of mechanics had managed to lay his hands on the head of a distributor very similar to the part my car was missing. In order to fit it to the engine, however, he had to cut new slots for it, a task that required the scrupulously detailed work of a goldsmith. Armed with a file and calipers, and singing gospel songs, he set to work. I watched his every movement with feverish impatience. Soon my parents would be back from their travels and find that my car had disappeared. I did not dare to imagine the explosion my disobedience would incur. I had already been threatened with being sent back to France on the first available boat. I spurred Eddy on with all the English words I knew, but the modification of the part proved to be more delicate than anticipated. On the sixth evening, with a sinking heart, I made the most painful decision of my brief existence: I would take the car home again. My parents were due back next day and the Nash must be in the garage to greet them. Tying a thick rope around the bumper, I got it ready for towing. It was almost midnight. A tropical storm streaked the night with flashes of lightning. Then the sky opened up, unleashing a deluge of tepid water. Within minutes the streets became torrents.

A thunderbolt more vigorous than the others plunged the garage and the whole neighborhood into darkness. No matter! My Balthazar in overalls worked on by the light of a bulb wired to a battery. Suddenly I heard him call: "Mr. Dominique, please push on the starter!"

I rushed to oblige. Despite the darkness, my fingers instinctively found the button I had so often activated in my static dreams. The familiar grumble of the starter made the steering wheel shake. The battery was fully charged and I sensed in the intensity of its grumble a cooperative will to induce the longed-for purr. By the light of a lightning flash I saw the nape of Eddy's neck shining with sweat as he bent over the inside of the hood. I released the pressure of my finger and counted to ten.

The dazzling figures of Larigaudie and Drapier standing on the running boards of their conquering Jeannette passed before my eyes. I begged for their urgent intercession with the god of mechanics. We absolutely had to hear the Nash's voice that evening! With a heart that pounded ever more heavily, I pressed the starter button.

"Mr. Dominique," cried Eddy's reassuring voice, "push on the accelerator too!"

Then the miracle occurred: an initial splutter, then a blast, then a deep, heart-rending music issued from the car's entrails, which the holes in the exhaust pipe punctuated with unexpected backfiring. A cloud of burned oil soon spread all over the garage, enveloping the car, Eddy and me in choking fumes. Eddy had intoned a whole canticle of thanksgiving prayers in which there was some reference to a shepherd thanking God for having revived one of his lambs savaged by a wolf. After numerous effusive expressions of gratitude, I pulled out of the garage and took off.

Canal Street, New Orleans's great boulevard, was certainly not the Burmese mountain range, but piloting the Nash without windshield wipers and almost without brakes through traffic disrupted by the downpour demanded almost as much skill. After forty-five minutes of hazardous navigation, I passed through the gates of our residence on Broadway. It was nearly five o'clock in the morning. Moments later the two headlights of a taxi appeared in the street.

My parents were back earlier than expected.

"What are you doing at this hour?" exploded my mother, who without waiting for an answer proceeded to knock me half-senseless with a blow from her umbrella.

I staggered to the car door to switch off the engine. In the ensuing silence my mother's anger became even more terrifying. My father, who abhorred confrontations, slipped away as my mother heaped threats upon me. I did not try to defend myself; my case was hopeless. I had indeed abused her trust. She had given me this toy provisionally to allay my craving for adventure. And I had fallen so much in love with the toy that I had brought it back to life.

A few hours later a locksmith came and secured the gate to the street with a double chain and two large padlocks. I bade farewell to the wide-open spaces, the highways that went on forever and all my fine dreams of freedom!

MY PURGATORY WAS TO LAST for fourteen months. On the morning of my sixteenth birthday, my mother came down to have breakfast with me.

"Happy birthday, son," she said, handing me an envelope. "I think you'll like this present."

I shrieked with happiness when I saw the two documents it contained. One was a brand-new car registration card for the Nash in my name, the other a certificate for the insurance policy my parents were offering me. I also found in the envelope a key to the padlocks that secured the gate. Wild with joy, I dashed to the telephone to call the two friends I had made party to my plan to go and paint mailboxes along the roads of Louisiana.

"Go and buy the paint quickly," I cried. "We set off tomorrow!"

Next day, with its trunk weighed down with cans of different-colored paint, the Nash emerged majestically from its prison.

Another article in the *New Orleans Item* was to endow our little expedition with all the glamour of an interplanetary flight. Wherever we went, our fame preceded us. People waited for us in front of their mailboxes or on their doorsteps. In Lafayette, Saint Martin, Pompon, Lafitte and all those places in Louisiana with picturesque names associated with memories of France, we became slaves to the paintbrush. Not only did people have us repaint their mailboxes, they invited us into their houses, wooden chalets built on pilings. They took us fishing on the bayous and fed us simmered casseroles of stuffed crab, eels and gumbo soup. It would have taken us the whole year and barrels of paint to exhaust the warmth of Louisiana's hospitality.

Sadly, a telegram from my mother brought our journey to a premature end. The Quai d'Orsay was recalling my father back to Paris to give him a position in the Foreign Affairs Ministry.

In the autumn of my sixteenth year I returned to France: to restrictions, unlit streets and the cramped confinement of our apartment in the rue Jean Mermoz which the wide-open American spaces had made me forget. I found myself back on the benches at the Condorcet *lycée*, with my head still full of

dreams, firmly resolved to escape for further adventures behind the wheel of some other old car.

Up Thermopylae in Reverse

I waited patiently for three years. But the new *coup de foudre* that
struck me one Sunday afternoon in an auto junkyard on the old
Orly Airport road made that long purgatory worthwhile. What
caught my eye was a radiator grille: the muzzle of a racing creature from a wilder age. That pretty little six-horsepower Amilcar open tourer, with its wooden bodywork topped with airplane
canvas, its red leather seats and benches, its steering wheel aris-
tocratically positioned on the right, its spoked wheels fixed to
the hub with a large chrome butterfly nut like those on racing
Bugattis and Bentleys, must once have been a proud sight.
True, not much remained of its original luxury. But the engine
roared out a waspish note that reawakened my appetite for adventure on the spot. After some hard bargaining I was able to
buy the old rattletrap for the sum of fifty thousand old francs,
not quite a hundred dollars.

That sum corresponded exactly with the advance I had just
received from the Paris publisher Bernard Grasset for my very
first book. *Un Dollar les Mille Kilomètres* (A Dollar Every Thousand Kilometers) was the story of the eventful journey I had
undertaken as a hitchhiker the previous summer across the
United States, Mexico and Canada. Having set out with thirty
dollars, I had covered 18,600 miles, earning my living as a window cleaner, lecturer, gardener, private detective and siren pol-
isher on a cargo ship.

The publisher Bernard Grasset had chosen my manuscript
and had written the foreword himself. "I do not claim to be introducing another Radiguet[1] here," he wrote. "I am not even
sure that Dominique Lapierre will make a lasting commitment

1. Raymond Radiguet, French author who wrote, at the age of eighteen, *The Devil in
the Flesh.*

to writing. He had something to say and knew how to say it. That is all."

A little man with a cigarette holder forever at his lips, Grasset, who prided himself on having published, among other shining lights, the four most important Ms of modern French literature—Malraux, Mauriac, Maurois and Montherlant—was my Amilcar's first passenger. He was a Sunday painter, and to please him I piled his easel, paint boxes and canvases into the backseat and took him up to the Meudon Hill, his favorite outlook onto the rooftops of Paris. One Sunday, French publishing nearly lost one of its leading figures. In the vicinity of Porte Maillot, the car door against which he was leaning suddenly fell off. There were no such things as safety belts at that time. Bernard Grasset let out a cry, lost his cigarette holder and nearly toppled out. I grabbed him by the sleeve at the very last minute.

The incident amused him so much that he made me his regular driver. Every Sunday that winter, the Amilcar would take us back to the Meudon heights. At intervals Grasset's voice would ring out: "Son, I've something to read to you!" He would then take out of his pocket a sheaf of paper, the last episode of the book he was writing about his conjugal disappointments. This Don Juan had never been happy in love. "Listen to this, son! . . ." He wrote with the same skill with which he launched his author's books. His reading was a great treat and he would often go on until evening when we got to Alberto's, the Italian bistro in the Latin Quarter in front of which the Amilcar would drop us. There we dined on minestrone and a cutlet à la Milanese, washed down with a bottle of Brunello that the proprietor, whom Grasset had known for twenty-five years, kept in reserve for him. I was eighteen. Established authors came over to greet him, glancing enviously at me in passing, as if to say: "What is Bernard Grasset doing with that youngster?"

With the help of his publisher's bright ideas, the youngster in question was making a respectable debut in the field of literature. That winter, his first book was Grasset publications' lead best-seller. Germany, Holland and Italy bought the foreign-language rights. The Paris daily *Combat* serialized it. *Le*

Monde devoted an entire half-page to it. Discovering I had a gift for speaking, Grasset requisitioned my Christmas and Easter vacations with lecture tours across France, Switzerland and Belgium. Persuaded that I would be better than any of his reps at convincing people to read my book, he filled the Amilcar with hundreds of copies that I was assigned to sell after each talk.

I had more prestigious and distant adventures in mind for my car, however, than having it act as a delivery van for my publisher. One day I suggested to Dominique Frémy, a classmate at the Paris Political Institute, that we drive my antique Amilcar from Paris to Ankara, Turkey. It would be a 3,700-mile adventure!

We left the Place de la Concorde scarcely one hour after the end of our exams. The car's springs buckled beneath the weight of the tins of cassoulet, ham and pâté, first-aid kits, snake-bite serum, water-purifying capsules, sun creams, insect repellents and the religious medals devoted to every saint in paradise with which our parents and well-wishers had packed our wretched Amilcar. We had managed to provide it with new tires, powerful headlights, a modern carburetor, camping equipment, a fire extinguisher and even a distress flare. To prevent the water in the radiator from boiling too frequently, we traveled at night for hundreds of miles. Via Genoa, Pisa, Rome, Naples and Brindisi, we cheerfully reached Athens, taking long stops along the way to visit museums, churches, palaces and archaeological sites. Everywhere we traveled the venerable car aroused tremendous curiosity. Every time we went through a town, swarms of scooters would provide it with a triumphal escort. When we stopped, we had difficulty extricating ourselves from the crowds that instantly surrounded us.

One day Frémy had the artful idea of exploiting the enthusiasm of our admirers to reinforce our finances. After parking the Amilcar on the cathedral parvis in Naples, we hid it from the eyes of the passersby behind a screen made out of our tent canvas. *"Cinquanta lire per ammirare la più bella machina del mondo!"*[2] announced Frémy with a juggler's glibness of tongue

2. "Fifty lire to admire the most beautiful car in the world!"

and an Italian accent worthy of a Vittorio de Sica film. A queue immediately formed. People went on filing past the old car until evening, caressing the torn canvas of its bodywork, prodding the rubber of its big wheels, going into ecstasies over its old-fashioned lamps. This lucrative exercise enabled us to buy tickets in Brindisi for the ferry to Greece.

Welcomed, petted and pampered by the priests from the Christian School in Athens, the Amilcar and its drivers spent a week preparing for the toughest 950 miles of our journey. No one had been able to provide us with any kind of road map from Thessaloniki to Istanbul. No such document existed. From the north of Greece to the Turkish border was *terra incognita*. To keep the engine cool, we decided to carry on traveling by night. On the evening of our departure all the good fathers of the Christian School were there. The father superior, a giant in a white cassock, insisted on our taking a heavy rope he had got ready for us.

"You can't imagine the mountains you're going to have to cross," he told us. "You'll be very glad to be able to get a tow."

Another priest arrived with his arms full of canned food. "For heaven's sake, take these provisions," he begged. "Because the local food could kill you."

We might have been about to take off for the moon. The father superior emptied a flask of holy water over the hood of the car, then gave us his blessing: "Lord, watch over our travelers. May your star guide them safely to their destination."

We had hardly left Athens before a particularly steep slope brought the unfortunate Amilcar's six horsepower to its knees. I downshifted into first gear to no avail, the car hung back, emitting a spectacular rattling noise. Frémy jumped out and set his back against the trunk to try and help the engine, but the car was too heavily loaded to climb such a grade. That was when my companion had a brilliant idea.

"Suppose we went up the slope in reverse?" he suggested.

I turned around just to give it a try. The effect was miraculous: our valiant car began to climb like a Tour de France bicycle rider. We continued on all that night under the stars, our heads uncomfortably turned backward, trying to steer a course by the beam of a flashlight. At dawn, after one final bend, we at last reached the summit. I stopped in front of a small chapel that marked the pass. Frémy struck a match to check our position on the map. I was impatient: "Where are we?"

My companion's face had lit up. "Guess!"

"On top of Everest?"

"No, pal, on the tip of Thermopylae."

After Thessaloniki, we were into the unknown. The Automobile Club in Athens had firmly advised us against approaching Turkey by the only existing road running along the coast at the foot of the mountains of Bulgaria. The route passed through an unsafe area overrun with communist guerrillas. To top it all off, sharp stones tortured our tires and the blades of our springs. We came to a bridge guarded by two strapping fellows armed with guns, their chests girded with cartridge belts like in Mexican films. Although they examined our passports suspiciously, they let us pass on our way. We drove with headlights on, trying to follow the ruts made by bullock carts on the side of the road. Suddenly the silhouettes of three men holding rifles stood out in the beam of our lights. Their fierce looks were not exactly reassuring. They pointed their guns at us. Were they communists or government supporters? The one who seemed to be the leader shouted orders. At once, his companions signaled to us to stop. There could be no question of doing as he said. I switched off the lights, jammed my foot on the accelerator and at the risk of disintegrating the Amilcar, crossed the bridge with a burst of speed. As I shouted to Frémy to "Bend your head!" a volley of bullets whistled past our ears. Fortunately we were already some distance away. I switched the headlights back on and just managed to avoid crashing the car into an enormous rock. Worn out, we stopped a few miles farther on and fell asleep under a tree.

At dawn we set off again. The road stopped at the banks of a river where was neither bridge nor ford. We emptied the car completely to make it lighter. Then, in our underpants, we got down into the water to level out the banks with a pick and pile up stones to make a way across that was roughly suitable for a motor vehicle. After four hours' labor, our hands bleeding and my back burned by a blazing sun, I got behind the wheel and cautiously began the descent to the river. To prevent the Amilcar from running out of control, every few inches Frémy placed wedges in front of the wheels. Soon the water was up to the hubcaps. A few more inches and the engine would be flooded: our extraordinary journey would be brought to an end. We reached the middle of the stream. The opposite bank was a little less steep. I tried to encourage Frémy, who was wading stoically through the mud.

"We're almost there!" I called.

I had scarcely uttered those words when one of the rear wheels skidded on a stone. Out of balance, the Amilcar nosedived and sank into two feet of water. The engine gave a last gasp and stopped. Fortunately I spotted some people working in the sunflower fields. I yelled for help and they came running from all directions. Although the unexpected sight of our poor, half-submerged car gave rise to open hilarity, a dozen men courageously agreed to be harnessed to the rope the good priest from the Christian School in Athens had provided. Others waded into the river to push from behind. Coordinated by my "Heave-ho!'s," they managed to retrieve the Amilcar and drag it onto the bank. I at once dismantled the generator and found to my dismay that its housing was full of water. Our engine would never start again unless we could find a baker's oven in which to dry out this vital organ. I questioned our rescuers in sign language. I must be quite good at mime because I was taken straight to the baker's in the nearby village. He was in the middle of putting some loaves of bread in his bakehouse oven. He surveyed the metal part I showed him with some surprise. The good man had manifestly never had to cook that sort of instrument before. Minutes later a truck entered the village square. Its driver, a rough, unshaven character with a mustache like Pancho Villa's, spoke a few words of Italian; we understood that he was going as far as the small town of Komotini, some twenty-five miles away, where there was a garage with a mechanic. He was willing to tow us there.

On that perilous expanse of broken road the operation promised to be quite an acrobatic feat. Frémy climbed into the truck with the mission of preventing the driver from going too fast; on the end of the rope, the Amilcar was likely to turn into an uncontrollable punching bag.

"Keep an eye on my headlights," I told my companion. "If I switch them on, you make the driver stop immediately."

The truck started up, spewing out a cloud of smoke that blinded me. I could no longer see even the hood of my vehicle. Abruptly stretched taut, the rope snatched at the Amilcar like a wisp of straw. Changing into second gear and immediately accelerating, the brute of a driver inflicted another jerk so violent that for a second time the car narrowly missed being smashed against the back of the truck. I put my foot down hard on the brake pedal to try and keep the rope taut, but very soon the pedal failed to respond. The truck gathered momentum. The car bounced from stone to stone, plunged into potholes, leapt from one side of the road to the other. It was like being on a raft battered by breaking waves. I expected to see my poor Amilcar disintegrate at any minute. I railed against Frémy and that damned Greek. The ordeal only got worse. The steering wheel seized up with the wheels pointing slightly to the right. I could no longer keep the car in line with the truck. One of the shock absorbers must have broken unless the jolting had twisted the axle. I switched on the headlights to give the agreed distress signal. I gave a blast of the horn, I shouted, I called upon Drapier and Larigaudie to come to the rescue. But the swirling dust must have hidden me from Frémy and the Greek. The truck continued careening on its crazy way. The Amilcar creaked, groaned and bumped. I was still desperately sounding my horn when its noise weakened and finally failed altogether. The battery had given up and thus so had the headlights. A slight slope. The driver changed gear and accelerated. I extricated my head from the windshield and yelled. Dragged along by the monster to which it was tied, the Amilcar assumed terrifying angles. I was certain it was going to turn right over. No doubt the end had come.

The truck came to a bridge at thirty-five miles an hour. It slowed down a little and I was unable to hold the car back. Even the emergency brake no longer worked. I was being carried along with the wheels locked to the right toward the river below. If I could not straighten out in the next few fractions of a second, our trip would end in disaster. My entire life flashed before my eyes. I yelled again but the dust and sand stifled my voice. The truck continued on its way. The only chance I had of saving my skin was to jump out of my doomed car. My fingers tore at the two clips that attached the top to the windshield, but I was unable to undo them. It was not possible to open the doors either: they were wired on. My destiny was tied to that of the car. Together, she and I would be dashed on the rocks of the river below.

Once more I applied all my strength to the spokes of the steering wheel, but the locked steering had no effect on the wheels. At that moment the towrope slackened. Left to its own inertia, the Amilcar headed for the abyss. That was when the truck suddenly picked up speed again, wresting the vehicle from the fatal drop right at the very last second. The Amilcar crossed the bridge with its two right wheels in the void, smashed the plank of the parapet and rebounded like a ball back onto the road. At last the truck came to a halt. Frémy and the driver came running. I hadn't even the strength left to hurl curses at my companion and the Greek. I collapsed onto the steering wheel, shaken by an attack of inconsolable weeping. The incident had broken me. One thing was sure: I was not made of the stuff of Paris–Saigon heroes. Not yet, at least.

THE AMILCAR SURVIVED its terrible injuries thanks to the assiduous attentions of the kindly mechanic in the small city of Komotini. Dried out and cleaned, the generator got its valiant engine going again. Two days later the magical sight of the first Oriental minarets appeared through our windshield. First Andrinopolis, then Istanbul welcomed the survivors of that infernal route like a princess dropped out of the heavens. The car's photo taken from every angle appeared on the front pages of the local newspapers and brought us all the warmth of Turkish hospitality and a shower of invitations. Then via Ephesus, Bursa and Izmir, we reached Ankara, the ultimate goal of our journey. Impressed by the age of our car, the president of the Turkish Republic offered us the opportunity to return to France with our vehicle aboard one of the passenger liners of the national shipping line. His gift could not have been more opportune: a telegram awaited me in Ankara. The directors of the Fulbright scholarships were offering me a scholarship to study at Lafayette College in Easton, Pennsylvania. A cabin had already been booked for me on the *Queen Mary*.

I fell into Frémy's arms. Going back to America was a sure way of soon getting back on the highway to adventure.

Honeymoon in a Chrysler Royal

The dear Marquis de La Fayette could rest happily in his tomb. The college a grateful America had named after him was a little gem. Built on a hill overlooking the charming Pennsylvania town of Easton and its Lehigh River, its gracious red brick buildings extended around a vast lawn bordered with maple trees and hundred-year-old oaks.

I was delighted. Lafayette College was situated only about sixty miles away from the dazzling city I had discovered at the age of fourteen: New York.

To escape from my gilded cage to that mirage, I needed a car. I set out in search of a suitable successor to the Nash and the Amilcar in the local secondhand dealers and wreckers. That was when it appeared before me, like a resurrected childhood memory. I rubbed my eyes. It had the same long streamlined hood as my uncle's blue Hupmobile in Châtelaillon, the same chrome horns beneath its nose, cone-shaped headlights and the same small steps to climb up to the same rumble seat! Despite the ravages of time, its interior exuded the same smell of leather, paint and Galalith that had fired my imagination as a child. It was a 1938 Chrysler Royal convertible.

I emptied my wallet into the hands of the flabbergasted

salesman and climbed back up the college hill as proud as Fangio bringing home the twenty-four-hour Le Mans trophy. On the evening of the next day I sped off to New York. Returning at dawn, I was off again that same evening. Two gallons of gasoline cost less than a glass of Coca-Cola. The Chrysler brought me freedom. And very soon love. In fact, with its help, I managed to capture the heart of a most attractive editor for the famous New York fashion magazine *Harper's Bazaar*. With the top down despite the cold, we took off every weekend to explore the admirable New England countryside, the frozen banks of the Saint Lawrence River with their picturesque French villages, the battlefields of lovely Virginia and a hundred other unforgettable eastern American landscapes, all so conducive to the blossoming of romantic love.

The apotheosis of my complicity with that car took place one morning of the following summer outside the monumental porch of New York City Hall. In accordance with American custom, I had decorated the Chrysler's hood, windshield and rumble seat with ribbons and white carnations for the occasion. That day I married Aliette, my pretty fashion editor. A few days previously, robed in a black gown with the ritual mortarboard on my head, I had sat with my Lafayette class to hear the commencement address delivered by Henry Luce, founder of *Time* and *Life*, before climbing onto the dais to receive from the college president the degree of bachelor of arts.

Dominique Frémy, the companion of my adventures in the Amilcar, had hitched a lift on a boat across the Atlantic to be a surprise witness to my marriage. Outside, the successor to the Nash and the Amilcar was waiting to take us—him, my wife and me—away on an expedition that the heroes of the Paris–Saigon run probably never envisaged for their Jeannette: a honeymoon as a threesome. Destination: Mexico City, some 4,300 miles from New York. Larigaudie had written that with a dinner jacket and a pair of shorts you could go anywhere. My young bride had taken the lesson to heart but made her own calculations as to the requisite number of each. I had all the difficulty in the world wedging her collection of suitcases full of evening dresses into the rumble seat. As for the dinner jacket I took along, I did wonder about its actual usefulness. We were traveling rough, with only three hundred dollars to spend, just enough to quench the Chrysler's thirst, provide us with sandwiches and buy our rooms in modest truck drivers' motels. Never mind! We were twenty years old and in love.

A Russian Kiss for a Tricolor Flag

"*Monsieur le Maréchal,* we'd like to travel across the USSR in a car with our wives. As we're unable to speak your language, we suggest that a young Soviet journalist couple accompany us to act as guides and interpreters. We ask you to grant us this exceptional authorization."

This scene took place four years later, in February 1956, under the rococo chandeliers of the great Hall of Saint George in the Kremlin where Moscow's dignitaries were hosting former French President Vincent Auriol and his wife. The individual with the white goatee whom I had just addressed looked at me in astonishment.

"By car?"

He was Marshal Nikolai Bulganin, president of the Council of Ministers, the highest authority in the Soviet Union. Next to him were Vyacheslav Molotov, minister for foreign affairs, Marshal Vorochilov and various other dignitaries who had been plunged into a similar stupor by my request.

Paris Match had sent me to Moscow to cover the visit of our former president. My work as a senior reporter for Europe's premier current affairs weekly satisfied my craving to witness history in the making. But it was still Larigaudie and Drapier's ideal that fired my fantasies. Even my most exciting assignments lacked the scent of adventure the heroes of Paris–Saigon-by-car had been able to conjure up.

One day, coming back by car from a story, I had turned to the photographer who was with me. "Jean-Pierre, does the idea of driving across the USSR during our next summer vacation tempt you?"

The guy to whom I put the question was one of *Paris Match*'s top photographers and my favorite working companion. A giant of a man with tousled fair hair, a face like that of an archangel, an eternal Leica around his neck, twenty-nine-year-old Jean-Pierre Pedrazzini epitomized the new generation of frontline reporters born out of World War II. His courage, his generosity, his modesty and his physique of a movie matinee idol gave him a special place with the magazine. I had been lucky to carry out my first assignment with him during the British elections. When the plane taking us to London roared onto the runway, I had seen Jean-Pierre make the same motion as bullfighters entering the arena: the sign of the cross. The reporter who had risked his life on so many dangerous assignments was not ashamed to show his fear.

The surprise of the USSR's supreme leader and the skeptical looks from his entourage were entirely predictable. No foreigner had ever been authorized to roam Soviet roads freely behind the wheel of a car. A Chicago dentist who had tried to "force" his way through the Soviet-Finnish border had seen his Jeep loaded onto a freight car and sent back to Finland. All the experts we consulted were quite explicit: never, in a country where individual travel was forbidden, would four members of a capitalist country be allowed to enter and travel freely. Why would the Soviets reveal the inadequacy of their road and hotel systems and the poverty of their countryside? Why would they permit their citizens contact with foreigners who could only spread subversive ideas? Why would they let tourists use routes that would inevitably, at some point or other, lead to a prohibited area?

Our plan engaged the interest of President Auriol, who was quick to talk to Nikita Khrushchev in person that same evening.

"Tovarich Nikita, do you know what this boy wants to do?" he said, pointing paternalistically at me. "He wants to wander about your country in a car! If I were fifty years younger, I'd go with him. You must give him permission."

With a thumping heart I waited for the first secretary of the Soviet Communist Party's reaction. He shook his head and a strange light came into his eyes as round as marbles. "Dear Mr. President, this is no time to put such proposals to me. I won't be able to sleep!"

The time for our summer vacation came. We had given up all hope of being given the authorization we wanted. Jean-Pierre and his young wife rented a sailboat in the Mediterranean, my wife and I a villa on the Spanish Costa del Sol. Our dream of venturing across the never-ending plains of the Ukraine, along the meanderings of the Volga, on the beaches of the Crimea, had gone out the window. Then a telegram arrived from Moscow.

"YOUR REQUEST GRANTED," it said. "YOU CAN ENTER USSR AT TOWN OF BREST LITOVSK. SUGGEST ITINERARY VIA MINSK, MOSCOW, KHARKOV, KIEV, YALTA, TIFLIS, KRASNODAR, ROSTOV, STALINGRAD, KAZAN AND GORKI. NOTIFY US OF DATE OF YOUR ARRIVAL AT BREST LITOVSK." I scrambled for a map. Miracle of all miracles: we were being offered an eight-thousand-mile jaunt across the western Soviet Union.

We needed a car that was up to such a long run. In the end we fell for a Marly eight-cylinder station wagon made by Simca. This elegant straw-and-gold-colored model was bound to please the Soviets. I had the name *Paris Match* inscribed on the fenders, the words "Across the USSR by car" on the doors and "French journalists," in Russian, on the trunk. We left a Paris in a state of festivity: it was Bastille Day. Three days later we arrived at the Soviet frontier post of Brest Litovsk. Our great adventure had begun. Among the group of uniformed officials waiting for us was a big fellow with an abundant shock of hair.

"My name is Stanislav Ivanovich Petoukhov," he informed us in impeccable French. "I am a journalist with *Komsomolskaia Pravda*, the Young Communists' daily. I have been designated to accompany you. My wife, Vera, will join us in Moscow. Welcome to the Soviet Union."

Flanked by two Jeeps packed with soldiers, we made our entry into the town where, on March 3, 1918, the Bolsheviks had rocked the history of the world by signing a treaty with

Germany that would leave them a free hand to lead a success-ful revolution.

Next day, in Minsk railway station's immense square, we had our first contact with the Russian crowds. A tidal wave. Dozens of faces pressed themselves against the windows of the Marly. At first we were observed with amazement, as if we were exotic fishes in an aquarium. A bearded *muzhik* who had stepped straight out of a Dostoyevsky novel at last decided to engage us in conversation. I understood that he was interested in the make and purchase price of our vehicle. A corpulent *babushka* in a head scarf was anxious to know whether the car belonged to us. Discovering the inscription "French journalists" on the trunk, a teenager planted himself in front of the bumper and recited a poem by Victor Hugo. Then, coming over to my win-dow, he asked us in a whisper for French newspapers. The pressure became such that Jean-Pierre had to start the car to extricate us. But the human sea immediately re-formed around us. For people who had been cut off from the rest of the world for so long, the appearance of that two-toned car with four "Martians" on board was a sight they could hardly believe.

We encountered the same curiosity, the same astonishment, everywhere we went on our long journey. Every time we stopped we were assailed, surrounded, submerged. Curious people would slide underneath the car to examine the sus-pension. We were constantly being asked to lift the hood so that people could view the engine. Heads came in through the windows to admire the interior. In Tiflis, Georgia, mounted police charged to repel the enthusiastic crowd; in Kharkov children took the windshield-wiper blades as trophies; in Kiev a taxi driver begged us to take him for a drive. We used up tens of gallons of water for the sheer pleasure of squirting the wind-shield washer, a piece of equipment unknown to Soviet cars. In Yalta an elderly lady even begged us to let a little air out of a tire so that she could "breathe the air of Paris." Radio Moscow had spread word of our expedition, and everywhere we went we were feverishly awaited.

Our arrival in Sukhumi, a seaside resort on the Black Sea, brought us a singularly moving encounter. A curly-haired man in his thirties picked his way through the hundreds of people besieging the car. When he got to our radio antenna, I saw him take our tricolor flag respectfully in his hands, then raise it to his lips and kiss it.

"I must absolutely speak to you," he whispered then in French with a surprising Marseille accent. "I'll come to your hotel at nine o'clock tonight. Unless the KGB arrests me in the meantime."

At nine o'clock precisely there was a knock on the door. Jean-Pierre had got out our only bottle of pastis. Before sitting down, the visitor meticulously inspected every nook and cranny of the room, moved the furniture, unhooked the paintings, followed the wires that ran along the wainscoting and examined any suspicious objects. Apparently reassured, he sat down in an armchair and lit a cigarette. I served him a generous pastis while Jean-Pierre turned on our tape recorder. We were not exactly at ease: it was always possible that we were being set up.

"My name is Georges Manoukian," he began. "I used to be a cobbler in Marseille. My parents are Armenians, but I am French." From the pocket of his shirt he took out a card. "Look: 'République Française.' That's my identity card." He drew closer to the microphone. "Mother, I can't tell you who I am, but I'm sure you'll recognize my voice. This is your son talking. Remember: I owe you two thousand francs you loaned me at the casino in Aix-en-Provence on Christmas Eve 1945. Mother, I beg you: go and see all our friends and relatives in the cobblers' street and tell them never to make the same blunder I did by coming to this country."

"Why did you make this 'blunder' yourself?" Jean-Pierre asked.

The Armenian replied briskly, smiling with all his gold teeth. "We were young and the ship was beautiful. We said to ourselves: let's go and do a stint there, and if we don't like it we'll come back. There were six thousand of us. Soviet propaganda, parents who encouraged us to go, the taste for adventure . . . When we reached Batum, they loaded us into cattle cars. They had promised us jobs, good salaries, houses, cars and all the rest. What they actually gave us was hell. You know, it would be more apt to say 'Go to the Soviet Union!' than 'Go to hell!' I had to steal in order to eat. Until the day came when I couldn't take any more and I decided to escape. One night I packed twelve cats into a bag on my back and set off for Turkey. When I got to the border and the dogs of the Soviet guards smelled my presence and barked, I released the cats. The dogs took off after the cats and I took the opportunity to jump in the river. Sadly, I was spotted by a sentry and recaptured. They gave me a journey in a barred railroad car to the Verkhoyansk camp, a corner of Siberia that passes for the coldest place on earth. I was condemned to ten years of hard labor. To shorten my sentence, I volunteered to be part of a unit that emptied the camp cesspools. The work was so revolting that every day counted for three. Because of the smell that permeated right into us, we were locked away in a separate barrack hut. I stayed there for three years. On my return to Soviet Armenia, friends helped me to buy an identity card on which there was no mention of my period in the gulag. Since then I've been living off little jobs here and there in the hope of getting permission to return to France."

Returning to France! There were six thousand French Armenians like Georges Manoukian desperately pursuing that dream. In the course of our journey we met dozens who begged us to intervene on their behalf. Their cases were tragic. All the diplomats we consulted in Moscow were unequivocal: the Soviets would never allow such fanatical enemies of the "socialist paradise" to leave. Two weeks later, when we passed through Sukhumi again on our way back from Tiflis, a woman with her face half concealed in the folds of a scarf approached our car. In a few words murmured in English, she told us that the police had arrested Georges Manoukian as soon as we left.

SEVEN YEARS LATER, at my Paris home one evening, I received a telephone call from Marseille. The voice on the end of the line had such a distinctive accent that I thought I recognized our Armenian from Sukhumi. It was not him, but his brother calling from the cobblers' street.

"Mr. Lapierre, I'm asking for your help. A miracle has just happened: my brother Georges has obtained his visa to leave the USSR, but the French authorities are now refusing him an entry visa for France! For pity's sake, do something! You remember: my brother was brave enough to kiss the French flag on your car in front of everyone. You published the photo in *Paris Match*. The Soviets didn't appreciate it. They sentenced him to eight years in camp beyond the polar circle . . ."—the man had difficulty containing his emotion—"and now the French don't want him."

I asked at once to meet a friend of my editor in chief who held a prominent position at the DST, the French equivalent of the FBI. I showed him the photograph of Georges Manoukian kissing our tricolor pennant and vigorously pleaded his cause. The official remained unmoved.

"My dear Dominique Lapierre, I'm surprised at your naiveté," he finally responded. "Surely you must suspect that if the Russians have released 'your' Manoukian, it's because they've made a deal with him. Your Manoukian is now a KGB spy."

I was amazed at the assertion. Cops have wonderful imaginations. I could not help thinking of that poor man describing his escape attempt with his cats and his three nightmarish years in the gulag emptying cesspools.

"That man might be a spy today," I said, "but I'm willing to guarantee you that after he's spent a fortnight with his family and friends in the cobblers' street in Marseille, the KGB will have to strike him from their files. He's bled too much for him to serve his torturer's regime for any length of time."

Shaking his head with a look of skepticism, the policeman assured me he would look into the case.

One evening three months later I found a magnificent bunch of roses outside the door to my Paris apartment. On the calling card were four words: "Thank you. Georges Manoukian."

THIRTY YEARS WENT BY. One day in 1993 I felt an urge to know what had become of the Armenian from Sukhumi. My wife consulted telephone information. She found three Georges Manoukians living in Marseille. I dialed the first number. There was no answer. I called the second. Someone replied.

"I'd like to speak to Georges Manou—"

I had not even finished saying "Manoukian" before a voice in the receiver burst out: "I'll bet that's Mr. Dominique Lapierre from *Paris Match!*"

A few days later I went armed with a bottle of champagne to greet the survivor of the gulag in the attractive apartment at 10 impasse du Gaz, to which he had retired. We drank to our poignant meeting in the Soviet Union. He no longer had his gold teeth, but he was otherwise much the same as when I saw him force his way through the crowd to come and kiss our small flag. On his return to France he had found a job with a Parisian shoemaker. But it was Marseille that was in his blood. He went back to the city he had dreamed about in his Siberian camp and opened up a cobbler's workshop. A letter I received from his wife at the beginning of 1996 informed me that Georges Manoukian had died of a heart attack while plying his trade. "Seeing you again was one of the last great joys of his life," she wrote.

Mechanics Straight out of a Tolstoy Novel

Each day the hazards of the Russian roads came close to shattering our poor car. Worst of all, however, was the foul, stinking juice we had to give it for fuel. We might have done better to fill it up with vodka. And yet it had got off to such a good start. We had been able to gorge it on a top-grade high-octane fuel at the Metropole Hotel garage in the Bolshoi Theater

Square in Moscow, not realizing that it would be the only time it would be treated to such nectar. There was only one garage that sold high-grade gasoline in the whole of the Soviet Union. Everywhere else, the low octane level and the impurities—sand, brick dust and rusty metal flakes—made the gasoline difficult for a modern Western engine to consume. The result was awful. In vain we filtered the liquid we were offered through all kinds of strainers (notably my grandfather's opera hat); the symphonic sonorousness of our eight cylinders was repeatedly reduced to a shameful backfiring. Deprived of a good half of its power, our car dragged itself along at the speed of the Gypsy caravans we met along the way. Ten, twenty times a day, we had to stop and clean the carburetor and blow through the nozzles. In Sochi, a seaside resort on the Black Sea reserved for *nomenklatura* dignitaries, the once-powerful engine expired with a series of gasps. What were we to do, nearly two thousand miles from the nearest Simca dealer, in a country where no foreign makes were represented and where there were no garages for private cars? Unanimous opinion was that the only solution was to take the unfortunate creature to the large local "engine hospital," as it transpired, the municipal bus depot where Slava, the Russian journalist accompanying us, assured me I would find "all the skill of Soviet technicians and the mechanical precision your patient needs."

The technicians in question, Vladimir Alexandrovich and Ivan Nicolayevich, were named after Tolstoy characters. At the entrance to their workshop, beneath a huge banner proclaiming "Onward to Communism," there was an honors board containing photos and names of the best workers. I was reassured to discover, under the effigies of Karl Marx, Lenin and Stalin, the portraits of Vladimir and Ivan. The Marly was in good hands! Especially since the director of the depot and his chief engineer, both in ties and business suits, had come running to the rescue of their overalled mechanics. After a detailed examination of the engine they went into a long consultation. The conclusion was somewhat frightening: the cylinder head would have to be removed and the sixteen valves reground and adjusted. Were these Russians who had never before touched a piece of foreign machinery capable of such surgery? Lost in this far corner of the USSR, I was brought to a sudden appreciation of the universal nature of mechanics. Without a word, with precise, almost instinctive movements, Vladimir and Ivan began to strip the engine.

Eight hours later, at midnight, as the Soviet national anthem resounded from the workshop's little radio, Vladimir and Ivan silently finished putting back the last bolt. The repairs were finished. Under the anxious gazes of the two drawn-faced Stakhanovites, I installed myself at the wheel. My trembling fingers felt the icy metal of the ignition key. Vladimir and Ivan watched my hand as if it were about to launch a *Sputnik* into space. They had worked so hard! I put an end to the suspense by turning the key. The engine started up. But I was too familiar with its music not to realize at once that the orchestra was missing half of its instruments. The two Russians' intrepid labors had been to no avail. Proper life had not been restored to our eight cylinders. I wiped away a tear of rage and turned off the ignition.

"We should call Boris," suggested Vladimir, admiring the small Eiffel Tower Jean-Pierre had just given him.

"Boris? Who's Boris?" we asked.

"He's the mechanic in charge of carburetors," translated Slava, proud to show us what wealth of specialists his country had.

The clock in the workshop indicated that it was almost one o'clock in the morning.

"And where might one find this expert at this time of night?" I worried.

"No problem," Ivan intervened. "He's on duty at the other depot. I'll go and tell him."

That was how the man who was our last resort appeared on the scene. He was a big fellow with glasses, who did not seem at all surprised at this nocturnal SOS. He listened at length to the faltering sound of the engine, depressed the accelerator several times and pronounced his diagnosis: "The fuel is not

circulating properly in the carburetor, which is blocked somewhere."

"Doctor" Boris disconnected the gasoline pipes and throttle
linkage and removed the carburetor much as one might remove
a heart. He placed it carefully on the workbench, took off the
float cover and removed the floats. In less than a minute, our
poor car's vital organ found itself dissected into a hundred tiny
parts. I wondered anxiously how Boris was going to put this
metal puzzle together again. He proceeded to subject every
screw, jet and recess of the float chamber, as well as every fuel
pipe, to a fierce blast of compressed air. Then he reassembled
the whole thing and placed the carburetor back in position. Before reconnecting the fuel inlet pipe, he took the precaution of
installing a small supplementary filtering device to stop impurities from getting through once and for all.

Ignition on. The engine roared. I could not believe my ears.
I clasped Boris in my arms while Jean-Pierre opened a bottle of
vodka. The Marly had been saved. The night ended with a
tour around the deserted streets of Sochi at sixty miles an hour.
Screeching around corners, with Grand Prix–style acceleration,
I shamelessly woke the whole town, addressing a flood of al-
leluias to Drapier and Larigaudie. Our magic dream could continue.

No incident could dispel the good humor of Slava, our Soviet colleague. Ever since our arrival in his country, our discreet, warmhearted companion who showed evangelic
patience with our insatiable demands had made it a point of
honor to translate the propaganda placards plastered all over
the landscape. "Peasants, learn skills," "We salute the world
with our outstanding work," "The Soviet people do their utmost for peace!" On one, a little girl with long blond braids
brandished a pick and exclaimed: "Let us master the art of
good farming." Farther on, a plump figure that bore a distinct
resemblance to Khrushchev in a straw hat held out an enor-

mous watermelon at arm's length and exclaimed in jovial
fashion: "Let us farm the USSR well." There were hundreds
of them. Slava assured us that all those placards had been put
up by the peasants and workers themselves "in order to put
pressure on our leaders."

This young man was a perfect product of the system, even if
he had only been a party member for three years. One day
when I was telling him about my reporting of the Korean War,
I plucked up the courage to sound out his knowledge.

"Slava, why, in your opinion, did the North Koreans invade
their neighbors in the South?" I asked him.

Slava's reddish cheeks became suddenly white. "But, Dominique, what are you saying? You know very well it was the
Americans and the South Koreans who attacked the North."

Twenty-eight years old, with a turned-up nose and green
eyes that sparkled like champagne, his wife, Vera, had joined
us in Moscow. She taught piano at a secondary school. It was
the first time she had met anyone from a capitalist country, and
set out to discover her own country. One day when we were
camping in the Caucasus, she gazed at length at the bowl in
which my wife was washing my shirt. The material the receptacle was made out of was new to her. Vera Petoukhov had
never seen plastic before.

THE NEVER-ENDING PLAINS of the Ukraine in the rain: a
vagabond impulse suddenly made me leave the main road and
make for the red roofs of a *kolkhoze* we could see some miles
away. How did the *muzhik* of the regime live? We wanted to
find out by getting ourselves invited into one of their homes to
stay with them for a few days. In Minsk we had done the same
with a railway employee; in Moscow, with a salesgirl from the
big GUM department store; in Tiflis, with a surgeon at the central hospital; in Gorki, with a worker from the Pobieda automobile plant. Never before had foreigners infiltrated the
privacy of the Russian people in this way. The car was our pass-

port. Who was going to close his doors to our mythical two-toned Western chariot?

Suddenly, however, I felt the Marly skid as if it had hit ice. The road was so soft the wheels lost their traction. The Ukrainian soil stuck to and finally sucked at the vehicle like a suction cup. The car ended up getting bogged down to its belly. Jean-Pierre rushed to immortalize the scene on film. Delighted, Slava clapped his hands like a small boy. His Communist Youth's daily had definitely not prepared him for this kind of adventure. Just imagine! A Soviet castaway lost in the middle of the Ukraine in a car with Paris plates, along with four young capitalists full of ideas worse than subversive! What a strange world it was! But our companion's euphoria vanished abruptly. Like us, he had just seen soldiers appear from all sides, pointing their submachine guns in our direction. A shouting officer rushed at Jean-Pierre to snatch his camera off him. My friend evaded him with a pirouette and the officer took a dive into the mud. Slava's fresh pink cheeks turned a pale yellow. He might well be one of the "happy few" with a party card in his pocket, but he knew that this slip of cardboard would be of no use to him in a confrontation with the military. Why were those soldiers with their shaven heads threatening us? Slava tried to find out. According to the mud-covered officer, we were in a forbidden military zone and we had committed the crime of taking photographs. The soldiers pushed us with the tips of their weapons toward a camp of barracks protected by barbed wire. They shut us in a kind of shed that reeked of rancid fat. Through a barred opening, I discovered what all the commotion was about: some radar equipment and several heavy artillery pieces were concealed under camouflage netting.

"Well, baby, you really chose a good spot to take your photos!" Jean-Pierre's wife remarked.

Photos or no photos, no travel agency could ever have provided us with such an experience. After two hours of anxious waiting, the door to our shed finally opened. Two officers from the military police, identifiable by their red armbands, had arrived from Kiev. They brought us into the main room. The two men, one fat and one very thin, settled themselves behind a table. Our interrogation began at once. The report that was read to us began thus:

We the undersigned Colonel Illysef, Lieutenant Major Trigou, Lieutenant Major Pietrov and Private Bielli declare that on August 13, 1956, at 1605 we saw a yellow and black vehicle approach the military base and stop. Several people got out of the car and took photos. The people concerned were:

1. The tovarich Petoukhov, Stanislas, who claimed he was a correspondent for *Komsomolskaia Pravda*, and who presented his identity card;

2. The tovarich Lapierre, Dominique, who presented his French journalist's card, according to which he was born in Châtelaillon-Plage, France, on July 30, 1931;

3. The tovarich Pedrazzini, Jean-Pierre, who, without any means of identification, claims he is also a French journalist;[2]

4. The tovarichi Lapierre, Aliette, and Pedrazzini, Annie, claiming to be the spouses of the above-mentioned citizens.

There followed six pages explaining that we had deliberately photographed the military targets in the zone where we had been arrested. We vehemently contested this assertion, but the fat colonel proved intractable. The discussion went on interminably. To put an end to it, Jean-Pierre opened up his camera, took out the incriminating film and held it out to the officer.

"Take it! We have no desire to go to Siberia," he declared. "You'll see for yourselves there are no military secrets on that film."

This time Slava turned from livid to crimson and translated. The officer shook his head with a smile.

"You're wrong," he objected calmly. "Siberia is very beautiful." After a pause, he added: "I spent seven years there."

---

2. In the USSR all foreigners had to hand in their passports at the reception desk of the hotel where they were staying for the entire duration of their stay in a city. Jean-Pierre had left his at our hotel in Kiev.

HAPPILY THAT WAS THE END of the affair. We were allowed to resume our trip. After three hundred miles of broken roads, torrents that had to be forded and various experiences of getting bogged down, the Marly reached the heart of the Caucasus. Our tricolor pennant fluttered from the top of a young oak tree between our tents. We were the first foreigners to camp in an area subject to rigid police regulations. All at once the iron curtain, the cold war, the proletarian revolution, the Red terror and the gulag seemed to us like creations of a disaster movie. Jean-Pierre lit a fire and cooked succulent *pasta alla carbonara* for us. Our wives took the washing down to the river. Slava sang old Russian melodies in his deep voice, with Vera accompanying him on the harmonica. We basked in utter euphoria. It was too good to last. The news of our passing spread throughout the region. "Delegations" of mountain dwellers and vacationers converged on us from all sides. We were showered with tokens of friendship. People protested that letting such distinguished guests sleep in a tent was no way to welcome them. We were given fish, honey, fruits. Above all, people admired the car. We handed out our last Eiffel Towers and silk scarves emblazoned with the Paris coat of arms. A tall, roughly shaven Georgian swore I would be his brother until death, seized my chin in his big callused hands and kissed me passionately on the mouth. Slava assured me this was a very old Georgian custom. The car acquired fresh messages of friendship traced in the dust on its bodywork. "France and the USSR are the two greatest tovarichi in the world," affirmed one of them. "Long live Yves Montand and Edith Piaf," proclaimed another. "The workers of Kharkov greet those of Paris." "Peace to the whole world". . . We gave up washing the car so that we could take all the messages from those warmhearted people back home, never realizing that our decision could incur a heavy fine. Soviet law in fact required all drivers to maintain their cars in a state of perfect cleanliness.

On our return to Moscow the dirtiness of the Marly created quite a sensation. Traffic police pursued us. Whistles signaled to us to stop. Police officers emerged from their boxes and ran their index fingers over the bodywork with a scandalized air. As it was difficult for us to tell each one in Russian why it was that we wanted to keep the dust and the inscriptions, I asked Slava to write a declaration for the benefit of the Greater Moscow Police on a piece of cardboard, telling them that the reason we had not washed our car was so that we could take back home a little bit of Russian earth and the innumerable tokens of friendship that people had marked on it.

The day for the long return journey had arrived. Slava was exultant: he had received permission to accompany us back to France. His paper had entrusted him with a huge black Zim, on the sides of which he had had painted in French "Moscow–Paris—Soviet Journalists." Unfortunately his wife, Vera, would not be able to take part in the trip. In order to quash any intentions her husband might have of taking advantage of being outside the Soviet Union to "choose freedom," the police authorities were holding her hostage. Slava found it quite natural that "Vera's school should have absolute need of her presence to teach its pupils the piano." A cameraman from Soviet television came in the young woman's place. We were sorry to leave our lovely Russian friend behind the iron curtain.

One morning in October, loaded down with tins of caviar, records, books and a whole collection of Russian nesting dolls given to us in Gorki, Rostov, Minsk, Yalta and elsewhere, the Marly set off from Red Square to the astonished stares of hundreds of people queuing to go into Lenin's mausoleum. Direction: Paris. Winter was already prowling over the vast expanses of the Ukraine. Everywhere, the local people had put on the quilted coats and felt boots that formed their cold-weather uniform. In three to four weeks the road would disappear under the white blanket of General Winter, conqueror of both Napoleon and Hitler.

The entire staff of *Paris Match* came running out into the Champs-Elysées to greet our return to the fold. Many representatives of the press, photographers, television and movie news cameramen were there too. Slava and his colleague could not believe their eyes: they were received like a tsar and his grand duke. A reporter and a photographer from *Match* were waiting to guide them across France. Our friend's first contact with our country was, however, offset by one small fiasco. Keen to appear friendly toward the policeman checking his passport at the border, Slava offered him a Russian cigarette, one of those *papirossi* with a long cardboard tip and very little tobacco in it. The Frenchman examined the cigarette with a disdainful sneer. "Here, my friend, we call that a stub."

We paid fond farewells to our car. I stroked its thick black Bakelite steering wheel and revved for one last time the engine whose music had given me so much joy and so many headaches. I consoled myself with the thought that after that vehicle there would, of course, be others in my life: I had celebrated my twenty-fifth birthday between Kharkov and Kiev. But I would always recall with nostalgia the deep, generous, sonorous sound that only the marriage of eight cylinders can produce. The Simca representatives invited me to drive it on the last leg of its great journey to the manufacturer's showroom on the avenue des Champs-Elysées where, like a creature returned from another planet, the Marly was going to be put on display to curious Parisians. A photo montage illustrating its adventures in the course of our eight-thousand-mile trip had been prepared to provide the backdrop for our proud car, still covered in the graffiti of friendship, written in the dust accumulated across the wide-open spaces of the Soviet Union.

The Death of an Archangel

Alas, history deprived us the pleasure of savoring our achievement. Fourteen days after our return, an uprising of Hungarian patriots took place in Budapest against the communist dictatorship oppressing their country. They managed to take over several of the capital's nerve centers. The insurrection spread to many parts of the city and then to other parts of Hungary. The communist world was on the brink of losing one of its bastions. The Soviets decided to intervene. While a convoy of armored vehicles marked with the Red Star set off for Budapest, a white Alfa Romeo leaving from Vienna forced its way through the Hungarian border and sped toward the burning capital. At the wheel, wrapped up in his trench coat, with his hair blowing in the wind and his Leica around his neck, a strapping fellow sang away at the top of his voice. Jean-Pierre Pedrazzini had responded unhesitatingly to *Paris Match's* editor in chief's call. He had closed his travel bag, kissed his wife, paid a brief visit to the office where I was sorting out the photographs of our journey across Russia. "See you soon, old man!" he had shouted before rushing to Orly to catch a plane to Vienna.

On October 30 he was in Budapest, outside the Communist Party HQ in Republic Square. Rebels were storming the building. Tanks flying the Hungarian flag appeared. The crowd applauded them and sang the "Marseillaise." Suddenly, however, there were screams of horror: the tanks were being driven by Soviet crews who proceeded to fire into the crowd. Jean-Pierre was hit by three bursts of machine-gun fire, in the legs, back and stomach. His fellow reporter, the Hungarian Paul Mathias, carried him in his arms to a Red Cross ambulance. "Watch out for the cameras! Have you got the film?" Jean-Pierre voiced his concern through chattering teeth. The ambulance reached the hospital to meet with a dreadful scene: hundreds of wounded and dying people were piled in the corridors, courtyards and even the cellars. There were no bandages, medicines, anesthetics. Jean-Pierre's courage in his awful suffering earned him everyone's admiration. He was only worried about one thing: his pictures. When a nurse came to give him a second

Achromycin injection, he refused it, knowing that the antibiotic was extremely rare: "Keep it! Others need it just as much as I do!"

Hungarian surgeons tried to close up the wounds that had devastated his belly, but they had run out of catgut, dressings and antibiotics. Only immediate evacuation could save Jean-Pierre. As soon as they were informed, the editors of *Paris Match* sent a rescue plane to Budapest. Dr. Dieckman, a skilled surgeon at a Paris hospital, volunteered to go and bring the wounded man back.

Just as the plane was about to take off to return to Paris, a Soviet tank positioned itself across the Budapest airport runway. From the newsroom at *Paris Match* I called the French ambassador to Moscow, with whom we had dined less than two weeks earlier, and begged him to intervene with the highest Soviet authorities to have the runway cleared immediately. The Soviet ambassador to Paris, the president of France, the prime minister, the Foreign Ministry were all alerted. In a matter of minutes a rescue chain was set up to save our colleague. The tank moved and the plane could take off. It would be the last aircraft to leave the Soviet-surrounded Hungarian capital. It landed at Le Bourget. We all waited apprehensively at the foot of the aircraft steps. On the pillow of the stretcher I saw a haggard face, covered with stubble, ghastly pale, and with eyes that had sunk into their sockets. A nurse was holding a transfusion bottle over his disheveled mop of hair. Jean-Pierre did not appear to be conscious. An ambulance took him to an emergency clinic in Neuilly. All the leading specialists summoned to his bedside shared the same opinion: he was too weak to withstand surgery. His body had first to regain some strength. By a cruel stroke of irony, his room, number 35, was the one in which Marshal de Lattre de Tassigny, one of France's liberators, had died four years earlier. The poignant photograph of the marshal in full uniform on his deathbed had been one of the first scoops Jean-Pierre had landed for *Paris Match*.

While my friend lay at death's door, Paris broke out in sympathy for the Hungarian rebels. The salesmen at the Simca showroom on the Champs-Elysées scrambled to hide the

Marly under a cover and remove the travel photographs for fear that people would smash their display window. I rushed to the hotel where we had put up Slava to make sure that, as a Soviet citizen, his safety was not under threat. I found the poor man on his knees on the pavement, using a pumice stone to frantically scrub the words "Moscow–Paris—Soviet Journalists" off the sides of his Zim.

"Dominique, they're going to set fire to our car and perhaps even kill us too!" he wailed, listening to the sound of cries of "Down with the USSR!" "Death to the communists!" coming from the nearby Champs-Elysées.

I told him the tragedy that had befallen Jean-Pierre. He seemed so upset I was afraid he was going to collapse.

"Soviet bullets!" I said. How ironic after the three months of friendship we had shared.

At these words, the lenses of his heavy glasses misted over with tears. He took both my hands and shook them with all his might.

"Poor Jean-Pierre," he murmured. "Poor Jean-Pierre."

"Dominique, I want to see my pictures!"

In between bouts of delirium, Jean-Pierre kept demanding to see his work. After tearing out the photograph showing him half-dead on a stretcher coming off the airplane, I brought him the special issue of *Paris Match* with all his pictures. It was to be his final consolation. His condition was deteriorating rapidly. His urea count had risen to 1.40 grams, a sign that his system was in the process of poisoning itself. All the same, he found the strength to ask his nurses to call Balzac 00.24, the telephone number for *Match*.

"Tell them to come and get me," he begged me.

I tried to calm him down. He was a devastating sight with his half-closed eyes showing only their whites. His cheeks and forehead had taken on a waxy tinge. He was listening for noises. At the slightest footstep in the room, his eyes would open and he would gaze anxiously around him. Spotting his sister, Marie-Charlotte, the person to whom he was probably the closest, he tried to sit up.

"Charlie, get me out of here!" he cried.

Then suddenly he was clutching my shoulders, pulling me toward him with extraordinary strength.

"Come on, Dominique. Let's go!" he moaned. "Let's go!"

Around midnight a nurse gave him an injection of morphine. He remained delirious, so they gave him a massive dose of Pentothal. At three in the morning it was hard to find a pulse. One hour later his breathing became more and more labored and irregular. The nurse put an oxygen mask over his face. At 4:40 A.M. he stopped breathing altogether. His sister laid a kiss on his forehead and closed his eyes.

I looked at my dead friend and realized I had said good-bye to my youth.

SLAVA PETOUKHOV RETURNED hurriedly to the USSR. The bloody crushing of the Hungarian revolution by his country's tanks and the death of Jean-Pierre had put a premature end to his dream of getting to know the France whose language he spoke with so much affection. The following February, *Paris Match* published over three issues the report of our journey across the highways of Russia, illustrated with Jean-Pierre's amazing photographs. In Moscow Slava was immediately penalized by the management of his newspaper and the police authorities who had assigned him to watch over us during our journey. How had he been so imprudent as to allow us so much freedom? He tried to redeem himself by writing a vitriolic article on the front page of the *Komsomolskaia Pravda*, denouncing the way in which I had reported our experiences and meetings with the Russian people. But his attempt to satirize "his French friends" was not enough to save him from inevitable punishment. He was sacked and exiled to Siberia for three years.

Today, Slava lives in Moscow, half paralyzed after an operation on his spine. He separated from Vera about ten years ago and married his nurse. I telephone him from time to time to talk about those happy days when we were young and discovering together his country's hidden universe.

The Spirit of Ecstasy

It was one of the most brilliant creations of twentieth-century man's genius. Since the beginning of the century when two British gentlemen, an aristocratic racing driver and an obsessive mechanic, combined their talents to spread their passion for cars into high society, the Rolls-Royce had been the ultimate symbol of motorcar perfection. The vehicle make favored by royalty, emirs, sultans, maharajas, heads of state, the sovereign pontiff, Hollywood stars and captains of finance and industry, Rolls-Royce cars had, in a myriad of forms and models, demonstrated their creators' ability to turn a car into a myth. The myth fed largely on legend. Was it not said that Rolls-Royce cars were so perfect that their hoods were sealed so that only their own mechanics could open them to service them? That all the parts were manufactured and fitted by hand? That it took a whole month to produce a single car? That no two cars were identical? That out of the sixty thousand Rolls-Royces made since the company's inception, some fifty thousand, approximately eight out of ten, were still running three-quarters of a century later?

Obviously such excellence had its price. Rolls-Royce cars were the most expensive in the world. The pale green eight-cylinder Corniche coupé with a 6.5-liter engine I was contemplating that October day in a London showroom cost a mere forty thousand pounds, the price of twenty-five Peugeots. Strangely there was nothing really exceptional about the lines of that vehicle, or of any of the other models on display. The Italian postwar designers had accustomed us to greater style and originality. Like all the other most recent models, the Corniche looked slightly cumbersome. Was that the secret of its majesty? I am more inclined to attribute it to the feature religiously preserved on all Rollses since the birth of the make: the superb chrome radiator grille reminiscent of the facade of a Greek temple. In a way it was the blazon of Rolls-Royce. The grille's height had diminished with the passage of time, but it had still maintained its emblem, a winged and almost naked woman taking flight. The artist who sculpted her had given her the beautiful name of Spirit of Ecstasy, but thereafter she was known simply as the Flying Lady. This shameless emblem on the automobile jewel of puritan England never ceased to astonish me.

Greedy curiosity drew me into the interior of the shop. In the same way that one longs to touch the beveled surface of a precious stone or caress the naked shoulder of a beautiful woman, I felt an irrepressible desire to run my hands over the bodywork and chrome of that Corniche coupé. I waited until the salesman was engaged in conversation with a visitor before gently feeling the wings of the Flying Lady, letting my fingers run down the folds of her veil. Then, slowly, I stroked the imposing chrome triangle of the grille with its badge bearing the intermingled initials and names of Rolls and Royce and below them, like the pipes of a celestial organ, the double flutes of the air ducts. Then my hands strayed to left and right to brush the twin headlights that looked like a ball mask concealing the eyes of a Venetian marchioness. In that way I toured the vehicle several times before daring to sit inside. What a feeling flooded over me when the door closed behind me, leaving me alone, almost in a reclining position, astounded by the richness of an interior that was finished in leather and precious wood. Something almost supernatural came over me as I touched the small wooden steering wheel and depressed the accelerator with my foot. I cupped the elm knob of the gearshift lever in my palm and fiddled with the switches for the air-conditioning, the radio with its eight speakers and the cruise control. I lowered the two marquetry trays built into the backs of the front seats for the benefit of the passengers in the rear. I moved my electrically controlled seat into every imaginable position. Comfortably ensconced in that all-enveloping seat, breathing in lungfuls of the delicious smell of leather, I gazed through the windshield at the long tapered hood, at the end of which soared the graceful Flying Lady. In my fantasy I could imagine the silence of the engine, a silence so complete, it was said, that in a Rolls-Royce the only sound heard was the ticking of the clock.

It was indeed the spirit of ecstasy! Far from being lulled into a state of relaxation, I felt myself being swept away by a desire to drive that magnificent car to the far reaches of the earth, to buy it for my fortieth birthday and the great new literary venture Larry and I were about to begin, which was to take us to India. India, the very country where Rolls-Royce cars had known their finest years.

Had I gone mad? Could I really sacrifice everything to the same passion for cars that had earned me a beating with my mother's umbrella at the age of fourteen? I did some brief calculations. The price of this Rolls-Royce amounted exactly to my share of the advance I had received from our publishers for the new book we had under way. I could just about afford this madness. Happy birthday, old boy!

Before tearing myself away from carpeting as thick as eiderdown to tell the salesman the news, I took the precaution of straightening my tie in one of the four courtesy mirrors and brushing down my blazer. Unfortunately I did not possess a bowler hat and umbrella to establish my credibility. Nor did I have a British checkbook to put down a deposit and so cement the purchase.

The salesman regarded me with polite condescension before addressing me with a "Good afternoon, sir. What may I do for you?" in a voice as lacking warmth as that of a railway conductor of whom I had inquired of a train time. The Rolls-Royce representative was a tall, skinny individual of about fifty with a blotchy complexion. He was wearing a white shirt with a stiff collar, a black vest under a black jacket and gray-striped trousers. He looked more like a butler in some country estate than a car salesman. It should be said that the cars he was selling were not for ordinary mortals. The austerity of his attire specifically underlined that point. I indicated the pale green Corniche at the far end of the showroom.

"I would like to buy that motorcar," I said, assuming my best British accent.

The salesman let out an "ooh" of amazement. His Adam's apple danced up and down his throat.

"You would like to purchase that motorcar?" he repeated, emphasizing each syllable, as if seeking to convince himself that he had heard correctly.

"That's correct," I replied.

He emitted several more troubled "Ooh!'s." It was obviously the first time in his life that anyone apparently so young and devoid of a waistcoat, umbrella and stiff collar had told him he wanted to buy one of his automobiles. He rubbed his chin several times, then asked me a question that, at the time, I found irrelevant.

"To which country do you intend taking this motorcar?"

He must have picked up a foreign intonation behind my truly British accent.

"India!"

The salesman's eyes rounded like billiard balls. If I had said the moon, he could not have been more surprised.

"India?" he repeated, paralyzed with astonishment.

A heavy silence ensued. He bowed his head as if I had hit him. Clearly he was deeply disturbed. He had never before had to deal with a client like me. People generally bought his cars to travel back and forth between London and some stately home in Yorkshire or the Highlands. And now here was some madcap talking of taking one of his motorcars to India!

"Did you really say India?"

There was a quaver in his voice in which I thought I discerned a hint of nostalgia. I nodded in confirmation. He shook his head several times.

"In that case, sir, I shall have to consult our export manager. He's the only one who can take responsibility for complying with your wishes."

He disappeared into an office next door. After a few seconds I heard him explaining on the telephone: "There's a foreign gentleman in the showroom who would like to buy a Corniche to take to"—he choked and then went on—"to take to India . . . I think, sir, that his request warrants your attention."

A few minutes later I saw a plump little man with a thin Charlie Chaplin mustache arrive, also dressed in black. A gold chain twinkled from his vest pocket. He greeted me with a touch of disdain.

"I understand you have expressed the desire to purchase one of our motorcars and take it to. . ." He stumbled over the word "India," just as the salesman had done, as if the connection of Rolls-Royce with that country was about as incongruous as anything could be. "The trouble is, sir, that we no longer have any agents in India," he continued. "Were you to be the victim of some mechanical problem, trivial as it might be, you would have to send your car to . . ." He motioned to me to follow him into a room where, hanging on the wall, was a map of the world dotted with red spots representing Rolls-Royce agencies. He hesitated and looked for the red spot nearest to the Indian subcontinent. "Sir, you would have to send your car to Kuwait."

At a rough estimate on the map, Kuwait must be at least eighteen hundred miles from New Delhi.

"I thought a Rolls-Royce never broke down," I objected, surprised.

"True, but mishaps can always occur," answered the little man, lowering his eyes. "And then there are maintenance procedures."

"You mean changing the oil?"

"Changing the oil, greasing, tire pressure, in short, all kinds of small checks and adjustments."

I had difficulty in keeping a straight face. "It seems to me that any Indian garage ought to be capable of changing the oil and carrying out those various routine procedures. As for the tire pressure: surely New Delhi air must be just as suitable for Rolls-Royce tires as London's?"

At my last remark the faces of my two interlocutors froze. Such impertinence with regard to a Rolls-Royce was unworthy of a would-be purchaser. I read all that in their reprobatory looks. The export manager found a way out.

"Sir," he said, "I shall consult the person in charge of our after-sales servicing. He is the only one who can tell us whether it is reasonable to take one of our motorcars to that part of the world. Would you be so good as to call in again late morning, tomorrow?"

I explained that I had to catch a train in an hour's time for Romsey, near Southampton, where I had an appointment with Lord Mountbatten for an interview in connection with my next book. "So I'd like the opinion of the gentleman in charge of after-sales service this very day," I insisted.

Neither the name of the last viceroy of India nor the mention of the fact that I was a writer had the slightest effect on the plump little man and his stiff-collared acolyte. At Rolls-Royce they were accountable only to God. All the same, the export manager agreed to call the man in charge of after-sales service. I witnessed the arrival of a third accomplice similarly dressed in black. His colleague's call had evidently disturbed him at his labors. He seemed in a very bad mood. The export manager gave him a summary of the situation. As I expected, he stumbled over the word "India" to the point of letting the glasses on his forehead slip down onto his nose. The two men then retreated into the adjacent office, leaving me alone in the company of the salesman.

Much amused by a situation that was becoming farcical, I took the opportunity to explore the rest of the showroom. Apart from "my" beautiful pale green Corniche coupé, there was a four-door Silver Shadow painted in what the British proudly call British racing green. Also on display was the very latest Phantom VI, similar to the one Her Majesty the Queen had just acquired for herself, with its 6.5-liter engine and its two independent air-conditioning turbines that allowed the front and the rear of the interior to be cooled separately. This vehicle for the royals cost over $150,000. I went back to caress the Flying Lady on the grille of my Corniche, surer than ever that she and I were destined to share a steamy love affair from one end of the earth to the other.

It was at this point that the two men in black emerged from

their deliberations. They rejoined me in front of the object of my concupiscence.

"We are sorry, sir," declared the export manager with the untroubled conscience of a magistrate sentencing a prisoner to penal servitude. "We cannot sell you this motorcar."

I acknowledged the blow with all the dignity I could muster, then, with rage in my heart, ran to Victoria Station to catch the train to Romsey. The purpose of the journey was to ask Lord Mountbatten about his first encounter with India when, in 1921, as a young ADC to his cousin, the Prince of Wales, he had traveled about the country playing polo with maharajas, hunting tigers and panthers in their forests and dining in ceremonial uniform on the terraces of their illuminated palaces. It was during that prodigious journey that young Louis had met, at a gala evening at the viceroy's, the lovely Edwina, who was to become his wife. In his private journal he had recorded the outstanding moments of his fantastic discovery of the Indian empire. Meticulous, well-organized man that he was, he had gathered together his notes and reflections in a red, leatherbound volume, which he agreed to entrust to me so I could copy out the most remarkable episodes. Back in Paris later that night, I immersed myself in engrossing reading. Much to my surprise, I discovered an account of a tiger hunt with the maharaja of Mysore, dated April 21, 1921.

"His Highness has turned one of his numerous Rolls-Royce cars into a shooting-break to enable his guests to shoot game from the most comfortable vantage point imaginable," Mountbatten had written. "That car is an unadulterated marvel. It crosses watercourses, goes up and down the steepest banks without even requiring a change of gear, goes through jungle, making light work of any obstacles. Oh, if only a Rolls-Royce representative had been there! How proud he would have been!"

That description made me inordinately happy. Clearly, like Drapier and Larigaudie's Jeannette, like my Amilcar and the Marly on the infernal roads of Greece and the Caucasus, a Rolls-Royce could rise to any challenge and make its way where there was no way. It was a salutary lesson for the undertakers in the London store! I photocopied that unforgettable page and placed it carefully in my briefcase.

Next time I traveled to the English capital, I rushed to the Rolls-Royce showroom. My Corniche was still in the same place in the display window.

The salesman in the stiff collar recognized me instantly. I asked him to call the export manager. When the latter arrived, I gave him the photocopy of the extract from the diary of the queen of England's uncle.

"These words, sir, were written by one of your most illustrious countrymen," I declared, pleased to have my revenge. "Allow me to give them to you. Read them. They explain without any shadow of doubt why you did not consider it prudent to sell me one of your motorcars. I'm afraid that today's Rolls-Royces are not as good as yesterday's."

MY UNPLEASANT EXPERIENCE with the Rolls-Royce representatives scandalized Mountbatten, who had been one of the most fervent Rolls-Royce users throughout his life.

"If they're not sure enough of their new cars to allow them to go to India, buy an old model," he advised me. "A good old Silver Cloud, for instance. Go to Frank Dale & Stepsons of Sloane Square. They're the biggest dealers in secondhand Rolls-Royces in the world. You'll find something to suit you there."

On a narrow door in a street off Sloane Square in Chelsea, a simple copper plate read: "Frank Dale & Stepsons." I rang the bell and, somewhat surprised at the ordinariness of the premises, stepped into a room filled with cigarette smoke. Sitting in a corner under a photograph of a race car, an elderly gentleman was reading the newspaper and drawing on a cigarillo. This was Frank Dale, owner of the garage. With his blazer and yellow-and-blue-striped tie, he looked very much part of the British Empire. He welcomed me pleasantly and motioned me to follow him. The door he opened revealed a sight that took

my breath away. No car museum, no collector of vintage vehicles, could ever have dreamed of assembling so many in one
place. They were all Rolls-Royces. There was a sumptuous Silver Phantom four-door convertible from the thirties, with enormous spoked wheels; a 1929 Silver Ghost open tourer, with
springs enclosed in a leather sheath, a windshield that could be
lowered and a tool case that looked more like a jewelry box; an
exquisite sky-blue convertible, with a cream canvas top held
half-open by two S-shaped chrome brackets like on the gen-
try's baby carriages. Beyond, an enormous ivory hood cast an
imperially majestic light over this extraordinary collection of
masterpieces. It was a four-door convertible that had once belonged to the American movie star Jean Harlow. She had apparently had the color of the upholstery made to match her
platinum-blond hair. Most of the models on display had won
prizes for elegance and cups for outstanding performance.
Even their model names were prestigious. They were called
Ascot, Deauville, Regent, Brougham, Pullman.

At the back of the garage there were also some Silver Clouds
of the fifties like those Mountbatten had recommended. The
souls of their former owners still seemed to occupy those
leather and rare wood jewel cases, and imbue them with a special life, resonance and warmth.

"Do you ever come by a left-hand-drive Silver Cloud?" I
asked my blazered guide.

"Alas, hardly ever! And when we do happen to find one, it
usually goes straight off to the United States."

"Lord Mountbatten has advised me to look for a car
equipped with an air filter sitting in an oil bath because of
India's many deserts and terribly dusty unsurfaced roads."

The garage owner looked at me agog. No customer had ever
expressed such a wish before. His surprise was understandable.
A Rolls-Royce was a world apart, a vehicle to which the usual
requirements of other cars did not apply, into which dust had
no more right to penetrate than external noises and smells.

"I'm afraid our cars are not usually fitted with air filters in oil
baths," responded Frank Dale, manifestly sorry to be unable to
satisfy this slightly eccentric client. He added with humor:

"Because of our climate, our purchasers tend to be more concerned with the reliability of the windshield wipers."

Good salesman that he was, he assured me that he would, however, set about trying to get me the rarity I desired. I promised to come back next time I was in London. In the absence of a left-hand drive, I could always acquire one of the many superb models that were actually available.

That was when Drapier and Larigaudie decided to spring a surprise on me. I had hardly got back to my hotel room when the telephone rang. I had difficulty recognizing the voice of the salesman I had just left. Abandoning the very last vestige of his British phlegm, he shouted down the phone:

"A miracle, Mr. Lapierre, a miracle! You had only just left the garage when a British doctor retired in France brought us his magnificent Silver Cloud. It's a left-hand drive, it has an air filter in an oil bath, it has air-conditioning and, to cap it all, it's registered in France ... Yes, Mr. Lapierre, its plates have a number 17 for the town of La Rochelle! Are you interested?"

"You bet!" I shouted back, half swallowing the receiver. "A thousand times yes! I'll be over to collect it this minute."

For a moment I remained thunderstruck by the extraordinary coincidence that seemed to me like an encouragement from heaven: La Rochelle! The cradle of my ancestors! Châtelaillon, where I was born, was only seven little miles away from the towers of the port of La Rochelle!

THE BRITISH DOCTOR'S SILVER CLOUD was painted in aristocratic black and gray. The distinction of its front end and its quiet power made it, to my neophyte mind, one of the most successful models in the whole history of the make. I never tired of the beauty of its lines that were all sobriety, elegance and virile power. It had the additional advantage of costing no more than five thousand pounds, scarcely more than a new Chevrolet sedan. In anticipation of the long Indian exile to which it was destined, together with my wife, Dominique, I spent an entire day familiarizing myself with its different parts. Dominique conscientiously wrote down in a notebook the instructions of the garage's chief mechanic. She drew diagrams of the bolts, screws and parts we might one day have to replace somewhere in a lost desert of Rajasthan or Deccan. This initiation into the secrets of my car was to be the first stage of my love affair with her. Before setting out on our great adventure, I added a small perfecting touch of my own: registration plates ending with 83, the number that corresponded with my paradise in the south of France. I was not a little proud to take these magic digits to such far-distant lands.

Return to the Land of Maharajas

As carefully wrapped in cotton wool as if it had been the Venus de Milo, my Rolls left Marseille packed up in a crate. Three months later I received it in the port of Bombay. Its first Indian night was spent in one of the majestic garages of the Royal Bombay Yacht Club that had formerly housed the Silver Phantoms and Silver Ghosts of the empire's high dignitaries. The next day, to the awestruck gazes and applause of passersby, children and street peddlers in the great square in front of the Gateway of India, I took the road to New Delhi, where Larry Collins was waiting for me. People's reactions reassured me. In Paris friends had been shocked that I wanted to travel about a country fraught with so much poverty in so luxurious a car. Well aware of the problem, I had hesitated for a while, then consulted my guardian angels. A remark made by Larigaudie in his book *La Route aux Aventures* had allayed my scruples. In his super-equipped Jeannette, the young adventurer had asked himself the same question. "Provided it is shared with others, there is no improper pleasure," he had written. The Rolls's long hood had scarcely left the center of Bombay before I realized that India was indeed sharing in my pleasure. Every time I stopped, I was surrounded, submerged, engulfed by an enthusiastic crowd. To guide me to the Indian capital nine hundred miles away and act as interpreter when the need arose, I had invited a young driver from the French consulate in Bombay to join me. His name was Ashok and he was a Hindu. Driving Arjuna's celestial chariot could not have made him more proud. But finding the way out of a huge and tentacular city like Bombay required knowledge of subjects besides mythology. I had to hire a taxi to come to our rescue and escort us out to the main road to Delhi.

Poor and brave Rolls! What an ordeal I had condemned you to. For hundreds of miles the road was a single lane. Every encounter with an oncoming vehicle became a deadly duel, a game of Russian roulette. Trucks automatically refused to give way. I had to hurl my two tons of vehicle onto the hard shoulder, risking shredding its tires, then get back onto the road. Some drivers seemed to be overtaken by a fit of madness when they saw the Rolls. They would let their hands off their steering wheels to clap them, blow their horns, resort to dangerous acrobatics. I saw heavily loaded trucks topple over into ravines or jackknife at full speed, and cars flip over like pancakes after overtaking me. Unfortunately I had to dismiss my driver after a few hundred miles. Seven hundred and fifty languages and dialects are spoken in India. As we traveled farther away from his part of the country, poor Ashok could no longer make himself understood. Fortunately, though, everywhere I went I found some veteran, some retired civil servant, who could speak enough broken English to give me directions. The natural kindness of the Indian people did the rest. I never felt lost.

WHAT A JOY IT WAS TO TRAVEL through India's thousand noises listening to Ravi Shankar's frenzied sitar or Bach's calming cantatas in the padded silence of a Rolls-Royce! In six months my car and I covered more than twelve thousand miles. All along the way, I conducted interviews, looked for documents and descriptions of locations and historical places and continued to research the new book Larry and I had started.

One day an almost imperceptible rattle began to trouble the usually inaudible purr of the engine. Would the oppressive heat, the poor quality of gasoline and the lack of regular servicing prove the three stiff-collared representatives in London right? I telephoned the only other owner I knew to be driving a Rolls-Royce in India: the British ambassador. He was eager to reassure me.

"I have my Silver Shadow serviced and repaired at a garage on Connaught Circus to my complete satisfaction," he informed me. "I'd recommend you take your Silver Cloud there."

"What's the name of the garage?" I asked, excited and eager to be vindicated.

The reply took the wind out of my sails. *"The British Garage."*

Dear old Albion! Twenty-five years after the pearl of your empire showed you the door, the best garage in New Delhi was still called the British Garage.

In striped tie and blazer, just like old Frank Dale in London, the Indian manager was a retired colonel. He listened to my account with rapt attention. I emphasized the fact that my car was functioning perfectly; the clicking noise was only a subjective and passing irritation, and not an indication of some deeper malady.

"We'll check," he assured me with all the seriousness of a doctor discussing with a patient.

All the garage workers had hurriedly congregated around my vessel to exchange enthusiastic comments. At the British Garage of all places, the appearance of such a beautiful English lady was cause for celebration! The manager asked me to open the hood and start the engine. He listened with scrupulous care as it turned over, then signaled to me to depress the accelerator. It was at half-speed that the insidious clicking became noticeable. You needed to listen carefully to make out the tiny noise. He straightened up and clapped his hands, whereupon a venerable Sikh with a gray beard and a scarlet turban appeared. He was the chief mechanic.

I was reassured; the Sikhs are the taxi, truck and airplane

drivers of India. Guru Nanak, the sacred founder of their community, had instilled a genius for mechanics into them. The old man sounded the Rolls-Royce's breathing in his turn. What I witnessed then was an extraordinary ritual only India, with its caste system, could come up with. His examination complete, it was the elderly Sikh's turn to clap his hands. Thereupon a young mechanic of "lower" birth, probably from the south judging by his very dark skin, brought out a screwdriver, pliers and an adjustable wrench on a tray. The elderly Sikh gingerly took hold of the screwdriver and buried his scarlet turban in the engine. I waited feverishly for the outcome of his dive. A long and muffled consultation then took place between the manager and his chief mechanic. They spoke in Punjabi. From the gravity of their faces, I realized that their diagnosis was unlikely to be optimistic. At last the manager turned to me:

"Mr. Lapierre, we would like to keep your car to give it a more thorough examination," he announced.

"A more thorough examination?" I repeated, suddenly panic-stricken.

This was what I had dreaded most. Here I was, risking getting my car back handicapped for life when it was only suffering from a temporary indisposition.

"How long would you want to keep the car for?" I asked anxiously.

"Oh . . . let's say . . . about a week," the manager responded after consulting his chief mechanic.

I spent that week in a state of frightful anxiety. In the hope of exorcising the image of my Silver Cloud in pieces on an Indian garage workbench, I took myself off to Kashmir. But neither the enchantment of boat trips on Srinagar Dal Lake nor the intoxicating discovery of the Shalimar gardens nor that of the treasures of local craftsmanship could take my mind off the British Garage. On the eighth day, with a pounding heart, I was at last reunited with my beloved. She looked even more beautiful and illustrious than when I had left her. The window was open and the key was on the dashboard. Without even waiting to sit behind the wheel, I reached out my hand to start the engine. There was not the faintest trace of a tremor from under the hood. I repeated the operation. In vain. My Rolls remained inert. Frantic in my distress, I ran to the manager's office.

"What have you done to my car?" I demanded through a blur of tears.

Without answering, the man adjusted his tie and stood up. When he got to the car, he asked me to lift the hood.

"Oh!" I remarked, dumbfounded.

The engine I had thought dead was running perfectly, but so silently it was inaudible. As for the clicking sound, a surge of the accelerator confirmed that, at the magic touch of the Sikh in the scarlet turban, it had completely disappeared. The elderly Indian had been the mechanic for the Rolls-Royces of the last British viceroy of India.

New Delhi–Saint-Tropez, the Magic Vacation of a Flying Lady

The culmination of my childhood dreams: thirty-five years after Drapier and Larigaudie, it was my turn to set out on my idols' *route aux aventures*. The time when, at the age of ten, I had devoured the account of their exploits, tucked beneath the bedcovers in my icy cold bedroom in the rue Jean Mermoz seemed so close! I was about to turn forty. I had filled the trunk of the Silver Cloud with all the notes and documents Larry and I had accumulated. New Delhi to Saint-Tropez was about six thousand miles on the map, a quarter of the way around the world.

Our arrival at the Indo-Pakistani border was quite an event. Since the last conflict between the two countries, it was only open for two days a week and then only for a few hours. Bad luck would have it that we arrived on the wrong day. But what border could remain closed to a Rolls-Royce? Indian Major Palam Sing and Pakistani Commander Habib Ullah came to an agreement to let us go through, and we opened our last bottle of champagne as a tribute to the unexpected cooperation of these mortal enemies.

It was thrilling to drive along the Great Trunk Road that had once linked, with a trail of asphalt, the whole of the northern Indian empire, from the Khyber Pass to Calcutta. I imagined Jeannette and my idols making their way, as we were, through the tide of trucks, buses, carts and cycle-rickshaws. In Lahore the driver of a tonga came so close to us that its wheel hub dented the hubcap of the front right wheel of the Rolls. I vowed never to polish out the slight scar left on the body of my car by a horsedrawn cart from the far side of the world.

Peshawar, at the gates of Afghanistan. The governor of the region invited us to dinner. I thought with pleasure of the account Larigaudie had given of his passage through that same city:

In Peshawar we dined with Sir George Cunningham, governor of the Northwest Province of India. A long, silent, almost unctuous Rolls-Royce, driven by two chauffeurs fallen from the enchanted chariot in *A Thousand and One Nights*, transported us to the palace. With a brief slapping of hands on rifle butts, the guards presented arms.

English lawns, a tennis court, a swimming pool, tropical trees lining sanded pathways, a mosaic pattern of blooming flower beds, sparkling white pavilions, buildings and gardens, stamped the might of England on the indigenous town that lay strewn about the palace like an assembly of matchbox models.

As you crossed the threshold you left India behind you. Had it not been for the silent passing of barefoot servants in their turbans, the reception room, then the dining room looked as if they had been furnished by an Oxford Street interior decorator.

Nothing had really changed since those lines were written. The charming Pakistani governor, a Cambridge graduate, seemed as British as his pre-independence predecessor. His whiskey came from the same Scottish Highlands. His guard presented arms with the same crispness as in the days of the empire.

Next day we crossed the historic Khyber Pass. Fierce-looking Pathan tribesmen who sometimes amused themselves by shooting the radiator caps off passing trucks witnessed with curiosity the passing of our majestic vessel. I offered up a prayer to Saint Larigaudie that they would refrain from using the Flying Lady as a target. Cut into the mountainside, traversing ravines and gorges by means of daringly constructed bridges, with a caravan route running alongside its entire length and military control posts dominating every stretch of it, the road intersected one of the world's most dangerous frontiers. I felt a twinge of emotion as I saw the coat of arms of the British regiments who had come here to defend this gateway to the empire engraved on the rocks of the mountainside. Around a last bend and past a customs post, a large sign proclaimed, "Welcome to Afghanistan. Keep to the right."

In Kabul, King Zahir Shah's personal guard did the honors for the Silver Cloud. The monarch had agreed to see Larry and me for a long conversation about the troubled times his country was going through. Less than six weeks later that gracious and cultured man who expressed himself in studied French would be banished from power by a coup d'état. Afghanistan would then sink into one of the longest and most terrible tragedies in its history.

We spent our last night in Afghanistan on the outskirts of the large town of Herat, in the only hotel before the Iranian border. The place was apparently a haunt for drug traffickers. Ever since the Shah of Iran had ordered carriers mercilessly shot, traffickers had been looking for new ways of conveying their merchandise. One of the tricks, we had been warned, was to hide packets of drugs in the bumpers or under the chassis of tourists' cars while their owners were asleep. The following night, all the traffickers had to do then was recover the drugs from the garage of the only hotel in Meched, the first stopping-off place in Iran.

On the strength of this warning I took the precaution of stopping a few miles from the border to make sure we were not transporting anything suspect. I put my hand inside the front bumper. To my horror, my fingers encountered a cellophane bag full of powder held in position with adhesive tape. I made a similar discovery in the rear bumper. Other small bags were stuck inside the fins and under the trunk. Larry, who had written a cover story on the French Connection in Marseille which had made him quite an expert, examined our findings and announced: "Chinese packaging." The white powder we were conveying thus came from China via Pakistan and Afghanistan. Larry estimated its value at several hundred thousand dollars. I rushed to stop the minibus in which a group of friends were escorting us from Lahore.

"Pierrot, search your vehicle from top to bottom," I told my old friend Pierre Foucault. "We've been stuffed full of heroin!"

While he set about inspecting his van with the help of his fellow travelers, I carefully examined one of the bags we found under the Rolls's trunk. The slightly granular texture of the powder surprised me. I thought heroin looked more like extremely fine talc. I opened one of the packets and tasted a little of the powder. It was salt. Everyone was taken aback, not least Larry. We opened the other packages: salt, nothing but salt. The passengers in the minibus, with my friend Pierrot as their ringleader, burst out laughing. They told us they had exhausted the hotel's entire supply of salt to play this trick on us.

"You bunch of bastards!" Larry shouted. "You might have got us shot for five packets of salt!"

RISING FROM A SPUR OF ROCK, a fortress stood guard over the desert: the border post with Iran. The commander of the post, a lordly man, bade us enter a vast vaulted room where divans, seats, walls and floors all merged in a profusion of carpets. Servants brought us glasses and ewers and we took tea with some bearded Afghans while our passports were being stamped in the office next door. There were no exit formalities and there was no search of the car, which the guards surveyed with an almost religious respect. On the other side, the man in charge of the Iranian frontier post received us with the same courteous deference.

Having reached northern Greece, the Rolls made a detour to Komotini to greet the mechanic who, twenty-two years previously, had brought the Amilcar back to life after the disastrous tow that had nearly smashed it to pieces. We fell into each other's arms like two brothers meeting again. The road on which I had very nearly perished had turned into a superb three-lane highway. As for the river where my antique open tourer nearly drowned, it was now straddled by a work of art almost as splendid as the Golden Gate Bridge.

From then on, the journey was easy going. We dawdled through Athens, Olympia, Delphi, Corinth, Naples and Rome. Thirty-two days, seventeen hours and twelve minutes after leaving the Red Fort in New Delhi, the signpost to SAINT-TROPEZ appeared within view of the Flying Lady. The speedometer showed 6,364 miles. Before driving the last two miles to the entrance to the Great Pine, I took my valiant troop for a pastis in the harbor. It was like returning home after a long sea crossing, like those made in olden times by the corsair ships, when navigators from this little port guided their crafts to the coasts of Africa and India. As I savored that moment of happiness, one of the fish sellers in the Place aux Herbes took a respectful look around my vessel. Staggered by the length of it, she suddenly looked up and remarked: "Good Lord, for a hulk like this, you'd need a parking meter for the front and another for the back!"

Since then, the beautiful car bought from Frank Dale's London museum has continued to be part of my life. Like an old couple that love has united for eternity, together we have covered many more thousands of miles, across France and Europe. It is now forty years old and I am sixty-seven. We both, thank God, are blessed with splendid health.

When I compare us to an old couple, I should record an episode that is inevitably part of the history of most long-standing marriages.

At the end of one recent summer, as I was leafing through a magazine specializing in vintage and collector's cars, I had the shock of my life. The photo in front of my eyes was of the 1938 Chrysler Royal I had had in my twenties, the honeymoon car I had bought for a hundred dollars from a wrecker in Pennsylvania. I recognized its every detail: the carnivorous radiator grille, the rumble seat in the guise of a trunk, the long running board, the chrome that looked like a mustache on the hood. Only the color was different. It was black. It was up for auction in the west of France. I called the auctioneer that very instant and put in a bid. One week later a secretary's voice informed me the car was waiting for me. I jumped on a train and got off at Poitiers, with my heart racing. It was the one! It was the car of my youth, in which I had driven across the United States and Mexico, the powerful convertible with the symphonic horn.

"You're going to cause holdups on the freeway!" the good-humored garageman predicted.

With a first stop at the Ile de Ré to visit a dear uncle of mine, and another at old friends' in the foie gras country of the Gers, in three days the Chrysler got me and my wife back to Ramatuelle to the admiration and bemusement of all the other motorists we met.

My Rolls-Royce bore me no grudge. The Chrysler and the Silver Cloud are now parked side by side like sisters, under the red tiles of a car shed built just opposite the room where I have my worktable. Like El Cordobés, I have only to look up and glance out of the window to see those two symbols of the joy I have experienced in life, and draw from them the inspiration for further dreams.

13

The Last Proconsuls of Victoria's Glorious Empire

We had just been served a superb Tatin tart as dessert when my host suddenly removed his thick tortoiseshell glasses and surveyed me with small, nearsighted eyes.

"So, Dominique, what subject are you and Collins going to tackle for your next book?" The man with the kindly voice had been my master and model at *Paris Match*. Every week during the 1960s and 1970s Raymond Cartier's articles had recorded world events with a level of inspiration and a wealth of information that enthralled millions of readers. As a young journalist I had had the good fortune to work for two years in New York alongside this highly professional man, who was as adept at revealing the secrets of the cold war or disclosing the reasons for the Soviet-Chinese breakup as he was at analyzing the Brigitte Bardot myth. He had applauded the success of *Is Paris Burning?* and approved of my decision to withdraw from *Paris Match* to try my hand at a literary and historic venture of the kind he himself worked on between major current affairs assignments.

Larry and I had just published *O Jerusalem*. That mammoth investigation into the birth of the State of Israel and months of arduous writing had left us down for the count.

"You know all too well, Raymond, there aren't too many subjects to which you want to devote four years of your life," I said. "Have you any suggestions?"

Cartier knitted his brows and leaned toward me as if to tell me a secret.

"My dear Dominique, when I was your age, I went to a remote village in North Bengal to interview an old half-naked Indian who had brought one of the most powerful empires of all time to its knees. His name was Mohandas Gandhi. Why don't you and Larry Collins tell the story of that Indian and the fall of the British Empire in India, the population of which at that time constituted a fifth of the human race? It happened in 1947, less than twenty-five years ago. Many of those who had a role to play in that tremendous page of history must still be alive. I'm sure you could find them."

Cartier saw my face light up with curiosity. He went on:

"August 15, 1947, is probably one of the most important dates of our time. That was the day on which India and Pakistan proclaimed their independence. On that day, in New Delhi and Karachi, in front of hundreds of thousands of men and women with dark skins and bare feet, the white man's domination of a whole section of the universe disintegrated. On that day, what was to be known as the Third World was born. After that August 15, 1947, the world would never be quite the same again. The people responsible for this upset are all extraordinary characters: first there's the little Mahatma that Churchill called 'the half-naked fakir.' Then there's Nehru, the man with the rose, a Brahmin aristocrat from Kashmir, an unadulterated product of the British educational system, who nevertheless spent a third of his life in British prisons. Next there is Mohammed Ali Jinnah, a sort of Asiatic de Gaulle, an inflexible and arrogant individual, who managed to procure Pakistan for the Muslim minority of India. Finally there's Lord Mountbatten, King George VI's cousin, the last viceroy of India, who was given the sad task of liquidating the jewel in the empire his great-grandmother Victoria had assembled. There, Dominique, you have all the ingredients of a classical tragedy with heroes that are far from ordinary. If I were your age, I'd start researching tonight."

Dear Raymond, I was never able to tell you that I called Larry as soon as I left your home, because shortly after that memorable dinner you were abruptly taken from us. That night, Larry was at his parents' home in Connecticut. A fortnight later we lunched in London with Lord Mountbatten, the last living protagonist of those great historic events. Our meeting took place at the home of our friends Geoffroy and Martine de Courcel, who were France's ambassadors to Great Britain at the time.

What a character Mountbatten was! His youthful manner immediately made me forget his seventy-two years. Tall, slender, as supple as a cat, his blue eyes twinkling with mischief and curiosity, there was nothing formal or stiff about that man who had been born with the century and had led so many different lives. I could imagine him galloping on his polo pony; clad in his grand uniform of first lord of the admiralty studded with stars, medals and gleaming shoulder knots; sporting his cap with the gold leaf of commander in chief of war operations in Asia; or in the tunic adorned with the stars and decorations of viceroy of India.

Mountbatten was delighted with our idea. He lamented the fact that his fellow countrymen had shown so little appreciation of his success as a decolonizer, that they had so relentlessly reproached him for the speed with which he had carried out his task. He felt the accusation unjust and undeserved. By extricating his country from the Indian wasps' nest without spilling a single drop of British blood, Mountbatten had saved Great Britain from one of those colonial wars of which France had made a specialty. Our project won his support all the more easily for the fact that we happened to be the authors of one of his favorite books.

"I reread *Is Paris Burning?* at least four times," he admitted to us. "That's how history should be related."

As soon as we finished lunch, we climbed into his Jaguar and he took us to Broadlands, his home near the village of Romsey in the south of England. It was to this magnificent residence in a setting of hundred-year-old oak trees that he had retired. On his worktable were piles of letters, for the most part from India or Pakistan, correspondence from strangers, from friends who had remained faithful or from former servants to whom he had been sending a small viaticum regularly for twenty-five years. Duna, his black Labrador, and Mistou the cat were his only companions in this warm inner room, full of Victorian furniture, velvety carpets and heavy curtains. Countless photographs displayed in silver frames—portraits of his family and the world's great leaders, war pictures, photos of missions and journeys—served as reminders of the rich life he had led. A portrait of Elizabeth II was affectionately inscribed *To my Uncle Dickie*. One photo showed the frail Mahatma Gandhi, swathed in his dhoti, in between Lord Louis and his wife, Edwina, when they were viceroy and vicereine of India; farther on were the newlywed Mountbattens on their honeymoon in Hollywood, surrounded by their friends Charlie Chaplin, Mary Pickford and Douglas Fairbanks. But the truly unique feature of the home lay in the basement, where the master of the house led us with undisguised pride. In its labyrinth of tunnels he had assembled all the professional documents and personal mementos he had carefully preserved in the course of his life. For Larry and me, impatient to embark on what was doubtless the most ambitious research project of our literary partnership, this was a real treasure trove. The documents and mementos not only recorded the peripeteia of decolonization; they were the history of our century.

Mountbatten opened a drawer at random. In it we found a bundle of letters yellowed by time. The first, handwritten, was signed by Nicholas II, tsar of all the Russias, inviting his young nephew Louis to come and spend the summer vacation of 1914 with his imperial cousins on the family yacht anchored in Saint Petersburg. Fifty-eight years later the blue eyes that had caused so many feminine hearts to flutter brightened perceptibly at the sight of this relic.

"I was madly in love with Grand Duchess Mary then," he confided. "She looked like a Gainsborough portrait."

Under that letter was an announcement. In it "Victoria, Queen of Great Britain, Ireland and the Dominions, Defender of the Faith and Empress of India," announced the birth of her great-grandson, Louis Francis Albert Victoria Nicholas of Battenberg."[1] That was on June 25, 1900. The century was six months old. Victoria reigned over the largest colonial empire of all times, a grandiose institution that the newborn infant would be called upon to dismantle half a century later.

The crowned heads that leaned over his cradle were members of his family. Charlemagne was a direct ancestor; among his uncles and cousins were Kaiser Wilhelm II, Alfonso XIII of Spain, Ferdinand I of Romania, Gustav VI of Sweden, Constantine I of Greece, Haakon VII of Norway and Alexander I of Yugoslavia. Europe's crises were family problems.

From another drawer, Mountbatten exhumed a packet of old envelopes covered with small penciled writing.

"Guess who wrote this scrawl," he asked with a laugh. "Mahatma Gandhi himself! The dear old man used to keep a day of silence every Monday. That day, he used to use the backs of the envelopes from his mail and a minute stub of pencil to communicate what he had to say to me. At least on those blessed Mondays, I didn't run the risk of any untimely declaration by the unpredictable Great Soul on his way out of my office."

We had already come to the very crux of our subject. When Mountbatten set foot on Indian soil on March 21, 1947, he was not yet forty-seven years old. The destiny of nearly 400 million people and the peaceful decolonization of history's largest colonial empire would depend on the trust the envoy from London and Gandhi could establish between them.

They were a strange couple, apparently opposite in every way. Mountbatten was a refined British aristocrat, elegant, athletic, a great military leader, a man whom fortune had blessed; Gandhi, on the other hand, was an elderly half-naked Indian, an apostle of nonviolence, living in poverty. By some miraculous alchemy, the Englishman and the Indian understood each other. Five months after his arrival, on August 15, 1947, India's last viceroy granted 300 million Indians and 80 million Pakistanis their independence. On the day he left India, dozens of men and women threw themselves in front of the wheels of his

1. Louis's father gave up his German name of Battenberg for the name of Mountbatten at the beginning of World War I.

carriage to prevent him from leaving. When one of the six horses in the team refused to move, a voice in the multitude cried out: "It's a sign from God, you should stay with us."

WE RETURNED TO BROADLANDS nineteen times, and every one of those visits was a real joy. Mountbatten had a phenomenal memory: he could remember the color of the rose Nehru wore in his buttonhole for such and such a meeting, or the brand of cigarettes Mohammed Ali Jinnah, the founder of Pakistan, chain-smoked. But, above all, we were fortunate that every memory, every event that occurred during the crucial weeks prior to India's independence, had been recorded in writing and stored in the meticulously ordered files in the depths of Broadlands' cupboards. Mountbatten had not received a sole visitor, made one move, been present at a single demonstration, nor had one telephone conversation without immediately dictating a report to one of the innumerable secretaries on his staff. The texts were so precise and so detailed that we were able to reconstruct situations as if we had been there ourselves.

Like all those close to him, we called the former viceroy "Lord Louis." Sometimes he orchestrated the most extraordinary surprises for us. During one visit he apologized for not telling us in advance that he had invited another guest to the meal that provided a respite from our work. We found ourselves having the pleasure of lunching with Prince Charles. From the appreciative way in which his great-uncle described our research, we realized we were providing Lord Louis with one of his last joys, that of reliving in minute detail the six months that were the high point of his career. He supported our venture in a way that exceeded all our hopes. One day he entrusted us with documents kept secret for twenty-five years. Documents that could, if made public, gravely disrupt relations between Great Britain and its former dominions. He even went so far as to intervene with his niece, Her Majesty the Queen, to induce her to grant an exception to the fifty-year embargo on certain state papers he considered indispensable to our work.

Mountbatten's punctilious interest in the smallest aspect of our research fascinated us. I discovered in New Delhi the sumptuous carriage in which, on August 15, 1947, the viceroy, his wife, Edwina, and Prime Minister Nehru had traveled through the celebrating Indian capital. I jotted down the name of the carriage manufacturer inscribed on one of the lamps. Six months later, after reading the scene in which we described the carriage, Lord Louis advised me of an error that had crept into the spelling of the manufacturer's name. In his recollection "It was Parker, not Barker." I at once checked my notes. He was right. Sure enough, I had written down "Parker." Our secretary had made a mistake in the transcript.

Often his sense of humor would spice up our stark and studious reconstruction of the facts with incidents that were comical or touching. He told us how on the night before India's independence, he had withdrawn to the solitude of his office. "I am still one of the most powerful men in the world," he thought. "For a few more minutes, from this office I shall still rule over a fifth of the human race." He was reminded of a story by H. G. Wells, "The Man Who Could Do Miracles." It was the story of an Englishman who had the power, for one day, to accomplish anything he liked. "Here I am, in my last minutes as viceroy of India," Mountbatten had said to himself. "I must do something exceptional, but what?" All of a sudden, inspiration struck. "I shall promote the wife of the nawab of Palampur to the rank of Highness."

Mountbatten and the nawab of Palampur, a small moslem state in west-central India, were old friends. In 1945, while staying with his friend the prince, Lord Louis had received a very peculiar request from the British diplomatic resident accredited to his host. The nawab had married an Australian, to whom the viceroy of the time obstinately refused to grant the title of Highness on the grounds that she was not of Indian blood. Yet the foreign woman had converted to Islam and enjoyed real popularity with the local people. The nawab had been heartbroken. But Mountbatten's intervention had been to no avail. London was fiercely opposed to Indian princes marrying foreign women. On the eve of independence, taking advantage of his last moments of supreme authority, Lord Louis therefore made the nawab of Palanpur's Australian wife a Begum, thus elevating her to the status of Highness.

THIRTY YEARS AFTER THIS EPISODE, as I was signing books after a lecture I had just given in Geneva, I saw a woman coming toward me. She was dressed simply, her wrinkled face wore no makeup and her gray hair was hidden by a scarf. She placed on the table a very dog-eared copy of *Freedom at Midnight*, the book we had written about India's independence, and timidly asked me to autograph it.

"To what name?" I inquired.

She hesitated. Then with a hint of nostalgia in her eyes, she replied: "To the begum of Palanpur."

After independence, she and her husband had left India to settle in Europe. The nawab had died in relative financial insecurity. The woman whom Mountbatten had made a Highness was now giving English lessons to rich Arabs living on the shores of Lake Geneva.

WE NEVER FAILED TO DISCUSS the often unexpected findings of our research with Lord Louis. One day we showed him a report of our meeting with the Indian doctor who in 1947 had treated the founder of Pakistan, Mohammed Ali Jinnah. Reading it made him blanch suddenly.

"I can't believe it!" he gasped. "Good God!"

When he looked up again, the blue eyes that were usually so calm were shining with intense emotion. He swiped the air several times with our sheets of paper. "If I'd only known all this at the time, the course of history would have been different. I would have delayed the granting of independence for several months. There would have been no partition. Pakistan would not have existed. India would have remained united. Three wars would have been avoided . . ."

Lord Louis was astounded.

The report described in detail a chest X ray we had discovered with Jinnah's doctor. The plate confirmed the advanced stages of tuberculosis. In the spring of 1947 Jinnah, the inflexible Muslim leader who had quashed all Mountbatten's efforts to preserve India's unity, knew that he had only a few months left to live.

IT TOOK US MORE THAN A YEAR to go through the mementos and archives of the principal British actor of our research. Before leaving England for India and Pakistan, we also wanted to meet some of the former administrators and military men of the prodigious empire over which Lord Louis had presided, those white Englishmen whom Rudyard Kipling claimed had been selected by whim of providence to "dominate poor lawless people." At the time this meant a small number of an elite: the two thousand officials in the Indian Civil Service and the ten thousand officers who commanded the Indian army. This handful of men had governed and maintained order in a country twice as populous as the whole of Europe. The infinite expanses of the Indian subcontinent had provided those Britons with something their own confined island shores could not give them: a limitless arena in which to quench their thirst for adventure. They arrived, young and timid, on the quays at Bombay. Forty years later they left with faces tanned by excessive sun, voices roughened by too much whiskey and bodies scarred by tropical diseases, panthers' claws, polo falls and bullets, but proud to have lived their dream in the world's last romantic empire.

For most of them the adventure had begun in the spectacular confusion of Bombay's Victoria Station. There, under the neo-Gothic arcades, they had experienced their first shock: contact with the febrile swarms of indigenous people, with the acrid, omnipresent smell of urine and spices and the burning clamminess of the atmosphere. They had discovered, to their astonishment, the complexity of Indian society at the station water supply where different taps dispensed water to Europeans, Hindus, Muslims, Parsis, Christians and untouchables. The sight of the dark green railroad cars of the Frontier Mail or the Hyderabad Express, with locomotives bearing the names of illustrious British generals, reassured them. Within the curtains of the first-class compartments a familiar world of seats with embroidered headrests and bottles of champagne chilled in silver ice buckets awaited them; a world in which the only Indians they were likely to encounter were the conductor and the waiters in the dining car. As soon as they arrived, the newcomers learned one essential rule: Great Britain ruled India, but the British lived there in a state apart.

The young administrators of the empire had lived through rough years. Detailed to distant outposts, often cut off from all civilization, without telegraph or electricity, roads or railways, they found themselves isolated in an unfamiliar world. At twenty-four or twenty-five they frequently became all-powerful masters over areas as vast as Scotland, with populations larger than that of Belgium. They inspected their districts on foot or horseback, going from village to village at the head of a caravan of servants, with a cohort of donkeys or camels to transport their office tent, their bedroom tent, kitchen tent, bathroom tent and a month's supplies. Every time they stopped, their office tent became the audience chamber for a court. Suitably installed behind a folding table, framed by two servants fanning away the flies, they dispensed justice in the name of His Britannic Majesty. At sunset, after bathing in a tub made of goatskin, they would ceremonially don their dinner jackets for a solitary meal beneath the mosquito net of the dining tent, by the light of a hurricane lamp, while all around them resounded the noises of the jungle, sometimes even a tiger's roaring. At dawn they would set off again to exercise "the white man's sovereign authority" elsewhere.

This apprenticeship prepared the imperial servants for accession to those islets of privileged lushness from which the imperial aristocracy governed India. Gilded ghettos for the British, the cantonments were literally foreign enclaves attached to the main Indian towns. Each had its own public gardens, its English-style lawns, bank, school, shops and church with a stone bell tower, replicas of the church towers of Dorset or Surrey. At the heart of these communities was that most British institution of all: the club. At the sacred hour when the sun disappeared over the horizon, His Majesty's worthy representatives would take their places on the lawns or cool verandas of these clubs to savor their "sundowner," the first whiskey of the evening, brought to them by barefoot servants in white tunics. Comfortably settled in leather armchairs, they would immerse themselves in the *London Times*, the pages of which—a month or more old—brought them distant echoes of the Commons debates, the exploits of the royal family, the events of London life and, above all, the announcement of the births, marriages and deaths of compatriots, from whom they were separated by a quarter of the surface of the globe.

This was the romantic, picturesque India of Kipling's stories. The India of white gentlemen in plumed helmets leading their squadrons of turbaned horsemen; the India of tax collectors lost in the torrid expanses of the Deccan plateau; the India of lavish festivities at Calcutta's Bengal Club; the India of polo chukkas in the dust of the Rajasthan desert and tiger hunts in Assam; the India of officers in red jackets, scaling the dizzy slopes of the Khyber Pass and pursuing the fierce Pathan rebels in blazing summer heat or winter blizzards; the India of a caste of men sure of their superiority, dining with their memsahibs on the lawns of their clubs.

Lord Louis sifted through his address book to help us find some of the survivors of this imperial dream. He also advised us to put a notice in the Times of London, inviting any former servants of the empire who had had exceptional experiences to contact us. The idea proved productive. We traveled all over Britain, from Suffolk to Surrey, Cornwall to Scotland, and Kent to Wales, on a pilgrimage to meet former members of the empire in India.

ONE DAY IN KENT I RANG the doorbell to a cottage occupied by the former colonel appointed by Mountbatten to Mohammed Ali Jinnah, the founder of Pakistan, to direct his military cabinet in the aftermath of independence. His name was William Birnie. Tall, fit, with the florid cheeks of a man fond of gin and whiskey, Birnie had spent several months in close proximity to the Muslim leader. He was a unique source of information about one of the principal players in the Indian imbroglio. Birnie had brought numerous keepsakes back from his spell in India, among them an impressive tiger skin spread out at the entrance to his living room. I stopped, subdued, before this ferocious-looking creature. Amused at my disquiet, the colonel took off his jacket, pullover and shirt. In a matter of seconds he was naked to the waist. A deep scar ran across his chest from his shoulder to his waist. The Englishman pointed one hand at the tiger's head and laid the other on his scar.

"Yes, that's him!"

One night when he was a young lieutenant on operations in the Central Provinces, he had had the absurd idea of killing one of the many tigers that prowled around the camp. He had tied a goat to the foot of a banyan tree. Then, with a light attached to the barrel of his gun, he had lain in wait in the undergrowth. After a few minutes he heard the noise of breaking branches followed by terrified bleating.

"I switched on my torch. A magnificent tiger had pounced on the unfortunate goat. I fired at once, but in the half-darkness I failed to bring the animal down. Instead of making off with the pain of the impact, the bastard charged at me without giving me time to fire a second shot. I just managed to turn my gun round and plant the butt in his throat. It was a desperate struggle at close quarters. He slashed me with his claws and I could see his teeth ready to mangle my head. My gun in his mouth eventually made him let go. He broke off the fight and disappeared into the night. I hurried to climb into the nearest tree. It had all been most uncomfortable."

"You must have been really relieved to find yourself alive up there on your branch," I offered.

"Not at all!" the Englishman protested vigorously. "I was furious! Do you realize that that bastard had decamped with my gun! A brand-new Holland & Holland I'd bought the day before for the astronomical price of fifty pounds!"

Next day Birnie and his comrades set off on elephant back in pursuit of the tiger. They found him after two days. Birnie was able to finish him off with a single bullet. But he never saw his beautiful brand-new gun again.

In a modest cottage in the Sussex countryside, I met Sir Frederick Burrows, the last British governor of Bengal. Nothing about this former trade-union leader suggested that from 1945 to 1947 he had been sovereign of an area more populous than Great Britain and Ireland put together. With its 65 million inhabitants, Bengal extended over more than six hundred miles, from the jungles of the Himalayan foothills to the mouths of the Ganges and the Brahmaputra. Calcutta, capital of the province, was the largest British city after London. Raj Bhavan, the governor's residence, was a splendid palace with 137 rooms in the middle of a thirty-acre park. Lavish parties had been given there. On these occasions, Sir Frederick would take his place on a purple velvet throne enhanced with gilding, surrounded by an array of ADCs and officers in dress uniform. The former governor who had once had a staff of five hundred liveried servants now only employed a local country woman to do his housekeeping.

Before my bemused eyes, he leafed through his photograph album, records of the final stages of British rule. He hid neither his nostalgia nor his bitterness from me. Britain might have given the people she governed their freedom, but she had been unable to stop them from killing each other as soon as she left. He told me with sadness how his own rule had come to an end. While Lady Burrows and he were closing their luggage in one wing of their palace, hundreds of rampaging demonstrators had invaded the rest of the building, pillaged the crockery and silverware, torn down the curtains and danced for joy in the reception rooms, landings and stairways. The last sight of their bedroom had remained engraved upon his memory: dozens of little dark men who had never slept anywhere but on the beaten earth, jumping about and bouncing up and down on their bedsprings as if on a fairground trampoline. The guards had had to open up a way through the throng to allow the governor and his wife to get to the launch where a patrol boat was waiting for them. The confusion of their withdrawal had not allowed for any good-byes. The last representatives of Victoria's empire had left Calcutta on the run.

Sir Frederick had kindly provided lunch as a break from our labors. The man who had had five hundred servants at his disposal brought in the dishes himself. At the end of the meal, he got up. Pointing to our plates and cutlery, he asked me: "Mr. Lapierre, would you regard it as an inconvenience if we were to continue our conversation in the kitchen over the washing up?"

LIEUTENANT COLONEL JOHN PLATT had been the last British officer to leave Indian soil. Boarding the launches moored at the Gateway of India in Bombay that morning of February 28, 1948, Platt and his men had put the final stop to the British imperial adventure. Twenty-five years later, by that time a general, he invited me to lunch in the impressive surroundings of the Army and Navy Club in London, to talk about that historic departure. He had commanded the first battalion of the Somerset Light Infantry, a regiment in which his father and grandfather had already won fame and which had fought continuously since 1842 on the frontiers of the Indian empire.

The regimental blazon sported a bugle and a crown surmounted with the inscription "Jalalabad," the site of a bloody
victory over the Afghan tribes in the last century.

This departure took place in a festive atmosphere. Platt and
his men went from parties to receptions, the last being hosted
by the new Indian management of the Royal Bombay Yacht
Club, into which, until independence day, no Indian, not even
a maharaja, had been allowed to enter. When the time came for
farewells, representatives of the Indian army gave the British
officer their new national flag with Gandhi's spinning wheel on
it, as well as a silver model of the Gateway of India, the first
monument seen by so many young Britons arriving from their
distant island. Platt also received a photograph, a tribute to the
old fighting camaraderie that prevailed between the Indians
and their former colonizers. It was a picture of an Indian soldier
receiving the Victoria Cross from a British general. In return
Platt presented them with a Union Jack in Chinese silk and expressed the wish that it should be displayed in the honor hall
of Bombay's new Indian garrison.

Next day the Somerset Light Infantry, in khaki shorts and
white puttees, marched across the vast esplanade in front of the
Gateway of India, where tens of thousands of inhabitants from
all over Bombay, from the slums and suburbs, had amassed.
Battalions of Sikh and Gurkha soldiers paid tribute as an Indian
naval band played "God Save the King." It was a glorious departure. "When my men and I arrived under the archway of the
Gateway of India, I heard singing from the crowd gathered in
the square and on the pier," he continued. "It swelled rapidly,
bursting forth from thousands of chests. It was 'Auld Lang Syne.'
Among those singing were old militants from the Congress
Party with their white caps. Some of those skulls probably still
bore the scars of truncheons wielded by our police! There were
women in saris, students in their college uniforms, beggars in
rags. Even the soldiers in the guard of honor mingled their
voices with the others. I can assure you, it was . . ."

I saw the general's eyes shining in the half-light. He could
not finish his sentence and drank his coffee in silence. I imagined the emotion of that final scene. I could hear the sponta-

neous singing on the esplanade, the poignant promise that
there would be an occasion "to meet again" with those depart-
ing British. A whole era was ending in front of the Gateway of
India; the era of decolonization was beginning, brought about
by the frail old man of whom Mountbatten had spoken so
much. Thirty-two years before, returning from South Africa,
Gandhi had passed through that same Gateway of India. That
day the future liberator was carrying under his arm his manifesto *Hind Swaraj (Indian Home Rule)*, which was to become the
bible of the struggle for independence.

After the departure of Platt and his battalion many ports in
the colonial world would witness ceremonies similar to that
held on February 28, 1948, in Bombay. But no other would be
steeped in quite the feeling described to me by the British
general. Launches took the Somerset Light Infantry out to the
troopship *Empress of Australia*, lying at anchor out to sea. The
commanding officer's baggage contained the skins of the four
tigers he had shot in the Indian jungles. Overcome with nostalgia like all the other passengers, the Englishman went up to
the bridge to take a last look at the luminous and grandiose metropolis of Bombay, laid out in a quarter-circle before him. A
hand on his shoulder jolted him from his melancholy. The
ship's radio had brought him a telegram. "Good-bye. Good
luck. Good hunting," the message wished him. Sent by the
Fox Hunting Club in Bombay, it was India's final farewell to its
colonizers.

IN A RED BRICK MANOR HOUSE in Wiltshire, I found the former
naval captain who had been Louis Mountbatten's senior ADC.
At the age of thirty-one Peter Howes had witnessed firsthand
the historic game of poker that, in the spring of 1947, had decided India's fate.

In Delhi the young officer's days began at six in the morning
with a gallop in the countryside in the company of the three
other ADCs.

"Lord Louis would often join us," he recalled. "The Indians we encountered were astonished to see their new viceroy out without an escort like any other sahib. From the moment he arrived he had put a new, personal stamp on Britain's relations with the local elite. For the first time, official dinners, which were my responsibility to organize, included more Indian guests than British. And for the first time, too, vegetarian dishes were served at the viceroy's table. After partition, when hundreds of thousands of starving refugees poured into the capital, Edwina put us all on short rations. 'India is dying of hunger,' the former vicereine declared. 'We must set an example.' Those of us who were young and sporting had the greatest difficulty coping with the restrictions. At nightfall we would slip away to the restaurants in Connaught Place to fill our rumbling stomachs.

"Mountbatten expressly wanted imperial rule to end with an apotheosis of pomp and glory such as India had never known before," Howes explained. "He arranged it so that the enthronement ceremony surpassed in splendor the coronation of British sovereigns in London. Posted at the foot of the monumental flight of steps leading up to Durbar Hall, the throne room at the heart of the viceroy's palace, detachments of the Indian army, navy and air force mounted a guard of honor. Their lances glinting in the morning sunlight, the horse guards in red and gold tunics, white britches and black riding boots formed a line of honor up to the entrance.

"I found myself at the head of the procession, some thirty paces in front of Lord and Lady Mountbatten," recalled Howes with nostalgia. "My comrades and I were wearing the ADC's superb ceremonial uniform: a scarlet tunic with gold buttons, white trousers and a helmet with a red plume. If only my naval comrades could have seen me in that outfit! When the procession entered the dimly lit room, trumpeters broke into a muted march. A few moments later, when Mountbatten came in, trumpets and lights exploded triumphally under the vaulting. It was fantastic. I thank heaven for having been lucky enough to experience such moments."

The young naval captain watched the viceroy and his wife

make slowly for their thrones surmounted by a crimson velvet canopy. All of India's elite were there. He recognized judges from the High Court in black robes and curling wigs; senior officials of the Indian Civil Service, the proconsuls of the empire, whose Anglo-Saxon pallor contrasted sharply with their young Indian colleagues; a delegation of maharajas glittering in satin and jewels; and, above all, Jawaharlal Nehru, the man with the rose, and some of his companions from the Congress Party, all wearing their white caps, the rallying symbol of those who had fought for independence.

The chief justice stepped forward and Howes watched Mountbatten raise his right hand and pronounce the oath that made him viceroy of India. Then the rumble of the cannon of the Royal Horse Artillery assembled in the courtyard rolled through the hall.

Howes remembered the few poignant words Mountbatten had addressed to the assembly of eminent persons gathered before him. "I have no illusions about the difficulty of my task," he said. "I shall need the greatest goodwill of the greatest possible number and I am asking India today to show me that goodwill. Avoid any word or action that might add to the number of innocent victims."

Guards threw open the massive teak doors. The young captain caught the majestic view of the ornamental pools and lawns stretching away to the heart of New Delhi. Suddenly he felt wild euphoria flood over him. To him that ceremony demonstrated the everlasting links between Britain and India. It would not be long before the young Briton's optimism was swept away by the tide of impatient Indian leaders passing through the ADC's room on their way to the office of the new viceroy to press the urgency of putting an end to British rule.

One day one such visitor nearly died in his arms. The overpowering air-conditioning that Howes had installed in Mountbatten's office to help cope with the tropical heat had turned the seventy-nine-year-old Mahatma Gandhi into an icicle. Called to the rescue, the captain swiftly carried the frail old man out into the garden to warm him up again. It would have taken very little that day for the critical negotiations going on between India and Britain to end in tragedy.

The Most Bitter Divorce in History

When they separated, India and Pakistan had to share between them a patrimony accumulated over centuries. It was his involvement in this gigantic process of allotment that formed one of Captain Howes's most moving memories. Bank holdings had to be divided; steam engines, dining cars and freight cars from the railways; typewriters, tables, chairs, spittoons and brooms from the ministries' offices; leggings, turbans and truncheons belonging to the police force. In Lahore an official divided the town band's instruments into two lots. He gave a trumpet to Pakistan, a pair of cymbals to India, a flute to Pakistan, a drum to India. Some allocations, such as those of the libraries, occasioned bitter disputes. Complete sets of the *Encyclopedia Britannica* were split up, the even-numbered volumes going to one state, the odd ones to the other. Dictionaries were split in half so that India inherited letters *A* to *K* and Pakistan the remainder of the alphabet. Where there was only one copy of a work, a clear decision had to be made. Thus men were seen to come to blows over *Alice in Wonderland* or *Wuthering Heights*. Elsewhere respectable officials were seen swapping an inkwell for a jug, an umbrella stand for a coatrack. The Muslims demanded the dismantling of the Taj Mahal and its transportation, stone by stone, to Pakistan, arguing that the mausoleum had been built by a Mogul emperor. On their side, the Indian Brahmins laid claim to the Indus River, which ran through the middle of Pakistan, because their sacred Vedas had been written on its banks twenty-five centuries previously.

Neither India nor Pakistan had hesitated to claim the gaudiest symbols of colonialism. The sumptuous white and gold viceregal train went to India. By way of compensation, Pakistan was given the official Rolls-Royce of the commander in chief of the Indian army and that of the governor of the Punjab. The most remarkable of all these divisions took place in the stable yard of Viceroy's House. At issue were twelve carriages. With their adornments laden with gold and silver, their glittering harnesses and their bedizened cushions, they embodied all the pomp and majesty that had both fascinated and outraged the raj's Indian subjects. Six coaches were trimmed in gold, the other six in silver. Breaking them up was out of the question. It was therefore decided that one of the dominions would receive the gold carriages, the other the silver.

"It was to me that Lord Mountbatten allocated the task of determining the beneficiaries," the former ADC told me proudly. "No simple task! For want of a better idea, I decided to put the matter to the toss. I summoned the two future commanders of the presidential guards for India and Pakistan to the stable yard. I asked one to call heads or tails, and I tossed a coin into the air. 'Heads!' cried the Indian. When the coin fell onto the courtyard paving, we rushed over to it. The Indian did not contain his joy. Chance had just allocated the golden coaches of Victoria's empire to the leaders of the future socialist India! Next came the distribution of the harnesses, whips, riding boots, wigs and coachmen's liveries. Soon there was only one piece of equipment left: the royal postilion's horn, of which there was only one example.

"I showed the two officers the instrument and said to them: 'This horn cannot be divided. So I have found a fair solution. I'm going to keep it.'"

At these words, I saw the former captain get to his feet with a roguish look. He walked around the living room and stopped in front of the fireplace. A formidable blast of a horn suddenly shook all the windows in the house. Howes brandished the instrument triumphantly.

"I never miss the opportunity to sound this horn. It reminds me of the most memorable days of my life."

ARMED WITH CLIPPERS, he was pruning one of the magnificent rosebushes growing on his property, a former priory attached to the ruins of a Gothic church in Warwickshire, not far from Birmingham. Of medium build, with thin lips, sparse gray hair carefully plastered over his temples and round metal spectacles on his slender nose, Sir Cyril Radcliffe had a cold, reserved air about him that scarcely invited confidences. Of all the veterans of the Indian epic, he had been the only one to show any reluctance to receive us. Strictly speaking, Sir Cyril was not a veteran of the imperial adventure. Indeed, his relationship with India had been rather the opposite of an epic. Twenty-five years previously the hand now delicately trimming a shiny-leafed Dorothy Perkins rosebush had cut up the map of the Indian subcontinent with scissors. As surely as a surgeon's scalpel, that vivisection had created two separate states, Pakistan and India, affecting the lives of nearly 100 million people.

The man to whom that terrible burden had fallen had no previous knowledge of India; he had never set foot in the country. Paradoxically it was precisely because of his ignorance that, one day in June 1947, the forty-five-year-old distinguished lawyer had been torn away from his London chambers.

"The summons came from the Lord Chancellor," he recalled. "He explained to me that the plan for the partition of India had failed to resolve the crucial problem of dividing up the Punjab and Bengal provinces. Realizing that they would never reach agreement over the siting of the new frontiers, Jinnah and Nehru had decided to entrust the responsibility to an Indo-Pakistani boundary commission. To preside over this commission they wanted a British lawyer with no experience of India, who would serve as a guarantor of impartiality. The Lord Chancellor thought I was the man to fit the bill."

"It was a considerable honor," Larry remarked.

Sir Cyril stiffened in his chair. "Dividing up those two large provinces was the very last thing I wanted to find myself called upon to do. I might have been completely ignorant of India, but I had enough experience to know that it would be a thankless assignment."

"The fact that at that critical point in their shared history two such staunch adversaries as Nehru and Jinnah had decided to choose a Briton was a tribute to Great Britain," I encouraged him. "Could you have refused?"

Sir Cyril uttered a sigh by way of response, then told us that an hour after his meeting with the Lord Chancellor, a high official from the India Office had come to unfold a map in front of him and show him the provinces he would have to divide.

"I knew vaguely that they were both in the north of the country, one in the west, the other in the east. I watched the official's finger run along the Indus River, skim the barrier of the Himalayas, go down to New Delhi, climb back up towards the Ganges, skirt the shores of the Gulf of Bengal . . . The sight of the two vast regions I was going to have to cut in half gave me vertigo."

Sir Cyril had arrived a few days after this meeting in the suffocating heat of New Delhi. Mountbatten placed at his disposal a bungalow within the actual viceregal estate. Immured behind its shutters, he had at once begun to trace on a Royal Engineers map the boundary lines that would separate the two huge populations. Deprived of any contact with the places or people he was dissecting, he could not have foreseen the impact of his surgery on areas teeming with life.

"I knew that water is a symbol of life everywhere, that whoever controls the water controls life," he told us. "And there I was, having to carve up irrigation channels, canal systems, locks and reservoirs on a map. I mutilated rice and corn fields without ever having seen them. I hadn't been able to visit a single one of the villages through which my boundary would pass, nor form any idea of the tragedy it would inflict upon poor peasants suddenly deprived of their fields, wells and roads. The equipment I had at my disposal was totally inadequate. I had no very large-scale maps, and the information provided on those I did have sometimes proved to be wrong. I noticed the Punjab's five rivers had an awkward tendency to run several miles away from the beds officially assigned to them by the survey department. The demographic statistics which were to be my base reference were inaccurate. They had been falsified by both parties to support their opposing claims."

There was something surreal about listening to this account in the comfortable, peaceful setting of that English residence. I looked at that decent, respectable man and had difficulty imagining how he could have been the involuntary architect of such a tragedy.

"Of the two provinces, Bengal and the Punjab, which was the one that gave you the least trouble?" asked Larry, anxious to find some redeeming memory in a somber story.

"Bengal, without a doubt. My only hesitation was over what to do with Calcutta. Jinnah had laid claim to it, which seemed justified to me from an economic perspective. But in the end the large Hindu majority of the population was, in my view, a more important factor than any other consideration. Once this principle had been established, the rest was relatively simple. My boundary was just a pencil line drawn on a piece of paper. In the tangle of marshes and half-flooded plains of Bengal there were no natural boundaries to serve as a frontier."

"And the Punjab?" I asked.

The mere name of the province was enough to make the barrister's eyebrows pucker. He mopped his forehead with his handkerchief.

"The whole area was a mosaic of different religious communities overlapping one another. It was impossible to delimit a boundary that would respect the integrity of the communities. I had to cut into the quick."

Sir Cyril remembered the torrid heat of those summer weeks and their cruel, enervating dampness. The three rooms in his bungalow were littered with maps, papers and reports typed out on hundreds of thin sheets of rice paper. When he worked in shirtsleeves, the pages stuck to his sweating arms, leaving strange stigmata on his skin: the imprint of someplace that might represent the hopes of hundreds of thousands of human beings. A fan suspended from the ceiling stirred up the overheated air. Then the sheets would start to swirl about the room in a symbolic storm which portended the sad destiny that awaited the villages of the Punjab.

"I knew from the outset that a bloodbath would follow the publication of my plan for partition. Massacres had already begun in the villages I was in the throes of dividing up. I had no contact with the outside world. If I ventured out to a reception or dinner, I would instantly find myself encircled by a crowd of people, assailing me with petitions."

Sir Cyril Radcliffe's cuts arrived on Lord Mountbatten's desk at midday on August 13, 1947, thirty-six hours before the official proclamation of the independence of the two states born of the partition of imperial India. Fearing the two countries would vehemently contest the London lawyer's arbitration, the viceroy ordered his conclusions to be kept secret until the day after the independence celebrations. Lord Louis had Sir Cyril's two yellow envelopes addressed to Jinnah and Nehru locked away in a safe. During the ensuing seventy-two hours, while the two countries gave themselves up to festivity, the location of their new boundaries remained locked in that safe like the evil spirits in Pandora's box. India and Pakistan were to be born without their leaders knowing the fundamental composition of their nations, the number of their citizens or the limit of their lands.

ON PAPER THE DIVISION might well have appeared acceptable. In reality it was a disaster. In Bengal the dividing line was to condemn both parties to economic ruin. While 85 percent of the world's jute grew in the area allocated to Pakistan, there was not one single factory to process it. The Indian sector, on the other hand, found itself without a single jute plantation but with more than a hundred factories and the only port from which to export it, Calcutta. In the Punjab the boundary divided the lands and people belonging to one of the most militant and united communities in India, that of the Sikhs. For the generations to come, the Sikhs in their despair would be the primary cause of a tragic instability that would threaten the unity of India.

As MIGHT HAVE BEEN FEARED, Jinnah and Nehru exploded with anger when they were made aware of the plan for partition drawn up by the envoy from London. The two leaders had, however, promised to accept his decisions and implement them. If their mutual anger proved the total impartiality of Sir Cyril Radcliffe, their condemnation of his handiwork was a clear disavowal. Disheartened, he responded in the only manner he considered appropriate: he refused the two thousand pounds he was to have received as fee.

The special plane that took him back to England a few days later flew over the Punjab he had just divided up. Beneath its wings, the largest migration in the history of humanity was under way. Dozens of columns of refugees fled along the paths and canals and across the fields toward the burning asphalt of the Great Trunk Road. Muslim villages that had greeted the birth of Pakistan with enthusiasm found themselves in India. Elsewhere, areas occupied by Hindus or Sikhs were now part of Pakistan. The lives of tens, even hundreds of thousands of people depended solely on a desperate flight to one or the other of the two new nations.

Some of the absurdities became quickly apparent. The supply sluice gates for some irrigation canals were in one country, while they actually flowed into the other. Sometimes the frontier ran right through the middle of a hamlet. Even houses were cut in two, their entrance on the Indian side and the back window opening out onto Pakistan. But, above all, Sir Cyril's scissors had left 5 million Hindus and Sikhs in the Pakistani half of the Punjab, and as many Muslims in the Indian part. Those desperate masses were to be gripped by a murderous frenzy.

"As I'd anticipated, northern India was to sink into a bloodbath," said the man involuntarily responsible for the appalling disaster in a voice full of sorrow.

ONE SUMMER'S DAY IN 1979, watching Lord Mountbatten get out of his car in front of the perron at Broadlands, I called to mind the image Charles de Gaulle had used in the last pages of his *Mémoires*. Would the "shipwreck of old age" ever befall this giant of a man? He had just celebrated his seventy-ninth birthday. Buckled and booted in his uniform of colonel in the Queen's Guards, his chest studded with all his decorations, his bearing haughty, his step triumphant, he looked just like the photo of the viceroy, thirty-two years earlier, striding toward the throne of India.

In the course of our conversations, we had at times broached the subject of death. Mahatma Gandhi's assassination, in particular, fascinated him: with his tragic end, the Indian leader had achieved what he had been unable to do in life: reconcile the Indian communities. This achievement, Lord Louis believed, had imbued his passing with a meaning and dimension that destiny only rarely granted. Although he never said so explicitly, he gave us to understand that he hoped the last chapter of his own life might similarly end in victory.

As he did every summer, Mountbatten was planning to spend his family holidays in his castle in Ireland. For thirty-five years he had been faithful to this corner of the great island he held dear: the village of Mullaghmore on the coast of Sligo. There, among his own people, surrounded by everyone's affection, he felt totally safe.

On the eve of his departure, Larry spoke to him on the telephone.

"Lord Louis, be careful over there," he urged. "You're a particularly tempting target for these IRA fanatics."

"My dear Larry," Mountbatten responded sharply, "your warning shows just how little you know about the situation. The Irish know very well what I think of the Irish question. I'm not in any danger."

Nearly every day, the former viceroy of India took those closest to him fishing on the *Shadow V*, a solid old fishing boat with an engine. That afternoon of August 27, there were seven on board. Lord Louis was at the helm and with him were his daughter Pamela and her husband, John Brabourne, their twins, Nicholas and Timothy, aged fourteen, their grandmother Lady Brabourne and an Irish sailor.

A few minutes after happily waving the *Shadow V* off as it left the harbor, the inhabitants of Mullaghmore heard an explosion. The boat had blown up. Fishing boats immediately went to the rescue. They brought back the three horribly mutilated bodies of Lord Mountbatten, his grandson Nicholas and the young Irish sailor. The other victims were taken to the hospital in critical condition. The British press gave voice to the anger and distress of the whole of Britain, describing the Irish terrorists as "bloody assassins."

While India flew its flags at half-mast and decreed a nine-day period of national mourning in honor of her first head of state, Great Britain gave the decolonizer of its empire a state funeral at Westminster. Unlike his wife, Edwina, who had asked to be buried at sea, Lord Louis was laid to rest near Broadlands. Eighteen years later, at the beginning of 1997, Thomas McMahon, the terrorist who had planted the bomb on board the *Shadow V*, was released from the prison where he was serving a life sentence.

Unfortunately Louis Mountbatten's assassination did not have the beneficial effect of Gandhi's. Often, during our meetings, Lord Louis had marveled at the way Westerners could so easily condemn Hindus and Muslims for the sporadic outbreaks of violence between their communities, "while in Northern Ireland, people of the same origins, worshipping the same God, have gone at each other for so long."

14

The Crucifixion of a Great Soul

Three centuries and seventy-three years after William Hawkins, captain of the galleon *Hector*, set foot on Indian soil to begin the British colonial enterprise there, the Franco-American team of Lapierre and Collins arrived in New Delhi to research how that enterprise came to an end. A friend had found us two adjoining houses in a new neighborhood at the far end of Shanti Path, the majestic avenue that runs right through the diplomatic enclave.

Outside the entrance to my house, the six servants engaged to work for me were waiting, lined up like an honor guard. I was amazed at how many there were. I had not yet learned that in India every task is assumed by a specific caste. My staff included a "bearer" or majordomo, a cook, a *dhobi* to do the washing, a "sweeper" assigned to the housework, a *mali* to maintain the garden and, finally, a *chowkidar* to guard the house. I was concerned about the cost of retaining so large a staff. My mind was soon set to rest. Altogether, their salaries came to less than eighty-five dollars a month. My questions about social security payment benefits were met with astonishment. Socialist India had no such system in place. I had, instead, to fulfill two obligations: first, provide my staff with tea and sugar, and second, outfit them with official uniforms. The bearer pointed out a man with a shaven head who presided over a sewing machine on the pavement outside. He was a tailor ready to make up uniforms to fit my retinue on the spot.

This bearer seemed very well informed.

"Sir, I am a Roman Catholic and my name is Dominic," he announced.

I was to learn that this way of immediately stating one's religion was typically Indian. Religion takes priority over all other forms of identification. The cook was a Muslim—just as well since I did not wish to be restricted to a vegetarian diet. The men in charge of the laundry and the garden were Hindus, but of very low caste. The guard was also Hindu. As for the servant employed to do the housework, known as the sweeper, a puny man with very dark skin, he was an "outcaste," an "untouchable." He performed what Indians considered the basest duties, among them cleaning the toilets.

Despite their different religions and "births," my six servants lived together harmoniously in the two staff rooms provided at the back of the house. A few days later I was surprised to find that I was actually housing a village of a good fifty people. In India a job and lodgings constitute such a bonus that all of my servants had immediately brought in wives, children, grandparents, uncles, aunts and cousins from all over the country.

Cosmopolitan as the capital of India was, the arrival of two sahibs, a memsahib and their offspring was still an event. I was swiftly to discover that one of the characteristics of life in India is the complete absence of privacy. We had no sooner taken up residence than the two doorbells began to ring. The first visit was from the milkman accompanied by his herd of buffalo cows, offering us milk, "drawn from the cow in front of you." Then a showman appeared with his bears, another with monkeys, then a cobra charmer with mongooses. All of them insisted on performing their acts in front of Larry's admiring children. Then came an uninterrupted succession of door-to-door salesmen offering carpets, fabrics, saris, basketwork, items made out of wood, stone, glass, papier-mâché, the innumerable products of the rich craftwork of the various Indian provinces. Sellers of dogs, birds and goldfish also turned up. Not to mention an ear cleaner, several hairdressers, a magician, an astrologer, a palm reader and a group of musicians and singing monks in brown robes, their foreheads streaked with multicolored powders. To crown this inexhaustible flow, a splendid elephant arrived with his beturbaned mahout, intent upon taking these maharajas from the West for a ride around the neighborhood.

NEW DELHI BECAME THE BASE camp for our Indian research. One evening a telephone call informed me that the much-loved only daughter of Pandit Nehru, the man who had been the first prime minister of independent India, had agreed to recapture with me the glorious but tragic hours of the summer of 1947. Twenty-five years after her father took control of a newly free state, destiny had placed an extraordinary burden on the frail shoulders of Indira Gandhi, that of governing the world's most populous democracy. From her monumental office on Raj Path, the imperial avenue opened by the British in the heart of the capital, this fifty-six-year-old woman reigned alone over 700 million people, almost a fifth of humanity. Every morning before going to carry out her crushing duties, in the garden full of roses and bougainvilleas of her residence on Safdarjang Road, she welcomed the ordinary people of India who came from all over the country to receive a *darshan* from their high priestess, a visual communion with the one who was authority incarnate. It was there that she received me.

Having arrived early, I watched with astonishment as this very fair-skinned woman in her flowing sari trotted about from group to group, meeting here some very dark-skinned peasants from the extreme south; there in unbleached cotton dhotis a delegation of railway workers from Bengal; farther on, a class of young schoolgirls with long braids; farther still, a gang of barefoot untouchable sweepers who had come from their far-distant province of Bihar. The "mother of the nation" spoke a few words to each group. She read the petitions proffered, responded with a promise and graciously went along with the ritual of photo souvenirs. Thus, as in the days of the Mogul emperors, the people who are the true fabric of India had access, for a magical instant, to the source of power.

Indira became caught up in my curiosity. That interview was to be the first of many. They all took place in the living room, which opened onto the park. The room had only one single adornment: a large portrait of Jawaharlal Nehru with a charming smile, a rose in his buttonhole and the white cap of the Congress Party militants on his head. I sought in vain a physical feature that father and daughter had in common, but their resemblance was probably more internal than obvious. I looked at her long, slender fingers and thought of the passionate letters she had sent him while he was immured in his prison cells. From Oxford, where she was studying, she had written to him: "Father, I love you, I kiss your hands. I am suffering with you. I am struggling with you. I admire you so much." After getting her degree, she had rejoined her hero and never left him again. Together they had embarked upon the last battles against British colonial power, trailing tirelessly about the country, haranguing the crowds in the rural areas and the poor neighborhoods under the scorching sun or in the monsoon tornadoes. Everywhere they went people came running, even if most of them understood nothing of what they were saying. It didn't matter! It was enough for them to see the emblem of Jawaharlal's white cap above the sea of heads.

At the age of twenty-one Indira had joined her father in the ranks of the Congress Party, the all-powerful independence party of which he had become the president. It was a step up the political ladder which she celebrated in prison where the British had sent her on a charge of subversion. Her incarceration had further strengthened the bond between her and her father.

On August 15, 1947, India broke its chains. Nehru was fifty-seven; Indira thirty. It was a triumphant day for both father and daughter more united than ever in the same fight for the advent of an India freed of its superstitions and its weights, a modern India that was to be more just and more fraternal. Nehru had just lost his wife to cancer. Indira moved in with him in the colonial residence on York Road, from which he ran a country threatening to disintegrate. Apart from the massacres in the north that were spilling rivers of blood, Kashmir, their ancestral homeland, was on the point of falling into the hands of Pathan tribesmen. The maharajas were threatening to reestablish the sovereignty of their kingdoms. Indira did not leave her father's side, watching over his health, giving him advice.

Indira Gandhi described to me those tragic unforgettable hours with haunting precision:

On the evening of August 14, my father and I had just sat down at the table for dinner when the telephone rang in the next room. It was only a few hours before my father was to proclaim India's independence on the radio. The connection was so bad that I heard him shouting to the caller to repeat what had been said. He came back looking deeply distressed. Unable to speak, he buried his face in his hands and remained silent for a long while. When he raised his head again his eyes were full of tears. He told me the call had come from the town of Lahore that partition had allocated to Pakistan. The new authorities had cut off the water supply to the Hindu and Sikh neighborhoods. It was a torrid summer. People were going out of their minds with thirst. Those women and children who ventured to go and beg for a bowl of water were immediately massacred by the Muslims. Already whole streets were being ravaged by fire. My father was devastated. I heard him asking himself questions in a voice that was scarcely audible. "How am I going to be able to speak to the country this evening? How am I going to be able to pretend that my heart is rejoicing over independence when I know that Lahore, our beautiful Lahore, is burning?"

Indira had tried to appease the father she loved so greatly. She had helped him to prepare his speech. She knew he would speak from the heart.

"But that telephone call had irreparably spoiled the triumphal moment," she added. "Even if the words sprang spontaneously to his lips, he couldn't take his mind off the vision of Lahore in flames."

Yet few historic speeches achieve the grandeur and nobility of the one Nehru delivered that night.

"Long years ago we made a tryst with destiny and now the time comes when we shall redeem our pledge," Nehru declared. "At the stroke of the midnight hour, while the world sleeps, India will awake to life and freedom. A moment comes which comes but rarely in history, when we step out from the old to the new, when an age ends and when the soul of a nation long suppressed finds utterance.... This is no time for petty and destructive criticism, no time for ill will or blaming others. We have to build the noble mansion of free India where all her children may dwell."

"My father had only just left the microphone when the clock over the speaker's stand in Parliament struck the twelve chimes of midnight," Indira recalled. "Then the wail of a conch shell reverberated through the hemicycle. It heralded the birth of the world's second most populous nation, and the end of the colonial era."

THE PRINCIPAL ARCHITECT of this historic victory did not take part in the festivities that night. He prayed, fasted and worked away at his spinning wheel at the other end of India, in the center of Calcutta, a city threatened with an outbreak of sectarian slaughter between Hindus and Muslims. To ward off this nightmare, Mountbatten had dispatched the only "army" at his disposal to Bengal—the Great Soul, with whom he had negotiated the decolonization of India. He was convinced that Gandhi's presence alone could prevent civil war, calm people's passions and restore reason to the residents of India's most violent city.

Fed by hunger, poverty and religious hatred, violence was endemic in the fetid, swarming confusion of the slums of Calcutta. Four years before independence, a dreadful famine had killed hundreds of thousands of people in the agglomeration that was without any doubt one of the greatest urban disasters on the planet. People had dragged themselves to the garbage cans and rubbish dumps to look for means of surviving, mothers had killed children they could no longer feed; men had eaten dogs, and dogs had devoured old people. The virus of religious hatred had brought a new dimension to this violence. One year before independence, conflict between the communities left more than 25,000 horribly mutilated corpses in the streets. Since then Hindus and Muslims had been eyeing each other in an atmosphere of distrust and terror. Every day brought its crop of victims. Armed with knives, revolvers, submachine guns, Molotov cocktails and iron hooks called tiger claws used to gouge out eyes, the two communities were preparing, during that month of August 1947, for the final bloodbath that haunted Mountbatten.

On August 13 Gandhi moved into an old balustraded house abandoned by its last owner to the rats, snakes and cockroaches. The refuse fouling it had been hurriedly swept away and the commodity that had drawn the Mahatma's attention to it repaired: a toilet, a rarity in the poor areas of Calcutta. It was there, in a house surrounded by stench, vermin and filth, that he launched himself into the mission assigned to him by the last viceroy.

WHILE LARRY FLEW OFF TO MADRAS, Bangalore and Bombay to meet several key participants in the events of 1947, I set off for Calcutta in the footsteps of Gandhi. Apart from his legs, the railway had been the only means of locomotion India's liberator had used in his incessant journeying about the country. He had always insisted upon traveling third-class, with the untouchables, lepers and peasants. Throughout his life his contact with the most underprivileged had enabled the Mahatma to identify with the nation's deep undercurrents.

"If you only knew what those whims of Gandhi's cost the British treasury!" Mountbatten told us. "We were so frightened he would be assassinated that all those travelers in the third-class compartments—untouchables, beggars, lepers—were police inspectors in disguise."

To understand the Mahatma better, I, too, climbed into a third-class compartment. It was a rough but rich experience! I shared my austere wooden seat with three lovely creatures dressed in brightly colored muslin saris. Their faces were made up with scarlet powder and sandalwood paste, but their very deep voices left me no doubt: my traveling companions were eunuchs. They were going to the grand pilgrimage that each year brings the 300,000 members of their community to the vicinity of Benares.

What an adventure it was to trundle along for two days at twenty-five miles an hour across the sun-baked expanses of the Indo-Gangetic Plain, in the suffocating heat, amid spatters of soot, shouting, weeping, the smell of incense, curry and urine and a prodigious riot of color, smiles, vitality and dignity. Gandhi was right: the best way to get to know and love a people is to travel in a third-class railway car.

The enormous caravansary of Howrah Station, facing Calcutta, where the Mahatma had alighted twenty-five years earlier, was still an encampment for refugees squatting on the platforms, in the lobbies, waiting rooms and on the sidewalks. Like the 1947 partition, the 1971 war between India and Pakistan had propelled millions of people, fleeing terror and slaughter, in the direction of Calcutta. I found myself projected into a gathering of the lame, the sick and the dying. Women with empty breasts were delousing children with inflated stomachs by the pale glow of neon strip lighting; urchins in rags were foraging through piles of rubbish, looking for something to eat; lepers hauled themselves about on boards on wheels, holding out their begging bowls; packs of mangy dogs curled up and slept. In the midst of all this disaster, there were also sights that pulsated with life. A cloud of coolies in red tunics trotted about in all directions, carrying pyramids of bundles on their heads; people selling nuts, fruit and cigarettes threaded their way through the crowd; a flood of cars and taxis hooted past, depositing travelers right at the door to their railway car; interminable queues jostled around the ticket offices. I was literally drunk with all the spectacles, dazed by the deafening cacophony of loudspeakers, of the shouting, of the calling, of the whistling of locomotives.

One strange discovery intrigued me. Why were there so many weighing machines in the station lobby? In front of each one was a crowd of people who were nothing but skin and bone. Why were they spending twenty precious paisa to know how much their wretched skeletons weighed? Finally I found out. On the back of the ticket that confirmed their destitution was their horoscope. In Calcutta only weighing machines dared to guarantee the promise of a better karma.

With the Last "Human Horses" on the Planet

I had managed to get a room at the Bengal Club. Until the end of the empire, a notice at the door to this temple to the white man's supremacy had announced that entrance to the club was prohibited to "dogs and Indians." The city's prosperous middle-class residents had taken over from their colonizers without rancor. They had left the portraits of their former masters on the walls of the drawing and smoking rooms. Barefoot servants, dressed in the livery and turbans of the old days, still served insipid mulligatawny soup and lamb with mint sauce imported from the mists of Britain to the tropics of Bengal, in crockery bearing the coat of arms of the East India Company. Every morning at 4:30 precisely, the elderly Muslim bearer assigned to my room, who had spent the night in the corridor ready to leap at my least requirement, brought me the traditional strong, hot and sweet early morning tea, with which every day in India begins. This rich beverage would propel me to the nearby Victoria Memorial Gardens for a morning walk. There I would find hundreds of potbellied merchants in their dhotis, plump matrons swathed in multicolored saris, students in trousers and white shirts and veterans in the legendary white caps of the struggle for independence. They gathered there to stretch their legs and await the sunrise, the primordial event that governs the life of so many Indians.

In a city perpetually paralyzed by infernal traffic jams, especially the narrow alleyways of the slums that Gandhi had managed to calm in 1947, I used a means of transport that all other cities in the former colonial world had long banned from their streets: a rickshaw. In Calcutta fifty thousand human horses still harness themselves to carts to transport people and goods. I made friends with one of them. Hasari Pal came originally from Bihar, a very poor province in the northeast. At thirty-five he had reached a record age for people in his profession, who, with lungs riddled with tuberculosis, rarely live past thirty. Like so many other peasants, Hasari Pal had been obliged to sell his only field to raise the dowry without which his daughter would have been unable to marry. Deprived of all resources, he had set out for the mirage city of Calcutta. A rickshaw puller from a neighboring village had given him shelter in the garret he shared with six other Biharis. Afterward the rickshaw puller had got him a job with his boss. After paying for the rent of his cart and the various cuts due to the middlemen, police and other parasites, Hasari was left with less than seventeen dollars a month to feed himself and his family, who had remained behind in the village.

One day I asked this poor drudge if I could harness myself to his rickshaw. Thunderstruck that a sahib should want, even temporarily, to change his incarnation to such an extent, he was eager to satisfy me. He showed me the marks of his palms on the shafts, where the paint had worn off. "You see, big brother, the important thing is to find the balance of the rickshaw in relation to the weight you're carrying. For that you have to put your hands in the right place."

Following his advice, I positioned myself between the shafts. It took the strength of a buffalo to get the contraption moving because, even empty, it weighed easily 180 pounds. My muscles strained to the point of tearing. My cheeks puffed out. Suddenly I felt myself propelled forward. It was an unreal sensation. To slow down or stop took even more strength than starting out.

My absurd experiment caused a sensation. Never in Bengali memory had a white-skinned human horse run through the streets of Calcutta. Hasari was exultant. The oppressed, downtrodden whipping boy, the slave who had been humiliated over so many thousands of miles, sat as a passenger on the narrow red moleskin seat. A pack of urchins escorted us, laughing. Hasari must have thought he was on Arjuna's mythological chariot pulled by its winged donkeys across the cosmos. Poor Hasari! He knew that in the jungle of traffic he was a mere pariah compared with the motor vehicle drivers, especially those in buses and trucks who took a sadistic delight in coming as close as they could to the rickshaws, asphyxiating them with their exhaust fumes, terrorizing them with their horns. I emerged from that adventure nearly broken, but full of admiration for the courage of those unfortunate victims of a rotten karma.

The Gospel According to a Great Soul

My lucky star stayed with me, even in the hellhole of Calcutta. I found two close companions of the Mahatma. They had not left his side during the dramatic days of August 1947 when his presence alone had prevented the city from degenerating into terror. Ranjit Gupta was one of the police officers in charge of his security; the Bengali writer Nirmal Bose had acted as his secretary. Both became my Sherpas, guiding me in the footsteps of the savior of Calcutta.

It was through a simple prayer meeting in the courtyard of his residence that Gandhi had made contact with the people of the capital of Bengal. He had always used these prayer meetings to spread his message to India during its long march to freedom. He then talked about the nutritional value of unhusked rice, the evils of the atomic bomb, the importance of regular bowel movements, the beauties of the Gita, the advantages of sexual continence, the iniquities of imperialism and the benefits of nonviolence. Transmitted by word of mouth across an entire continent, those daily addresses had been the cement that held his movement together, and the gospel of the Mahatma, India's Great Soul.

Now, in the courtyard of his tumbledown house in the center of a city pervaded by hatred, he was preparing to speak at his last prayer meeting of the colonial era. Throughout that day he had received Hindu and Muslim delegations and explained to them the peace agreement he intended to offer Calcutta. The presence of several thousand people suggested that he had been heard.

"From tomorrow we shall be delivered from the bondage of British rule," he declared. "But from midnight today India will be divided. Tomorrow will be a day of rejoicing, but because of partition, it will be a day of mourning as well."

He warned the faithful that independence would place a heavy burden on all their shoulders.

"If Calcutta can embrace an ideal of brotherhood and return to reason, then perhaps all India can be saved. But if the flames of fratricidal strife envelop the country, how can our newborn freedom survive?"

The elderly prophet's appeal spread like wildfire. In the human jungles of Kelganda Road, in the dock area all around Sealdah Railway Station, the leaders of the Hindu and Muslim bands of thugs sheathed their knives and, together, hung Indian flags from the streetlamps and windows. Sheiks opened up their mosques to the worshipers of Kali, the goddess of destruction and patron of the city for Hindus; the latter invited their Muslim neighbors into their temples. Long-standing enemies embraced each other in the middle of the street. Children from the two communities exchanged toys and sweets.

All through Independence Day, Hindus and Muslims continued to flock to the Mahatma's residence. Every half hour, he was obliged to interrupt his meditation and his spinning to show himself to the crowd. He had not prepared any congratulatory message for the people he had led to freedom. The day when, because of partition, 80 million Indians left India to found another nation was for him a day of intense suffering.

To a group of political leaders who had come to seek his blessing, he said simply, "Be wary of power, for power corrupts. Don't fall into its trap. Don't forget that your mission is to serve the poor in the villages of India."

NEXT DAY, MORE THAN 30,000 people congregated in front of the platform for his prayer meeting. On the days thereafter there were 100,000, then 200,000, then 500,000, Hindus and Muslims together in an ocean of brotherhood, chanting slogans of unity and solidarity, exchanging cigarettes, cakes and sweets, sprinkling each other with rose water. On August 29 more than a million massed together on the immense esplanade of the Maidan to listen to their prophet.

It was too good to last. Suddenly, on the morning of August 31, after sixteen days of unexpected calm, the virus of religious hatred flared up again in Calcutta. There, as elsewhere, the infection had been spread by news of atrocities committed in the Punjab. A vague rumor intimating that a young Hindu had been beaten to death by Muslims in a tram set light to the powder. Fires, murder and pillaging rekindled the civil war.

The elderly prophet was shattered: the "Calcutta miracle" had been no more than an illusion. Shocked, he refused all food and immured himself in silence.

"I am praying for light. I am searching in my innermost depths," he confided simply.

A few hours later he announced that he was going on a hunger strike to force Calcutta to return to reason.

A hunger strike! It was a paradoxical weapon to brandish in a city where death from starvation was the fate of so many wretched people. But Gandhi's whole life was marked with victories brought about by his public fasts. This time he declared he would keep up his sacrifice all the way to his death. In order to save millions of innocents, he was prepared to lay down his life.

Thousands of people rushed to his house.

"Either peace will be restored in Calcutta, or I shall die," he repeated unceasingly.

His strength declined rapidly. By dawn on the third day, his voice was little more than an imperceptible murmur and his pulse was so weak that those around him feared the worst. As word of his imminent death spread, Calcutta was seized with anguish and remorse.

Prominent Hindus, Sikhs and Muslims compiled a communal declaration, solemnly promising to prevent the rebirth of religious hatred in the city. Mixed processions of Muslims and Hindus marched through the most violent slums to restore order and calm. The definitive proof that a new wind was sweeping through Calcutta came at noon on the third day, when twenty-seven gang leaders from the central districts presented themselves to India's liberator. Heads bowed, their voices vibrant with remorse, they admitted their crimes, asked Gandhi's forgiveness and begged him to end his fast. A few hours later one of the most infamous thugs confessed his bloody acts, then told the Mahatma: "We are prepared to submit willingly to any punishment you choose if you will only put an end to your sacrifice." To prove their sincerity, he and his acolytes opened the folds of their dhotis and allowed a shower of knives, daggers, "tiger claws," sabers, and pistols, some of them still red with blood, to fall at the old man's feet.

At 9:15 in the evening, on September 4, 1947, after his seventy-three-hour ordeal, Gandhi ended his fast by taking a few sips of orange juice. He had previously addressed a warning to the leaders of the various communities clustering around his bedside.

"Calcutta holds the key to peace throughout India. The least incident here could produce incalculable repercussions elsewhere. Even if the world goes up in a conflagration, you must see to it that Calcutta is kept out of the flames."

The message was received. This time the "Calcutta miracle" would endure. India's most restive and bloodthirsty city would remain true to its promise and to the elderly prophet who had been prepared to lay down his life for her.

GANDHI WAS ABLE TO RETURN to New Delhi. To be better assured of his protection, Nehru moved him in with an industrialist, G. D. Birla, who had a palatial mansion overrun with climbing roses in the heart of a residential area. Today it is one of the most moving sanctuaries I have ever visited. Everything there has been religiously preserved. But "everything" does not mean very much: India's Great Soul possessed virtually nothing. Next to the narrow charpoy that served him as both bed and chair can be seen his small spittoon and the wooden spinning wheel that was the emblem of his message to the Indian masses. On a bedside table lay his round, metal-rimmed spectacles, his false teeth, his eight-shilling Ingelsol pocket watch, the theft of which once made him cry, and the few books that reflected the eclecticism of the prophet of reconciliation: the Hindu Bhagavad Gita, a copy of the Koran, *Practices and Precepts of Jesus* and a collection of Jewish meditations. There is also a fetish statuette of three monkeys covering their ears, eyes and mouth with their hands, symbolizing what was for Gandhi the secret of wisdom: "Hear no evil, see no evil, speak no evil." In the bare-walled room a French window opens out onto the garden. On the path leading to the lawn, footprints in colored cement mark the Mahatma's last strides. The footsteps stop thirty yards farther on, at the top of three steps and in front of a stele adorned with flowers that are changed each day. It is here that the apostle of nonviolence met his assassin on January 30, 1948, at seven minutes past five in the afternoon.

The situation Gandhi found in New Delhi was worse than what he had experienced in Calcutta. While waiting to be evacuated to the promised land of Pakistan, the Muslim residents had grouped together in barracks and forts. They were dying in the hundreds, of hunger, sunstroke, typhoid, cholera. Not daring to come out of their refuges, they threw their dead to the jackals outside the walls. Some streets in the old city were killing fields. The magnitude of this holocaust broke the elderly sage's heart. Overcoming his extreme weakness, he visited the refugees to try and appease them, preaching the values that had always been his inspiration: love, nonviolence, truth and an unshakable belief in a universal God. But talking of forgiveness and brotherhood to men who had seen their children slaughtered, their wives raped and their parents murdered, to people who had touched the depths of despair, had become an impossible challenge.

I WENT BACK DAY AFTER DAY to the room in Birla House where Gandhi had suffered and prayed for the salvation of India during the last 101 days of his life. To steep myself in the atmosphere that had surrounded him during that distressing autumn of 1947 and the winter of 1948, I took with me a number of photographs dating from the period. They showed the aging leader stretched out on his woven rope bed, his stomach covered by a mud poultice. Kneeling solemn-faced at his bedside was Nehru, his spiritual heir. In one of the pictures I recognized the disheveled head of Pyarelal Nayar, the indefatigable secretary who for forty years committed to paper the Mahatma's every action, gesture, thought and word. In another photo were Manu and Abba, his great-nieces, with their tresses and their round metal-rimmed spectacles. The two of them never left their holy master. They slept near him, massaged him, prayed with him, prepared his poultices, gave him his enemas, nursed him when he had diarrhea and ate with him out of the same begging bowl.

The circle of people around the old man also included a smiling young woman with short hair. At thirty-two Sushila Nayar had kept an eye on the vital functions of the half-naked body stretched out before her. She had been the Mahatma's private doctor. She agreed to return to the poignant setting of his room to conjure up for Larry and me the tragic day when the Great Soul signed his death warrant.

"*Bapu* [Father] decided to resort once more to the weapon he had used to save Calcutta," she told us. "On January 12, 1948, he announced he was going on a hunger strike until death in the hope that the violence would stop and the Indian government would respect its obligations to Pakistan.

"That evening he had a last meal: two chapatis, an apple, goat's milk and three-quarters of a grapefruit. When he had finished, he led us out into the garden for a small prayer meeting. He seemed cheerful and sanguine. He had recovered his optimism. I concluded the little ceremony by intoning the Christian hymn that always moved him, ever since he heard it in South Africa. All together we sang 'Your Cross, Lord, Is My Joy.' Then *Bapu* went back to his room, lay down on his charpoy and dozed off. His last great challenge had begun."

Ashes in the Waters of the Indus

The presence in the capital of hundreds of Indian and foreign journalists gave the Mahatma's latest challenge even greater impact than his Calcutta fast. Part of the population, however, took his act as a provocation. The situation in New Delhi was explosive. The city had been invaded by Hindu refugees who were spreading their hatred of Muslims and crying vengeance. They were seizing mosques and Muslim houses and slitting the throats of their occupants. And now Gandhi was threatening to give his life to force Hindus, Sikhs and Muslims to be reconciled! And to make this act of blackmail worse, he wanted India to pay the sums of money it owed to Pakistan.

His attitude provoked immediate revolt among a small group of extremists living in Poona, a city in central India. They belonged to the Hindu Mahasabha, the "Great Hindu Gathering" nationalist party. The fanatics and their leader, journalist Nathuram Godsé, editor of the *Hindu Rashtra* (Hindu Nation) newspaper, harbored a dream of rebuilding a great Hindu empire stretching from the sources of the Indus to those of the Brahmaputra, from the snows of the Himalayas to the beaches of Cape Comorin. Their guru, Vir Savarkar, a sixty-five-year-old theoretician of Hindu racial supremacy and a partisan of violent action, professed an unrelenting hatred of Muslims.

With their eyes riveted to his newspaper's teleprinter, Godsé and his companions blanched at the news of Gandhi's latest hunger strike and the conditions he had laid down for breaking it off. Many times Godsé had publicly proclaimed what a deliverance the disappearance of the man who preached understanding between Hindus and Muslims would be. Gravely he turned to his companions and announced: "We must get rid of Gandhi."

Sixteen days later, on January 30, 1948, Nathuram Godsé put those words into action by shooting three revolver bullets into India's Great Soul as Gandhi was preparing to hold his prayer meeting.

"The light has gone out of our lives and there is darkness everywhere," exclaimed Nehru, giving voice to the grief of the nation.

"Mahatma Gandhi has been assassinated by his own people for whose redemption he lived," lamented the front page of the *Hindustan Standard*. "This second crucifixion in the history of the world happened on a Friday—the same day as Jesus was put to death 1,915 years earlier. Father, forgive us."

Nathuram Godsé was apprehended, revolver in hand, at the scene of his crime. He put up no resistance. The capture of his accomplices followed shortly afterward.

We managed to get hold of the reports written by the police officers responsible for investigating what was described as "the murder of the century." They did little to allay our curiosity. How had it been so easy to assassinate Gandhi when he was protected day and night by dozens of guards? Why had fanatics registered in the police criminal records in Poona not been arrested when they had made no secret of their intentions? Why had the police in New Delhi, who were aware of a conspiracy and even knew the identity of the conspirators, not communicated their information to their colleagues in Poona and Bombay? Was it simply a matter of negligence? Or of a deliberate complicity to let India dispose of its Mahatma? In 1960, twelve years after the incident, an official commission of inquiry was set up to shed light on the strange behavior of the Indian police at the time. Unfortunately, by then most of the officials concerned had died. The commission was content to conclude that Mahatma Gandhi's security had not been adequately enforced and that the police inquiry at the time had not been conducted "with the diligence a crime against his life required."

THE MAHATMA'S ASSASSIN, Nathuram Godsé, and his principal accomplice, Narayan Apte, were hanged. The four other conspirators were sentenced to life imprisonment. One day in March 1972 Larry and I were startled to find an insert on the front page of the *Times of India*. The four conspirators had just been released for good behavior. This providential act of clemency provided us with the opportunity of making some spectacular encounters.

Larry set out on the heels of Vishnu Karkaré, who had already resumed the management of the Deccan Guesthouse in Ahmadnagar in the Maharashtra. Meanwhile I went off in hot pursuit of Gopal Godsé, the murderer's brother. I eventually found him on the third floor of an old house in the suburbs of Poona. He was a rather distinguished-looking man in his fifties, with carefully combed white hair, who wore his long white shirt with elegance. Conscious of being a historic figure, he was pleasant, even warm, entirely disposed to answer my questions unreservedly. The veranda where he received me was decorated with a huge map of India incorporating the area of Pakistan. A string of lightbulbs marking the course of the Indus River wound its way across the upper part of the map, while a large photo of his assassin brother garlanded with flowers was stuck in the center. There was no remorse or regret in the precise, detailed answers Gopal Godsé gave me. I was surprised to hear him pronounce Gandhi's name with reverence. He added the suffix "ji" to it, which in Hindi gives an affectionate connotation to a surname. "Gandhiji" here, "Gandhiji" there, I could hardly believe my ears. What about Gandhiji's ideal of nonviolence?

"My dear friend, you must remember Hindu women had to burn themselves alive to escape the infamy of being raped by Muslims, and Gandhiji told them that the victim was the victor."

After twenty-five years in prison, Gopal Godsé's anger was still intact.

"Gandhi's nonviolence threw Hindus to the mercy of their enemies. Hindu refugees died of hunger and Gandhi exalted their sacrifice, defending their Muslim oppressors. How long could we go on putting up with that? Yes, how long, my dear friend?"

Godsé invited me to the ceremony that, every November 15, commemorated his brother's execution. He had placed on a pedestal in front of the large map of India a small silver-plated urn containing Nathuram's ashes. The latter had actually asked, on the eve of his execution, that his ashes "be kept until such time as they could be scattered on the waters of the Indus flowing through a country at last reunited under Hindu domination." All members of the murderer's family, women and children included, together with several disciples of Vir Savarkar, the Hindu guru who had inspired the conspirators, were present. Doleful sitar music accompanied by the beating of a tabla soon filled the room. At the bidding of the master of the house, the participants raised their fists and swore, before the funeral urn and the portrait of the assassin, to reconquer the "severed section of our motherland"—Pakistan—and to reunite India under Hindu rule. With a calculated sense of dramatic timing, Godsé then opened a chest from which he took some clothes.

"Here is the shirt Nathuram was wearing the day he killed Gandhiji," he announced, exhibiting a bloodstained khaki tunic, a reminder of the truncheon blows he received when arrested.

Next he displayed the trousers and sandals. Everyone came

and bowed respectfully before these relics. Godsé then read his brother's will. While the sitar and tabla resumed their melancholy playing, the participants came up one at a time to prostrate themselves, candle in hand, before the ashes. Each one waved the candle several times around the urn before raising it to the luminous serpent that symbolized the Indus River. In unison, they all repeated their promise to reconquer India's lost land.

FORTY-NINE-YEAR-OLD FORMER TERRORIST Madanlal Pahwa had settled in Bombay. He was the one who had first tried to kill Gandhi by setting off a homemade bomb at the foot of his prayer platform. After two days of diligent tracking, I at last flushed him out in a neighborhood on the city's outskirts inhabited by Hindu refugees from Pakistan. It was impossible not to recognize him: he had the same thick black head of hair divided by a side parting, and the same fine mustache as on the mug shots taken twenty-five years earlier by the police. Madanlal was the only one of the conspirators to have been driven out of his home by partition. Having lost everything and known the suffering of exodus, he had assumed the leadership of a commando of Hindu fanatics, which had massacred hundreds of Muslim refugees in the trains taking them back to Pakistan. Following his abortive assassination attempt, he had been arrested, and after two days of intensive interrogation, had supplied the names of all his accomplices. It was through him that the New Delhi police had known, two weeks prior to the assassination, that a group of terrorists were in the capital to kill Gandhi. They had even had detailed descriptions of them all.

At first Madanlal received me with mistrust. In the end, however, the interest I showed in his latest activities won him over. He had switched to a somewhat unexpected business: toys. He was most proud of a compressed-air rocket that went some three hundred feet up in the air and came down on the end of a parachute. He offered me the opportunity to become his agent in Europe "to compete there with the damned Japanese exports."

Still in Bombay, I managed to find the most disturbing of all that brood of assassins, the former arms dealer Digambar Badgé, who had provided the revolver for the crime. With his long beard, he looked more like a holy man than a revolutionary. Since his release from prison, Badgé, too, had taken up an unusual occupation. Having spent years selling devices designed to inflict death, now he was making an accessory to protect people from it. With the help of his elderly father, he "knitted" coats of mail like those worn by knights in the Middle Ages. These bulletproof vests were much prized by hired assassins, strikebreakers and politicians on all sides. His order book was full for the next two years.

"Do you have any French clients?" I asked him.

He assumed a sly expression. "Not yet. But our meeting could alter that, couldn't it?"

Damned assassins! Their readiness to talk to us gave me an idea. Why not take them all back to New Delhi and have them go through the motions of their crime on camera. I weighed the dangers. The Indian police themselves had had to give up all ideas of reconstructing the crime during the investigations for the trial for fear of bloody and vengeful reactions. I went to Poona to suggest the trip to Gopal Godsé. Would he think I was being provocative and throw me out? I had scarcely revealed my plans before I saw his head wagging from left to right with a pleased expression.

"It's a very good idea." Then suddenly he scowled. "But only if we can take our families along."

I bought tickets for everyone, and a week later we met on the platform of Victoria Station in Bombay next to the Frontier Mail leaving for New Delhi. It was like going on an outing with relatives I just happened to meet. They called me "dear brother" or "Mr. Dominique" and had me taste the innumerable delicacies, pastries and provisions they had brought along in baskets. Godsé, Karkaré and Madanlal claimed it was the same train they had caught twenty-five years previously to go and assassinate Gandhi. To reduce the risk of their all being arrested together, Nathuram had taken a plane.

"We had arranged to meet in Delhi in the garden of the temple to the goddess Lakshmi," Godsé proudly recalled.

After a forty-eight-hour journey, I took them back to the same garden. I had hired a cameraman and a soundman to whom I had taken the precaution of not revealing the identity of the persons with me.

Godsé took Karkaré over to the huge pink-painted sanctuary of the temple and showed him the bell hanging over the door. "Remember? We rang it before going to collect our thoughts at the goddess's feet."

The wives listened, smugly admiring and proud, to their husbands' explanations. They could have been a squad of old soldiers returning to the battlefield where they had won a medal. Beyond the sanctuary there was a small wood.

"That's where Nathuram tried out our revolver," Karkaré explained. "Fortunately there was no one about. Not knowing whether Gandhiji would be sitting or standing when Nathuram fired at him, we practiced the procedure for both positions. We selected a tree. One of us squatted down against the trunk to give an idea of the silhouette Gandhi would present in the sitting position. We drew around it with a piece of chalk. Nathuram backed away about ten yards and fired five times. All the bullets went home."

Godsé took us then to the central railway station cafeteria where, on the eve of the murder, they had shared a Pantagruelian feast.

As the assassins had done that day in January 1948, we next caught horse-drawn carts to Birla House, Gandhi's residence. Floods of visitors were silently walking through the rooms and garden. The walls of that much-venerated house were covered with photographs of the Mahatma at every stage of his life. Pilgrims paused with a particular respect in his bedroom. They followed the steps leading to the small stele that stood on the spot where he had been assassinated. They meditated on the great lawn where he had held his last prayer meetings. Was I not profaning this sacred place by bringing back the men who had so odiously defiled it?

I was asking myself the question when I heard a voice calling my name. I turned around and recognized the curator of the house, a distinguished Brahmin who had taken a lively interest in our historical research work.

"Dear Mr. Lapierre, I see that you have company today!" he exclaimed amiably. "You even have a film crew with you! Won't you introduce me to your friends?"

Cold shivers ran down my spine.

"With pleasure," I said, trying to conceal my disquiet. "Allow me to introduce Mr. and Mrs. Gopal Godsé, Mr. and Mrs. Vishnu . . ."

As I rattled off the names of Gandhi's assassins, I saw the curator's features distort. Was he suddenly going to have a stroke? Overcoming his surprise, he gave me a somewhat forced smile before inquiring: "Mr. Lapierre, would you like us all to go to my office?"

We entered the spacious ground-floor room where Larry and I had so often listened to him recapture the last hours of Gandhi's life. A servant brought chairs and we sat down in front of his worktable. What was he going to do? Pick up his telephone and call the police? Throw these undesirable visitors out? The curator sank into his armchair, overwhelmed by the unexpectedness of the situation. His silence lasted several minutes. Finally he sat up again and his eyes brightened. I waited for the worst.

"What will you have to drink?" he inquired. "Tea or Kampa-Cola?"

A LITTLE WHILE LATER I was standing with the assassins on the exact spot where Nathuram Godsé had been standing on January 30, 1948, at seven minutes past five when he killed Gandhi. The camera was directed point blank on his brother.

"The garden was black with people," recounted Gopal

Godsé. "Gandhiji was several minutes late. Suddenly we saw people parting. The procession was arriving. Gandhiji was walking at its head, leaning with both hands on his great-nieces. Nathuram had positioned himself on the path leading to the prayer platform. It was an ideal position. I saw him get his revolver out of his pocket."

Our presence had attracted a crowd of pilgrims. Among them were many Sikhs in their distinctive turbans. What would their reaction be when they learned the identity of the man the camera was filming?

Gopal Godsé went on, unruffled: "Nathuram did his best to conceal the revolver between his joined palms and bowed respectfully before Gandhiji, saying '*Namaste, Bapu*' [Greetings, Father]. Then he drew one of the girls away to avoid wounding her and fired: once, twice, three times. Gandhi whispered, '*He Ram!*' [O God!], and sank slowly onto the grass. It was all over."

At those words, I saw a tall, fierce-looking Sikh rummaging feverishly in the folds of his waistband. I was convinced he was looking for the dagger all members of his community carry. I could already see the blade glinting in the sunlight. He was going to cut the three criminals' throats, and possibly the cameraman's and mine along with them. In that way he would avenge the hundreds of millions of Indians who remained inconsolable at the loss of their Great Soul.

I was wrong. Gandhi had died too long ago. What the fierce Sikh was looking for in the folds of his waistband was not the dagger of vengeance. He held out to Godsé a piece of paper and a pen. He wanted his autograph.

They Were the Proud Collectors of Women, Rolls-Royces and Elephants

The architects of Indian independence, Gandhi and Nehru at their head, had made no provision for them in the new India. Yet the 565 Hindu maharajas and Muslim nawabs reigned as hereditary and absolute sovereigns over a third of India's territory and approximately a hundred million of its inhabitants. Princes such as the nizzam of Hyderabad and the maharaja of Kashmir headed states as sizable and as populous as the larger European nations. Their princely confraternity included both some of the richest men in the world and monarchs with incomes as modest as a stallholder's in the Bombay bazaar. Experts had calculated, however, that each had an average of 11 titles, 5.8 wives, 12.6 children, 9.2 elephants, 2.8 private railway cars, 3.4 Rolls-Royces, and 22.9 tigers killed.

Rich or not so rich, the Indian maharajas constituted in any case an unusual aristocracy. According to Rudyard Kipling, "these men had been created by Providence to provide the world with picturesque settings, tales of tigers and grandiose spectacles." Accounts of their vices and virtues, their extravagance and prodigality, their whims and their eccentricities, had enriched humanity's folklore and amazed a world craving for exoticism and fantasy. Before the winds of history swept them away, the richest of these unique aristocrats had traveled through life on the flying carpets of some Oriental fairy stories. Their passions were hunting, polo, palaces, women, jewels and cars. Of these last, their favorite was naturally the queen of cars, the Rolls-Royce.

Larry Collins decreed that the passion I shared with them for Rolls-Royce clearly qualified me for the responsibility to research the maharajas. In 1947 Mountbatten had used his charisma and influence to persuade these monarchs, many of whom were his friends, to voluntarily give up their sovereignty and hand over their states into the basket of Indian independence. Talking to some of the men who had been involved in this collective act of hara-kiri was to be a most fascinating experience.

THE SIKH MAHARAJA YADAVINDRA SINGH, last titular prince of the state of Patiala in the northwest of India, still occupied, together with a few servants, the pinnacled palace built by his ancestors. His garages, which in 1947 had harbored a fleet of twenty-seven Rolls-Royces, now accommodated no more than one locally manufactured Ambassador and an antique French de Dion-Bouton. This relic, dating back to 1898, bore the significant number "Patiala 1," because it had been the first car to be imported into India. Singh, a tall man of six feet three inches, a lover of cricket and polo, had espoused himself to the new India on the day after independence, becoming one of its most respected diplomats. On entering the extravagant apartment where I was to stay as his guest, I noticed a sheet of paper placed on the bedside table. It invited me to mark the space opposite the various forms of transport available to me during my stay. Did I wish to travel in a carriage? By car? On a sedan chair? On horseback? Or on an elephant?

Yadavindra Singh had ascended the throne of the state of Patiala on the death of his father in July 1938. His coronation gave rise to seven days and seven nights of festivities and celebration. His peers came from the four corners of the country, and a representative of the British Empire had pinned on his turban the precious stone that established the young prince's allegiance to the Crown. It should be said that the young prince of Patiala was succeeding one of the most colorful personalities in a caste that abounded in legendary figures.

With his colossal stature, weighing 290 pounds, a mustache that curled up like the horns of a gallant bull, a splendid black beard carefully rolled up and knotted at the back of the neck in the Sikh manner, sensual lips and an arrogant air, his father, Sir Bhupinder Singh, known as "the Magnificent," seventh Maharaja of Patiala, looked as if he stepped out of a Mogul engraving. Sir Bhupinder epitomized all the splendor of the Indian maharajas. His appetite was such that he required over forty pounds of food a day, and he would happily consume two or three chickens at tea time. He adored polo. Galloping away at the head of his "Patiala Tigers," he had brought back trophies from playing fields all over the globe to fill his palace display cases. To make such achievements possible, his stables housed five hundred of the finest specimens of the equine race.

From his earliest adolescence Bhupinder Singh had shown the liveliest aptitude for another form of diversion equally worthy of a prince. The care he manifested in the development of his harem eclipsed even his passion for hunting and polo. He chose new additions himself on the basis of their attractiveness and their lovemaking skills. In its heyday Patiala's royal harem numbered 365 wives and concubines, one for each day of the year.

During the torrid Punjab summers, a number of them would position themselves each evening by the swimming pool, young bare-breasted beauties in the company of whom the prince would have a swim. Sacks of crushed ice brought from the Himalayas by a regiment of coolies cooled the water. The ceilings and walls of the private rooms were decorated with scenes inspired by the erotic temple bas-reliefs for which India was famous, a whole catalog of amorous positions guaranteed to exhaust even the most imaginative mind and the most athletic body. A large silk hammock enabled His Highness to pursue the intoxicating pleasures suggested by the activities of the figures on his ceiling, while suspended between heaven and earth.

To satisfy his insatiable desires, the inventive sovereign had resolved to regularly renew his ladies' charms. He threw open his palace to a whole retinue of perfumers, jewelers, hairdressers, beauticians and dressmakers. Top plastic surgeons were invited to come and reshape his favorites' features in accordance with his whims and the dictates of the fashion magazines he had sent from London and Paris. To stimulate his ardor, he had converted one wing of his palace into a laboratory to produce aphrodisiac perfumes, lotions, cosmetics and philters.

But no man, not even a Sikh as generously endowed by nature as Bhupinder Singh the Magnificent, could satiate the appetites of 365 beauties languishing behind the moucharaby of his harem. His alchemists had to compete with each other's ingenuity. They devised clever concoctions based on gold, pearls, spices, silver, herbs, iron. For some time the most effective potion was a mixture of carrots and sparrows' brains. When the effects of these preparations began to fade, Sir Bhupinder Singh had specialists brought over from France, a country he thought expert in matters of love. Treatment with radium was unfortunately to prove as ephemeral in its effect as the magic potions. Sir Bhupinder the Magnificent died at the premature age of forty-five—of exhaustion.

ONE OF HIS SUCCESSOR'S FIRST decisions was to close the paternal harem. Yadavindra belonged to a new generation of princes who were less colorful, less extravagant and less extraordinary than their elders, but more and more conscious of the precariousness of their privileges and the need to reform the customs of their kingdoms.

In fact, the India of the maharajas and the nawabs had another face, a face sometimes overlooked because of the excesses and eccentricities of a few princes. The Maharaja of Kapurthala, whose palace, which looked like a small Versailles, contained an ashtray pinched from the Hôtel Negresco in Nice, had equipped his kingdom with roads, railway lines, schools, hospitals and even democratic institutions, turning it into a modern, liberal state that was the envy of the provinces directly administered by the British. The Maharaja of Bikaner had transformed certain parts of his Rajasthan desert into a veritable oasis of gardens, artificial lakes and flourishing developments placed at the disposal of his subjects. The Muslim principality of Bhopal had granted women a degree of liberation unparalleled anywhere else in the Orient. The state of Mysore had the most highly regarded science university in Asia. A descendant of one of history's greatest astronomers, a learned man who had translated the principles of Euclidean geometry into Sanskrit, the maharaja of Jaipur had turned his capital's observatory into a study center of international renown.

The Indian princes had been the most zealous instruments of Britain's domination of India. They had accepted the suzerainty of the king-emperor as represented by the viceroy, abandoning control of their external affairs and their defense to him, in exchange for their internal sovereignty. They had spared neither their money nor their blood in the course of two world wars. They had raised, equipped and trained expeditionary corps that had won glory on all fronts under the Union Jack. During World War I, the Maharaja of Bikaner, himself a general in the British army and a member of the War Cabinet, sent his cameleers to attack the German trenches. On September 23, 1917, the Jodhpur Lancers took Haifa from the Turks. In 1944, under the leadership of their young maharaja, a commander in the Lifeguards, sepoys from the pink city of Jaipur cleared the slopes of Monte Cassino and opened up the Allied armies' route to Rome. In recognition of the courage the maharaja of Bundi had shown leading his battalion in the depths of the Birman jungle, he was awarded the Military Cross.

The British showed their appreciation of these faithful and unsparing vassals by showering them with honors and decorations. The maharajas of Gwalior, Cooch Behar and Patiala were granted the signal privilege of forming a mounted escort of ADCs for Edward VII during his coronation celebrations. Oxford and Cambridge awarded honorary degrees to a whole series of princes. The chests of the most deserving sovereigns were adorned with the glittering medals of orders newly created for the occasion—the Star of India and the Order of the Indian Empire.

It was, above all, by the subtle grading of an ingenious and original form of recompense that the suzerain power best knew how to show its gratitude. The number of cannon shots that greeted an Indian monarch was an indication of his place in the princely hierarchy. The viceroy had the power to increase the number of salvos in recognition of exceptional services, or to reduce it as a sign of punishment. Five sovereigns—those of Hyderabad, Kashmir, Mysore, Gwalior and Baroda—were entitled to the supreme honor of a twenty-one-gun salute. Next came the states with nineteen, then seventeen, fifteen, thirteen, eleven and nine guns. For 425 humble rajas and nawabs reigning over small kingdoms almost forgotten on the maps, there was no salute at all. They were India's forsaken princes, men for whom the cannon did not thunder.

Cannon or no cannon, however, that summer of 1947, India's maharajas and nawabs had all found themselves gathered under the same ensign, marking an irreversible farewell to a bygone age.

15

Men, Women and Children Who Are the Light of the World

After two years of enthralling discoveries in India, I felt the need to thank her. The success of *Freedom at Midnight*, the book born of our exciting research, gave me the means to do it. I decided to give part of my royalties to an Indian institution working for leper children. I made my way to Calcutta, which, I knew, harbored several thousand victims of that cursed disease.

At five-thirty one morning my wife and I knocked on the door of a large gray building in the very heart of the city. Calcutta was just awakening. At the entrance, a wooden board announced: "Mother Teresa." The Saint of Calcutta would certainly be able to recommend an institution in need of the money I had brought. A young Indian sister in a white sari with a blue border opened the door to us. A famished-looking old man tried to slip in through the narrow opening, but the nun pushed him gently away, telling him in Bengali where the nearest aid center was. Then she led us to the chapel on the first floor, a vast room where about a hundred young novices in white saris were reciting psalms, drowned out by the din of trams and trucks passing along the avenue outside. The only decoration was a simple wooden crucifix surmounted by the inscription "I thirst" on the wall behind the altar.

I immediately recognized the legendary, wrinkled figure kneeling on an old darned jute sack, her lips moving in uninterrupted prayer. As soon as Mass was over, Mother Teresa joined us in the parlor. The fatigue of a life of deprivation, exhausting journeys around the world and sleepless nights had not diminished the radiance of her expression, full of faith and love. I told her the reason for our visit.

"Mother, I know that what we have brought is only a drop in the ocean of need . . ."

"But if that drop were not in the ocean, the ocean would miss it. And it is God who has sent you," she interrupted with amused gentleness.

A walking catalog of all the city's wretchedness, the nun did not need to think for very long to know who was in urgent financial need.

That same evening, a European of about forty, dressed in an Indian shirt and cotton trousers, turned up at our hotel. In twelve years Englishman James Stevens had wrested more than a thousand leper children from poverty and death in the slums of Calcutta. He had once had a prosperous business, selling shirts and ties, but had sold everything he had and given up his comfortable existence in England to devote his life to saving children otherwise doomed to total destitution. The home he had founded on the outskirts of Calcutta was called Udayan, a Hindi word meaning "resurrection."

Our visitor's cheerfulness and florid complexion were a facade that masked the crisis he was going through: he was on the verge of closing his refuge and sending the 150 children it harbored back to their misery. He had exhausted all his personal resources and had been unable to find financial support to maintain his work. A small island of hope in the depths of hell was about to disappear.

In the days of the British, Barrackpore had been a smart residential suburb. A few oases of greenery sheltering once-grand residences, vestiges of imperial splendor, still survived amid the modern industrial activity. It was in the large paneled living room of an old colonnaded Palladian house, its paint peeling after the rigors of the monsoon, that James Stevens and his boys received us next day.

We arrived at the most important time of the day: lunchtime. The 150 children were sitting cross-legged on the ground. With their hands together, eyes closed, concentrating intently, they were singing away in shrill voices. In front of each brown head was a banana leaf containing a small mountain of rice, a few pieces of meat and some lentil puree, a balanced helping of healthful food still unknown to 400 million Indians. Stevens was singing the grace too. It was a prayer by the great Bengali poet and friend of Mahatma Gandhi, Rabindranath Tagore. "All that is not given is lost," it asserted. When they had finished singing, James said a short invocation in Bengali. A hundred and fifty small hands then descended on the food, to work the various ingredients into an initial small ball that was immediately raised to their mouths and gulped down. But for the sound of chewing, there was complete silence. Every face was focused on a sacred act, every mouthful was scooped up with gravity, every movement carried out with dignity.

James took us next to the dormitories that were also used as classrooms and places where judo, yoga and gymnastics were taught. A smiling picture of Jesus, another of Vishnu and a sura from the Koran adorned each room. One wing of the house harbored the workshops where the children learned to become tailors, mechanics and electricians, skills that would guarantee them a job when they left the center and enable them to help their families out of destitution. In India a single job can save as many as twenty people. On the walls of the infirmary small posters denounced some of the prejudices relating to leprosy. No, leprosy is not fatal. No, it is not necessarily contagious. No, it is not hereditary. No, it is not a shameful disease. Yes, it can be treated. Yes, you can be cured of leprosy.

Three times a week an Indian doctor came from Calcutta to give the occupants of the home appropriate treatment. One in five children arrived there with early symptoms, generally depigmentation of the skin in several places on his body. At their age mutilation was rare. Intensive sulfone-based treatment got rid of those initial signs in less than a year. But leprosy was only one of many diseases to affect children who came from slums where there was no hygiene, from squalid compounds where they competed with cockroaches and rats for food. They suffered from nutritional deficiencies that brought with them a whole litany of illnesses: rickets, tuberculosis of the lungs and bones, malaria, amebiasis. Some even had xerophthalmia, a night blindness caused by lack of vitamin A.

James Stevens had performed his first rescue operation with an old van on loan from Mother Teresa, on July 21, 1969, the same day three men landed on the moon. He had driven into the Pilkhana slum near the great Howrah Station. The leper colony was confined to the farthest reaches of the neighborhood, and initial contact was difficult. The Englishman knew only a few words of Bengali and Hindi. He had to use sign language to persuade the parents to entrust their children to him so that he could treat, feed and clothe them, and teach them to read and write.

"I shall never forget that first day," he told us. "The parents looked at me suspiciously, as if I wanted to steal their children and take them away to be slaves in some foreign country. The resistance put up by men and women who had nothing was heart-rending."

At the back of a hovel where several families lived crowded together, James Stevens had noticed a boy of about ten, dressed in rags. He was living with his mother, a poor widow who had no fingers and whose face had been eaten away by leprosy. He already had a few lesions on his skin. The Englishman gave the wretched woman to understand that he wanted to take care of her son and treat him. She shrugged her shoulders as if to say: "He'll never stay with you!" Stevens learned from neighbors that the child was a proper little savage who would sometimes disappear for months on end. To everyone's surprise, he agreed to go off with the Englishman and so became the first occupant of the Resurrection Home. His name was Budi Ram. In a matter of months he learned to read and write and became one of the most gifted pupils in the auto-mechanic workshop. He was so capable that his benefactor sent him to complete his apprenticeship at a highly respected technical school in the Punjab. When he graduated, he was immediately snapped up by the Escort tractor firm to supervise the execution of an important contract in Nepal. With his first savings, Budi Ram bought a plot of land in the countryside near Calcutta and built a house there for his mother to live in. She would never again have to shake her begging bowl on the platforms of the nearby station.

Not far from there, Stevens won over another little wildcat. Laxman Singh was eight years old, lived alone and fed off the refuse in the garbage dumps. It took the Englishman weeks to get to know his story. He had been four or five when his parents took him and his brothers and sisters to the festival of the goddess Durga, the Hindu patroness of Calcutta. In the throng he had become separated from his family. He would never see them again. Spotting the lost child, a passerby had taken him home and turned him into a servant, forcing him to do all the most arduous chores about the house. In the end Laxman had run away. He had survived by petty theft and small jobs in the eating places and tea stalls of the huge city. When James picked him up, he had a patch of leprosy on his left cheek. Swollen with worms, his stomach looked like a balloon. He was also suffering from ulceration of the cornea. Could he be cured? Dr. Sen at the home did everything he could. Laxman Singh would later become one of Air India's best mechanics.

That first evening, Stevens took home nine boys and two little girls aged four and ten. Six of them already had the stigmata of the terrible disease. He sat them down in a circle on the floor of the living room and gave them a meal. He had cooked some rice, lentils and a little fish himself. The children surveyed this feast with stupefaction. They had never seen plates so full. The Englishman sat on the floor among them and began to eat. Winning over these escapees from hell was difficult. It was worst at night. The frightened little creatures at first refused to drop off and when at last sleep did overtake them, it was only to plunge them into horrible nightmares. Their screams of horror were intermingled with fragmented sentences, suggesting the terrifying visions that haunted their dreams. There were tigers, evil spirits and *bhuts*, ghosts. James used to go from one to the next, sponging their sweating foreheads. Remembering he had been a tenor in an amateur opera group, he sang them melodies from *Rigoletto* and *La Traviata* and songs from his native Yorkshire; eventually the children settled down.

With the passage of the days, life became more ordered. Soon the home had some thirty boarders. Chand, an eleven-year-old boy found on the docks, was suffering from tuberculosis of the ganglia and got around on a board on wheels. A few months of vitamin-intensive food and rigorous medical care produced a spectacular improvement. The leprosy was checked, the tuberculosis stopped. Children who weighed half the normal weight for their age when they arrived were restored to balanced growth. Chand was able to walk again, first with crutches, then without any help. Another child had open heart surgery. James gave his blood for the transfusions. These victories soon manifested themselves in one very revealing sign: the children in the Resurrection Home had started to laugh again.

The generosity of the fair-haired "big brother" soon became known throughout the leper colonies. His van was assailed as soon as it appeared in the alleyways. By the end of the year, the home had fifty young Hindu, Muslim and Christian inmates. Stevens told us about the first Christmas.

"They had all decorated the house together and made a magnificent manger. An Ashoka tree served as a fir. I dressed up as Santa Claus and gave each one a present. We had prepared a real banquet. For the first time in their lives they tasted something their parents had been too poor to give them: a chicken curry with vegetables, and an orange."

A new phase began then. James opened a school divided into two sections: one for the Bengali-speaking children, the other for those who spoke Hindi. They all came together after classes for singing, yoga and craft lessons and maintenance work on the house and garden. For his older protégés, James created apprentice workshops where each child could learn a trade. He introduced us to Sultan Ali, the son of a rickshaw puller who, at the age of eleven, was already a champion on his sewing machine. He was almost cured of his leprosy. Like many Muslims, he wanted to become a tailor. This practical orientation was also particularly useful for those unable to follow normal academic studies because malnutrition at an early age had impeded their brain development.

In 1972 James Stevens put down definitive roots in the country to which he had given his heart. He married Lallita, a Christian teacher, originally from the Punjab. With their son, Ashwini, they lived the life of the children in the home, sleeping on mats rolled out each night on the bare floor, sharing their meals, their joys and their troubles, praying with them to the Hindu gods, to Allah the merciful and to Jesus.

In 1979 a gift from the Swiss organization Frères de Nos Frères enabled James to buy two hectares of land in the open countryside and build a bungalow for the children and two huts to house the school and the dispensary. In an area protected from urban pollution, he envisaged creating a small farm to provide the home with vegetables, eggs, poultry and even fish from a pond. Unfortunately his own funds had been exhausted, and the charitable organizations that had supported him had committed themselves elsewhere. Tirelessly James sought other financial support, but to no avail. He had to borrow money at extortionate rates just to feed his children.

James admitted to us that he was going to have to close the home and send his protégés back to the horror of their hovels. Devastated by the news, my wife, Dominique, took out of her bag the bundle of dollars we had brought with us.

"This initial donation will enable to pay off your debts," I said, and before really thinking, I added: "We will fight to see that you never have to close the Resurrection Home."

That commitment was to change our lives.

ON OUR RETURN TO FRANCE, I founded an association, Action Aid for Lepers' Children of Calcutta, the initial aim of which was to provide financial support for the work of that unknown Englishman.[1] To publicize its existence, I told the story of the Resurrection Home in the magazine *La Vie*. At the end of my article I appealed to readers:

1. See Appendix.

"If one thousand of us were to send every year about fifty dollars—the price of a good meal in a restaurant—together we could save 150 children from the misery of their slums."

A few days later our building superintendent rang our doorbell. She was livid.

"The postman has just dumped five mailbags in the lobby," she announced. "They're all for you. What should I do with them?"

We carried them up to our fourth-floor walk-up apartment. We called friends and relatives to the rescue to help us go through a flood of envelopes that brought words of encouragement almost always accompanied by a check or a money order.

"Our little Marie is one month old today," wrote one couple. "Her birth is a call to life and we want her to be a sign of joy and sharing. Our friends and family have replaced the traditional welcoming gift to Marie with a contribution to James Stevens's work in Calcutta. Here is the total sum of our gifts. We know it is a drop in the ocean but it is a token of life."

A couple from Normandy confided that the baptism of their son Simon had been an occasion for them to stop and think about the fate of other children not lucky enough to be born in a rich country. "So we asked our families, friends and Christian community to make Simon's baptismal present a gift to the children of the Third World, and more specifically those of James Stevens's Resurrection Home."

Madeleine Maire, of a small city in the east, sent the proceeds of a collection taken among the relatives and friends who came to keep vigil over her husband after his death. "Jean-Marie was a mountain guide," she wrote. "On September 13, 1981, he was swept away by an avalanche in the Mont Blanc massif of the Alps. He was a good and devoted man who cared about others. I would like James Stevens's children to know they will not be abandoned."

One writer enclosed with her gift a photo of three dark-skinned children obviously full of the joy of living. "We feel concerned," he said, "because we have adopted two Indian children from Pondicherry and a little girl from Guatemala. They bring us so much happiness that we would like all the world's children to have a happy future. Keep up your good work with courage. We are with you in spirit."

A grandmother had sent all her savings.

An inconsolable mother who had just lost her daughter wanted the money she would have spent on her dead child to "help other children to grow up and learn to smile."

"I have taken all my money out of my piggy bank to give to the children in Calcutta," wrote Laurent, a boy of twelve. "It isn't much but I will think of them as soon as I can send some more."

Hundreds of children like Laurent broke open their piggy banks. Sometimes a whole class sent what they had collected. Marie-José Hayes, aged nineteen, sent half her first wages, and her mother added a check in memory of her son Jean-Louis, "who died five years ago in a motorcycle accident while going to a charity meeting. He dreamed of a more just and brotherly world. On behalf of him I shall continue to support you."

"I am just a housekeeper," someone else confided, "but I shall happily work a few extra hours for the children of your Mr. James."

Minimum-wage earners went without the little they had, elderly people shared their savings. One anonymous person put a wad of treasury bonds in an envelope, another gentleman sent two hundred-franc notes (forty dollars) with a message asking James Stevens to accept "a little of our superfluity to enable all his children to live."

One envelope contained a check with this explanation: "I have just received the sum of 44,000 francs (nine thousand dollars) from my insurance company in compensation for a theft. I am sending it for James and his children."

Some people offered to adopt a child; others to go to Calcutta and work unpaid in the Resurrection Home.

"We are aged between nine and ten," the pupils of one school wrote in a collective letter, "and we talk a great deal about those who are less fortunate than ourselves. Tell the Calcutta children that we care about them and will help them all we can. Above all, tell Mr. Stevens not to lose heart."

The association I had just formed suddenly found itself supported by nearly three thousand donors whose address cards soon filled several shoe boxes. All I had to do then was send our friend James the telegram of a lifetime: "Resurrection Home saved. You can even take fifty more children. We're coming."

A Fete Among the Lepers

Under a banner proclaiming in large red letters, "Welcome to our brother and sister Dominique and Dominique," fifty brown heads were waiting for us at the Calcutta airport. The warmth of this tribute was kept up at the home where the children had arranged a program of dancing, games and sporting events. James had invited their parents to join in the festivities. Nothing could have made us more intensely conscious of the bonds that would from then on unite us with our Indian family. Those fathers and mothers whose offspring burst with life had lost their feet, fingers or noses. But they were monuments of dignity.

To help us understand how valuable Resurrection Home really was, James invited us to go with him to the leper colony where he had picked up his first inmates and where he was now taking two boys, Raju and Mohan, to visit their parents. From the outside there was nothing to distinguish it from the slum on the edge of which it was located. It was, however, a very particular kind of ghetto. No healthy slum dweller ever ventured inside. Crammed ten or twelve to a room, the six hundred lepers lived there in total segregation. A Dantesque vision of disfigured faces, feet and hands reduced to stumps and wounds that were sometimes purulent and covered with flies. Under improvised shelters, on the bare earth or on mats, those ravaged beings busied themselves with their daily tasks. The sight was nothing compared with the smell. The combined stench of putrefaction, alcohol and incense was enough to make our stomachs heave. And yet, as so often happens in India, the sublime coexisted with the unbearable: in the midst of all the rubbish and the excrement, children played with marbles and shrieked with laughter.

Our arrival set the colony in an uproar. People lame and

blind, with one arm or one leg, came rushing for a *darshan*, a visual communion, with big brother James and his friends. They smiled at us and there was nothing forced or imploring about those smiles. Some clapped their wasted hands to applaud. Others jostled with each other to get closer and touch us. Young Raju introduced us to his mother, a slip of a woman who was dreadfully mutilated. She had no fingers left and her ravaged face looked like a mummy's mask. But her brilliant smile made you forget her disfigurement. My wife, Dominique, clasped her in her arms. The gesture was doubly surprising. Not only did it transgress the usual Indian reserve, but above all it was directed at one of the "accursed ones," a pariah among pariahs.

Our visit turned into a fete. A group of musicians gave us an aubade with flutes and tambourines. Outside the door to one hovel, an old man who was almost blind pushed a three-year-old child he had just adopted in my direction. The man used to beg outside the temple to Kali when, one morning, that rickety youngster sought refuge with him, like a lost dog without a collar. Sick and destitute as he was, he had taken the little boy under his wing. A little farther on, we were amazed at the sight of a little girl massaging the emaciated body of her younger brother with fingers that were still healthy. In a compound four men were playing poker. The cards flew about between their stumps before tumbling to the ground amid a chorus of exclamations and laughter. How could so much vitality, so much joy, spring from so much abjection? Those people were life, LIFE in capital letters, life pulsating and bustling and throbbing in the same way that it throbbed everywhere else in Calcutta. Many of the occupants of that leper colony came from Bengal, Bihar, Orissa and the south. Most of them had never received any treatment.

James was feted as the big brother sent from heaven. Young girls put garlands of marigolds around his neck. The families of the boys from Resurrection Home had decorated the entrances to their shacks with carpets of *rangoli*, magnificent geometrical designs drawn out on the earth in ground rice and colored powders. The appearance of their benefactor gave rise to a most dramatic scene. A young woman in a yellow sari let go of her crutches to throw herself at his feet and wipe the dust from his sandals before touching her forehead and then her heart. James bent over to help her to get up again while Dominique gave her back her crutches. The poor woman's right leg had been amputated at the knee. Her face, still intact, had the pure beauty of a Raphael Madonna. A small boy with rickets was clinging to the folds of her sari.

"*Dadah* [Big brother], take him, I beg you, take him, for the love of God!" the leper woman implored in Bengali.

She explained to James that her husband had left her and that she had nothing to give her children to eat. We were devastated. I wanted to tell our English friend to agree to the mother's request, that we would find a few dollars necessary to take her child, that in Europe and America there were families who would give of their abundance to save that child from his tragic plight. But I did not dare intervene. James was the one who lived in Calcutta, not me. He was the one who daily confronted the misery of its inhabitants. The suspense went on. I could see that James was torn. Several dozen lepers had formed a circle around us. The nauseating discharges and the heat were making the air unbreathable. Dominique's face had turned white. James took the child in his arms and talked softly to him. His mother's face lit up with a dazzling smile. How beautiful that woman was!

"Thank you, *dadah*," she said, saluting him with her hands joined together, then touching her forehead and her heart.

I thought of Mother Teresa's saying: "To save one child is to save the world."

The Kingdom of the Poor

With its rectilinear alleyways, its small shacks built around small courtyards and its flat tiled roofs, the rest of the slum looked like an urban village. According to municipal statistics, it was one of the densest concentrations of humanity on the planet: seventy thousand people were packed into an area not much bigger than three football fields, in an atmosphere so pol-

luted that our eyes and throats immediately smarted with it.
They lived in hovels without water, electricity or windows,
along alleys edged with open drains. I could imagine that place
scorched by the blazing heat of summer, awash with the monsoon floods, its alleyways and shacks turned into pools of mud
and excrement. I imagined the stench, the diseases, the epi-
demics caused by the presence of buffalo cows confined to
filthy stables, and spread by the hordes of rats, cockroaches and
other vermin. James Stevens told us that the life expectancy
here was under forty. Nine out of ten people had less than one
rupee a day, about three U.S. cents, with which to boil a little
rice. The inhabitants of the slum were nearly all peasants who
had been driven from their land by one or other of the climatic
scourges—droughts, cyclones or flooding—so frequent in that
part of the world. To me the place was an antechamber to hell.

James led us through the teeming alleyways to the far end of a
compound. There, in a hovel six and a half feet by five, with no
water and no electricity, no windows and no furniture, not even a
cot, lived a forty-four-year-old Swiss. His extreme pallor, his thinness and his long Indian shirt made him look like some dropout
on the road to Kathmandu. His name was Gaston Grandjean.

"Sorry, friends, tourists aren't welcome here!" he called out
on seeing us.

Poor Gaston! How was he to know that the arrival of this foreign couple was to dramatically alter his life?

For twelve years the nurse Gaston Grandjean and the Indian
social workers he had trained to serve the poorest of the poor
had been working tirelessly in that overpopulated neighborhood. Unsanitary conditions, malnutrition, superstition and
lack of hygiene gave this other white "big brother" no respite.
It had taken several months, however, before he had been accepted. At first, people had wondered what could ever moti-
vate someone from a country as rich as Switzerland to come and
share their extreme poverty. Word went out that he was working for the police, that he was at the same time a CIA spy, a
Maoist mole and a militant missionary out to convert people to
Jesus Christ.

No one really knew how this son of a factory worker's family of Valais, near Geneva, had ended up in that Indian slum. As an adolescent he had wanted to be a missionary, but the White Fathers in Freiburg had discouraged him because of his precarious health. He had thus gone to work in the coal mines of northern France with the Algerian, Turkish and Yugoslav immigrants, and subsequently in a steelworks in the Paris area. A discovery he made then enabled him to channel his will to devote his life to the poor.

Founded at the end of the last century by a priest from Lyon named Antoine Chevrier, the Prado Fraternity brings together religious and consecrated laypeople who have taken a vow to "join the poorest of the poor and the most disinherited where they are, live the same life as they do and die with them." Fired by this ideal, the young Swiss joined the ranks of the Prado. He studied Spanish and Portuguese in the hope of being sent out to the slums or the *favelas* of South America. But it was to India that he was asked to go after he had completed his medical training.

With a haversack containing only a copy of the Scriptures, a razor and a toothbrush, he landed in India in the winter of 1972. Several days later he settled in a hovel in this slum of Calcutta. The successful treatment he gave to the almost blind girl next door, his indefatigable generosity without proselytizing in any way, gradually overcame the slum dwellers' distrust. Gaston's reserve toward us promised to be more difficult to overcome. Fortunately an incident came to our aid. The Swiss had just started his daily clinic at his makeshift dispensary when a little girl came running in.

"*Dadah*, come at once!" she cried, out of breath. "Sunil's dying."

The nurse handed the baby he had been examining back to his mother, grabbed his first-aid kit, sprang out into the alleyway and, seeing us, asked: "Have you got a car?"

It took us over an hour to get to the slum where the dying youth lived. A robust young man of twenty, used to pulling heavy loads on his cycle rickshaw, he was now no more than a fleshless specter. His eyes had rolled back and were showing only the whites. His dignified mother was crying quietly as she

mopped his forehead and cheeks. The poor boy had sep-
ticemia, blood poisoning. He was breathing erratically. A trickle
of saliva came from his mouth. He seemed very near the end.
His family was grief-stricken. Gaston filled a syringe with
Coramine to stimulate his heart, but he had difficulty administering the injection because there was nothing but skin and
bone left on his body.

"We know a clinic where a German doctor has just arrived,"
I said. "Perhaps he—" The Swiss interrupted me: "Take him!
Who knows! I'll take care of his parents."

Dominique sat in the backseat and I placed the dying young
man in her arms. For miles traffic jams in a city in a permanent
state of congestion reduced us to a walking pace just when
every minute, every second, counted. Sunil's breathing became
more and more irregular. Dominique stroked his motionless
face as if to inject some of her own life into him. "Hang on,
hang on, little brother," she murmured.

Our driver attempted acrobatic maneuvers to make up a few
dozen yards. The small temple that was our landmark appeared
at last and, immediately afterward, the passageway leading to
the clinic. I leapt out of the car and went through the assembly
of lame and sick besieging the consultation room. A young fair-
haired European was in the process of examining a child with
a swollen stomach.

"Doctor, there's a dying man in our car. I beg you, come
quickly!"

The German doctor stood up without asking any questions.
He took Sunil from my wife's arms, then said calmly: "Thank
you, I'll see to him."[2]

---

2. It was only several months later, on the occasion of another visit to Bengal, that
we learned the epilogue to our rescue attempt. Suddenly, on a small dike running
between two rice fields, we saw a cycle-rickshaw pedaled by a big athletic-looking
fellow. Someone said to us: "That's Sunil!" The boy jumped off his machine and
rushed over to us. His father and mother came running shortly afterward. We were
overwhelmed. For the first time in my life, I had the strange feeling I had contributed directly to saving a human life.

THAT SIMPLE ACT OF SOLIDARITY earned us some consideration on the part of the Swiss nurse. In his eyes we were no longer tourists who had come to dip our toes into exotic poverty before returning to our comfortable security. He welcomed us with a friendly smile when we went back to see him. That day, an emaciated Indian, swathed in a blue-checked dhoti with a cotton shawl around his neck, was sitting cross-legged in his room, praying in front of a picture of the Holy Shroud of Turin hanging on one of the walls. Krishna was Gaston's closest neighbor, a former sailor from the south. One shore leave he had found himself washed up in this slum. Although a Hindu, he came regularly to gather his thoughts in front of this picture of the scourged Christ that reflected so well the suffering of the occupants of the neighborhood. *"Ram . . . Ram . . . Ram . . ."* (God, God, God), he repeated unflaggingly in between the fits of cavernous coughing that racked his frail frame. He lived in the room next door with his wife and their five children. He was in the final stages of tuberculosis. Three times Gaston had taken him to Mother Teresa's home for the dying. Three times he had reemerged with enough strength to walk home.

Convinced of the sincerity of our feelings for India and our genuine desire to show her our gratitude by helping the most destitute, Gaston agreed to introduce us to his kingdom of the poor. Was that kingdom just a dung heap? It was more like a frenetic ants' nest. Everywhere you went, outside every hovel, at every street stall, in a succession of small workshops, people were busy selling, haggling, manufacturing, improvising, repairing, sorting, nailing, gluing, piercing, carrying, pulling or pushing. Here children were engaged in cutting up brass sheets to make cooking utensils; there teenagers were making firecrackers, slowly poisoning themselves by handling toxic substances. Near Gaston's home, tucked away in premises with no lights, men, shiny with sweat, laminated, welded and adjusted pieces of ironwork amid a smell of burning oil and white-hot metal.

Next door in a lean-to with no ventilation, a dozen old men sat cross-legged and rolled *bidis*, the tiny Indian cigarettes.

"They nearly all have tuberculosis!" Gaston pointed out. "They don't have the strength to work a press or pull a rickshaw anymore, so they roll cigarettes. Provided they don't stop at all, they can produce up to thirteen hundred a day. For a thousand *bidis* they get less than fifty rupees [$1.70]."

A little farther on, five workmen were using pickaxes to enlarge the access to a workshop in which they had forged a ship's propeller at least six feet in breadth. They shifted the monster and levered it onto a cart. Three coolies then braced themselves in a desperate attempt to get the cart moving. In the end the wheels turned. The workshop boss seemed relieved that he would not have to engage a fourth coolie to deliver the merchandise, but I shuddered to think what might happen to those three wretches when they reached the bottom of the ramp leading up to Howrah Bridge.

How long would it take me to discover all the places where slaves of all ages spent their lives making springs, truck parts, bolts, airplane fuel tanks and even turbine gears to a tenth of a micromillimeter? My head reeled: a whole workforce with unimaginable skill, ingenuity and resourcefulness was assembling, reproducing and repairing every possible part, every possible type of machine.

"Nothing is ever thrown away here," commented Gaston. "Everything is always reborn as if by some miracle."

After two hours of exploring, we felt quite dizzy. That slum was a laboratory of survival. We went back next day and on the following days to make new discoveries and meet more of the people of light who lived there. People like Bandona, the radiant twenty-two-year-old Assamese nurse with her slit eyes who had come from the high Himalayan plateaus to relieve suffering and whom the inhabitants of the slum had nicknamed Angel of Mercy. Or the simple soul who walked about naked, bestowing his blessing on passersby. Or Margareta, in her white sari of widowhood, who took into her hovel the orphaned children of neighbors who had died of disease. Or Ashish and Shanta Gosh, a young couple who spent their free time dressing the wounds of lepers; or the adorable little Padmini, who, although barely eight years old, got up at dawn every day to do her part to ensure her family's survival.

One morning, wanting to know where Padmini went so early, we followed her. She climbed the nearby railway embankment to gather from between the tracks the bits of coal that had fallen from the locomotives during the night. Her mother would then sell this miserable bounty and buy a little rice to prevent her children from dying of hunger. Like all Indian girls of her age, Padmini would then see to the domestic chores. She fetched water from the fountain, scoured the cooking utensils, cleaned the family's only room, washed her younger brothers' and sisters' faces, deloused them and mended their ragged clothes. Of all those tasks the most moving was the daily massage she gave the family's last-born, little Santosh. Padmini would sit down on the edge of the alleyway and lay the child out in her lap. She would moisten her palms with a few drops of mustard oil and begin to massage. Skillful, supple, attentive, her hands would move up and down the length of the skinny body. Working turn and turnabout in waves, she would set off from the baby's flanks, move across his chest and come back up to the opposite shoulder. A flame burned in the look that passed between the little girl and the baby; it was if they were talking to each other with their eyes. Padmini would next turn her little brother onto his side, extend his arms and massage them gently. Then she would take hold of his hands, kneading them with her thumbs. His stomach, legs, heels, the soles of his feet, his head, the nape of his neck, his face, nostrils, back and buttocks were all successively stroked, vitalized by the supple, dancing fingers. It was a hymn to life, a vision of tenderness and love, the apotheosis of which was the beautiful smile of that child who knew how to mother long before she could be one.

Another of Gaston's young protégés took us to the scene of his daily exploits: Calcutta's municipal garbage dump. Nissar was nine years old and had never been able to go to school. He earned his living by ragpicking. Along with dozens of other boys and girls, in the blazing sun and unbearable stench, they foraged with bare hands through the piles of rubbish brought by the yellow municipal trucks, in the hope of finding debris they could sell. Nissar and his friends had no reservations about crawling over the refuse to slip in behind the bulldozer scoop in order to be the first to explore the various forms of manna. Each had his or her specialty. Nissar used to pick up the bits of plastic, others dealt with the glass, wood, paper, metal, rags, old toothpaste tubes, used batteries or rubber. At the end of the day, they took their baskets to the secondhand dealers who came to the spot to buy their pitiful harvest for a few rupees.

Among the many who welcomed Gaston to the hazards of the alleyways, the most enthusiastic was a gnome with a short beard. Nicknamed Gunga (the Mute), he was bursting with life and joie de vivre. He had arrived in the slum after a terrible flood in which he nearly drowned. Every evening a family gave him a plate of rice and a corner of roof beneath which he could sleep. Gunga became our friend too. The way he shrieked for joy whenever he saw us made us daily more attached to the poignant humanity of the neighborhood.

In the midst of all that seeming squalor, I was to find more courage, more generosity, more smiles and ultimately perhaps more happiness than in our affluent West. Gaston told us that a while after his arrival, some of the neighbors had come to see him in his room.

"Big brother," one of them had said, "we would like to think with you about doing something useful for the people who live in our slum."

Something useful? In a place where tuberculosis, leprosy and dysentery were rife, where all the diseases of malnutrition reduced life expectancy to one of the world's lowest levels, there was everything to be done. They needed a dispensary and a leper clinic. They needed to distribute milk to children with rickets, install wells with drinkable water, increase the number of latrines, evict the cows and buffalo that spread tuberculosis.

"I suggest you sound out the people around you to find out what they want most," Gaston replied.

The result was made known three days later. What the men and women of the slum wanted first was not to fill their bellies. The food they hungered for was primarily intellectual. Above all else they wanted a night school, so that their children who worked in the workshops and tea stalls during the day could learn to read and write.

Gaston invited the families to find a venue that could be used as a classroom and suggested putting the money some passing friends had left him toward wages for two teachers. It was probably the only school of its kind in the world. Too small to take more than about twenty children at a time, it remained open from early evening until dawn.

AFTER *Is Paris Burning?*, ... *Or I'll Dress You in Mourning, O Jerusalem* and *Freedeom at Midnight,* historical accounts that had recorded the struggle of millions of people for liberty, I felt it was time for me to tell the story of the daily struggle of seventy thousand unknown people in a slum of Calcutta: the saga of the voiceless ones unlucky enough to be born into that unfortunate part of the world, but whose courage, love, faith and dignity were examples to all people of our times; especially to those of us who are well off, but who can no longer see the value of things—those of us who forget all too often to appreciate how fortunate we are.

I knew that with *The Fifth Horseman*, our last literary venture together, Collins had developed a taste for writing fiction and that he had in mind an idea for a novel about an episode in World War II.[3] We could always get together later to retrace other great historical events. My wife, Dominique, enthusiastically supported my idea, all the more so because I had decided to give half of my prospective royalties to James Stevens's Resurrection Home and other humanitarian undertakings designed to improve the living conditions of the slums.

On my return to Paris, I contacted the various French and foreign publishers of the successful books I had written with

---

3. His book was to be called *Fall from Grace*. It was a great success and was adapted for television.

Larry. All would have preferred to see me embarking on another great historical research venture with my American partner. All except my French publisher Robert Laffont, an ally whose support was as faithful as it was unconditional, and my American literary agent, Morton Janklow, who, on reading the synopsis, assured me that this project could well be "one of the greatest book successes of the end of our century." The hyperbole made me smile.

It did, however, encourage Dominique and me to pack our bags again and return to Calcutta.

Three Michelin Stars

To plunge straight into the reality of the world I was going to explore, I decided to spend my very first night investigating with Gaston, right in the very heart of his slum. He arranged to meet me outside the movie theater on the Great Trunk Road. The building was being besieged by a noisy crowd. For half a rupee, about one and a half U.S. cents, people came here to forget the hunger gnawing at their stomachs.

"The Michelin Guide inspectors haven't yet honored us with a visit and it's very wrong of them," Gaston said to me mischievously, determined to show his slum in the best possible light. He burst out laughing. "This evening we're going to dine at the local Maxim's."

"For a holy man who's become an apostle of the poor, you seem very much in touch," I marveled. "You even know about Maxim's!"

The setting made our exchange seem totally surreal. We were seated on opposite sides of a table under a lightbulb black with fly specks, in a smoke-hung room furnished with a dozen tables, all occupied by workmen and coolies. An exhausted fan stirred the torrid air, heavy with the smells of frying. Enthroned at the back of the room on a wooden stool, the owner, potbellied in his vest, stirred the contents of an enormous pan in which the dish of the day, a buffalo hide stew, was simmering.

"For one rupee (three cents), you have all the protein in the world there," commented the Swiss, burning his fingers on the food as he made as firm a small ball as he could.

It was difficult to tell exactly what it was that we were eating, but Gaston went on extolling the virtues of the spiced gelatin that set my palate on fire. I had often wondered what induced Indians to abuse condiments to such a degree. One evening in an eating place in Madras I found the answer. The smell coming from the kitchen left me in no doubt. The meat being served was rotten. But it was spiced with so many chilies, so much pepper and curry, that no one realized it. Through the ages, spices in India had made up for the lack of refrigerators.

The walk through the slum to Gaston's room after our meal was an unforgettable experience. At every step, people greeted joyously the "big brother" who had come from the West to share their plight. Some were content to just touch his clothing with respect. Barefoot in his three-rupee sandals, his figure swathed in a cotton loincloth, he was the apostle who knew how to nurse them, calm them, relieve them, cure them.

Now and then, an open door in a mud wall would reveal in the semidarkness some thirty children crouched around a paraffin lamp, reciting the letters of the alphabet and learning to count, under the supervision of a bearded mullah or a Hindu teacher in a white cap. Ever since the Swiss had created his first school, small classrooms where children studied in two-hour turns had multiplied.

Gaston's room had a festive air about it. In honor of my coming, Nirmala, the eldest daughter of the Hindu Krishna, his neighbor with tuberculosis, had drawn a large lotus flower in chalk on the beaten earth floor and decorated the icon of Our Lady of Tenderness on the small oratory with a garland of jasmine petals. She had also lit the candle next to the open volume of the Holy Gospels. There was nothing unusual about such attentiveness. Nowhere had I seen so much respect for the manifestations of God as in that slum. Everyone there was steeped in a surprising spirituality. I had noticed that every time the muezzin called for prayer from the minaret of the local mosque, women would come out on their doorsteps and recite verses from the Koran. At all hours of the day, you could hear people in the alleys and passageways chanting the Hindu *om . . . om . . . om. . .* , the mystical invocation that brought contact with God and inner peace. Gaston himself would regularly sound off oms, from time to time adding the name of Jesus.

"For me, it's a way of joining the prayer of the poor who are permanently approaching God in this wretched slum," he explained.

Gaston slept on the bare-beaten earth. He kept his few possessions—some linen, his shaving brush and razor, his Jerusalem Bible—in a tin chest which the cockroaches had managed to penetrate. In summer the monsoon cataracts that caused the latrines and drains to overflow and transformed the slum into a pool of excrement forced him to take refuge on some wooden scaffolding erected on bricks. The absence of any window obliged him to leave the door open at all times. For nine months of the year the temperature in the room was over a hundred degrees Fahrenheit, with humidity that reached almost 100 percent.

I was lucky: it was winter, a winter that Gaston and the slum dwellers considered icy. At night the thermometer went down to fifty degrees, a polar temperature for people with bare feet and no warm clothing, who slept on the ground on mats in damp hovels. On the corners of the alleyways, the residents burned bits of refuse to try and keep warm. Worst of all was the pollution that the layer of cold air forced back onto the slum. Every evening the thick smoke released by the cow dung cakes used for cooking imprisoned the whole quarter in an acrid veil that burned eyes and throats. The sound of the coughing fits that racked people's lungs dominated all others.

Once the cow dung stoves had been extinguished, the din assumed its usual level. This was a deafening cacophony, a confusion of ever-strident women's voices, children's cries, disputes and altercations between the customers of the illicit saloon set up by the local godfather at the end of the passageway, the various public loudspeakers' attempts to outbid each other, the whistles of trains rolling past the slum, the throb of machines in the neighboring workshops, a passing band, barking dogs, the call of street vendors, men exhibiting bears or monkeys, snake charmers . . .

Gaston sat down in the lotus position, his legs folded back under his thighs, a position quite uncomfortable for Westerners who have not practiced yoga. I clicked my tape recorder on to capture the concert of noises assailing us. Gruff masculine voices were also coming from the room opposite ours. Intrigued, I decided to go and have a look. Sitting in a circle, four people dressed in brightly colored saris played cards by the light of a hurricane lamp. Their cheeks were made up with scarlet powder, and at the slightest gesture, their wrists jangled with the movement of innumerable bracelets.

"You never thought you were going to spend the night in the company of eunuchs?" Gaston inquired roguishly.

"Eunuchs here?"

"Of course! Even in your eccentric paradise of Saint-Tropez you wouldn't be so lucky!"

"Why lucky?"

"Because eunuchs play a very important role in the life of the slum. Hindus credit them with purificatory powers, among them the capacity to wipe from newborn babies the sins accumulated in their previous incarnations. Families never fail to call upon their services when there's a birth. And they charge a small fortune every time."

My presence had aroused the curiosity of these unusual neighbors. One of them got up to bring us lighted incense sticks, which he placed in front of the icon of the Virgin. A sweet, slightly sickly smell spread through the room. With this gesture the eunuchs paid homage to the holy man who lived in the compound and to his visitor.

With his head and shoulders wrapped in a maroon woolen shawl, his eyes closed and his face turned toward the image of Christ on the wall, deliberately deaf to all external noises, Gaston invited me to share in his prayer of thanksgiving "for the joy we have been granted of being together."

"Jesus, thank you for welcoming Dominique into this place where so many of your children are suffering," he began in a low voice. "Thank you for having given him the desire to bear witness to what he will see and feel among all the martyred innocents here in this slum, who daily commemorate your sacrifice on the cross." At that point in his invocation a rat with a huge tail made its appearance in the corner of the little oratory, just in front of the incense sticks the eunuch had brought. Its assertiveness amazed me. It was just as if it had come to join in our prayer. Gaston, who had not even noticed its presence, went on:

"Jesus of this slum, you, the voice of the voiceless ones, you who suffer in them, permit Dominique and me to say to you this evening, along with all those around us, that we love you." It was midnight. The discussions and disputes had gone quiet, as had most of the children's crying, the coughing fits, the dogs' barking and the whistle of locomotives. A fragile silence enveloped the dormant slum. I folded up my shirt and jeans to form a pillow and stretched out on the mat that my host had borrowed to protect me from the damp ground. His room was scarcely longer than me. After a last look at the picture of the Holy Shroud, Gaston blew out the candle and bid me a "Good night, brother!" in the tones of an old soldier addressing a young recruit about to spend his first night in a frontline trench.

The term "brother" touched me on two counts. First because it came from someone who had made fraternity his life's ideal. Second because of the solidarity it expressed for the forthcoming night's adventure. It was indeed to be an adventure for me. I had had occasion to sleep in some unusual, even dangerous places—beneath the stars in an African jungle full of lions and elephants, in a Korean paddy field faced with Chinese machine guns, on rough oceans—but never in the gulag of suffering of a Third World slum. Did I have the right to share the slumbers of those immured people, condemned to live here until their dying day, when I would be spending the following night in a comfortable room in a residential area? Suddenly my overnight stay assumed an almost improper light.

An incident put an end to my inner debate. My companion was already asleep when a frenzied saraband broke out above our heads. I struck a match and discovered a troop of rats chasing each other over the bamboo framework of the roof, emitting piercing cries as they rushed down the walls. I leapt to my feet and, despite my desire not to disturb Gaston's sleep, set about chasing away the intruders with blows from my shoes. But as soon as I had chased some away, others appeared through the holes in the roof. What could I do with such an invasion? Finally I gave up. Repugnant as it was, this cohabitation was part of the general order of things. I was just a visitor; I had no right to change it. I lay down again. Gaston was still sleeping the sleep of the innocent.

Almost immediately thereafter, I felt something moving in my hair. I struck another match, shook my head, and an enormous, hairy millipede fell out of it. Fervent admirer of Mahatma Gandhi's nonviolence that I was, I crushed it pitilessly. Only next day would I learn the nature of the beast: a scolopendra, a creature with twenty-one pairs of legs whose sting could be as venomous as a scorpion's. I lay down for a third time. In the hope of achieving a little serenity, I reeled off a rosary of oms, but I could feel a curious coming and going on my legs. A third match to light the candle and this time I saw cockroaches. They were everywhere, on the walls, on the joists, around the icon of the Virgin, on the pages of the Gospel, on the bundle of clothes I was using as a pillow. What could I do? I was prepared to have another go at them with the soles of my shoes. But what would be the point? There would always be more. I lay down again. By the flickering, almost ghostly light of the flame, I saw then on a bamboo joist in the roof a spectacle worthy of New York's Belmont racetrack. A lizard was pursuing an enormous cockroach that was making off as fast as it could. I urged the lizard on like the most enthusiastic of race-goers. On the point of being caught, the insect made a fatal mistake. It took refuge under the belly of a fat tarantula whose hairy body made a superb shield. Overjoyed at the prospect of this unexpected prey, the spider seized the intruder between the roach's legs and plunged the two claws with which its abdomen was armed into its body. Then it sucked it down like an egg. A few minutes later the cockroach's carapace dropped onto me. When I woke up I found several cockroaches similarly emptied of their substance.

The Martyrdom of the Innocents

After those various interludes, I finally fell asleep. But it was to be only a brief respite. Around one o'clock in the morning, I was awakened by groans coming from one of the hovels in the compound. Soon their rhythm was stepped up and I heard rattles. Gaston had woken too.

"It's Sabia," he sighed, "the son of the Muslim woman across the courtyard. The poor kid is dying of bone tuberculosis in dreadful pain. I've done everything I can to try and save him . . . everything."

His explanation distressed me greatly. I had allowed myself to be taken in by those deceptive smiles and convinced myself that these people could joyfully rise above their misfortune. Sabia's rattles opened my eyes; the slum was a place of the damned. How could Gaston's apparent resignation be right? I questioned him fiercely.

"How can you, you who believe in God, accept that He would permit that innocent child's agony in a place already overrun with suffering?"

For a long while Gaston listened to the moaning.

"Unfortunately I don't have any adequate answer to give you," he said finally. "I've been at a loss myself, faced with the pain of that child. In the beginning I used to plug my ears so I wouldn't hear his rattles. Like Job, I was on the verge of anger. Even in the Scriptures I found no explanation for the fact that God could allow it to happen. How can you tell a child writhing in pain: 'Blessed are you, the poor, because yours is the kingdom of heaven. Blessed are those who weep today, for tomorrow you will laugh. Blessed are the hungry, for you shall be fed.' You can't."

"Is that all Jesus has said to the suffering?" I asked.

"Jesus showed his compassion to the suffering. He suffered

with them. But it's true, he didn't say very much to them," acknowledged Gaston.

He also admitted that it had taken him several nights before he could listen to Sabia's cries. And several more to hear them not just with his ears but with his heart. He had felt himself torn between his faith as a committed Christian and his revolt as a man. "Do I have the right to be happy, to sing praises to God, while that intolerable ordeal is going on next to me?" he had asked himself. Unable to share his dilemma with anyone, he had resorted to prayer. Every night when his neighbor's child started to groan, he had begun to pray. One morning, when he could take no more, he had gone to the hospital in Howrah and bought a dose of morphine.

"His disease might be incurable, and my prayer might have failed, but at least Sabia should be able to end his life without suffering," he said.

His little neighbor's illness went through several weeks of remission. His mother, who earned a few rupees by making paper bags out of old newspapers, kept saying that God had saved her son.

"For my part, I didn't dare believe in a miracle," Gaston admitted. "Sadly I was right. Three nights ago his agony began again."

The groaning had stopped: Sabia must have fallen asleep. The precarious silence of the compound lasted only a few moments. All of a sudden music blared out from a transistor in a nearby room. I looked at my watch: it was four in the morning. The noise drowned out the coughing fits that started up again. At the other end of the compound, a cock began to crow, then there was the noise of buckets and children's squeals. The compound was awakening. Its residents were already going off to attend to "the call of nature." The nearest toilet had been overflowing. Since yesterday, people were wading through excrement. The municipal cesspool cleaners were on strike. Those who did not want to go too far from here had to relieve themselves in the open drain that ran alongside the housing.

Gaston used to go to the latrines that had recently been installed three alleyways away from the compound. For relative privacy the public convenience was sheltered by a cabin. At half past four in the morning, several dozen people were already lined up. Everyone greeted the big brother with his small crucifix hanging from his neck, but the arrival of another sahib in jeans and sneakers provoked lively curiosity, all the more so because in my ignorance of the country's customs, I had committed a blunder: I had brought with me a few sheets of toilet paper.

"To these Indians, you're a barbarian," Gaston explained, delighted to enlighten me. "How can they fail to be surprised that you want to collect up a defilement expelled by your body and then leave it for others?"

Showing me the tin of water he had in his hand, a young boy gave me to understand that I should give myself an intimate wash before cleaning the toilet. I realized that, sure enough, everyone had brought small cans full of water with them. Some even had several that they were pushing forward with their feet as the line progressed.

"They're queuing for other people," Gaston told me. "It's one of the thousands of little jobs in the slum."

A man with his head muffled in a shawl darted to the front of the line, tin in hand. He looked in considerable discomfort. Everyone stepped aside to let him pass. Dysentery attacks and their urgent and merciless manifestations were common. I myself was to benefit from an unexpected free passage when a young boy planted himself in front of me and signaled to me to go directly to the cabin without waiting for my turn. I was surprised at this favor. Gaston questioned the youngster, who promptly pointed at my wrist. "*Dadah,*" he responded, "you have a watch, so you must be in a hurry."

I had to step over a pool of excrement to get to the public convenience. The stench caught me by the throat. That people could remain good-humored amid so much abjection seemed quite extraordinary to me. They laughed and joked, especially the children, who brought the freshness and gaiety of their games to the cesspool. After the trials of the night, that escapade nearly finished me off.

That first experience of sharing the life of the slum was not yet over, however. When I got back, the compound was already in full swing. Mothers were shouting reprimands at their children. Little girls came back from the fountain, carrying buckets so heavy their spines were twisted. Others were using ash to clean utensils from the previous night's meal, or lighting braziers so that wreaths of smoke soon imprisoned the compound in an asphyxiating cloud.

Outside Sabia's room, two boys were clearing a blocked drainpipe with a piece of bamboo, scraping the gutters and pushing the excrement away to the outside drain. A tiny tousled little girl ran barefoot among the piles of rubbish, at which a pack of mangy dogs was scratching furiously. Wherever I looked, life burst forth. It was washing time. People who had spent the night ten or twelve to a vermin-infested hovel were reborn to light as if it were the world's first morning.

Women managed to wash themselves all over without revealing a single patch of nudity. From their long hair to the soles of their feet nothing was missed, not even their saris. They took the greatest care oiling, combing and plaiting their hair, before adorning it with a fresh flower, picked God knows where. Children cleaned their teeth with twigs dipped in ashes, old men polished their tongues with strands of jute, mothers deloused their children before soaping their little naked bodies even in the bitter cold of that winter's morning.

Deciding to let me discover the subtleties of local custom for myself, Gaston had told me nothing about the Indian bathing rituals. I undressed, as I had seen the men do, down to my underpants. I took my tin full of water and a bit of the locally made soap Gaston had loaned me—a small ball of a mixture of clay and ash—and I went out into the alleyway to squat on my heels in the typically Indian position that was so difficult for me to maintain. I had taken off my shoes, soiled with excrement, poured a little water over my feet and began to scrub my toes vigorously when the elderly Hindu who kept the tea shop just opposite called out to me in horror.

"Brother, that's not how you should wash yourself! You should start with your head. The feet come last when you've cleaned all the rest."

I was about to stammer some excuse when a little girl appeared. I recognized my friend the exquisite Padmini, the one who got up at four in the morning to go and pick up bits of coal from along the railroad tracks. The sight of this half-naked sahib sprinkling himself with water amused her so much that she burst out laughing.

"Why are you scrubbing yourself so hard, *dadah*?" she asked. "You're already so white!"

A Cathedral of Heroes

Gaston agreed to take me on his morning round. First he was going to see young Sabia, whose groaning had haunted me during the night. His mother welcomed us with a radiant smile. She sent her eldest daughter to fetch two small cups of tea from the elderly Hindu in the alleyway and invited us into her home. I hesitated for a few seconds on the threshold before plunging into the half-darkness.

The little Muslim boy lay helpless on a mattress made of rags, his arms folded, his skin pitted with ulcers crawling with flies and his legs half bent back over his fleshless torso. Gaston approached him with a syringe of morphine in his hand. The child opened his eyes. A spark of joy lit up his gaze. I was completely taken aback. How could a smile like that spring from that martyred being?

"*Salam*, Sabia," said Gaston.

"*Alaikoum salaam, dadah!*" responded the child in a feeble voice. "What have you got in your hand, a lollipop?"[4]

We entered another compound. A mother presented the big brother her child, with rickets and an inflated stomach. Aged about two but looking no more than six months, it was a pathetic little emaciated thing. "Fourth-degree malnutrition," Gaston mumbled. "He has suffered from such deficiency since

4. Sabia died a few days after that visit. His body was carried to the Muslim cemetery, draped in a velvet shroud and followed by all the occupants of the compound, Hindus included.

birth that his fontanels haven't closed. His skull has been deformed by lack of calcium. His dolichocephalic features are obvious. With this degree of malnutrition, a large proportion of his gray cells have probably been destroyed.

"Even if we manage to save him," the Swiss added, pulling a small bag of vitamin-enriched flour out of his haversack, "he'll always be mentally retarded."

Hearing that the big brother was there, a little girl came running, carrying her younger sister astride her hip. The infant had been a victim of meningitis. Gaston had managed to save her but she was still mentally deficient. The father, who was a coolie in the big Burra Bazaar market, the mother and all the brothers and sisters surrounded the handicapped youngster with so much love that Gaston had never been able to commit her to a home for retarded children. She was wonderful. She gesticulated, smiled and prattled away. She, too, was life with a capital *L*.

Next stop was an obscure passageway between two hovels, near the mosque. Stretched out on a charpoy, a very young woman spat into a pitcher with dark red stains on it. Fever burned in her eyes. She could hardly breathe. She had terminal tuberculosis. Every morning, Gaston came and gave her an injection. He spoke to her. The sick woman answered, but a cavernous cough interrupted their dialogue. Two half-naked children were playing marbles at the foot of her rope bed.

Two alleyways farther on, Ashu, a boy of eleven curled up on a jute sack, was waiting for his big brother to call. His family was too poor to pay for any kind of shelter, so they squatted on a veranda with a crumbling roof. Gaston had saved Ashu from tubercular meningitis. At first he was completely paralyzed. In three years of treatment and rehabilitation his big brother had taught him how to move his arms again. Every week, he paid for his transportation in a rickshaw to a specialist center. Gaston dreamed that the boy might have a hip replacement.

That morning, as every morning, the Swiss apostle's pilgrimage ended in a hovel near the railway line with a Christian leper woman who was blind. The poor woman was so emaciated that I could see her skeleton through her shriveled skin. Behind her, from a nail in the mud wall, hung a crucifix; over the door, a niche contained a small statue of the Virgin Mary, blackened with smoke. She was forty years old at the most. Some sixth sense alerted her to Gaston's arrival. As soon as she sensed his approach, she tried to sit up. With what was left of her hands, she smoothed her hair in a moving gesture of coquetry. Then she arranged a place beside her, patting a cushion made out of rags in readiness for her big brother. The widow of an employee of the Calcutta municipal council, she spoke a little English. Her four grandchildren were asleep on a threadbare mat at the foot of her charpoy.

"Good morning, brother!" she called out, beaming.

"Good morning, Grandma!" replied Gaston, removing his shoes. "I've brought my friend Dominique, a French writer, with me to see you today."

"Good morning, brother Dominique!" the blind woman exclaimed.

I greeted her in my turn. She held out her emaciated arms to Gaston, brought her stumps to his face and allowed them to wander over his neck, cheeks and forehead. There was more love in the gentle touch of that ravaged flesh than in all the embraces of the world.

"Brother, I wish so much the good Lord would come and take me," she declared then. "Why can't you ask him to?"

"If the good Lord keeps you with us, Grandma, it's because he still needs you here."

The leper woman joined her stumps in an attitude of prayer that had nothing suppliant about it. Gaston told her about our visit to young Sabia.

"Tell him I'll pray for him."

"I've brought you the body of Christ," the Swiss then announced, taking out of his pocket a consecrated Host.

She opened her lips slightly and Gaston placed the Host on the tip of her tongue after pronouncing the words of the Eucharist.

"Amen!" she murmured.

I saw tears flowing from her blank eyes. Her face had lit up with intense joy.

"Thank you, *dadah*. Thank you, *dadah*," she repeated.

The four little sleeping forms had not stirred. When Gaston got up to go, the leper woman raised her rosary to him in a gesture of salutation and offering.

"Be sure and tell all those who are suffering that I'm praying for them."

That evening, Gaston Grandjean would jot down in his notebook:

"That woman knows her suffering is not useless. I affirm that God wants to use her suffering to help others to bear theirs." A few lines later he would conclude: "That is why my prayer for that poor woman can no longer be sorrowful. Her suffering is like that of Christ on the cross; it is positive, redemptive. It is hope. Every time I come out of my sister the blind leper woman's hovel, I do so revitalized. This slum should be called the City of Joy."

THE CITY OF JOY! Before I so much as wrote the first word of my book, I knew what the title would be. Despite the curse that seemed to weigh upon it, the slum was indeed a cathedral of joy, vitality and hope. If I needed convincing, Gaston's compound was an ideal observatory. It was, above all, the kingdom of children. Their carefree spirit, their zest for life, their magical smiles and dark faces with mischievous expressions, colored their drab surroundings with beauty. Gaston never stopped reminding me that if the adults there managed to keep their hopes up, it was because of the children. "Without them the slum would be nothing but a slough of despond," he said. Day by day, I discovered the extent to which those children contributed to everyone's survival. In vain, Article 24 of the Indian Constitution had stipulated that "no child may be put to work in a factory or mine, nor employed in any dangerous positions." The youngsters of the City of Joy slogged away like their elders, at the most arduous tasks, in a multitude of factories and workshops. Their docility, the dexterity of their small hands and the meager salaries they were paid often made them preferable to adults. The few rupees they brought home to their parents meant the difference between total starvation and their family's precarious survival.

What activity, what to-ing and fro-ing, went on from dawn till dusk! At every moment some bell, gong, whistle or voice would announce the arrival of a street salesman or juggler. In the space of a few seconds the miserable courtyard and its surrounding hovels would be turned into a theater and fairground. I had difficulty keeping track of all the participants in this incredible metamorphosis. The list was endless. Exhibitors of bears; monkey, goat, mongoose, rat, parrot and scorpion trainers; cobra and viper charmers; verse chroniclers, puppeteers, bards, storytellers, fakirs, mimers, conjurers, acrobats . . . all brought enchantment to adults and youngsters alike with their performances.

The festivals that could disrupt the slum at any time were even more amazing. I had the opportunity to take part in the ceremony of shaving a newborn baby's head, that of a father giving his baby its first solid food when it was six months old, and a celebration for a young girl's first period. For all their poverty the castaways of the slum knew how to preserve their culture, traditions and taste for festivities: festivities that wrested them from reality for a day or a week; festivities for which they fell into debt or went without food; festivities that were a better vehicle for religion than any catechism, and that set hearts and senses aglow with the magic of song and ceremony. I eventually got lost in this perpetual display of celebrations.

One morning I found the neighborhood workshops suddenly transformed with altars brimming over with flowers. That day the workers of the City of Joy were celebrating the festival of Vishvakarman, the god of artisans. The slaves of the previous day now sported gleaming shirts and brand-new *longhis;* their wives had got out their ceremonial saris, preserved with such difficulty against the voraciousness of the cockroaches in the family coffers. The children were resplendent, dressed up like little princes and princesses. From street to street the joyful saraband of wind instruments and drums took over from the din of machinery over which a Brahmin priest officiated, ringing a bell with one hand and carrying a purificatory flame in the other to bless all the tools of trade. Every workshop had a sumptuously decorated statue of the god on display. People who had nothing gave themselves up to the magic of their culture. The workers and their families went from place to place, marveling at the statues. Everywhere loudspeakers spilled out popular tunes, and fireworks punctuated the libations.

Of all the festivals that transfigured the slum, none seemed to me more in communion with its poverty than the celebration of the birth of Jesus. If ever the message "God made man to save humanity" reverberated somewhere on this earth, it was in that slum. Bethlehem and the City of Joy were one and the same. Christians were few in number, but garlands of fairy lights and streamers decorated their newly whitewashed homes. Loudspeakers relayed carols. For everyone the most beautiful symbol of that magical night was the giant luminous star dangling on the end of a bamboo cane over Gaston's hovel. His Hindu and Muslim neighbors had had the idea of hoisting this symbol into the sky, as if to say to all the occupants of the slum: "Don't be afraid. You're not alone. This night when the Christian God was born, a savior is among us."

The "savior" in question invited Dominique and me to spend the evening with him among his destitute brothers. With his head and shoulders wrapped in a shawl against the bitter cold, he led a prayer vigil for some fifty of the faithful, gathered in a compound where several Christian families lived. He spoke in Bengali. My little tape recorder captured his words.

"It is because the poor are the only ones to know the riches of poverty that they can rise up against destitution, against injustice and against suffering," he said. "Brothers, if Christ chose to be born among the poor, it is because he wanted the poor to teach the world the good news of his love for humanity."

I watched the faces turned toward this big brother who had come from the other side of the world. They listened to him as the crowds that gathered around Jesus must have done, or those who thronged around the preachers of the Middle Ages.

"Brothers and sisters," Gaston continued, "you are the ones who bear the torch of hope today. I, your brother, promise you that the day will come when the tiger will sit down with the little child, when the cobra will lie down with the dove, when all people of all countries will feel they are brothers and sisters."[5]

IT WAS QUITE CLEAR: not only were those poor people managing to remain human, but also they were becoming what Gaston called "models of humanity." They gave me a good illustration of this on the eve of my return to France after two years of research. I was with Gaston in his room, sitting cross-legged in front of the Holy Shroud for a farewell prayer, when a brass band going past in the alleyway made us jump. Behind the musicians marched a procession of men, women and children dressed in festive attire. Gaston did not know what divinity or event was being honored that day. He asked his neighbor Krishna. The tuberculosis patient seemed very surprised at our ignorance.

"What, big brother, you don't know? Today we're celebrating the birth of spring."

The birth of spring! In this slum where I had not seen one single tree, one single plant, one single flower, one single bird, one single butterfly . . .

5. Gaston would tell us that as he spoke these words he was thinking of a photograph of the American pastor Martin Luther King, Jr., meditating in front of a Christmas manger. In the caption to the picture published in a magazine, Dr. King explained that, while standing before the manger, he had had "a dream that one day in the red hills of Georgia, the sons of former slaves and the sons of former slave owners will be able to sit down together at the table of brotherhood." That Christmas Eve, Gaston had felt himself caught up in the same dream. One day, he was sure, rich and poor, slaves and masters, executioners and their victims, would all sit down at the same table.

Before we tore ourselves away from Calcutta, Dominique and I witnessed an event that showed us that the exodus of millions of poor peasants to this mirage city was not necessarily inexorable. That one day the exodus might stop. That its course might even be reversed.

Two young occupants of the slum, Ashish and Shanta Ghosh, came to tell Gaston that they had decided to return to their village. Ashish and Shanta were Hindus. Good-looking, healthy, bright, they spent their spare time dressing lepers' wounds. Under her red cotton veil with its decorative floral patterns, the young woman looked like a Mogul princess. She was the eldest daughter of a landless peasant from an isolated village in the Ganges Delta. To provide for his family, her father used to collect wild honey from the forest in the Sundarbans. One day he did not come back. He had been carried off by one of the man-eating tigers in the jungle that ate over three hundred "honey pickers" a year. It was at the little local primary school that Shanta had met the curly-haired youngster who was to become her husband. Twenty-six-year-old Ashish (Hope) was the son of an agricultural day laborer.

The couple's story was almost unique: they had married for love. Their challenge to all the dictates of tradition had caused such a scandal that they had been obliged to flee their village and take refuge in Calcutta. After starving for a year, Ashish had found a job as a monitor in a center for handicapped children. Shanta had become a teacher at a school in the suburbs.

On the birth of their first child, they had chanced upon their El Dorado: a room in a Hindu compound in the slum. Two regular salaries of two hundred rupees (each about seven dollars) might not seem very much, but in the City of Joy it was a fortune.

For three years the young couple saved up, rupee by rupee, to buy two acres of land near their village. They had a pond dug to breed fish and set up a rudimentary irrigation system to provide a second crop in the dry season. Above all, however, they wanted their return to their village to bring some benefit to the other residents. Ashish planned to create a peasant cooperative. "With water, the Bengal earth can yield at least three crops," he told me one day. As for Shanta, she wanted to open up a primary school and a craft workshop for the women.

The announcement of their departure gave rise to feverish excitement in the compounds. After several years, to most of the slum dwellers, the dream of returning to their villages seemed an unrealizable utopia. That a young couple might voluntarily give up the unheard-of luxury of two regular incomes to go and plant rice surpassed all expectations. Strangely enough, it was back home in their village that the reaction to the Ghoshes' plans was most hostile. "When the goddess Lakshmi puts oil in your lamp, it's a crime to put out the flame to go somewhere else," the boy's parents decreed furiously. They even threatened to use force to prevent him and his family from returning to the village.

One morning at dawn the Ghoshes and their children piled their things into a rickshaw and left. Gaston and I accompanied them as far as the bus station. As Ashish was climbing into the coach with his wife and children, he turned to the man who had shared his family's suffering in the slum.

"Big brother," he said in a voice choked with emotion, "you know we're Hindus, but it would really mean a lot to us if you would give us the blessing of your Jesus."

Suppressing his tears with difficulty, Gaston raised his hand and said: "May the Lord Jesus Christ bless you and give you his peace, for you are the light of the world."

THAT LONG, DIFFICULT and sometimes painful period of research will remain one of the most powerful experiences of my life. It made me adapt to situations I had never previously encountered. It made me realize that people could rise to inhuman living conditions with a smile; that they could work like beasts of burden with only a few balls of rice in their bellies; stay clean with less than a pint of water a day; light a fire in the monsoon downpours with just one match; and fan their faces while they slept in the blazing heat of summer. Before being adopted by the downtrodden people of that slum, I had to familiarize myself with their customs, understand their fears and their difficulties, know their struggles and their hopes and gradually initiate myself into the riches of their culture. Along the way I discovered the true meaning of the words courage, love, dignity, compassion, faith and hope. I learned to thank God for his every benefit, to listen to others, not to be afraid of death and never to despair. It was undoubtedly one of the most enriching experiences a man could have.

It changed my life, my vision of the world and my sense of values. I now try not to give so much importance to petty, everyday problems, like finding a parking space. The fact that for months I lived alongside people who survived on only a few cents a day made me discover the value of the least little thing. I no longer leave a hotel room without turning out the light, I use a bar of soap to its very end, I avoid throwing away anything that might be used or recycled.

That unique experience also taught me the beauty of sharing. In two years I never came across a beggar in the alleyways of the City of Joy. Of all the people I met, not one held out his or her hand or asked for any kind of help. Quite the opposite, people only gave to us. In fact, I often had to prevent men and women who had nothing from sacrificing their last resources in order to welcome us in accordance with the generous rituals of Indian hospitality. My interpreter informed me one day that a woman I was going to interview had given up the small gold ring in the ala of her nose. She had pawned it with a usurer-jeweler to buy a little coffee and some sweets and cookies for us. To prevent this kind of sacrifice, Dominique came up with a characteristically Indian solution. Every time we entered a compound, she would announce through our interpreter that I was unable to accept anything to eat or drink because it was my fast day. I was afraid people would worry about my depriving myself of food so frequently. I was wrong. I should have thought of Mahatma

Gandhi and the mystique of fasting in India. Even the starving of the slums offered the gods one day of voluntary abstinence a week.

All the same, when we left we brought with us a mountain of carefully wrapped gifts from our brothers and sisters in the City of Joy. Two large additional suitcases could scarcely contain all their tokens of love and generosity.

I LEFT THAT INHUMAN METROPOLIS with twenty notebooks full of writing, hundreds of hours of recorded interviews and two thousand photos. I knew I was taking away the most remarkable piece of research of my entire career as a writer. As soon as I got home, I ensconced myself at the Great Pine. It took me several days to get used to the calm and softness of the heavenly Saint-Tropez countryside. Every morning, before starting to write, I tried to get back to the teeming atmosphere of Calcutta, to its noises, its smells, its colors. I showed myself dozens of slides and listened to miles of tapes of the bustling life I had recorded. I would jangle the bell given to me by Hasari Pal, my rickshaw-puller friend who had used it to proclaim his presence among the roaring Calcutta traffic. For me that sound symbolized all the heroism of this planet's last "human horses." That small round bell was to become my talisman. I never fail to slip it into my pocket when I'm about to set off on a journey.

Urgent Needs Met in a Few Months

It took me over a year to tell the epic survival story of the inhabitants of the City of Joy. Though I had been convinced of its absorbing interest, I was nevertheless surprised at the enthusiasm with which it was received. Far from discouraging people, the adventures of a poor community confronted by the worst adversity were welcomed as testimonies of love, courage and hope.

"The book is a detonator that showed me the triumph of love over evil and suffering in its full glory," a lawyer from Paris wrote to me. "This book is a love song, a cry of joy, a lesson in kindness and hope for all the people of our time," wrote one reviewer from the *New York Times*, while another stated: "The heroes of the City of Joy revive in us the taste for God and for all the values that are tending to disappear."

I received nearly 200,000 letters. A number of messages were accompanied by support for our charitable work: a bank draft, a money order, on one occasion even treasury bonds. Sometimes, too, a small parcel would arrive with a pendant, a gold ring or earrings in it. One envelope contained two wedding rings taped to a sheet of paper. "We have worn these rings for thirty happy years," an unsigned note explained. "Sell them. They will be of more use to the people of the City of Joy than on our fingers." This gesture gave Dominique an ingenious idea. Instead of selling the wedding rings, she took them to India along with other gold jewelry we had been given. A local jeweler turned them into pendant earrings and nostril studs to suit Bengali taste. Those humble ornaments provided a modest dowry for some very poor girls Gaston knew. Without such a viaticum they would never have been able to marry.

MY AUTHOR'S ROYALTIES enabled me to respond instantly to several pressing requests for financial assistance. A small clinic—created in a particularly destitute area of the Ganges Delta by a former Muslim terrorist whom Gaston had won over to charitable work—was short of everything. Almost all of the hundreds of skeletal people who laid siege to it each day went away without treatment, medication or food. Yet the eradication of tuberculosis had been proclaimed "a national priority" by the Indian government. Epidemiological studies had established that a third of the country's inhabitants were afflicted with this scourge, primarily because of malnutrition and lack of hygiene. In the countryside surrounding the Ganges Delta, the figure increased to one in two people. The father of a family was generally the first to be affected, then the children and mother. In the absence of any medical infrastructure, the disease created an ideal opportunity for healers, sorcerers and country pharmacists selling potions and pills stolen from hospitals in Calcutta. To buy such medicines, patients had to sell their crops, then their cow, their fields, their huts, and finally trek off on foot to Calcutta. No hospital would take them. When the "red fever" struck, it meant certain and swift death.

The former terrorist's clinic was established to combat the death rate. But it needed a full-time doctor and nurses, a pathology laboratory, a microscope, a radiology unit and stocks of antibiotics. It needed a concrete building to withstand the onslaughts of the monsoon and the scorching sun, and the pillaging of thieves for whom an ordinary box of aspirin tablets was prize booty. We were able to satisfy all these emergency requirements in a few months. I went myself to negotiate the purchase of radiology equipment from the Siemens representative in Calcutta. The arrival of this ultra-sophisticated apparatus in the far reaches of the countryside provoked the sort of stupor a UFO falling out of the sky might have occasioned. For the X-ray machine to function, unfortunately it needed electricity, a lot of electricity. That rural area being as yet devoid of any such advantage, I besieged the office of the Bengal minister for energy to ask for a priority cable. My efforts became so bogged down in bureaucratic obstacles that I had to resort to a weapon Gandhi used against the British. I threatened the minister that I would call a press conference to announce that the author of *Freedom at Midnight* and *The City of Joy* was backing his humanitarian appeal with a hunger strike outside the door to his office. Three days later a squad of workmen was planting the first posts and stretching out the cables. In ten days the line was in place. We still, however, needed the authorities to supply it with electricity. Another threat brought the first kilowatts, a victory that Wohab, the former Muslim terrorist, and

Sabitri, the young Hindu woman who ran the clinic, celebrated by doing a first X ray. The resulting image showed the bones of their four hands grasping each other by the wrist, a symbol of sacred union which they made into the logo of their aid committee. Ten years and twenty thousand X rays later, tuberculosis had disappeared from twelve hundred villages in the region, and 100,000 sick people were cured. Fifteen tons of vitamin-enriched flour were distributed; 541 drinking-water wells and nearly 1,000 latrines were dug.

When they inaugurated the clinic's new installations, Wohab and Sabitri planted a young acacia tree in the courtyard. At the foot of it they placed a plaque with its name. They called it *Dominiques' Tree*. From then on the acacia became a personality in our lives. It sent us a postcard regularly. "Big brother and big sister Dominique, I have been well watered," said one of them. "I have grown more than forty centimeters. Soon I shall be able to provide the sick with shade. Come back soon! I'm pining for you."

A French priest who looked after several hundred handicapped children from very poor families in homes on the outskirts of Calcutta and in the north of Bengal also asked for our help. Some of his inmates who had polio or bone tuberculosis could only get around on boards on wheels. Others who had Down's syndrome, cerebral palsy or other physical and mental handicaps would never be completely autonomous. There were also deaf-and-dumb, blind and autistic children. These youngsters needed the help of a large and experienced staff, which doubled the cost of keeping them. Father François Laborde was not content merely to pick them up from the streets, clothe, feed and care for them. He also offered them the chance to be reborn to an almost normal life. No sight could better help you appreciate how much love and hope those homes stood for than seeing the infinite patience with which young *didi* in saris got the inert arms and legs of those disabled youngsters moving again, rekindled the minds of retarded boys, taught embroidery to little blind girls and introduced dancing to children who had been deaf from birth. I immediately assumed responsibility for providing for 125 of those children, together with the building of a first school.

Significant as it was, what I did was by no means unique. With all its countless ramifications, Indian society could show extraordinary solidarity. I was constantly discovering charitable associations and aid and development organizations. They stemmed from churches, clubs, temples, sects, confraternities, unions, castes, sports teams, schools and factories. Gaston knew them all. One day he introduced us to a young Muslim who had been born and bred in his slum. Twenty-six-year-old Mohammed Kamruddin had devoted his life to relieving distress in his neighborhood. By day he worked as a nurse in a clinic, and at night he responded to the emergencies of the alleyways and compounds. The young man spoke and wrote impeccable English and displayed an inquiring mind and a degree of culture that were staggering for someone who had known no horizons but the open drains and the leprous facades of his neighborhood. Thanks to some medical books Gaston had obtained, Kamruddin had managed to qualify as a doctor in homeopathy. His dream was to open up a clinic in an even poorer slum in a farther Calcutta suburb. He was bursting with other projects. All of them were directed at the very roots of poverty and underdevelopment: Kamruddin wanted to start crèches, primary schools, vocational training centers, libraries, craft workshops. He wanted to organize a system for borrowing cooking utensils, crockery and tents for marriage celebrations, he wanted to sink wells and latrines, and fit drains. He wanted to build a whole village to take in families of Himalayan refugees living in squalid shanties, destroyed each summer by the monsoon.

One by one we helped that young Muslim doctor to fulfill all his dreams. He would build his village: fifty dwellings with water supply and toilets, and two large community halls for religious ceremonies, educational meetings and an apprentice workshop for girls and abandoned or widowed wives. He would even create a home for handicapped young people there. The village would add to the 650,000 other villages of India. Kamruddin baptized it "The Dominique & Dominique City of Joy Village."

Other extraordinary people Gaston trained also received our vigorous support. Shukesi, an enterprising Bengali nurse, knew as much about medicine as any specialist in Calcutta's hospitals. The clinic she ran practically alone in the middle of a rural area of the southern delta drew all the suffering people from twenty-five miles around. With nothing but a little alcohol, forceps, a scalpel and a few medicines, she treated six hundred patients a day. The sight of those heart-rending processions will haunt me forever. Mothers brought children covered with boils, abscesses, anthrax, alopecia or scabies. One case in three had gastroenteritis and parasites. The most unbearable spectacle was that of rickety babies with inflated stomachs. At a year old they weighed less than six and a half pounds. There were also emergency cases: bites from rabid dogs or snakes, accidents, knife wounds, burns, fits of madness and poisonings. One day a young Hindu woman showed Shukesi a light patch on her pretty face. A prick with a pin in the center of the patch was enough for the nurse to diagnose leprosy. Many came because a miracle was their only hope: people with cancer, acute heart disease, people who were mad, blind, mute, paralyzed and deformed. Fortunately there were also reasons to smile. One day a patient turned up brandishing a prescription several years old: the label read that as he was suffering from metastatic cancer in its terminal stages, he should take six aspirin tablets a day. Another patient respectfully produced a twenty-year-old chest X ray showing cavities as big as a fist. The young nurse always took the time to listen, reassure and give each person a comforting smile. The daughter of poor peasants, she herself had known what it was to be in distress: her husband had abandoned her while she was pregnant, making off with the clinic's cashbox and the few gold trinkets that had made up her modest dowry.

Thanks to *The City of Joy* and the support of its readers, our little Indian sister would also be able to fulfill her dreams. She gave a hundred untouchable children a chance in life by building a school for them and providing two protein- and vitamin-rich meals a day. She constructed a home for sixty physically and mentally handicapped children. She launched vaccination campaigns against smallpox, tetanus and tuberculosis. Soon a thousand children suffering from malnutrition received a food supplement every week. The most poverty-stricken, the oldest, the handicapped, the widowed, in short, all the distressed in the area, received financial support from her to start up some small undertaking: open a shop, raise chickens or set up a handicraft workshop.

To all these talents, Shukesi added that of being a superb *cordon-bleu* cook. Her fried eggplants and cardamom rice will remain among our unforgettable gastronomic memories.

AMONG THE CENTERS I was able to support with my royalties was, of course, the institution that had first sparked our humanitarian commitment. The Englishman James Stevens's Resurrection Home became a proper campus. It expanded by several acres of land, and four separate cottages were built where the children found running water, showers, electric lighting and, courtesy of a Calcutta businessman, a luxury unimaginable in their leper colonies—fans to cool the sweltering heat of summer nights. Thanks to the newly acquired land, James was able to implement one of the projects that had for so long been close to his heart: that of making the home and its 250 children almost self-sufficient in rice, vegetables, fruit, fish, eggs and poultry. A symbolic victory over India's ancestral curse—hunger.

A Crusade to Defend the Money of the Poor

Some disappointments, some setbacks and much pain were nevertheless concealed behind the balance of our successes. Helping is not easy. Sending a check is an infinitesimally small undertaking in comparison with the administration involved in such financial support. It is not enough to send money; the integrity of its use must be guaranteed. I made certain our association Action Aid for Lepers' Children of Calcutta would operate without any paid helpers. Dominique and I decided to absorb all the office costs so that my royalties and the readers' donations are sent, in their entirety, to the people for whom they are intended. For more than eighteen years this relentless effort has taken up half of our time.

As soon as we sent the first funds to India we learned to be vigilant. Banks not used to giving saddled our transfers with heavy exchange commissions and other handling charges. Since the threat of a hunger strike was unlikely to have any effect on their directors, I had to come up with other arguments to induce them to lower the exorbitant costs of banking procedures. Nearly every day I won some case. Every victory enabled us to save one or even several children. In India itself, our first fight consisted of getting the best exchange rates. According to the bank and the mood of their managers, a dollar could be worth thirty rupees one day, thirty-one rupees another and thirty-two rupees on yet another. In the case of $100,000, that could mean many more children snatched from destitution.

We also had to see that the beneficiary accounts for our transfers were credited immediately, which was rarely the case. As in any developing country, the arrival of the smallest amount of money is an occasion for a string of small profits. Sometimes it was a matter of actual misappropriation. A transfer of forty thousand dollars disappeared one day between Paris and Calcutta. After six months of investigating, I eventually found out that the sum had been retained by a bank in Bombay. I made a detour to the great Indian port and rushed to the head office of the establishment concerned. I went straight into the manager's office. I could tell from the polar chill that prevailed in the room that I had come to the right door. In India the more refrigerated an office, the more elevated the position of the occupant. I introduced myself.

"Sir, for six months your bank has been withholding forty thousand dollars that belong to the poor of Calcutta," I raged, showing him the faxes my own bank in Paris had sent me. "I would like to know why."

The man rose from his chair. His face flushed with extreme embarrassment. "I'll pay interest, Mr. Lapierre! I'll pay interest!"

He pressed a bell and three officials in suits and ties made their entrance. The manager ordered them to look into the matter urgently. The three men went out and returned five minutes later.

"Sir," declared the eldest, "the day the sum in question arrived, the Reserve Bank of India had not fixed the exchange rate between the dollar and the rupee. So our foreign currency department did not know what exact rate to apply."

I could hardly believe my ears. The cold was making me want to sneeze more than laugh, but the scene was comical. I was subjected to a torrent of apologies.

"How much interest are you going to give the poor of Calcutta to make up for your unbelievable negligence?" I demanded.

"Twelve percent!" blurted the manager in a wild fit of generosity.

"That's not enough!"

"Fifteen percent!"

"That's still not enough."

The three employees and the manager exchanged stupefied looks.

"I can't go any higher than that."

"I demand at least seventeen percent. The money you kept was meant for leper children. I'm appealing to your generosity."

The manager held out his hand. "Agreed: seventeen percent."

FAR MORE SERIOUS was the Indian government's sudden decision to prohibit the receipt of foreign subsidies. By this restriction the central government hoped to deprive the Sikh organizations seeking independence in the Punjab and the Muslim militants in the center of the country of the foreign donations that enabled one group to buy arms and the other to build mosques. For the beneficiaries of our own aid it was a disaster. Overnight they found themselves without money to buy food for the children in the homes, medicine, X-ray plates, bricks, cement and tiles for our new buildings and the linings for wells and latrines; or to pay the doctors', nurses', social workers' and schoolmasters' wages. We were strangled. I had to borrow several thousand rupees from Indian friends and change all our personal cash to give our organizations under threat of expiry a gasp of oxygen. Our staff showed exemplary generosity. Nurses, teachers, social workers and all the people with small jobs at the centers agreed to carry on working without touching their salaries for months. Their heroism spurred me to move heaven and earth. I besieged ministers in New Delhi with photograph albums showing the hundreds of leper children who had been cured and educated, the tuberculosis sufferers who had been treated, the food that had been distributed, the drinking-water wells that had been sunk and the villages that had been rebuilt after the last cyclone. I pleaded desperately for this aid and development work to urgently receive the funds it needed to survive. One day I succeeded in forcing my way in to see the minister for justice. It so happened that he was from Calcutta and had read *The City of Joy*. Bless the man! A few days later all our centers received, like a lifesaving monsoon, the money they had been waiting six months for.

I HAD TO LEARN TO DEAL with all sorts of difficult situations: the Bengali Communist Party wanted to use our Resurrection Home to employ a batch of its militants; two tax inspectors assigned to check one of our clinic's accounts demanded a bribe; solar-powered pumps meant for poverty-stricken villages deprived of water in the dry season were diverted by the company that checked and signed for their delivery; customs officials appraised at three times its actual value a Peugeot van donated for a priest who sank wells for the poor in the Madras region.

The saga of that van is a good example of the absurd situations in which Indian bureaucracy can ensnare its people. One day when Dominique and I were showing a group of European and American friends around Madras, I asked Jesuit Father Pierre Ceyrac to come and talk to us at our hotel about the India our privileged traveling companions would never know: the India of the villages where he sank his wells, the India sung and revered by Mahatma Gandhi. I had an idea in the back of my mind. I knew this apostle transported the building materials for the wells in an old Peugeot van in which he must have covered ten times the distance from the earth to the moon. That old rattletrap was on its last legs. It so happened that Bertrand and Christiane Peugeot were part of our group. I had no doubt that once they had met this apostle, their company would grant us a significant discount on the purchase of a new vehicle.

Father Ceyrac knew how to talk about his India with words that reduced us all to tears. After the meal, I offered to walk him back to his van; I took our Peugeot friends along with us. The priest tried to dissuade us from going out in the extreme heat.

"I parked my car a long way away," he apologized.

We insisted and fell into step with him. Our shoes sank into the melting asphalt. The glare was such that we were walking almost blindly. It was over a hundred degrees.

At last we reached the priest's old jalopy. He got behind the wheel. The poor vehicle no longer had windows, and its doors were hanging on by bits of wire. He gave us a friendly good-bye wave and pressed the starter. A series of splutters were audible but the engine refused to start. The priest persisted. To no avail. Then we saw his face, trickling with sweat, appearing at the window.

"She must be cold," he said.

Three months later a ship unloaded a brand-new van on a pier in Bombay. It was white and bore the name of Father Ceyrac. As a gift from his friends in France, it had been bought at an exceptionally good price. As ill luck would have it, because of an incorrectly completed importation form, customs officials fell on it like vultures. In vain I scrambled from office to office. Three years went by. I was no longer sure that the vehicle even existed anymore. Had it been resold on the sly to some local mafioso, dismantled bit by bit or reduced to dust by the concerted assaults of the monsoon and the tropical sun? One day I felt an impulse to find out. I took a taxi with Dominique and went to look for it in the Bombay dockyards. It was as if we had wandered into a Fritz Lang film! Endless docks, enough warehouses to house half the population of India, a galaxy of oil reservoirs as far as the eye could see. There were slums everywhere and small bazaars teeming frenziedly with people amid mountains of containers, cases, sacks, and bales. After exploring for two hours, exhausted, covered in dust and half choked by the fumes, we decided to turn back. Suddenly my attention was drawn to a red registration plate, in between two piles of crates on a quay. We rushed over to the spot. There it was, its tires flat, its bumpers in a gangue of grime and its hubcaps reddened with rust. It was there; dirty, unrecognizable, but it was there! And apparently intact. By chance, the warehouse keeper spoke some English. He was a Muslim. His name was Saïd.

"Saïd, you see this vehicle? It belongs to a holy man who has given his life to the poor of India. It is to enable him to transport the materials needed to sink wells in villages in Tamil Nadu."

Saïd surveyed the pile of dust and filth in a silence that was simultaneously apprehensive and respectful.

"You're a holy man too," I went on, placing my finger on the small Koran hanging around his neck. "So you must look after that car as if it were your own sister. You must clean it, wash it, make it shine. You must cover it with a tarpaulin, properly inflate the tires, turn the engine over. You must treat it like a member of your family. And in the meantime, I for my part am going to do what I can to have it sent to the holy man it is meant for."

"You can count on me, brother," said Saïd, wagging his head. "I'll do everything you said."

I gave him my name and address, without holding out too many illusions. When the monsoon broke, he hurriedly sent me a postcard: "Don't worry, brother, I have draped a tarpaulin over the car. It is clean and sparkling like a begum's ring. It's waiting for you to come and fetch it."

Months went by. The customs officers remained implacable. I decided to go right to the top. I requested an audience with the prime minister, Rajiv Gandhi. We had met several times when I went to Safdarjung Road to interview his mother, Indira, for *Freedom at Midnight*. I was convinced that this warm, open man, so uncharacteristic of the Indian political world, would agree to take a few minutes away from his burdensome duties to listen to me. He did.

"Those bureaucrats should be hanged!" he concluded. "You can tell your holy man that he will receive his vehicle very soon."

Three days later Father Ceyrac's van at last escaped the clutches of those who had kept it for so long.

A Chief of State Among the Poor and a Poor Man Among the Rich

It was winter. A disastrous winter. There had not been so much rainfall in the south of France for fifty years. The Saint-Tropez peninsula had been reduced to a sponge. It was bitterly cold and damp. In short, our spirits were not running high. Dominique and I had just made a painful decision. Our commitments in the Calcutta slums and the destitute areas of the Ganges Delta were requiring more and more substantial sums of money. My royalties, the generosity of thousands of readers and the talks I was invited to give all over Europe and America were not enough to make ends meet for an aid budget that now approached half a million dollars a year. We decided to put the Great Pine up for sale and move into the more modest and more easily maintainable house that we had built at the lower end of our property for our old age.

Giving up the Great Pine was a sad prospect. So many memories bound me to every nook and cranny of that house, built bit by bit with the royalties from successive books. Moving eleven rooms full of books, papers, furniture, objects and mementos brought back from so many journeys into a house a third of the size would force us to make heart-rending choices. But would we, in the first place, find a buyer? The real estate crisis and that dreadful season were hardly conducive to a swift sale.

That was when the telephone rang.

"This is the Palais de l'Elysée," said a harsh voice. "I am putting you through to the protocol department."

The speaker on the other end of the line informed me that François Mitterand, the president of France, wished to invite my wife and me to accompany him during his forthcoming state visit to India. The presidential itinerary was to include a stop in Calcutta. The president wanted to take the opportunity to meet some of the people I had portrayed in *The City of Joy*. Could I arrange for him to do so?

Ten days later Dominique and I stepped onto the impressive

red carpet that ran from the VIP lounge at Charles de Gaulle Airport to the Concorde that was to take the president of France, his staff and guests, to India. Before taking his seat in the specially designed cabin, François Mitterand greeted each of his fellow travelers.

"For you, going to India is a bit like going home!" he suggested kindly, before adding with warmth: "Going back to Calcutta with the author of *The City of Joy* is a real joy."

Going back to Calcutta? When François Mitterand was elected first secretary of the Socialist Party in 1971, he had wanted to spend two weeks in a developing country. So he had ended up as an assistant nurse in a clinic run by a French priest in Calcutta.

Eighteen years later that state visit to India was to provide him with an opportunity to see again a city that had left such an impression on him. Rajiv Gandhi, India's prime minister, loaned him his personal Boeing 737 for that leg of the journey, as the runway at Calcutta airport was too short to accommodate the presidential Concorde. After two hours over the dried expanses of the Ganges valley, we flew over the lush Bengali countryside. Then, all at once, I recognized the neo-Gothic bell tower of Saint Paul's Cathedral, the enormous stone wedding cake of the Victoria Memorial, the race course and the old red double-decker buses crawling through Maidan Park. We were arriving in Calcutta.

Before landing, the plane described a circle around the buildings of the old Dum Dum air terminal. A sea of dark heads swarmed around the terminal that had been festooned with a line of flags. On the edge of the runway waited a superb row of turbaned horsemen, the famous Bengal lancers glorified by Hollywood films, together with a military band and a guard of honor in bedizened uniforms. All the color of romantic India was gathered around the officials in white dhotis and their wives in saris, to receive the head of a country that had once vied with Britain for possession of those imperial borders. After the somewhat reserved official welcome in New Delhi, the Indian masses were at last going to give the French president the exuberant Asian welcome he longed for.

Words cannot describe my embarrassment a few minutes later when, as we left the terminal, François Mitterand discovered that the crowds were not there to greet him; that the placards, banners and pieces of calico we had seen from the air proclaimed "Welcome Dominique and Dominique." The welcome committee was made up of former tuberculosis patients who had been saved from a premature death by the royalties from *The City of Joy*.

The president had the good grace to be very sporting. Before climbing into his car, he whispered in my ear: "In Calcutta you're the one who deserves people's applause."

I left the official cortege to jump in a taxi. I had an urgent appointment. The Bellevue Clinic was Bengal's most modern hospital. It was also the most expensive. Only rich businessmen, company directors and high dignitaries in the local communist government could afford the luxury of its MRI cobalt machine, its operating rooms, its qualified staff and its air-conditioned rooms. But for the first time in history the clinic had an indigent among its patients. The winter pollution and overwork had got the better of Gaston's lungs. He had been found unconscious. No hospital had wanted to take this sahib dressed like a poor man whose pockets contained not even a ten-paisa coin. It had taken the intervention of a doctor friend of James Stevens to have him admitted as an emergency case to the Bellevue Clinic. The fact that he was semicomatose had made his admission possible; if he had been conscious, Gaston would never have agreed to enter an establishment for the rich where the price of one day's care was more than a rickshaw puller could hope to earn in six months of exhausting labor. Just as I had been about to leave Paris, a distressed telephone call from a friend in Calcutta had warned me that the clinic was demanding immediate payment of a substantial deposit.

The clinic's director was not in his office. His secretary informed me that he was in a meeting with the owner of the hospital in the next room. That was my chance! I rushed to the next door, knocked and, without waiting for any response, entered a vast room over which an opulent woman in a mauve muslin sari presided from behind a desk. She gave me an angry look. I begged her to excuse me and introduced myself. My name in association with the title of my book *The City of Joy* elicited a broad smile. Without giving her the time to wonder at my intrusion, I took her hand with its fingers dripping in rings and declared:

"Madam, your clinic has the honor to number among its patients a saint, a man who has given up everything to devote his life to the poor of your country, to relieve their wretchedness and bring them his love. This apostle has been worn out by the task. Three days ago he was found half-dead. No hospital wanted anything to do with him. Friends managed to have him admitted here. Since then your doctors have been struggling to save him. But today they're threatening to throw him out."

Knowing how important the sacred is in India, I begged: "Madam, go and see this sick man in his room, receive a *darshan* from this man of God. He is as great as Mahatma Gandhi, as great as any of India's sages. His blessing will bring you happiness . . ."

What would I not have said to save Gaston!

"It is always a lucky opportunity," I went on, "to contribute to the saving of a life. This one has been entrusted to you by destiny to enrich your karma. I ask you to grant him the gift of his recovery in your fine clinic."

The words "destiny" and "karma" seemed to have an impact. The opulent lady questioned her director in Bengali. There was a brief exchange. Eventually she rose from her chair and responded to my request with one single word.

"Granted!"

Scorning the elevators as too slow, I climbed to the fifth floor on foot and rushed to room 519. Dressed in a pale blue shirt, Gaston lay stretched out on the bed with his head propped up on two pillows. Several IVs suspended from supports were instilling a flicker of life into his wasted body. An oxygen mask was attached to the wall to ward off any further bouts of suffocation. He looked pale, emaciated, exhausted. Nevertheless my arrival brought a mischievous smile to the corner of his lips.

"Gaston, I bring you greetings from the president of France!" I exclaimed. "Above all I bring you greetings from the owner of this clinic, who is giving you your treatment as a present. You can let yourself be cajoled, pampered and petted by the nurses. You can take all the medicines they bring you, eat everything they serve you. Everything, you hear, everything is on the house. Rest assured you're not depriving the poor of a single rupee."

He made an effort to speak.

"Thank you," he began, "but I want to leave here and go to a hospital where anyone can go . . ."

A spasm shook him. I gazed at his inert body and wondered for an instant whether Gaston was not in fact dead. Then I caught the irregular wheezing of his breath. A nurse came in to attend to him and I withdrew.

On my way downstairs I thought of all the discussions I had had with him about his health. How many times I had tried to convince him that his life was more important than his death, that his passing would create a yawning abyss for all the destitute whose survival depended on his presence, and for those who, far away, fought to support what he was doing. I thought of every time I had heard him say that his life was in God's hands and that his main problem was not living but "being able to look the people around me in the eyes, without feeling ashamed."

THAT AFTERNOON AT FIVE O'CLOCK, most of the principal heroes of the *The City of Joy* came to have tea with President Mitterand in the library at La Martinière College. Founded in the eighteenth century by an aristocrat from Lyon, the institution educated the elite of Bengali youth. Among the guests were James Stevens and his wife, as well as François Laborde, the French priest with whom the president had worked as a volunteer medic in 1971. I had adopted several of the homes he had founded for handicapped children. It was moving to see gathered around the same table the president of France, a wealthy Western nation, several of his ministers and advisers, and on the other side, those poorly dressed, thin people consumed by their ideal of love and sharing.

On the plane that took us back to Bombay next day, François Mitterand, profoundly affected by his experience in Calcutta, asked me how France could help those he had met. I immediately reeled off a few ideas.

"And in the meantime, *Monsieur le President,*" I added in a jocular tone, "you might show them our country's admiration by awarding them all the Légion d'Honneur!"

Six months later the suggestion became a reality.

CALCUTTA HAD BECOME our second home. On one of our frequent visits a huge surprise awaited us. The communist mayor, K. K. Basu, and the 250 members of his council were intent upon receiving us in the festival hall of their old Town Hall, decorated with gigantic welcoming banners. In his introductory speech the mayor expressed the "gratitude of Calcutta" for the way in which I had revealed to the world "its people's virtues of courage, vitality and hope." By way of thanks, the elected head of the great metropolis had decided to make Dominique and me honorary citizens and present us with the gold medal of the city. Deeply moved, I responded that it was in the name of all the heroes of the slums, of all the rickshaw pullers, of all the people of light we had been fortunate enough to meet in that magical city, that we accepted the medal. First and foremost the medal was theirs. It was in honor of the men, women and children who, each day, showed the world that "if adversity is great, as the great Bengali poet Tagore had written, man is even greater than the greatest adversity."

The most extraordinary tribute I was to receive on that memorable day, however, was a document that showed the impact my book had had on the city administrators. The development program they had drawn up for Calcutta was entitled "Calcutta—City of Joy—Projects for Tomorrow." Among the first plans to change people's living conditions was the daily distribution of two gallons of drinking water to every one of the 3 million inhabitants of the slums.

THE WHOLE OF CALCUTTA was soon to parade under the title "City of Joy," the phrase I had borrowed from Gaston to describe the exemplary values of one of its most squalid districts. Soon, on the way out of the airport and into the city, visitors would be greeted with signs saying "Welcome to the City of Joy" in huge letters. Paint manufacturers bought whole pages of newspaper advertising space to announce that their products were going to "repaint the city into a City of Joy"; dissatisfied citizens cried out to their elected members: "When are you going to turn our city into a real City of Joy?" Even the Marxist government used the appellation as a slogan. "Come and invest in the City of Joy," proclaimed its official propaganda, anxious to wipe out the Bengali capital's execrable reputation in international business circles.

"Blessed Is He Who Enjoys God's Mercy"

There was, all the same, one shadow that hung over our love affair with India. The man who had opened the doors of the City of Joy to us had not managed to obtain what he most desired—Indian citizenship. Gaston had married the people of India. He had identified himself with their joys, their suffering, their fears and their revolt. He struggled with them, prayed with them, hoped and wept with them, in a way that possibly no other outsider had ever done. The *dadah* was indeed a brother to all the unfortunate people of the city. Alas, this fact was unrecognized by a small handful of xenophobic and suspicious officials at the Bengal Ministry for Internal Affairs. They obstinately refused to grant the "Swiss big brother" the country's official gratitude, they refused to take him into the bosom of the Indian family. All the efforts Gaston had undertaken to obtain his Indian citizenship were systematically rebutted. Yet Gaston had scrupulously fulfilled all the obligations the law imposed on foreigners. He had learned to read and write an Indian language fluently, given proof of his residence and work in the country for more than five years, put his tax position in order, published his "notice of application for citizenship" in the newspaper, obtained the necessary number of sponsors and satisfied a thousand other niggling formalities.

But behind the red brick facade of the Writers' Building, a score of hostile bureaucrats continued to wonder what could possibly induce a citizen of one of the world's richest countries to become Indian. With repeated summonses to the headquarters of the police who dealt with foreigners, humiliating interrogations and scarcely veiled threats not to renew his visa, the authorities did their utmost to torment the unfortunate apostle of the slums.

Convinced that only a decision from New Delhi could put an end to this injustice, I made application after application. Dominique had put together comprehensive briefs that I religiously submitted to any officials I visited. I pleaded Gaston's case with each one of them with the aid of a passionate speech that never failed to move. I showed them photographs, talked in detail about his work for his Indian brothers, enumerated the success stories and cited examples that sometimes made the most hardened officials' eyes water. I always finished my presentations with an expression of my conviction that "India could only be richer, more brotherly, more fortunate, if it were to take such an exceptional person to its bosom."

This desperate crusade went on for two years. At last, one day the slum postman brought Gaston a yellow envelope bearing the stamp of the Ministry for Internal Affairs. He opened it with a pounding heart.

"My God," he trembled, "I bet the government's throwing me out."

Anxiously he scanned the type. Suddenly his eyes fell on words he had to reread several times before he grasped their meaning. "The Government of India hereby grants the said

Grandjean, Gaston, the certificate of naturalization and declares that after swearing an oath of loyalty at the time appointed and according to the regulations prescribed by the law, he will be entitled to all the privileges, prerogatives and rights, and subject to all the duties, obligations and responsibilities of an Indian citizen."

Gaston would tell us that he suddenly felt as if the heart of the whole slum was beating in his chest. Seized with vertigo, he leaned against the wall of his room and closed his eyes. When he opened them again, he took hold of the little metal cross he wore around his neck. He gazed at the two dates his mother had had inscribed upon it, that of his birth and that of his entry into the Prado congregation. His eyes burning with tears of happiness, he considered then the small blank space in front of the name he had had engraved several years previously. He had chosen that name a long time ago to be his surname as an Indian citizen. In Hindi as in Bengali, Dayanand means "Blessed is he who enjoys God's mercy." The term summed up perfectly his communion with the humble, the poor and the downtrodden of India. In front of that name that would from now on be his, he would have engraved the date of his definitive entry into the great family of his Indian brothers. That date was the third most important of his life.

The proverb I had discovered in the torrential rains of the monsoon had once again proven to be right. There are always a thousand suns beyond the clouds.

EPILOGUE

Gaston spent his first days as an Indian citizen in a state of euphoria. However, before he was entitled to a green passport stamped with the three lions of Ashoka, the emblem of his new homeland, he had to satisfy a formality that proved to be more complicated than he had anticipated. Indian regulations require all naturalized citizens to provide a certificate from the embassy of their country of origin, confirming that they have handed back their passport. So Gaston caught the train to New Delhi. His visit caused quite a stir in the Swiss embassy offices. Never before had a citizen of the confederation expressed the desire to give up his precious nationality for that of a Third World country. The ambassador tried in person to persuade this strange compatriot of the importance of holding on to his passport. Gaston refused categorically and finally managed to extract the certificate required by his new homeland.

GASTON'S DEFINITIVE MARRIAGE to India reinforced our commitment to supporting him. In July 1997 Dominique and I were fortunate enough to be able to help him fulfill a project that had been very close to all three of our hearts for several years. If there is one part of the world that is deprived of any kind of medical aid, a place where the inhabitants are so poor they cannot even muster the ten cents a ferry ticket costs to go and consult a doctor or a bonesetter on the mainland, it is the fifty-seven islands in the Gulf of Bengal, off the Ganges-Brahmaputra Delta. Those densely populated islands are always the first victims of the cyclones that periodically lay waste to this part of India. The soil is salty and yields only one crop of rice a year. To save their families from starvation, many of the peasants are obliged to gather wild honey in the immense mangrove forests of the Sundarbans that border the extremity of the delta, along the frontier with Bangladesh. Daily covered by the tide, this area is inhabited by a particularly ferocious species of tiger. Every year three hundred wild-honey pickers, like the father of young Shanta whom we had known in the City of Joy, are devoured by these man-eating tigers. The animals lead a semi-aquatic existence. They swim, feed on fish, even attack crocodiles, and they have no reservations about approaching boats and seizing any fisherman imprudent enough to sleep on the deck. If they spot a man on a forest path, they will follow him for days. They always attack from behind. To try and scare off these pursuers, the peasants who harvest the honey wear masks that look like human faces on the backs of their heads, fitted with an electrical system to make their eyes sparkle. The forestry department has even positioned dummies wired up to batteries at various points on the reserve. At the slightest contact the animal receives a charge of three thousand volts. No one has yet been able to explain the extreme ferocity of these creatures. Their taste for human flesh may be attributable to the fact that they often feed off human remains from the funeral pyres along the Ganges. Because wood is so expensive, the inhabitants of the region cannot always burn their dead completely, so they throw their remains into the river. The current then carries them to the edge of the forest.

Apart from tigers, tuberculosis, cholera, malaria and all the diseases of malnutrition ravage these unfortunate islands. Only a dispensary boat capable of travel from island to island would be able to ameliorate the situation. In addition to emergency operations and care of the sick, such a mobile clinic would also make it possible to conduct vaccination programs and campaigns to prevent tuberculosis and promote health education, family planning and hygiene. This project could mean a whole sanitary and social revolution for the region. To be really effective, the boat would have to be equipped with a portable X-ray unit and a generator, a rudimentary operating room and a solar-powered refrigerator to store vaccines and medicines. The team would have to be made up of two doctors, a dozen nurses and a competent crew.

The cost of such a project was far beyond our resources. How were we to find the $100,000 necessary? "God will provide," Mother Teresa used to say every time a difficult situation arose requiring a particular financial outlay. In the case of our dispensary boat, God used a young Dutch couple as his intermediaries. The owners of the Amsterdam-based Merison company, one of the world's largest distributors of household goods, Alexander and Suzanne Van Meerwijk, had heard one of my lectures. They came to Calcutta to visit our various relief centers. The work being carried out filled them with such enthusiasm that they decided to mark the hundredth anniversary of their enterprise in a very special way. Instead of investing in expensive celebrations, they gave us a check for $100,000 to enable us in November 1997 to launch what now bears the name of "Merison–City of Joy Boat Dispensary."

This initiative, probably unique in India and perhaps even in the rest of the Third World, proved so successful that the inhabitants of the area requested that we launch a second boat to help more islands. Thanks to the generosity of two citizens of the small state of Andorra, Pere and Maria Lluisa Roquet, we were able, in November 1998, to inaugurate a second boat-dispensary that bears their names. A fleet of eight similar boats would actually be necessary to cover the basic medical needs of the 350,000 inhabitants of the 57 islands of this wretched region of our planet. It's a goal Dominique and I are determined to fight for with all our energies.

THE DIFFICULT DECISION we had taken to sell our Saint-Tropez house, the Great Pine, to raise the necessary funds to continue our work in India was carried out without too much pain. Our departure was made easier by the geographical proximity of the more modest house into which we moved, and above all by the quality of the family who purchased the Great Pine. They were an Italian couple who had long shown their concern for the underprivileged. They had set up The Fondazione Benedetta d'Intino, a treatment and rehabilitation center in Milan for physically and mentally handicapped young people.

PINECONE, THE SPANISH MARE on whose back I had meditated and dreamed for so many years, as together we gamboled across the untamed hillsides above the bay of Saint-Tropez, passed away at the ripe old age of thirty-two. I had ridden her only two days prior to her death. She had retained the impetuousness that had so charmed me twenty-five years earlier in the Draguignan abattoir yard. Sensing her end approaching, she lay down on her side and called me with a chorus of whinnying. I had never seen her other than upright, ready to bite, kick or set off on a gallop. I knelt down beside her and took her head, surmounted by a white patch, in my hands to give her a long embrace. Always otherwise so spirited, she abandoned herself now, unflinching, to my grasp. Tears flowed from her large bright eyes now full of sadness. I realized she was saying goodbye to me. In defiance of all the evidence, I encouraged her with my voice to get to her feet. She started, managed to raise her neck and head, and get up onto her knees. Her hindquarters trembled, but she could not lift her rump. Exhausted, she fell back onto her side. Her eyelids fluttered several times. She panted for a few seconds, then her breathing stopped. It was all over. My wonderful companion had gone to animal heaven, taking with her one of the happiest pieces of my life.

In the neighboring stall, the white mare born of her love for Preferido, the murdered stallion, pawed the ground impatiently. I saddled her up at once and set off at a gallop to drown my grief in the hillsides trampled by the hooves of her unforgettable mother.

BEFORE CLOSING THE PAGES of this narrative, I would like to share with the reader three moving experiences that, in the twilight of my life, remain engraved upon my heart with particular intensity. All three took place in India, the land that has taught and given me so much.

The day after the publication of *Freedom at Midnight* I received an invitation. The little untouchable girls at a school in the ashram founded by Mahatma Gandhi on the banks of the Sabarmati River when he began his crusade to drive out the British, wanted to make my acquaintance. I harbored a very special affection for that place so steeped in memories of the Great Soul, where I had spent many days studying documents relating to the beginnings of his work. The schoolgirls were waiting at the entrance for Dominique and me, with superb garlands of yellow marigolds which they hung around our necks until we nearly suffocated. It was then that I was given what was possibly the most moving tribute I would ever receive in my career. The pupils had copied out with chalk on a blackboard the episode from *Freedom at Midnight* in which Larry and I had recorded Gandhi's last meditation on the morning of his death. Beneath the text and in large, clearly detached letters, they had written "Thank you."

No expression of gratitude could ever equal that "Thank you" addressed to a foreigner by those young untouchable daughters of India's prophet. We went into the ashram. Under a vast awning, a prayer platform had been set up. The headmaster of the school invited my wife and me and the few foreign friends who were with us to take our places on it. I was so moved that I had difficulty telling those young Indian girls that the Mahatma belonged to all the people of the earth, that my friends and I all felt, like them, that we were children of Gandhiji, and that this meant that we were bound together in a special way. The headmaster translated my words into Gujarati as I spoke and I saw the little girls' eyes burn with an ever more intense light. Then I invited them to sing the hymn by Tagore that Gandhi had so often hummed at the outset of his pilgrimages for peace and reconciliation among his Indian brothers. "If they do not hear your call, walk alone, walk alone" sang a chorus of childish voices at the top of their lungs.

IT WAS OUR FRIEND PADMINI, the little girl who went out at dawn every day to pick up the bits of coal off the railroad tracks, who was to provide me with a second unforgettably emotional moment. *The City of Joy* had just come out in Bengali. Every evening, the residents of the slums gathered in a courtyard around the Muslim mullah and a Hindu schoolmaster to listen to a reading of the story of their life and their struggle against adversity. Discovering that we had returned to India, a group of residents wanted to give us a welcoming celebration at the entrance to their neighborhood. "Welcome home in the City of Joy," proclaimed a white and red banner hung above our heads from one side of the alleyway to the other. A little girl emerged from the group with a big bunch of flowers in her hand. It was Padmini. She was radiant.

"Big brother and big sister Dominique, accept these flowers from all of us," she declared as she offered us her bouquet. "Today, thanks to you, we are no longer alone."

ONE DAY IN 1985 a surprise awaited me in New York. The newspapers announced that Mother Teresa and a small group of her Indian sisters from Calcutta had just arrived in Manhattan to open a home for AIDS patients with neither money nor family. This time the Third World was coming to the rescue of the rich West. I rushed to the home. The Saint of Calcutta had given her establishment the beautiful name of "Gift of Love." In the entrance hall a large poster proclaimed Mother Teresa's philosophy of life to the sick and those visiting this waiting room for death. She had written the text one night during the monsoon, many years previously when she was caring for lepers in a clinic on the banks of the Ganges. Each statement of her credo struck me as the most important invitation a person today could ever encounter.

Life is an opportunity, avail it
Life is a beauty, admire it
Life is bliss, taste it
Life is a dream, realize it
Life is a challenge, meet it
Life is a duty, complete it
Life is a game, play it
Life is costly, care for it
Life is a wealth, keep it
Life is love, enjoy it
Life is mystery, know it
Life is a promise, fulfill it
Life is sorrow, overcome it
Life is a song, sing it
Life is a struggle, accept it
Life is a tragedy, brace it
Life is an adventure, dare it
Life is luck, make it
Life is life, defend it.

APPENDIX

Thanks to royalties and my lecture fees, and thanks to the generosity of my readers and friends belonging to the association I founded in 1982, it has been possible to initiate and maintain the following humanitarian work in Calcutta and its surrounding area.

1. The assumption of complete and continuing financial responsibility for 250 leper children at the Resurrection Home; the construction of a fourth building to provide for 50 children; the purchase of a plot of land to extend the agricultural development to make the home more self-sufficient.

2. The assumption of total and continuing responsibility for 125 physically handicapped young people in the Mohitnagar and Maria Basti homes.

3. The construction and equipment of the Backwabari home for severely mentally and physically handicapped children.

4. The extension and reorganization of the Ekprantanagar home in a destitute suburb of Calcutta, providing shelter for 140 children of seasonal workers at the brickworks. The provision of drinking water on tap has transformed the living conditions in the home.

5. The provision of a school near Ekprantanagar home to educate not only the 140 children who board there but also 350 very poor children from the nearby slums.

6. The reconstruction of one hundred huts for families who, in November 1988, lost everything in the cyclone that hit the Ganges Delta.

7. The assumption of total responsibility for the clinic in Bhangor and its program to eradicate tuberculosis, which covers several thousand villages. (There are nearly 100,000 consultations annually.) The installation of fixed X-ray equipment in the main clinic and the creation of a mobile unit for diagnostic X rays, vaccination, treatment and nutritional care.

8. The creation of three medical units in the isolated villages of the Ganges Delta, providing not only medical treatment and a program to combat tuberculosis but also programs for prevention, diagnosis, education, vaccination and family planning, as well as "eye camps" to restore sight to patients with cataracts.

9. The sinking of tube wells for drinking water and the construction of latrines in numerous villages in the Ganges Delta.

10. The assumption of responsibility for the rural treatment center in Belari, serving more than 90,000 patients a year from hamlets devoid of any medical aid.

11. The creation of, and assumption of total responsibility for, a school and two medical (allopathic and homeopathic) centers in two particularly poverty-stricken slums on the outskirts of Calcutta.

12. The construction of a "City of Joy" village to rehabilitate homeless Himalayan refugees.

13. The construction of, and assumption of complete responsibility for, a home for abandoned children in Palstunda, near Bangladesh.

14. The provision of ten solar-powered water pumps for ten very poor villages in the states of Bihar, Haryana, Rajasthan and

Orissa, to enable the inhabitants to grow their own food even in the dry season.

15. The assumption of responsibility for a workshop to rehabilitate lepers in Orissa.

16. The dispatching of medicine and provision of seventy thousand high-protein meals for the leper children at the Udayan home.

17. The launching of two dispensary boats to take medical aid to the people of the fifty-seven islands in the Ganges Delta.

18. Various undertakings for the underprivileged and lepers in the state of Mysore, abandoned children in Bombay and Rio de Janeiro, Brazil, the occupants of a village in Guinea, Africa, and abandoned and seriously ill children in a hospital in Lublin, Poland.

How You Can Help Us to Continue Our Humanitarian Work Among Some of the World's Most Underprivileged Men, Women and Children

Because of lack of resources, the association Action Aid for Lepers' Children of Calcutta, which I founded in 1982, can no longer finance all our urgent priority undertakings.

Unless we find new sources of support quickly, we shall have to close several homes, clinics and schools run by admirable staff in the service of the poorest of the poor.

We have, furthermore, an ongoing serious worry. What would happen if tomorrow an accident or illness were to prevent my wife and me from meeting the needs of the various centers we finance?

There is only one way to address this eventuality: turn our association into a foundation.

The capital from this foundation would have to be capable of providing the necessary annual revenue to fund the work of the seven charitable organizations we support. In order to generate the minimum $330,000 needed each year, we would need an initial capital sum of at least $8 million.

How are we to raise that sort of capital if not through the contributions of a multitude of individuals?

Eight million is eight thousand times a thousand dollars. For some people it is relatively easy to give a thousand dollars to a good cause. Some people could probably give even more. But for the vast majority of friends who have spontaneously given to us after reading *The City of Joy* and now *A Thousand Suns*, or hearing one of my lectures, and who often faithfully keep up their generous support, it is much too large a sum.

One thousand dollars, however, is also twice five hundred dollars or four times two hundred and fifty dollars, or five times two hundred dollars, or ten times a hundred dollars or even a hundred times ten dollars.

Such a sum can be raised from several people at one person's initiative. By photocopying this message, by spreading the word, by joining with other family members, friends and colleagues, by setting up a chain of compassion and sharing, each one can help to keep this work alive and bring a little justice and love to the poorest of the poor.

The smallest gifts count for as much as the largest. Isn't the ocean made up of drops of water?*

—Dominique Lapierre

* I would like to remind the reader that Action Aid for Lepers' Children of Calcutta makes it a rule to have no overhead costs. All the money received is sent to the centers for which it is donated.

All that is not given is lost

ACTION AID FOR LEPERS' CHILDREN OF CAL-
CUTTA
26, Avenue Kléber
F-75116 Paris
France
Banking account number 730 3001 0801
Barclays Bank, Agency Kléber
24, Avenue Kléber, F-75116 Paris, France
Bank Code: 30588; Agency Code: 61081—Rib 33

You may benefit from a tax deduction on your U.S. income tax
by sending a check to:

CITY OF JOY AID INC.
c/o Marie B. Allizon
7419 Lisle Avenue
Falls Church, VA 22043
Fax: (703) 734-6956
Taxpayer identification number: 54-1566941

By saving a child,
by giving him the possibility to learn how to read and write,
by giving him a training,
it is the world of tomorrow that we save.

- Rescuing, curing, feeding, clothing, schooling and
training ten leper children for one year costs $3,000.
- Digging one drinking-water tube well in the saline
areas of the Ganges Delta costs $500 to $2,000.
- Curing one hundred tuberculosis patients costs $2,000.

Dominique Lapierre's humanitarian organization has *no*
overhead costs. Each dollar received goes entirely to Calcutta
to serve a priority action.